MISSIONS
AND
MONEY

The American Society of Missiology Series, published in collaboration with Orbis Books, seeks to publish scholarly works of high merit and wide interest on numerous aspects of missiology — the study of Christian mission in its historical, social, and theological dimensions. Able presentations on new and creative approaches to the practice and understanding of mission will receive close attention from the ASM Series Committee.

American Society of Missiology Series, No. 15

MISSIONS
AND
MONEY

Affluence as a Missionary Problem... Revisited

Revised and Expanded Edition

Jonathan J. Bonk

ORBIS BOOKS

Maryknoll, New York 10545

Third Printing, May 2011

Library of Congress Cataloging-in-Publication Data

Bonk, Jon, 1945-
    Missions and money : affluence as a missionary problem revisited /
Jonathan J. Bonk. – Rev. and expanded ed.
        p.   cm. – (American Society of Missiology series ; no. 15)
    Includes bibliographical references and index.
    ISBN-13: 978-1-57075-650-4 (pbk.)
    ISBN-10: 1-57075-650-3
    1. Missions – Theory. 2. Wealth – Religious aspects – Christianity.
3. Christianity and culture. 4. East and West. 5. Missions. I. Title.
BV2063.B63 2006
266'.0231722 – dc22
                                                         2006026286

To
Paul and Lila Balisky
— missionaries in Ethiopia for thirty-eight years —
mentors, friends, manifestly righteous servants of their Lord

Contents

Preface to the ASM Series

The purpose of the ASM (American Society of Missiology) Series is to publish — without regard for disciplinary, national, or denominational boundaries — scholarly works of high quality and wide interest on missiological themes from the entire spectrum of scholarly pursuits relevant to Christian mission, which is always the focus of books in the Series.

By *mission* is meant the effort to effect passage over the boundary between faith in Jesus Christ and its absence. In this understanding of mission, the basic functions of Christian proclamation, dialogue, witness, service, worship, liberation, and nurture are of special concern. And in that context questions arise, including, How does the transition from one cultural context to another influence the shape and interaction between these dynamic functions, especially in regard to the cultural and religious plurality that constitute the global context of Christian life and mission?

The promotion of scholarly dialogue among missiologists, and among missiologists and scholars in other fields of inquiry, may involve the publication of views that some missiologists cannot accept, and with which members of the Editorial Committee themselves do not agree. Manuscripts published in the Series, accordingly, reflect the opinions of their authors and are not understood to represent the position of the American Society of Missiology or of the Editorial Committee. Selection is guided by such critera as intrinsic worth, readability, coherence, and accessibility to a range of interested persons and not merely to experts or specialists.

The ASM Series, in collaboration with Orbis Books, seeks to publish scholarly works of high merit and wide interest on numerous aspects of missiology — the scholarly study of mission. Able presentations on new and creative approaches to the practice and understanding of mission will receive close attention.

The ASM Series Committee
JONATHAN J. BONK
ANGELYN DRIES, O.S.F.
SCOTT W. SUNQUIST

Foreword

Missions and Foreign Money

Walbert Bühlmann, O.F.M., Cap.

Even though money and spirit are quite different realities, no one will claim that they have no relation to each other. Even Jesus used an apostle, Judas Iscariot, as "keeper of the funds" (John 12:6) — though admittedly Judas proved untrustworthy. The case of Judas, in fact, clearly illuminates the ambiguity of the relationship between money and the world of Christian spiritual ideals since earliest times.

As is the case with long-established churches, "mission" churches founded and supported by Northern churches in the South cannot exist without money; but neither do they necessarily thrive if money is available in abundance. Dramatically illustrating and calling attention to this problem, we have in our hands a penetrating discussion of missions and money by Jonathan Bonk, a Canadian Mennonite. A basic argument of this book is that an imbalance in the relative wealth of evangelizer-missionaries and those among whom they work distorts the transmission and inculturation of the Gospel. Professor Bonk makes a cogent argument for this thesis, chiefly as it applies to Protestant missions, and especially to those from North America. I commend his book to all persons interested in the spread of the whole Gospel in the whole world.

While the book discusses this question in its Protestant dimensions, it also has Roman Catholic aspects, which are too often passed over in embarrassed silence or are unacknowledged. I elaborated on this in several chapters in my book *The Coming of the Third Church* (Maryknoll, NY: Orbis Books, 1977). It is my belief that conclusions similar to those drawn by Jonathan Bonk for Protestant missions can also be reached concerning the Catholic Church's mission work. But it is not the purpose of these few pages to draw these conclusions in any detail. Rather, a few general observations on this theme will be elaborated to ensure that the issue is faced squarely.

It may be helpful to observe that the terminology surrounding "missions" is itself disturbing to us Catholics. Commonly, we understand the term "missions" to mean territories which Rome has assigned to various mission organizations in the system formerly known as the *jus commissionis*. Under this system of entrusting territories, these mission organizations, usually religious orders or clerical societies of apostolic life such as the Franciscans or the Paris Foreign Mission Society, bore virtually complete responsibility for administering "their" missions.

Thus they sent missionaries to them, collected the necessary funds for them, and endeavored to build up church communities in their missions.

These organizations succeeded so well that, in great measure, almost everywhere today we find Catholic parishes with native bishops, priests, and religious. Vatican Council II recognized this and spoke not only of the "one, holy, Catholic church," but began speaking of "the communion of many local churches." As a result of this, in 1969 the *jus commissionis* system was ended and these missions were raised to the status of dioceses, each with its own bishop who had authority even over expatriate "missionaries" in the service of the local church.

Thus it seems anachronistic to Catholics today to speak of missions, and for indigenous Christians in such local churches "missions" sounds a bit patronizing. But the problems of missions and money and authentic inculturation of the Gospel are no less acute even if the terminology is somewhat passé.

It would be a serious mistake for Roman Catholics to think that money issues similar to those discussed by Professor Bonk have not in the past distorted their mission activity, or that it does not today have an effect on both the extensive and intensive growth of Southern churches. And facing that problem may well be important for Northern churches to discover deeper dimensions of Christian truth about the relationship of human communities and wealth.

For the independent Protestant churches described by Jonathan Bonk — churches today sending thousands of young people into mission — the word "mission" does not connote anything like "entrusted territories." For such Protestants the term simply denotes a group of people who go out "on mission" in the name of Jesus. But their great zeal for the Gospel does not relieve them of the responsibility of reflecting upon the potential of money to corrupt the inculturation of the message.

In his own day, Jesus is recalled as having had a simple solution to the money problem for his apostle missionaries. His commissioning mandate (see, for example, Luke 9:1–6 and 10:1–9 and parallels) is inherently fascinating in its idealism. It both engages one totally and portrays a life freeing missionaries from every care for the sake of the Gospel of the arrival of the Reign of God: "Take nothing for your journey, no staff, nor bag, nor bread, nor money — not even an extra tunic" (Luke 9:1).

Down through the ages, that ideal was maintained as an ideal and even physically approximated by missionaries in times when "sending churches" and missionaries were not immeasurably wealthier and more powerful than those to whom they were sent. For example, in 596 Pope Gregory the Great sent St. Augustine and his band of Benedictine monks to England as missionaries. Sixth-century Irish-Scottish monks lived a life much like that of the apostles when they came as missionaries to the European continent. Similarly, St. Francis of Assisi (died, 1226), who was influenced by the ideals portrayed in the Lucan passages quoted above, lived in complete poverty and detachment. He sent his religious as missionaries to Morocco and Egypt with the admonition: "Cast your burden on the Lord; he will sustain you," echoing the spirituality of Psalm 55:23 and 1 Peter 5:7. Although it may verge on romanticizing the past to say so, one suspects that these earlier generations of missionaries knew that wealth was itself a problem. That insight has largely been lost in the modern age. Perhaps a post-modern age will be capable of recapturing the spiritual wisdom of the ancient insight, the tradition of which was kept by the early monks and mendicants.

With the European discovery of the New World and subsequently with the development of reliable means of transoceanic travel in the eighteenth century, this monastic and mendicant heritage of suspicion of money developed into something quite different. The dangerous memory of poor, itinerant heralds of the Gospel of the Founder of Christianity was almost totally domesticated. In addition, unlike the medieval Benedictine and Franciscan missionaries, modern missionaries — Protestant and Catholic — found themselves laboring under the burden of colonial and imperial systems. Perhaps more dangerously, psychologically they worked amongst peoples whose material culture most Europeans and North Americans looked down upon and whose spiritual culture few Westerners appreciated. Instead of sharing totally *as equals* in the life of their people in the Lucan spirit, modern missionaries created mini-European and American "stations" in exotic lands and often had their wives or cadres of dedicated religious sisters to provide a familiar hearth for them when they returned home from their day's exertions. Relative to standards of living in their homelands, such stations were modest; relative to standards among the peoples they sought to evangelize, these stations were often luxurious.

Simply "going there" was viewed as an immense sacrifice by the countrymen and relatives of these missionaries. No American or European, it was commonly thought, could live at the level of the "locals." But it was probably very seldom considered that if the missionary *could not* do so, that incapacity might cause serious disturbances in the evangelization and inculturation process.

The manner in which money is raised in the North for missions in the South is not a question of purely theoretical relevance. Vatican Council II raised it in a way that was easily forgotten, even though it forthrightly criticized the begging system heretofore used in mission fundraising. In the Conciliar Document on Missions (*Ad Gentes*) the bishops observed that missionary activity, "the greatest and holiest work of the Church" (art. 29), should be financed by having a set portion of the budget of all local churches directed to missionary activity (art. 38). The goal of the Council's directives was that the financing of evangelization efforts needed to be planned. The wisdom of that directive is clear, but it does not go to the heart of the matter in the way Jonathan Bonk points us: to ask even more basic questions about the affluence of Northern-based missionaries in the South. Going one step further, remembering the monks and early mendicants, one might ask if money in mission is so important and open to so many abuses that it needs careful attention lest its gathering and dispersing corrupt the message, the messenger, and reception of the Gospel. It must be admitted that the Council itself thought only of greater efficiency and providing *more* material resources for missions, not of the deeper questions. Indeed, this entire issue has been dealt with nowhere as thoroughly and painstakingly — in regard to its deeper ramifications — as we find it treated in Professor Bonk's book.

It is not too radical, I think, to ask: Is the flow of large amounts of money from North to South still needed? Should the status of the young church remain humble and its growth proceed only as local economies grow? Would such a step lead local Christians to exert greater efforts toward sociopolitical and economic development and liberation than they do when, for example, they seek all the funds for a new pastoral ministry training center abroad rather than raise half or even more locally?

While not wanting to attack the notion of international Christian solidarity, the practical ambiguity of Northern financial support of Southern evangelization efforts simply must not be passed over in silence. We have the historical examples of an untold number of schools, churches, and hospitals founded and built by both Catholics and Protestants in their missions. Without question they did a lot of good, but they also created the impression that the mission/evangelization enterprise is performed by a mighty transnational religious corporation. The Christian missionaries of India became known as managers of schools and hospitals, yet not as masters of the spiritual life. Here one must think of Jesus, who did not let himself be impressed by the magnificence of buildings in the Holy City. Consider his reply to the disciple's exclamation: "Look, Teacher, what large stones, what buildings!" The reaction of Jesus was: "Not one stone here will be left upon another; all will be thrown down" (Mark 13:1–2).

Reflecting on the challenges contained in the person and message of Jesus is as difficult for Catholics as it is for Evangelicals. No one needs to cast a stone at anyone else, but perhaps we can help one another understand the particular nature of the problems we face individually as churches. Jonathan Bonk is immensely helpful in this.

The extremes of poverty and wealth in today's world are a real scandal. "Scandal," in the weak sense of the word's common use, means "shocking." What needs consideration is whether the scandal may be *real scandal* in the classic sense — leading people astray and corrupting them, even if unconsciously. Put in the form of a question that flows naturally from Professor Bonk's book: "Does money today so obfuscate interchurch relations as to distort the Gospel? For both members of long-established and younger churches?"

We Christians know we are called to work toward a climate where a reasonable contentment with a more modest living standard must become the norm. But when our very evangelization efforts — moving from the North to the South — involve us in funding church projects and development projects that undoubtedly benefit people, questions still need to be raised: Do not *even the best* of such projects run the risk of undesirable consequences?

The church, we easily say, does not exist for itself, but is founded as a sign of hope for the world. And we know that Christians did not receive the command to construct buildings but to invite peoples to discover their fellowship as forgiven, Spirit-enlivened believers under God in Jesus as the Christ. This is the task of God's people, that all may live more worthily in the sight of God and their fellow human beings.

Money is and will always be important and necessary for the life of churches. Nevertheless, it must be allocated in the right proportions and with full knowledge that — under present world conditions — it is not merely neutral, but dangerously liable to corrupt the evangelization process. Until a short time ago it was a one-way street between Western churches and the Southern missions. In the North was the rich, charitable, teaching church; in the South were the poor, needy recipients of Northern Christian largesse. In the past twenty-five years that relationship has been transformed into a highway with two-way traffic. We are no longer dealing with one-sided mission help, but with a need for a frank and critical exchange of insights between churches that can and should occur on several levels. That process receives an extremely insightful assist in the work of Professor Bonk. I only hope that the entire church will have the wisdom and courage to take up his invitation to reflect seriously on this important question.

Foreword

An African Viewpoint on Wealthy Missionaries

Zablon Nthamburi

I grew up near a mission station where for many years I interacted and rubbed shoulders with missionaries. At that time, missionaries were the only people who had good and decent houses, clean piped water, telephones, electricity, and serviceable automobiles. They were able to employ quite a number of people in the neighborhood as cooks, ayahs, gardeners, messengers, and menials of various kinds who did many of the more tedious household chores for them. There was no doubt that they were privileged ones, envied by less lavishly endowed neighbors who would have embraced Christianity at once had they been assured that such immense affluence and wealth were part of the package. What brought about disillusionment and resentment to a young Christian community was the feeling that they had been conjured into believing that, by becoming Christians, their material and social statuses would dramatically improve. The missionary was, by local standards, a very wealthy person. People could not understand why, with so much wealth, the missionary seemed unwilling to share with those who were poverty stricken.

In *The Gospel and Frontier Peoples,* John Mbiti describes African converts as beggars of Christian spirituality, ideas, cash, and personnel. As he puts it:

> African Christians still regard the missionary or his home church over-seas as "omniscient" in all matters pertaining to Christian faith; as the "omnipotent" in money and wealth.[1]

What Mbiti means is that African Christians expected so much from rich mission-aries because they could see the rich baggage of a missionary who was arriving for a new appointment. They wondered why on earth should a single person have so much while most people lived in deprivation. Even chiefs, considered wealthy by local standards, would visit a missionary for the purpose of acquiring a part of his astonishing wealth. Such affluence gave the missionary leverage and power in the community. Reflecting on this phenomena, Jean-Marc Ela wonders how the

---

1. R. Pierce Beaver, ed., *The Gospel and Frontier Peoples* (South Pasadena, CA: William Carey Library, 1973), 81.

Church can evangelize without being an incarnational institution sharing the life of the people, since that is the locus par excellence of the mediation of Scripture, the fertile ground of all experience of prayer, and the celebration of salvation in Jesus Christ.[2]

The witness of self-denial, lived out in authentic imitation of Christ, places us at the very heart of the Gospel. It locates us at a pivotal point where we are able to proclaim the saving power of God in a credible manner. The mere possession of a creed and articles of faith does not break down the wall of separation between poor and rich, slave and free; nor does orthodoxy ensure the operation of the Spirit in relationships between rich and poor within the Church. Together, excessive affluence and obsessive orthodoxy produce spiritual neuroticism.

Missionaries have been stunned and astonished to discover that their resources, job security, and Western lifestyle elevate them to the ranks of the rich in most communities. The stark contrast with those among whom they serve — who are often poverty-stricken and have little hope of improving their lot — hits them like a bombshell. Because of innate human egocentrism, it is only discerning missionaries who are able to realize the degree to which their lifestyle contradicts the biblical message. The effectiveness of the Gospel is hindered by insensitive affluence that makes social relationships not only difficult but embarrassing; for as long as there is an economic gap between missionaries and their converts, fraternal fellowship is difficult to maintain. In the end, the Gospel that the missionary tries to proclaim is watered down, not intentionally but watered down nonetheless.

Traditionally, Christian missions in the developing countries were undertaken from positions of power and affluence. Missionaries appeared as heroes among their own people; religious literature and missionary pamphlets bolstered interest in a missionary "vogue" that was not only heroic but fascinating. This literature, with its fantasies of faraway lands where exceptional persons performed mighty deeds, attracted many to the missionary vocation. As Adrian Hastings observes, at the beginning, the Baptists were not numerically or socially a powerful community. Their numerical growth, however, coincided with the growth of American neocolonial interest in Africa and the rise of Baptist social status in the United States. While at the beginning they were concerned about the poor, they have now "lost that objective status of disinterestedness and, perhaps, sympathy with the underdog which they previously possessed."[3]

In *Missions and Money* Dr. Bonk addresses himself to an extremely important concern in mission work. As he most articulately shows, the modus operandi of Western missionaries reflects the increasing prosperity of their homelands in a world where the gap between rich and poor is widening. Such affluence cataclysmically isolates missionaries from the cutting edge of missionary endeavors, rendering their efforts futile.

---

2. Jean-Marc Ela, *African Cry*, trans. Robert R. Barr (Maryknoll, NY: Orbis Books, 1980), 71–80.

3. Adrian Hastings, *A History of African Christianity 1950–1975* (London: Cambridge University Press, 1979), 228.

Dr. Bonk writes from a vantage point within the inner circle of missionary engagement, being a son of missionaries with whom he lived in Ethiopia for many years, and as a missionary in his own right, faithfully witnessing to the saving power of Jesus Christ and reflecting this in his own life. The sincerity with which he writes is genuine and endearing not only to evangelicals but to all Christians whose concern it is to share the truth of the Gospel. The reader will be attracted not only by the lucid and vivid nature of this book, but also by its radically biblical orientation and down-to-earth illustrations. The book challenges us not to resignation, but, through the enabling power of the Holy Spirit, to struggle to remove a dangerous contradiction from Western missionary endeavors. Dr. Bonk encourages us to adopt the incarnational model of mission, rejecting the easy power and prestige of affluence by an act of deliberate self-emptying. This book is a must for all people interested in doing Christian mission in a Christian way.

Introduction to the Revised Edition

My interest in the relational dynamics of material and social disparity in close social proximity, with particular attention to its Christian missionary dimensions, was probably inevitable. As a child of missionary parents, my most formative years were spent in Ethiopia, where, until I reached my later teens, I absorbed the values and assumed the entitlements of white, expatriate material and social privilege. Reminiscent of the privileged subjects of Robert Coles's famous *Children of Crisis* series, I confronted the burden of my own privilege, subconsciously at first, and later consciously.[1] The boarding school that I attended stood as an unapologetic bastion of Western privilege, with Ethiopians permanently relegated to kitchen, laundry, garden, and custodial roles. At the tinkle of a small bell at the head table, a barefooted servant would patter in from the kitchen, white apron scantly concealing his own threadbare clothes. The school was surrounded by a chain-link fence, intended to keep the entitled in and the unentitled out. Aware that we were members of a privileged superior class, we accepted, expected, and sometimes demanded the obsequious deference shown to us by "them," including adults. In our play and discussion, Ethiopians were subjects of curiosity, sometimes the objects of ridicule, and occasionally admired for their stoicism in the face of poverty and persecution; but they were seldom friends, and even more rarely social peers.

Returning to Canada in 1960 to continue my education, it would be fourteen years before I would return to Ethiopia — this time as a missionary with the Sudan Interior Mission. My wife and I were assigned to work in Tigre Province, administering a sixty-five-member multinational relief and development team working with survivors of the famine that would precipitate the collapse of Ethiopia's ancient monarchy, and the murder of its last emperor, the venerable Haile Selassie.

---

1. Robert Coles is a professor of psychiatry and medical humanities at Harvard Medical School, a research psychiatrist for the Harvard University Health Services, and the James Agee Professor of Social Ethics at Harvard College. In the 1950s he began listening to American children. The results of his efforts — published in five volumes between 1967 and 1977 — constitute one of the most remarkably perceptive social studies ever undertaken on this continent. Heard in their own voices were America's "children of crisis": African American children caught in the throes of the South's racial integration; the children of impoverished migrant workers in Appalachia; children whose families were transformed by the migration from South to North, from rural to urban communities; Latino, Native American, and Eskimo children in the poorest communities of the American West; and the children of America's wealthiest families confronting the burden of their own privilege. The five volumes in the series, published by Little, Brown (Boston) between 1967 and 1977, include: *Children of Crisis: A Study of Courage and Fear; The South Goes North; Migrants, Sharecroppers, Mountaineers; Eskimos, Chicanos, Indians;* and *Privileged Ones: The Well-off and the Rich in America.*

By this time theoretically egalitarian, and naturally predisposed to criticism of
Western mission modus operandi, I ensured that each member of the team —
an internationally eclectic mix of medical doctors and nurses, hydrologists and
water engineers, agriculturalists and mechanics, drivers and cooks, evangelists
and interpreters — received an equal share of the financial pot. We worked and
lived together both in the field and at the home base. I regret to recall that my not-
always-subliminal attitude vis-à-vis fellow missionaries sometimes bordered on
that of the infamous Pharisee in our Lord's parable, whose self-consciously conspicuous piety compared so unfavorably with that of the wretched tax collector
who prayed nearby (Luke 18:9–14).

With the deposition of the emperor came a palpable shift in media portrayals
of Western foreigners, including missionaries. As its military junta (the *Derg*)
proceeded to move the country from oppressive feudalism to enlightened socialism, the euphoria of its citizens was palpable. For the first time in several
millennia, peasant farmers could contemplate the prospect of owning their farms
and reaping 100 percent of what they sowed. Absentee landlords were to be a
vestige of the past. Millions faced the happy prospect of literacy as the country's
students poured out of the cities and towns and into the countryside to teach
reading and socialism. Students, in turn, would learn to respect the peasantry and
hard manual labor.

Following our stint in northern Ethiopia, my wife and I were assigned to Kaffa
province in the south, where coffee is thought to have originated. Here we worked
with a number of established congregations within several days walking distance
of Bonga. Our primary role was to lend support to the work of evangelists serving under the auspices of the Kale Heywet [Word of Life] denomination. The
church, sensing in the emerging stress on literacy an ideal opportunity for service, seconded Christian teachers and their families to assist in congregational and
community literacy in the hinterlands of the province. Poverty-stricken local communities were encouraged to construct simple single-room schools for which the
mission agency would supply corrugated roofing and blackboards, while teachers
engaged by the Kale Heywet church would provide instruction. As the presumably neutral foreigner, residing not far from a small town that boasted both a
post office and a telephone, the missionary's role was to liaise between the Kale
Heywet Church and the literacy teachers, serving as their communications and
financial conduit. The monthly stipend for each family was roughly equivalent
to eight U.S. dollars, with no benefits. To my personal net monthly income of
twelve hundred dollars, in the meanwhile, were added such benefits as medical
insurance, a semifurnished house, travel funds, and educational opportunities for
my children.

I derived quiet yet smug satisfaction from my self-perceived ability to work in
fraternal, nonpatronizing ways with my Ethiopian colleagues. Our home was as
open to them as theirs were to me. While vaguely disquieted by the conspicuous
material inequities that marked our economically and socially disparate lives, I
gave little thought to what could or should be done about it. An unwritten code
among foreign missionaries obliged one to toe the line when it came to wages

and other forms of remuneration. To break rank would set a dangerous precedent, exposing colleagues to invidious comparisons and putting enormous pressure on the cash-starved Kale Heywet denomination to do the same. It was commonly understood and frequently observed, furthermore, that increased compensation rates would "spoil" Ethiopian employees, rendering them unsuitable for church or mission duties.

Shortly following the departure of our senior — and I must add, exemplary — missionary colleagues, government teachers initiated a national strike, temporarily paralyzing the regime's literacy and socialization efforts. Although privately employed educators did not participate, several of the Kale Heywet teachers with whom I worked were arrested and required to show proof that they were legitimately employed by a recognized organization. Since the Kale Heywet denominational headquarters was hundreds of miles away, where its leaders were absorbed with myriad Marxist-revolution-related challenges of their own, I provided the beleaguered teachers with identification cards bearing the imprimatur of the mission society. At their request, ostensibly to reinforce their claim to be in active good standing as teachers, I also provided them with signed and dated receipts indicating the amount of their monthly reimbursement. These receipts, like their identification cards, bore the seal of my mission agency. With these documents in hand, the teachers returned to their several posts, more secure and apparently relieved.

Several weeks later the local bailiff served me with a lengthy indictment, initiated by the very teachers to whom I had recently rendered service. Charging that I was a "running dog capitalist and exploiter of the people," the document went on to enumerate twenty-three separate misdemeanors, climaxing with the charge that I had defrauded them of one-half of their contracted wages. My protests that the teachers were not in fact employed by me or by the mission, but by their denomination, were met with flat denial, the teachers offering as proof their SIM identification cards and compensation receipts. When I countered that contracts detailing the agreement between each teacher and the Kale Heywet denomination would support my contention, and that these could be found in the elementary school office filing cabinet, my accusers retorted that I was lying, and that there were no such contracts. Inspection of the filing cabinet revealed it to be empty. The contracts and everything else had disappeared.

Mission personnel policies clearly stipulated that Ethiopian employees be reimbursed a monthly minimum of what was then the equivalent of sixteen U.S. dollars, yet the receipts that I had signed provided damning proof that these men had been receiving only half of that amount. From all appearances, I had been pocketing the rest. Justice required that the teachers be compensated for back pay and damages. This, together with several similarly vexing experiences, drove me from Eden. Having until then concealed myself behind the scanty fig leaf of Western cultural entitlement, my material plenty in the context of relative destitution began to assume its rightful theological significance, and I stood exposed to myself in ways that had long been evident to my Ethiopian colleagues.

Denial and the reassuring rationalizations to which I had once had recourse were stripped away. I understood as never before why the rich dare not risk living in close social or physical proximity to the poor, and why, when circumstances oblige them to do so, they must protect themselves and their possessions with walls, gates, bars, dogs, armed guards, the society of the similarly privileged, and — if necessary — lethal violence or even war.

This experience provided me with an opportunity to regard myself from the vantage point of the poor among whom I lived and with whom I worked. My ruminations eventually resulted in the book *Missions and Money: Affluence as a Missionary Problem,* drafted during a 1987–88 sabbatical at Yale University, and published by Orbis in 1991 as number fifteen in the American Society of Missiology Series. Now in its eleventh printing, and badly out of date, the book nevertheless continues to be among the few attempts to address the issue, and is used for missionary training and orientation purposes across the English-speaking world.

Of the scores of letters that I have received from missionaries in the twenty years since I first began to write on the subject, scarcely any have manifested outrage or defensiveness. More typically, my correspondents have thanked me for providing them with a way of clarifying an issue that has long troubled them. Many have asked how they can become members of the "Fellowship of Venturers in Simpler Living" — a stillborn association that never went beyond a few sentences in the concluding chapter of the first edition. It was an idea that I had borrowed from Daniel Johnson Fleming's 1933 publication, *Ventures in Simpler Living,* and from his later *Ethical Issues Confronting World Christians,* both published by the International Missionary Council in New York (1935). I have had to confess that the envisaged "Fellowship" never materialized. Perhaps this edition of the book will serve as a modest amends for this unintentional failure.

Exploration of the roots of poverty and elucidation of the supposed wellsprings of affluence were not the purposes of the book then, nor are they its focus now, as important as these subjects might be.[2] Nor *was* it or *is* it my intention to address the immensely complex, ideologically polarizing questions swirling around missiological debates about dependency and interdependency. Rather, my attempt has been and is to show how both the effectiveness and the integrity of decent, well-meaning missionaries and mission organizations can be compromised when theory and practice are demonstrably at odds with those of the Lord they proclaim. This book is not about economic theory, but about the challenge of living *Christianly* in contexts of dire economic deprivation and destitution. Its argument may be summarized as follows:

---

2. Stephen C. Smith estimates that "There are on the order of one million programs around the world attempting to reduce poverty,..." in his book *Ending Global Poverty: A Guide to What Works* (New York: Palgrave Macmillan, 2005), xi. Smith is Professor of Economics at George Washington University, where he directs the Research Program on Poverty, Development, and Globalization. His material is based on the *World Bank Development Report: Attacking Poverty,* World Development Report 2000/2001 (New York: Oxford University Press, 2000). Equally gloomy is the most recent report of the World Bank, *World Development Report 2006: Equity and Development* (Washington, D.C., and New York: World Bank and Oxford University Press, 2005).

- Western missionaries frequently discover themselves to be relatively wealthy within their ministry contexts due to historical, economic, and cultural factors that cannot be replicated by the poor.

- It follows that what the Bible says *to* and *about* the rich, it says *to* and *about* such missionaries. *Wealth* and *poverty* are among the most frequently recurring themes in our Christian Scriptures.[3]

- While gross economic inequity in close social proximity poses profound relational, communicatory, and strategic challenges for missionaries, more serious are the complex ethical questions that challenge wealthy followers of Jesus in contexts of profound poverty. These questions emerge from scriptural teaching on the relationship between rich and poor, and between God's people and their possessions.

- Since the Christian faith is above all a relational faith, lived out in specific social and cultural contexts, verbalization of "the real Gospel" by missionaries who make a comfortable living from their religion is potentially obscured, subverted, or contradicted by the *good news of plenty,* of which they themselves constitute "exhibit A."

- Missionaries have tended to "adopt" (slip into) one of four possible responses to this state of affairs: (1) associate primarily with those of approximately equal social and economic privilege; (2) assume a simple lifestyle that it is hoped belies the extent of their privilege, whilst surreptitiously maintaining the benefits of Western entitlement in critical areas such as medical care, transportation, education of children, and retirement; (3) shift the debate from the moral/ethical dimensions of missionary affluence to the realm of mission strategy, focusing on the relative advantages of church independence as compared to dependence or interdependence; and, less frequently, (4) adopt a radically incarnational lifestyle, giving up privilege and living as those among whom they serve.

- While each of these approaches can be sufficiently beneficial as to be defensible, in this book I am proposing a fifth approach: assumption of the biblically informed and contextually delineated status of the "righteous rich," as delineated in my concluding chapter, and elucidated in the biblical essays by Christopher J. H. Wright and Justo González. The best way forward, I argue, is to learn how to function as "righteous rich" as opposed to "unrighteous rich" missionaries, within the socioeconomic contexts in which service is rendered. The status of "righteous rich," together with its concomitant roles, must be defined contextually but informed biblically.

- In the context of Protestant evangelicalism, neither conventional missiologies nor on-field orientations adequately prepare aspiring missionaries to address or even acknowledge the ethical compromises so conspicuously evident in the lives and ministries of those who — in St. Paul's words —

---

3. See the article by Jim Wallis, "A Bible Full of Holes," appearing in *The Mennonite* (November 21, 2000): 6–7.

"*peddle the word of God for profit*" (2 Cor. 2:17) in contexts of poverty. It is vital that the institutions and agencies committed to the missional Church address the issue in all of its complexity directly, deliberately, persistently, and biblically through training, mentoring, and policy. It is my hope that this book will serve that purpose.

When the first edition of the book appeared, I resolved to refrain from either teaching or lecturing on the subject, unless invited to do so. It is a vow I have maintained. The result has been seminars and lectures given in both academic and mission circles in Korea, Norway, Denmark, Scotland, Ecuador, New Zealand, the United Kingdom, Canada, and the United States. Thanks to Professors Peter Kuzmic and Timothy Tennent, for the past several years I have conducted annual seminars on the subject for M.Div. and D.Min. students at Gordon-Conwell Theological Seminary. I have been humbled to learn that a number of seminary and college instructors make my book required reading, and that students are obliged to provide written critical responses — which are sometimes forwarded to me. At an academic conference on the theme of "Missions, Money, and Privilege" hosted by the University of Edinburgh in July 2004, I listened with mild chagrin to a young scholar whose presentation, "From Powerless to Powerful: The Role of South Korean Missions in Relation to the Bonk Paradigm of Missions and Money," elucidated perceptions of my views and their concomitant implications that were somewhat unfamiliar to me.

In addition to the credits noted in my introduction to the first edition, I must mention the names of those without whom this revised edition would not have been possible. To Wisnu Sasongko, OMSC's artist in residence for 2004–5, I am indebted for the striking cover art — an evocative rendering of one of the characteristics of the earliest community of Christ-followers, singled out for notice by St. Luke in Acts 4:34 — "There was no needy person among them." I thank Meredith Farmer, my Yale Divinity School student intern for 2004–5, for cheerfully enduring the tedium of digitalizing the entire text of the first edition. To Matthew Kustenbauder, also a student at Yale Divinity School and part-time admissions assistant at the Overseas Ministries Study Center, must go credit for updating the tables in chapter 1. Finally, it is because of the patient persistence of my good friend Bill Burrows, managing editor of Orbis Books, that this book appears only one year later than I had initially intended.

To all of these must go my thanks, but not the blame, for this book.

Introduction to the First Edition

To speak of the affluence of missionaries in the context of a North American society that has become obsessed with consumption and with the mad pursuit of an ever-higher standard of living may seem oddly incongruous. If there are any North American Christians who have consistently exemplified the path of discipleship described by Jesus following his encounter with the rich young man recorded in Matthew 19:16–30, they are our foreign missionaries. Who more than missionaries have literally "left houses or brothers or sisters or father or mother or children or fields" for Jesus' sake? In the popular mind, the North American missionary is a living thesaurus on the word "sacrifice"! And for good reason, too. The sacrifices made by missionaries going abroad from the shores of the wealthy nations have been real.

But here we have a paradox. Missionaries who bid farewell to the good life in North America and Europe have frequently, upon arrival in the country of their destination, found themselves regarded as rich! Their personal resources, employment security, benefits, and lifestyle choices combine to make them the envy of those among whom they serve — whose life circumstances make them relatively poverty-stricken, and whose lifestyle options are severely limited by their lack of resources.

Several years ago, I tentatively explored some of the positive and negative implications of such disparity in a series of lectures and in articles appearing in two journals widely read by missionaries around the world.[1] The letter response was such as to confirm in my mind that the relative affluence of missionaries sent out from North American churches is of sufficient significance to warrant further investigation of the negative and positive, overt and covert, effects of the resulting economic and social disparity upon the accomplishing of the missionary task.

Often, after I have lectured on this subject, missionary reaction has been understandably defensive. But inevitably, as the discussion of the issue continues, missionaries have related personal anecdotes, reinforcing the central thesis that the relative affluence and security of our Western missionaries frequently constitutes a serious obstacle to the furtherance of the Gospel.

Surprisingly, a number of missionaries have chided me for not making the case against missionary affluence strong enough. Typical was the letter from W.E.C. missionary Patrick Johnstone, author of *Operation World.* "I have just

---

1. See Jon Bonk, "Affluence: The Achilles' Heel of Missions," *Evangelical Missions Quarterly* 21, no. 4 (October 1985): 382–90; and "The Role of Affluence in the Christian Missionary Enterprise from the West," *Missiology: An International Review* 14, no. 4 (October 1986): 437–61.

been reading your article on the Achilles Heel of modern missions. . . . Make it stronger; we want courageous missionaries who will battle through to a simpler lifestyle, and even to a Henry Martyn 'My love shall wait' commitment!"[2]

A church planter with Churches of Christ in Uruguay wrote commending me for "hitting the nail on the head." Affluence, he said, "has been the overwhelmingly greatest hindrance to my work in Montevideo."[3]

A researcher in evangelism with the Presbyterian Church in Canada Board of Congregational Life pointed out that the issue of economic disparity was "a very important area for home missions as well as our foreign missions," and gave illustrations from her denomination's experience with inner-city populations.[4]

After eight years in Irian Jaya, a missionary couple, in a letter to the alumni director of the institution where I teach, wrote:

> The greatest challenge we face in ministry in Irian is the day to day struggle against our far superior standard of living, the status and wealth we have, in comparison to the primitive people God has given us to minister to. They clearly are aware of the "gulf between" and desire to attain to that standard of power and wealth they see in us. We sought to cut back, and live more simply than most missionaries in Irian Jaya. But the struggle remains. So opposite of the example of Incarnation given us by Christ. But also easy to justify. Missionaries do it every day.[5]

Some will be disappointed to discover that this is not a "how-to" book. There are no easy answers to the perplexing and sometimes ministry-destroying effects of missionary affluence. But to deny that the problem exists is to manifest a willful myopia verging on blindness. And to refuse to confront an issue simply because it is too complicated to permit easy analysis or resolution is the height of folly. As I hope to demonstrate in the first three chapters, Western missionaries have seldom been unaware of the relative economic and material advantages which they clearly enjoy when abroad. Furthermore, many have selflessly put both themselves and their means at the disposal of those less fortunate than themselves. Some — though not many — have manifested quite remarkably the gracious spirit of their Lord, for the sake of others making themselves poor, that these through their poverty might be made rich (2 Cor. 8:9).

But missionaries sent into all the world by the affluent churches of the West usually do not — in any literal or deliberate sense — make this their modus operandi. Western missionaries reflect the increasing prosperity of their homelands in a world where the gulf between rich and poor is widening, where the rich are becoming proportionately fewer, and where the material prospects of the majority of peoples are dismal indeed. Missionaries from North American churches in particular have attained a level of prosperity unimaginable to the vast majority of the peoples among whom they serve. It will be the argument of this book that

2. Letter, Johnstone to Bonk, February 26, 1985.
3. Letter, Waddell to Bonk, November 7, 1986.
4. Letter, Strickland to Bonk, December 17, 1986.
5. Letter, McAllister to Loge, April 16, 1987, Irian Jaya.

this insular prosperity, while enabling the Western Church to engage in numerous expensive, efficient, and even useful activities overseas, has an inherent tendency to isolate missionaries from the cutting edge of missionary endeavor, rendering much of their effort either unproductive or counterproductive, or both.

This book has not been an easy one to write. As the son of missionaries who spent the best part of their lives in service to the people of Ethiopia, as one whose closest friends include numerous missionaries, and as one devoted to the task of sharing with the world the good news of Jesus as Savior and Lord, it is with a deep sense of personal humility and unworthiness that I write, for I am well aware of the deep and often sacrificial commitment to service characterizing many missionaries.

Nor should my criticism be interpreted as disloyalty to the cause. Those who speak or write are frequently tempted to say what people want to hear, instead of what needs to be said. Those seeking advice often manifest a marked preference for advisors whose words echo their own opinions. One man recently explained that he preferred the Unitarian Church over others he had tried because it was open-minded, and made no awkward religious demands on him. It is an all too human tendency. Most of us — even missiologists and ecclesiastics — prefer the soothing optimism of possibility thinking to the discouraging pessimism of the prophet who declares that unless there is repentance, there is no hope (cf. Isa. 30:9–11). American psychologists, having "proven that positive people outperform pessimists," have linked forces with business to find or create "supersalesmen."[6] This preference for positive thinkers is by no means restricted to the business world.

In ancient times, as now, the powerful frequently found it convenient to kill or otherwise dispose of those who spoke the truth, and would willingly listen to the counsel only of those whose opinions were in striking and flattering agreement with their own! Thus, Balak, the king of Moab, hired Balaam to curse the Israelites (Num. 22); Ahab and Jezebel, smarting from the words of the prophets of Yahweh, attempted to obliterate them — somehow imagining that ignorance of the truth would change the facts (1 Kings 18–22). The men of Anathoth tried to destroy Jeremiah, in this instance the one through whom the Lord revealed His immensely unpopular will (Jer. 11:18–23; cf. 6:13–15; 8:14–16; 38); and Pashhur, the chief officer in the temple of the Lord, had Jeremiah beaten and placed in stocks for speaking words given to him by God Himself (Jer. 20). Our Savior was killed because the truth he lived and proclaimed was too threatening to the vested interests of both the religious establishment and the political radicals of his day. Paul and the other apostles met similar fates, as the truth which they spoke came into conflict with powerful political, economic, or religious "powers that be," who stood to lose a great deal if the truth were to prevail.

Such behavior is not the exclusive prerogative of the mighty. Even we ordinary folk, with our modest but intensely personal stock in the status quo, are reticent to give our attention to those who speak of the need for repentance —

---

6. See Jill Neimark, "The Power of Positive Thinkers: How One Company Created a Work Force Full of Optimists," *Success* (September 1987).

our repentance. The human inclination, attested to by the sorry record of history, is to gather around us "a great number of teachers to say what our itching ears want to hear...to suit [our] own desires" (2 Tim. 4:4). As members of the Body of Christ, sent into the world to do and to be all that God sent Christ into the world to do and to be, our response to God's message should not be to do away with the medium. Rather — like David, as the shatteringly painful truth of Nathan's message came home to him — we should respond in a constructively repentant way to what God is saying to us. Any other course of action is more than deliberate disobedience; it is spiritual suicide.

It is my intention to speak the truth, insofar as I am able to discern it. This book is an attempt to explore, however inadequately, one aspect of Western missionary life and ministry which has for a variety of reasons been virtually ignored in the writing and teaching of most contemporary missiologists. The conscience, someone once said, is like a sundial. The person who shines his flashlight on it in the middle of the night can get it to tell him any time he wants. But when the sun shines on the dial, it can only tell the truth. That our consciences have been infected by the highly contagious hedonism characterizing Western societies cannot be denied. It remains to be seen whether the infection is lethal.

The argument of the book will evolve along the following lines: Beginning with a description of the nature, scale, and context of missionary affluence, it will be argued that the sense of entitlement with which Western missionaries regard their personal material and economic advantage can be traced to the very beginnings of the modern missionary era, and remains deeply embedded — for good and for ill — at the very core of Western missionary thinking, strategy, and policy. Some of the varied consequences — foreseen and unforeseen, deliberate and accidental, profound and incidental, positive and negative — of this disparity will be explored. An examination of some of the relational, communicatory, and theological challenges facing the rich missionary will then follow. And finally, an attempt will be made to point to the narrow way out of the mire of personal affluence — a difficult way, certainly — but a hopeful way that has been and is being followed by tens of thousands of missionaries...some of these Western.

Despite Jesus' insistence that "no prophet is accepted in his home town" (Luke 4:24), in this book I speak as an evangelical, primarily to evangelicals. Others of the household of faith are welcome to listen and are invited to contribute, of course. But if the language and the agenda of this book seem sometimes strange and unfamiliar, I beg you to bear with a fellow disciple.

Made possible by the cheerful support of my dearest and most loyal sojourners — Jean, Susie, and Jimmy; by the salaried sabbatical leave granted me by my school, Winnipeg Bible College and Winnipeg Theological Seminary; by the generous financial support of the Earhart Foundation; by the hospitality of the Overseas Ministries Study Center; and by the vast libraries and helpful personnel at Yale University; this book is dedicated to those who read their sundials by the Son who is the true Light of the world, rather than by the lights of the world.

Part I

THE CONTEXT OF WESTERN MISSIONARY AFFLUENCE

In an economic variation of the David and Goliath theme so dear to the Christian heart, the last two hundred years have witnessed David (Western missionaries) wearing Saul's armor and carrying Saul's weapons, marching against a Goliath (the mission field) clad in a skin and armed with only a few stones and a sling. The economic might has been on the side of missionaries from the West — in some instances representing multinational mission agencies whose annual budgets exceed those of the host governments themselves and constituting those countries' most significant source of foreign exchange.

Part 1 of this book, comprising chapters 1 through 3, attempts to show that neither missionary affluence itself nor missionary thinking about affluence takes place within a vacuum. Historical, cultural, and rational influences have changed and continue to exert a powerful effect on that Western missionary theory and practice which touches upon the personal stewardship of money and possessions in the context of poverty. In chapter 1 the fact and the scale of Western missionary affluence are briefly outlined. Chapter 2 shows how each succeeding generation of Western missionaries is culturally conditioned to redefine personal material "needs" according to a continually escalating standard that most of the world's population can only regard as wildly inflated. Chapter 3 demonstrates that missionaries are rational creatures, making quite deliberate economic choices for the best of personal and strategic reasons.

1

1

The Fact and the Extent
of Western Missionary Affluence

The wealth of the rich is their fortified city, but poverty is the ruin of the poor.
— SOLOMON

Western missionary awareness and acknowledgment of relative personal afflu-ence are not new. Indeed, even a cursory study of missions history reveals as commonplace a self-conscious sense of superiority on the part of missionar-ies, deriving from and proven by the fact of — it was thought, providential — economic advantage.[1]

One hundred and forty-five years ago, in an essay that won its author two hundred guineas, missionary weal was accepted as a natural concomitant of Brit-ish material prosperity, the climax of a slow but steady evolution from days when the nation had been "as obscure among the nations...as Africans [then were]." But now, Moffat modestly continued, "We have become rich in a variety of acquirements, favoured above measure in the gifts of Providence, unrivaled in Commerce, preeminent in arts, foremost in the pursuits of philosophy and science, and in all the blessings of civil society."[2]

In his Donnellan lectures at the University of Dublin twenty years later, William Walsh echoed Moffat. Though doubtless well read, Walsh confessed that he could not think of another nation "since the days of Israel" so highly favored as Britain.[3]

On the American side somewhat later, but no less confident, Josiah Strong, general secretary of the Evangelical Alliance, was only one prominent voice among many at that time proclaiming the inauguration of the final age in world

---

1. Jonathan Bonk, "'And They Marveled...': Mammon as Miracle in Western Missionary Encounter," in James R. Krabill, Walter Sawatsky, and Charles E. Van Engen, eds., *Evangelical, Ecumenical, and Anabaptist Missiologies in Conversation: Essays in Honor of Wilbert R. Shenk* (Maryknoll, NY: Orbis Books, 2006), 78–87.

2. Robert Moffat, *A Missionary Prize Essay on the Duty, the Privilege, and Encouragement of Christians to Send the Gospel to the Unenlightened Nations of the Earth* (Newcastle: Pattison and Ross, 1842), 50. The author of this essay should not be confused with the more famous London Missionary Society missionary of the same name.

3. William P. Walsh, *Christian Missions: Six Discourses Delivered before the University of Dublin, being the Donnellan Lectures for 1861* (Dublin: George Herbert, 1862), 51.

history. An unabashed proponent of racial manifest destiny,[4] Strong could foresee a time in the near future when, he said, "the mighty centrifugal tendency inherent in [the Anglo-Saxon race] and strengthened in the United States [would] . . . [with its] unequaled energy, with all the majesty of numbers and the might of wealth behind it . . . spread itself over the earth."[5]

Neither the strategies nor the outcomes of Western Christian missionary endeavors for the past two hundred years is possible to understand apart from the massive economic and material superiority enjoyed by missionaries, vis-à-vis majority populations of those regions popularly designated as "mission fields."

Fifteen years in Egypt (1954–69) with the United Presbyterian Church of North America convinced missionary Bernard Quick of this fact. A further five years of wide-ranging research on the subject confirmed that the modus operandi and the modus vivendi of American missions in Egypt were not isolated cases. To the contrary, in Quick's own words, "Economic power is still the most crucial power factor in the Western missionary movement. It is still the most important way that the Western missionary expresses his concept of what it means to 'preach the Gospel.' "[6]

Missiologist Harvie Conn, addressing delegates to the joint meeting of the American Association of Bible Colleges (AABC) and the Association of Evangelical Professors of Mission (AEPM) held in Chicago in October 1985, argued that the most significant of four pressing issues confronting modern mission endeavors was the growing disparity between shrinking rich populations and the burgeoning poor. He wondered how, as partakers of the wealth and security enjoyed by the relatively few, Western missionaries could sit where the majority of this world's peoples sit — poor or absolutely poor, with no prospects beyond destitution.[7]

The statistical dimensions of this economic disparity are not difficult to document. A variety of resources, each in its own way, reveal the breathtaking scale of the economic gulf separating the populations of rich nations from those of the poor. The most commonly used indicator of international economic comparison

---

4. It is important to remember that late-nineteenth-century racism exemplified by Josiah Strong was not peculiar to Christians; indeed, as I have attempted to show elsewhere, the racism of Christians — being based, as it was, upon the doctrine of monogenesis — was far less sinister than the scientific racism of the times, with its "survival of the fittest" assumptions and its varied theories of polygenesis. See Jon Bonk, " 'All Things to All Persons?' — The Missionary as a Racist-Imperialist, 1860–1910," *Missiology: An International Review* 8, no. 3 (July 1980): 285–306.

5. Josiah Strong, *The New Era; or, The Coming Kingdom* (New York: Baker & Taylor Co., 1893), 79–80; and *Our Country: Its Possible Future and Its Present Crisis* (New York: Baker & Taylor Co., 1885), as cited in Sydney E. Ahlstrom, *A Religious History of the American People* (New Haven, CT: Yale University Press, 1972), 849. See also Sydney Ahlstrom's chapter, *"Annuit Coeptis:* America as the Elect Nation. The Rise and Decline of a Patriotic Tradition," in *Continuity and Discontinuity in Church History: Essays Presented to George Huntston Williams on the Occasion of his 65th Birthday,* ed. F. Forrester Church and Timothy George (Leiden: E. J. Brill, 1979), 315–37.

6. Bernard E. Quick, "He Who Pays the Piper . . . : A Study of Economic Power and Mission in a Revolutionary World" (unpublished manuscript, Princeton Theological Seminary, n.d.), 52.

7. Harvie Conn, "Missions and Our Present Moment in History," an address to the Joint October 29–November 1, 1985, Meeting of the American Association of Bible Colleges (AABC) and the Association of Evangelical Professors of Mission (AEPM) held in Chicago.

is Gross Domestic Product (GDP) per capita, which measures the total market value of a country's goods and services — equal to total consumer, investment, and government spending — divided by the country's population for that year. Dollar figures for GDP are converted to international dollars using purchasing power parity (PPP) rates and are not adjusted for inflation. An approximately equivalent amount of goods and services in each country can be purchased with an international dollar.

As obviously crude and potentially misleading standards for comparison, GDP and PPP must nevertheless serve as the most satisfactory tools available to economists attempting meaningful international economic comparisons. However hazy the resulting view, Table 1 on the following page hints at the staggering dimensions of the economic gulf separating wealthy and poor nations in our time.[8] When it is remembered that such studies of relative national wealth do not reflect the inequitable distribution of this wealth within the country itself, no matter how sophisticated the methodology, and that missionaries have typically focused on the lower social and economic echelons of society, the conclusion is well warranted that the economic inequity between Western missionaries and the people among whom they work is probably even greater than aggregate statistics indicate.

According to estimates appearing on Anup Shah's "global issues" web site on April 3, 2006, using figures based on purchasing power parity, approximately 50 percent of the world's population lives on less than two dollars a day.[9] Approximately one-sixth of the world's adults cannot read a book or sign their name. Long-term trends indicate that income ratios dividing rich and poor countries have been steadily increasing for the past two hundred years, as indicated by the table below:

1820	3 to 1
1813	11 to 1
1950	35 to 1
1973	44 to 1
1992	72 to 1

As the World Bank's *World Development Report 2006* observes, inequities between nations or within communities are mirrored in disparate access to health, education, and employment opportunities.[10] According to the same report, while absolute poverty rates have declined over the past twenty years, so that an estimated 400 million fewer people lived on less than one dollar per day in 2001 than in 1981, during the same period "the number of poor people in Sub-Saharan Africa almost doubled, from approximately 160 million to 313 million."[11]

---

8. See "EarthTrends Data Tables: Economics, Business and the Environment," at *www.earthtrends .wri.org/pdf_library/data_tables/ecn3_2005.pdf.*

9. See *www.globalissues.org/TradeRelated/Facts.asp.* Lant Pritchett makes the same point in his article, "Divergence: Big Time," *Journal of Economic Perspectives* 11, no. 3 (Summer 1997): 3–17, although his ratios are based on GNP rather than PPP.

10. *World Development Report 2006: Equity and Development,* 55–69.

11. Ibid., 66.

TABLE 1
Income and Poverty 2005 for Select Countries[12]

	GDP Per Capita PPP (international $2002)	Percent of Population living on less than $1/day	Percent of Population living on less than $2/day	Human Poverty Index (100 = highest)
Asia	4,684			
(excl. Middle East)				
Bangladesh	1,695	36.0	82.8	42.2
Cambodia	2,001	34.1	77.7	42.6
China	4,577	16.6	46.7	13.2
Indonesia	3,223	7.5	52.4	17.8
India	2,681	34.7	79.9	31.4
Japan	26,937			
Korea	17,161			
Philippines	4,171	14.6	46.4	
Thailand	7,009	2.0	32.5	31.1
Europe	18,097			
Denmark	30,943			
Finland	26,186			
France	26,921			
Germany	27,102			
Hungary	13,869	2.0	7.3	
Norway	36,596			
Romania	6,556	2.1	20.5	
Russian Federation	8,269	6.1	23.8	
Spain	21,457			
Sweden	26,048			
Switzerland	30,008			
Ukraine	4,887	2.9	48.7	
United Kingdom	26,155			
Middle East &	5,994	2.4	29.9	
North Africa				
Sub-Saharan Africa	1,779	46.5	78.0	
Congo, Dem. Rep.	621	n.a.	n.a.	42.9
Ethiopia	745	26.3	80.7	55.5
Ghana	2,141	44.8	78.5	26.0
Kenya	1,018	23.0	58.6	37.5
Nigeria	919	70.2	90.8	35.1
South Africa	10,152	7.1	23.8	31.7
Uganda	1,486	n.a.	n.a.	36.4
Tanzania	579	19.9	59.7	36.0
Zambia	839	63.7	87.4	50.4

12. The second chapter of *World Development Report 2006: Equity and Development*, "Inequity within Countries: Individuals and Groups," shows that the world's highest levels of internal inequity are found in African and Latin American countries. See *World Development Report 2006: Equity and Development* (International Bank for Reconstruction and Development/The World Bank: Washington, DC: World Bank and New York: Oxford University Press, 2006), 28–54.

TABLE 1 (continued)
Income and Poverty 2005 for Select Countries

	GDP Per Capita PPP (international $2002)	Percent of Population living on less than $1/day	Percent of Population living on less than $2/day	Human Poverty Index (100 = highest)
North America	53,138			
Canada	29,484			
United States	35,746			
Central America &	7,347			
Caribbean				
Costa Rica	8,817	2.0	9.5	4.4
El Salvador	4,887	31.1	58.0	17.0
Guatemala	4,058	16.0	37.4	22.5
Haiti	1,623	n.a.	n.a.	44.1
Honduras	2,579	23.8	44.4	16.6
Mexico	8,972	9.9	26.3	9.1
South America	7,333			
Argentina	11,083	3.3	14.3	
Bolivia	2,459	14.4	34.3	14.4
Brazil	7,752	8.2	22.4	11.8
Colombia	6,493	8.2	22.6	8.1
Ecuador	3,583	17.7	40.8	12.0
Peru	5,012	18.1	37.7	13.2
Venezuela	5,368	15.0	32.0	8.5
Oceania	21,348			
Australia	28,262			
New Zealand	21,742			

Those among the nearly 400,000 (346,270 short-term and 45,617 full-time) North American Protestant missionaries serving in 211 different countries who happen to be based in wealthier nations would, of course, find themselves at the other end of the inequity equation, as a comparison between Table 2 and Table 3 below would indicate. Nevertheless, the uncontestable fact remains that most Western missionaries are virtual Rothschilds by the economic standards of the world's general population.

Not surprisingly, financial figures provided by North American Protestant agencies simply serve to accentuate the economic power represented by North Americans — including missionaries.[13] While per capita expenditure varies widely between agencies, North American missionaries are on the whole wealthy by majority global standards.

---

13. Western consciences have frequently derived solace from the conviction that "non-Western people don't need as much, because money goes further in their countries." At the same time, one hears that missionary salaries must be increased to keep pace with higher and constantly inflating costs of living in these same countries.

TABLE 2
Countries with More than 50 U.S. Mission Agencies Reported[14]

Country	Number of Agencies	Full-time U.S. Personnel	Country	Number of Agencies	Full-time U.S. Personnel
Mexico	159	1,657	Honduras	69	273
India	155	305	Peru	68	491
Philippines	133	1,278	Romania	64	291
Brazil	112	1,403	Ghana	64	160
Kenya	106	1,032	China	64	350
Russia	96	589	Asia — General	63	2,330
United Kingdom	89	714	Colombia	62	346
Japan	86	921	Uganda	61	278
Ukraine	77	336	Bolivia	60	416
Germany	76	601	Ecuador	57	568
Spain	73	497	Nigeria	57	229
South Africa	73	447	Costa Rica	55	263
France	72	584	Argentina	55	281
Thailand	72	404	Australia	52	352
Haiti	72	225	Hungary	51	283
Indonesia	71	727	Taiwan	51	289
Guatemala	70	350			

Such numbers do not, of course, translate directly into missionary salaries. Mission organizations are usually involved in a broad range of overseas programs, including medicine, education, community development, agricultural assistance, aid and relief, literature production, support of national churches, and technical assistance of various kinds.[15] Nevertheless, such data do indicate the resources which — in the eyes of host peoples — missionaries represent, to some degree control, and benefit from personally.[16]

By the standards of a majority of the world's population, missionaries from Western lands, reflecting the culturally prescribed material entitlements of their consumer cultures, grow ever more rich. As recently as August 17, 2005, the "basic support" of a missionary family — personal friends assigned to South Africa with a well-known mission society — was pegged at $4,344 per month. An additional estimated $600 in monthly "ministry funds" was also needed, on top of "outgoing funds" in excess of $19,000.[17] However inadequate $60,000 per annum might be for sustaining a North American family at levels of minimal social and

---

14. Dotsey Welliver and Minnette Northcutt, eds., *Mission Handbook 2004–2006: U.S. and Canadian Protestant Ministries Overseas,* 19th ed. (Wheaton, IL: Evangelism and Missions Information Service [EMIS], 2004).

15. See the "Ministry Activity" indices on 315–45, 499–507 of *Mission Handbook 2004–2006.*

16. Although the first edition of this book included a table showing "Annual Actual or Recommended Per Missionary Salary/Support Levels of Select North American Agencies" (10), I have chosen not to include such a table in this edition, since mission agencies tend to be somewhat reticent to divulge such information, and, furthermore, utilize widely varying approaches in calculating missionary salaries.

17. In an email dated August 17, 2005. This support would cover salary, administration, health care, and pension.

TABLE 3
U.S. Mission Agencies Reporting
$10 Million of More Income for Overseas Ministries[18]

U.S. Mission Agency	Number of Overseas[19] Personnel	Reported Income for Overseas (including gifts in kind)
World Vision, Inc.		$447,313,000
Southern Baptist Convention	5,437	197,866,000
Wycliffe Bible Translators	3,907	86,551,480
Assemblies of God	1,708	177,262,833
New Tribes Mission	1,496	32,247,000
Campus Crusade for Christ	1,096	123,279,000
Christian and Missionary Alliance	722	24,743,649
TEAM — The Evangelical Alliance Mission	675	23,540,000
Seventh Day Adventists General Conference	573	62,973,862
CBInternational — formerly Conservative Baptist Foreign Mission Society	558	19,155,068
SIM USA	557	26,670,750
Baptist Mid-Missions	495	19,200,000
Africa Inland Mission International	456	15,062,725
Evangelical Free Church Mission	352	17,120,282
UFM International	312	NR
Avant Ministries — formerly Gospel Missionary Union	257	8,200,000
SEND International	222	11,458,957
CAM International	210	6,260,000
OMF International	187	5,000,000
Eastern Mennonite Missions	140	3,078,974
WEC International	135	3,044,824
World Baptist Fellowship	130	5,600,000
Baptist General Conference	127	8,572,110
South America Mission	94	3,277,763
Child Evangelism Fellowship	72	4,460,518
Mennonite Mission Network	72	5,686,027
MBMS International — Mennonite Brethren Missions/Services	53	1,088,272
Brethren In Christ Mission	36	1,117,069
Samaritan's Purse	19	111,797,883
Africa Inter-Mennonite Mission	16	696,591
Reformed Baptist Mission Services	16	301,517

material entitlement in a bicultural, intercontinental ministry, their compensation guarantees them a place among the privileged in the social hierarchy of South Africa.[20]

18. These figures are from the *Mission Handbook 2004–2006*, 29 and 69–303, passim. Canadian income and personnel are not included.

19. This figure does not include nonresidential mission personnel, who are fully supported U.S. mission staff, and who travel to foreign countries for at least twelve weeks per year on operational aspects of the overseas ministry, but who do not reside in the country or countries of their ministry.

20. It is important to note that the actual salary received by a missionary with a given agency will usually be pegged to the given regional or national cost of living. While many of those working with independent or Interdenominational Foreign Mission Association (IFMA) associated agencies — so-called faith missions — are chronically undersupported, a significant number have access to special "ministry" accounts upon which they may draw for ministry-related expenses such as motor vehicle,

In North America, there seems to be no escaping from the one-way (up) material entitlement escalator whereby one generation's luxuries mutate into another generation's needs. Peter C. Whybrow noted that "As America's commercial hegemony has increased and our social networks have eroded, we have lost any meaningful reference as to how rich we really are, especially in comparison to other nations."[21] Given the extent to which the Christian community is infused with the values of the dominant culture, it would be surprising indeed if Western missionaries were somehow exempt from these powerful influences. As David Hesselgrave recently observed, "In 1998 the total income reported by mission agencies in the United States came within a hair's breadth of ... $3 billion. By 2003 this had increased to over $3.75 billion. Nevertheless, most missions and missionaries continue to report a serious need for support. What are we to make of this state of affairs?"[22]

In conclusion, the United States and Canada are indisputably wealthy nations. Whatever their culturally conditioned perceptions of minimal entitlement, missionaries from these countries are considered well off in most parts of the world. However crude or inadequate the figures cited in the tables above might be, the fact remains that most of the peoples among whom North American missionaries work would gladly trade economic places with them; and conversely, few missionaries would willingly trade places with the peoples among whom they work. Any Western missionary — even a very young missionary — can take for granted a whole range of material accouterments, security provisions, lifestyle choices, and educational options that are beyond the wildest dreams of most of the globe's human inhabitants. Members and missionaries of the North American Church are, beyond doubt, a "People of Plenty."[23]

Just what this means is the subject of later chapters. But one thing is certain: neither the direct effects nor the indirect side effects of missionary affluence have ever been entirely positive. With the weal comes also the woe. As we discuss in chapters 4 through 6, outside observers have been generous in their criticism of missionary lifestyles abroad. Nor have missionaries themselves been blind to the

---

a refrigerator, a power generator, etc. Denominational missionaries, such as Southern Baptists, receive supplementary allowances for such things as U.S. housing, longevity, outfit and refit, furlough transportation, local leave, and children's education, in addition to comprehensive medical insurance, life insurance, and retirement grants. The overall support package is reviewed regularly on the basis of the U.S. Department of State Indexes of Living Costs Abroad, Quarters Allowances, and Hardship Differentials. While Southern Baptist missionaries may be the envy of the missionary world, it is important to remember that relative to local and regional standards, even the poorest Western missionary is well off.

21. Peter C. Whybrow, *American Mania: When More Is Not Enough* (New York and London: W. W. Norton, 2005), 38–39. Whybrow is the Judson Braun Professor of Psychiatry and Biobehavioral Science and the director of the Jane and Terry Semel Institute of Neuroscience and Behavior at the University of California in Los Angeles. George Packer's opinion piece, "When Here Sees There," appearing in the April 21, 2002, issue of the *New York Times Magazine,* is a poignant reminder of the global impact of media inundation of poor countries with pictures of America's "glittering abundance and national self-absorption."

22. David J. Hesselgrave, *Paradigms in Conflict: 10 Key Questions in Christian Missions Today* (Grand Rapids: Kregel Publications, 2005), 228.

23. This is the title of a book by David M. Potter, *People of Plenty: Economic Abundance and the American Character* (Chicago: University of Chicago Press, 1954).

Hydra-headed, complex nature of the problems attendant upon the possession and enjoyment of luxury by those who get paid to speak for God. David Picton Jones, one of the few early missionaries of the London Missionary Society to survive the rigors of East African life long enough to master the local language, interpreted his failure to win converts as an unintended consequence of his personal affluence. "Our life," he wrote to the secretary of the London Missionary Society (LMS), "is far above them, and we are surrounded by things entirely beyond their reach. The consequence is, that they ... *cannot* follow us...."[24] James Gilmour, a contemporary of Jones working with the same agency in China, placed the blame for missionary impotence on their expensive, European style of life.[25]

As the twentieth century progressed and some of the unforeseen and unwelcome side effects of economic disparity became increasingly apparent, Gilmour's lament was joined by a small but vocal chorus of more official missionary voices. A result of the 1928 World Conference at Jerusalem was the establishment (in 1930) of the International Missionary Council of the Department of Social and Economic Research and Counsel, under the direction of J. Merle Davis. Its mandate was "to collect and distribute information on the economic and social developments which challenge the Gospel of Christ and limit the growth of His Kingdom among the younger churches."[26]

Energetic pursuit of this mandate resulted in a series of studies which constituted a significant part of the agenda for the Tambaram Conference of 1938. "Economic Disparities on the Mission Field" was the title of the first chapter of Davis's report. "Economics create an immediate source of misunderstanding in the relationship of the missionary with his people," concluded Davis. As he explained,

> The missionary comes from a world where salaries and expenditure are immensely greater than those prevailing in his new field of work. He is looked upon as the representative of a wealthy and powerful organisation. On arrival in his field the missionary puts into operation a new standard of economic values.... To the average national the missionary appeared not so much as the exponent of a new religion or way of life as a possible source of personal economic improvement.[27]

While the aim of these studies was to gather the kind of information that would enable younger churches to become self-governing, self-supporting, and self-propagating, the problem of missionary affluence always lurked just beneath

---

24. A letter from David Picton Jones (Uguha) to Ralph Wardlaw Thompson (London), December 2, 1884, located in the Council for World Mission Archives (Central Africa-Incoming-5/5/C) at the University of London.

25. See Richard Lovett, *James Gilmour of Mongolia: His Diaries, Letters and Reports* (London: Religious Tract Society, 1893), 211–13.

26. From the Foreword of *The Economic Basis of the Church, Preparatory Studies and Findings, Meeting of the International Missionary Council, at Tambaram, Madras, India, December 12–29, 1938*. See "The Madras Series," vol. 5, ed. J. Merle Davis (New York: International Missionary Council, 1939).

27. See J. Merle Davis, *The Economic and Social Environment of the Younger Churches, The Report of the Department of Social and Economic Research of the International Missionary Council to the Tambaram Meeting — December 1938* (London: Edinburgh House, 1939); a partial list of the specific studies may be found on 225–27.

the surface, and warranted a short chapter in the department's official report to the International Missionary Council in 1938.[28]

Excerpts from an editorial that appeared in the Calcutta-based *Baptist Missionary Review* provided an unambiguous distillation of the essential problem: "A village congregation growing up in the shadow of a mission station's foreign-built domes and towers is impressed from the beginning with its own economic weakness and develops a feeling of helplessness and futility."[29] Nevertheless, the fundamental thrust of the conclusions and recommendations of the studies said little about the personal affluence of Western missionaries; nor does there appear to have been any suggestion that the West might be overdeveloped. The goal appears to have been simply to place national churches on an independent financial footing.

It was Daniel Johnson Fleming, professor of missions at Union Theological Seminary in New York, who seems to have spoken for those who saw in missionary affluence more than simply an awkward obstruction to national church independence. In a book entitled *Ventures in Simpler Living,* written in acknowledgment of those ministry and credibility dilemmas which are a fact of life for Western missionaries whose material and economic resources are excessive by indigenous standards, Fleming chronicled and assessed a variety of practical missionary responses to the issue.[30] Two years later, he argued that "Differences in Standards of Living" was one of the great ethical issues facing world Christians,[31] a theme that he more fully elaborated in his book *Living as Comrades,* published in 1950.[32]

The message of these books seems to have sunk without a trace. Following World War II, with the swelling of North American missionary ranks from fewer than 19,000 missionaries in 1953 to over 400,000 in 2004, the item has virtually disappeared from missiological agendas.[33] This is at least partly due to the fact that the largest proportion of the new missionaries were associated with agencies that were either new and unaware of the mission tradition and experience of the Confessional church agencies, or which regarded with suspicion all churches, mission agencies, and missionaries associated with the ecumenical movement. The unhappy result was a failure to benefit from more than a century of collective mission experience. Whatever the reasons, economic and material disparity has not been high on the agendas of either independent evangelical

---

28. "Economic Disparities on the Mission Field" is the title of chap. 3 of *The Economic Basis of the Church,* 25–35.

29. Ibid., 31.

30. Daniel Johnson Fleming, *Ventures in Simpler Living.* The book, written in 1933, appears to have been published by Fleming himself, being printed by the Polygraphic Company of America, New York, and made available through the International Missionary Council, New York.

31. This is the title of a chapter in his book *Ethical Issues Confronting World Christians* (Concord, NH: Rumford Press, 1935, to be obtained from the International Missionary Council, New York), 109–22.

32. Daniel Johnson Fleming, *Living As Comrades: A Study of Factors Making for "Community"* (New York: Published for the Foreign Missions Conference of North America by Agricultural Missions, Inc., 1950).

33. *Mission Handbook 2004–2006: U.S. and Canadian Protestant Ministries Overseas,* 12–16.

agencies or those associated with the Interdenominational Foreign Mission Association (IFMA), the Evangelical Foreign Mission Association (EFMA), or the Fellowship of Missions (FOM).

Desultory references to missionary affluence continue to appear in both academic and popular missiological writings from time to time. Professor Harry F. Wolcott, after closely studying the behavior of American missionaries in Africa over the course of his 1970–71 sabbatical year, observed:

> Problems related to money plague and obsess many urban missionaries. They always have too much of it, and they never have enough. Their standard of living makes them seem wealthy wherever they go and results in constant conflict for them when they hold back so much of what they have for themselves. An anthropologist critical of missionaries recalled the old saw that they set out to do "good" and often end up doing "well."[34]

Wolcott was certainly not hostile to the Christian missionary enterprise and made his observations while under the auspices of a mission agency himself. This concern with money had little to do with any profligacy on the missionaries' part. On the contrary, their material and economic resources were seldom, if ever, adequate — and often scarce; their possessions were meager; and their spending habits with regard to food and clothing, frugal to a fault.[35] Missionary self-consciousness about their resources and lifestyles derived from the obvious fact of relative affluence in the African context — a state of affairs with which, as Christians, they were intuitively uncomfortable.

A Lausanne movement mini-consultation on reaching the urban poor was convened in Pattaya, Thailand, from June 16 to June 27 in 1980, under the chairmanship of Rev. Jim Punton. The resulting report, *The Thailand Report on the Urban Poor*,[36] was a response to evangelical concern for the poor. Nevertheless, there is little evidence so far that evangelical mission agencies have made the implementation of the report's excellent recommendations a priority. It may be a simple case of willing spirits, but inadequate flesh. Powerful mission agencies and their missionaries have been either unwilling or unable to pay the price. It continues to be the Catholics who work in the world's worst slums.

Dana Jones has captured the feelings of anguished guilt and helplessness experienced by many Western missionaries in the context of poverty. The daughter of missionary linguists in Mexico who had returned to the United States several years earlier, Dana went back to Mexico City at the age of sixteen, where she

---

34. Harry F. Wolcott, "Too True to Be Good: The Subculture of American Missionaries in Urban Africa," *Practical Anthropology* 19, no. 6 (November–December 1972): 252.

35. Ibid., 253. William Reyburn and Jacob Loewen discussed social dynamics disparity frequently and creatively in the pages of *Practical Anthropology*, but mission agency policy has seldom, if ever, attempted to address the issue.

36. The report is no. 22 of a series of Lausanne Occasional Papers emerging from the Consultation of World Evangelization held in Pattaya, Thailand, June 16–27, 1980. The full title of the report is: *The Thailand Report on the Urban Poor: Report of the Consultation of the World Evangelization Mini-Consultation on Reaching the Urban Poor* (Wheaton, IL: Lausanne Committee for World Evangelization, 1980).

hoped to renew contact with Celia, her closest Mexican childhood friend — now married and the mother of a child. Here, in her own words, is her story:

> As we rounded a curve in the road, I spotted Celia's house and my heart sank. The entire house was the size of my bedroom. The walls were made of cariso (a type of wild cane that resembles bamboo) and held together with strips of tree bark. The roof was thatched with maguey plant leaves, and an old beer crate served as the door.
>
> I approached the dark little doorway and called Celia's name. In a few seconds she emerged. I had grown so much in the years since I had seen her that I towered above her now and had to bend down to hug her. She was a little shy, but was glad to see me. Her eyes looked tired, and her shoulders sagged. I heard a baby cry inside and she went back in to see what was the matter.
>
> I ducked my head and started to follow Celia until something made me change my mind. When my eyes adjusted to the semi-darkness, I could make out her husband lying on a straw mat on the dirt floor ... obviously drunk. The smell of cactus liquor permeated the air. I quickly stepped back out into the sunlight and stood there blinking and feeling embarrassed. Then Celia reappeared, carrying her baby son.
>
> His little nose was streaming, and she wiped at it with her blouse. His diapers consisted of a strip of a cast-off shirt. Not that Celia wasn't a good mother, but being clean was a luxury for her family. The closest well was half a mile away, and the water had to be carried in buckets. She offered me her only little chair, but I insisted she use it instead. My heart went out to Celia as I realized how our differences had become so obvious over the years. Her life had become so desolate and mine so full of potential.
>
> Suddenly, my perspective was changed. I realized how blessed I was and how thankful I should be. I thanked God for education, good nutrition, health, clothing, and for living in America.
>
> I deeply wanted to help Celia, but I felt powerless. I turned and looked at Diago, my little guide, and wondered what his life would be like. Then I realized that God could help me to make a difference. More than anything, these people need the hope that God can give them, and I want to deliver this message to people like Celia.
>
> Knowing Christ may not improve living conditions for this group of people, but Jesus can surely help them through difficult times and help them rise above their circumstances.
>
> The next morning, I took a bag of baby clothes to Celia's house. No one was home, but I left them there — along with a promise.[37]

While the mixture of outrage and guilt, pity and relief, helplessness and optimism conveyed in this story are common to any Westerner who has lived in proximity to the poor, and while missiologists write endlessly about the subject of poverty and development, the subject of missionary affluence in the context

---

37. Dana Jones, "The Road to Celia's," *Evangelical Beacon* 60, no. 16 (August 31, 1987): 12–13.

of disparity — and of its impact upon the effectiveness of Western strategies — is not on the agenda of most, if any, of the North American agencies committed to fulfilling the Great Commission.

As a consequence, Western missionaries, although growing numerically and thriving financially, increasingly find themselves at a loss in relating the Good News to the swelling numbers of this world's absolutely poor — those, for example, who inhabit the slums of the great cities of Asia and Latin America. Despite all the talk of reaching the unreached, it is not North Americans who are doing the actual reaching. That task — as has perhaps ever been the case — is being carried out by the missionaries of poorer churches who demonstrate in their own lives the truth that Jesus is the way, the truth, and the life for the poor, the destitute, and the hopeless — and not just for the rich.

These poorer missionaries are seldom acknowledged as missionaries in the West. Since they are not associated with any agency other than their sending churches and since their cross-cultural missionary endeavors are restricted by the bounds of their own countries, they are referred to as national evangelists. But it is they who are on the cutting edge of the expansion of the Kingdom today. While missionaries from the affluent West get on with the expensive and complicated process of living comfortable and secure lives in a Third World context, their national counterparts take the Word and make it flesh, dwelling among peoples who see in their frail flesh the glory of a living Savior, full of grace and truth.

In summary, the affluence of Western missionaries is a fact. Furthermore, the economic and material gulf between Western missionaries and the rest of the world is widening, not narrowing. Finally, although there have been many who throughout most of the period referred to as the "William Carey Era" in missions have acknowledged the fact of disparity — and there have been some who have regarded this disparity as an often significant obstacle in accomplishing Christian missionary objectives — scarcely any North American Protestant agencies, and very few North American missionaries, have made rectification of this problem a priority in their missiological agendas. The following chapters constitute a modest attempt to begin the process of redressing this lack.

2

The Historical and Cultural Context of Missionary Affluence

*Whoever loves money never has money enough; whoever loves wealth is
never satisfied with his income.* — SOLOMON

*He had a great respect for money and much overrated its value as a means
of doing even what he called good: religious people generally do.*
— GEORGE MacDONALD

And whatever happens began in the past and presses hard on the future.
— T. S. ELIOT

Material and economic abundance has been a hallmark of the modus operandi
of Western missionaries throughout the past two centuries. In sharp contrast to
their apostolic counterparts of the first century, portrayed by St. Paul as being
"on display at the end of the procession, like men condemned to die in the
arena" (1 Cor. 4:9), missionaries from Europe and the Americas have — with
some notable exceptions — manifested escalating levels of economic and material
entitlement beyond the dreams of a majority of the world's population.

Correspondingly, as I try to show in chapter 5, the strategies of Western missionaries have become increasingly reliant upon expensive technologies which,
while contributing to personal velocity and creature comforts, seem to have
contributed little to missionary effectiveness. Indeed, reminiscent of the seven
churches described by St. John in the first three chapters of his Revelation, the
Church seems invariably to exhibit more signs of vitality among the poor than
among the rich. Take Africa, for example, a continent that gluts Western media
gristmills with bad news about poverty. The phenomenal growth and the vitality
of Christianity across that continent cannot be attributed to any kind of material
prosperity. As Lamin Sanneh recently observed, "Muslims in 1900 outnumbered
Christians by a ratio of nearly 4:1, with some 34.5 million, or 32 percent of
the population. In 1962 when Africa had largely slipped out of colonial control, there were about 60 million Christians, with Muslims at about 145 million.
Of the Christians, 23 million were Protestants and 27 million were Catholics.

17

The remaining 10 million were Coptic and Ethiopian Orthodox."[1] Forty years later, the number of Christians in Africa had multiplied by six to nearly 380 million, overtaking the Muslim population to comprise an estimated 48.37 percent of the approximately 800 million total population.[2] Between 1900 and 2000, the Roman Catholic population in Africa increased a phenomenal 6,708 percent, from 1,909,812 to 130,018,400. Catholic membership has increased 708 percent over the last fifty years.[3] All this on a continent that has become a byword for poverty, material scarcity, and political-social instability![4]

The Western missionary enterprise, meanwhile, is utterly and fatally dependent upon the accoutrements of affluence. This is hardly surprising, given the cultural and religious "womb" in which it was conceived, and the social and historical environment in which it was and is nurtured. Born and bred in the economic abundance of the West, the character, outlook, values, preoccupations, and strategies of missionaries have naturally been deeply affected. For as David Potter noted fifty years ago, material plenty as a basic condition of American life "has had a pervasive influence upon the American people... [exerting] a profound effect upon the character of the individual members of the society."[5] Writing a full fifty years later, psychiatrist Peter Whybrow offers a perceptive but deeply troubling analysis of the American materialistic treadmill as a kind of clinical mania in which the craving for material rewards in an economy of superabundance is a fatal addiction for which there is no known cure.[6] Even though few Western missionaries would disagree with such critiques, few American churches or denominations have seriously attempted to counteract its ethically and socially deleterious implications.[7]

Missionaries have tended to feel uncomfortable whenever they have been on the "rich" side of invidious economic comparisons. But the varied effects that their relative affluence has had upon the theory and practice of missions, and its impact upon those who have seen, heard, and responded to their comfortably incarnated Gospel, have not gone unnoticed. "It is not a coincidence that the greatest mission-sending nations have also been the nations possessing the greatest store of material resources and the highest standards of living," concluded J. Merle Davis, commissioned by the International Missionary Council (IMC) to

---

1. Lamin Sanneh, *Whose Religion Is Christianity? The Gospel beyond the West* (Grand Rapids: Wm. B. Eerdmans, 2003), 16.

2. Patrick Johnstone and Jason Mandryk with Robyn Johnstone, *Operation World: 21st-Century Edition* (Carlisle: Paternoster Lifestyle, 2001), 20–21. According to *Operation World* figures, Muslims constituted 41.32 percent of Africa's population in 2001. Annual growth rates for Christians and Muslims in Africa are estimated to be 2.83 percent and 2.53 percent, respectively.

3. Bryan T. Froehle and Mary L. Gautier, *Global Catholicism: Portrait of a World Church* (Maryknoll, NY: Orbis Books, 2003), 5.

4. See Dana L. Robert, "Shifting Southward: Global Christianity since 1945," *International Bulletin of Missionary Research* 24, no. 2 (April 2000): 50–58.

5. David M. Potter, *People of Plenty: Economic Abundance and the American Character* (Chicago: University of Chicago Press, 1954), 76.

6. Peter C. Whybrow, *American Mania: When More Is Not Enough* (New York and London: W. W. Norton, 2005).

7. George Packer, "When Here Sees There," *New York Times Magazine*, April 21, 2002. See *www.globalpolicy.org/globaliz/special/2002/0421media.htm.*

direct a series of extensive studies on the social and economic life of younger churches during the 1930s. Indeed, so naturally concomitant were material abundance and missionary activity in missionary thinking of the time that Davis, when asked by an Indian whether the Gospel had ever been "carried by a people of low economic standards to a group living on a higher economic level," was unable to think of a single instance, "unless it was the witness of the Christian slaves in the Roman Empire to their pagan masters."[8]

An article appearing some years ago in the *Los Angeles Times Magazine* referred to modern American missionaries — with their "computers, and air force and millions of dollars in financial support," as a "new breed."[9] The author was right about the affluence of missionaries from North America, but he was wrong in thinking that they are a "new breed." For it is only within the past two hundred years that Christian missions have come to be regarded as the special prerogative of rich Christians. It is true that Western mission agencies typically operate from a noticeably substantial financial base — sometimes out of headquarters "worthy of multinational corporations" — using expensive technologies to generate a plethora of maps, graphs, and statistics, in support of money-reliant strategies. But these have been a hallmark of Western missiology ever since the publication of William Carey's famous *Enquiry*[10] more than two hundred years ago.

If missionaries traveling from Western shores initially had neither computers nor an air force, they were still as a general rule reasonably well equipped by their standards. The London Missionary Society (LMS) expeditions into East Africa, for example, required the engagement of hundreds — sometimes approaching thousands — of native carriers, often for months on end, to transport missionary goods from the coast to inland destinations.[11]

Financed by a five-thousand-pound gift from Robert Arthington,[12] on July 25, 1877, the little party of six LMS missionaries embarked on the 830-mile journey from the coast to Lake Tanganyika. The 28,500 pounds of supplies and equipment were to have been conveyed by oxcart, but the dreaded tsetse fly made short

---

8. J. Merle Davis, *The Economic and Social Environment of the Younger Churches: The Report of the Department of Social and Economic Research of the International Missionary Council to the Tambaram Meeting — December 1938* (London: Edinburgh House, 1939), 1.

9. David DeVoss, "The New Breed of Missionary," *Los Angeles Times Magazine* (January 25, 1987), 14–18; 20–23; 34–35.

10. William Carey, *An Enquiry into the Obligations of Christians to Use Means for the Conversion of the Heathen* (London: Hodder & Stoughton, 1891 [reprint of 1792 edition]). Carey's book, while modest by the scale of the studies generated by contemporary missiologists, nevertheless constitutes the "source" of a continuing genre of Western missionary literature that reached its apogee with the publication of the *Encyclopedia of World Christianity,* ed. David Barrett (London: Oxford University Press, 1983).

11. I tell the story in my chapter " 'And they Marveled...': Mammon as Miracle in Western Missionary Encounter," in James R. Krabill, Walter Sawatsky, and Charles E. Van Engen, eds., *Evangelical, Ecumenical, and Anabaptist Missiologies in Conversation: Essays in Honor of Wilbert R. Shenk* (Maryknoll, NY: Orbis Books, 2006), 78–87. See Thomas O. Beidelman, "Contradictions between the Sacred and the Secular Life: The Church Missionary Society in Ukaguru, Tanzania, East Africa, 1876–1914," *Comparative Studies in Society and History: An International Quarterly* 23, no. 1 (January 1981): 73–95. Beidelman's comments on these caravans (79–82) are most helpful.

12. Elizabeth May, *Central Africa* (London: London Missionary Society, 1908), 15. See also A. M. Chirgwin, *Arthington's Million: The Romance of the Arthington Trust* (London: Livingstone Press, 1935).

work of the oxen before they had scarcely begun, giving the missionaries no choice but to make the thirteen-month journey on foot, in the company of 868 African carriers.[13] The "list of requirements" later forwarded by missionaries to the LMS in London was thirty-four pages long, and included everything from "camp equipage" and "shooting material" to "food, drink and condiments."[14]

Despite their impressive array of goods, disease and death prevented the first party of missionaries from establishing a mission. A second expedition, and then a third, also failed because of the high mortality rate, and it was only the fourth expedition, reaching Ujiji in February 1883 after a harrowing, nine-month overland journey from the coast, that succeeded in establishing the mission.[15]

One of the missionaries reported that he and his fellow missionaries were regarded with

> ...a high degree of admiration, because of...supposed royal blood... [and] because they were under the impression that we were wizards.... They had very peculiar ideas about white men [believing] that God was wide awake when He created the white man, but had fallen half-asleep when He came to create the black man. This accounted for the white man's superiority to the black in appearance, knowledge, and wealth. It was freely said that there was no red blood in our veins, which accounted for our skin being white. They were accordingly under the impression that they could

---

13. For background on the LMS's decision to utilize oxen, see the *Report of the Rev. R. Price of His Visit to Zanzibar and the Coast of Eastern Africa* (London: LMS, 1876); see also Edwin W. Smith, "The Earliest Ox-wagons in Tanganyika: An Experiment Which Failed," *Tanganyika Notes and Records,* no. 40, 1–14, and no. 41, 1–15 (1955).

14. Arthur W. Dodgshun, "Central African Expedition Lists of Requirements" (n.d.), SOAS, Council for World Mission Archives, Central Africa-Incoming-2/1/B. A similar list compiled by missionary physician E. J. Southon was issued as a pamphlet, "Hints to Missionaries Proceeding to Central Africa" (London: Printed for the Directors [of the London Missionary Society] by Yates and Alexander, 1880). As Johannes Fabian points out, European travelers and explorers in Africa traveled with huge entourages and often tons of equipment. See his *Out of Our Minds: Reason and Madness in the Exploration of Central Africa* (Berkeley and London: University of California Press, 2000). Francis Galton's *The Art of Travel* referred to in note 22 below is a cornucopia of information and advice to travelers, and includes a comprehensive catalogue of equipment useful in "wild countries."

15. The first contingent of missionaries arrived in 1877, crossing from Zanzibar to Ndumi, where they prepared for the expedition that was to convey them and their considerable goods overland by ox cart. There were six in the original party: Rev. Roger Price, from South Africa, chosen to lead because of his experience and known expertise with oxen; Captain E. C. Hore, J. B. Thompson, A. W. Dodgshun, E. B. Clark, and W. Hutley. Since their departure coincided with the advent of the rainy season, it was a disaster from the very beginning. Tests undertaken during the dry season to ascertain the presence of the dreaded tsetse fly had been negative; but with the rains came the pesky fly, so that most of the oxen died almost immediately. With the permission of the Directors, nearly nine hundred carriers were commissioned to convey the expedition's goods on foot. With Price and Clarke, in the meanwhile, having returned to their old stations in South Africa, leadership devolved upon J. B. Thompson, a missionary from South Africa. No sooner were they established at Ujiji than Thompson and Dodgshun both succumbed to malaria. Hore and Hutley carried on, to be joined in 1879 by Dr. Joseph Mullens, William Griffiths, and Dr. Philip Southon. Mullens, the foreign secretary of the LMS, died almost immediately. David Williams and Southon died within two years, while Walter Stephan Palmer and Hore returned to England. Only Griffiths, enfeebled through illness, remained — sustained by the prospect of reinforcements. See David Picton Jones, *After Livingstone: The Work of a Pioneer Missionary in Central Africa* (London: Privately Published by Dorothy Picton Jones, 1968), 16–22; and Jonathan Bonk, *The Theory and Practice of Missionary Identification, 1860–1920* (Lewiston, NY: Edwin Mellen Press, 1989), 48–49.

not kill us, as they could kill a black man. A lad told me one day that a white man was the same color as the air, and that it was impossible to see him until you were right up against him. They admitted that we were fair of face, but we had very ugly feet. It was evident that they believed our boots to be an essential part of us, which served us in much the same way as hoofs did a horse.... We were so different from them in every way. Not only were we white in colour but we covered our bodies with thick, and to their mind costly, clothing; we lived in houses which were more magnificent than their palaces.[16]

Even the most common objects were a source of wonder to Jones's African neighbors. With the arrival of his first child, Jones fashioned "a simple and crude perambulator" consisting of "a long box with four wheels," two of which came off of an old plough, and two of which he fashioned from wood. "People came from long distances to see that perambulator," Jones reported, "and exhibited their wonder and admiration over and over again, most of them putting their right hand on their mouths, to express amazement or unspeakableness."[17] On another occasion, while opening some boxes of clothing that had been shipped from home, they came upon an English doll that someone had sent for his little daughter, Hilda. Jones describes what happened: "When the 'boys' who were watching with wondering eyes the unpacking of the box saw this they started up in terror, and ran away at high speed from what they believed to be a ghost; and it was a long time before we could persuade them to come back."[18]

Jones found that almost everything he owned amazed or startled Africans. Pictures of animals, a portrait of the Prince of Wales, and even the most common household objects evoked amazement. "They would sit in the verandah for hours and gaze at the various household objects," Jones reported. They were particularly taken with his "small five shilling clock." Its ticking sound filled them with curiosity. Jones describes the ensuing scene:

"This," I said, "is the thing that tells me where the sun is. And it tells us where the sun is even on a cloudy day. It speaks to us always, day and night. Kalanda Kasikolo! — Wonder of wonders!" Then I handed it to one of them so that he might inspect it more closely. He examined it minutely. Then putting it to his ear, he declared with much excitement, "Of a truth, I hear his heart beating!" And all gazed upon it with a mixture of admiration and fear, just as they would regard a living thing.... There was

---

16. Picton Jones, *After Livingstone*, 39.
17. Ibid., 40.
18. Ibid. "They come in crowds to see the wagons, and they think us a most wonderful people.... They all seem to have a wholesome dread of us," wrote missionary David Picton Jones from Mabisi on October 1, 1887, in a letter to Joseph Mullens, general secretary of the London Missionary Society (School of Oriental and African Studies [SOAS]–Council for World Mission Archives [CWM]–Central Africa-Incoming-1/1/E). On November 14, with construction of a missionary residence well under way, he reported to Mullens's successor, Ralph Wardlaw Thompson, that "Many...look in as they pass,...lift their hands in amazement,...[and] exclaim, 'the white man! The white man!'" (SOAS, CWM, Central Africa-Incoming-7/2/D).

always something to see at the white man's, and something to hear from him. "Ah — h — h!" the natives would often say. "The white man — He is a powerful wizard, and is beyond understanding." They believed that our ability to read and write was derived from some potent magic. "Give us the magic," they would say, "and we will do the same thing."[19]

Missionaries then, as now, recognized that such astonishment could be parlayed into Christian conversion. With their pale skin and their extraordinary material culture, missionaries constituted a kind of Great Exhibition, attracting Africans from great distances. Particularly impressive were their homes. Fellow Welshman David Williams — who would succumb to malaria scarcely one month later — described his partially constructed house as "an object of great admiration to the Amwezi," so amazing that his rank had risen from a "little master" to "*Bwana Makabua* — great master." This was because, he confided in a letter to the home secretary, "the greatness of a man here [derives from] ... his property, especially his dwelling place."[20]

The adequately equipped LMS missionary to Central Africa found it necessary to take food, cooking utensils, trunks, tents, tools, medicines, sometimes boats, and barter goods sufficient to sustain life for several years in an environment as dangerous to the white man's health as it was uncivilized.[21] Missionaries, of course, were not unlike their fellow countrymen in this regard, taking their cue from the advice of such notables as Sir Francis Galton, president of the Royal Geographical Society, and an expert on survival in "wild countries."[22] The sheer volume of material goods required by Protestant missionaries proceeding to Asia and South America was, when measured against local standards, similarly grand.

Western missionaries seldom take vast supplies with them these days. But it would be a mistake to think that they are not at least as lavishly supplied as ever. Western "staples" — vehicles, clothing, building supplies, gadgets, food, furniture — all are available in most countries, albeit only to those few who can pay the exorbitantly inflated prices demanded of them. It is no secret, for example, that the price of automobiles in some countries is double, even triple

---

19. Picton Jones, *After Livingstone,* 42. By certain local standards missionaries were conspicuously impoverished. "The first characteristic of the chieftain," Jones observed, "was his wealthiness; and his wealth consisted chiefly in wives and cattle. Some of the chiefs had dozens of wives; those less blessed followed their example as closely as they could. Women stood for wealth, inasmuch as the husband paid for each wife a certain dowry, consisting of cattle, cloth, or horses" (36).

20. Letter from David Williams to Ralph Wardlaw Thompson, written in Urambo, August 10, 1881, in SOAS, CWM, Central Africa-Incoming-4/2/C. The house made a different impression on Williams's successor, Walter Hutley, who reported in his September 12, 1881, letter to the home secretary that he had been obliged to demolish it because it was "planned badly ... built badly ... [and] dangerous." SOAS, CWM, Central Africa-Incoming-4/3/A.

21. See E. J. Southon, "Hints for Missionaries Proceeding to Central Africa," a forty-nine-page pamphlet prepared for the London Missionary Society. Southon, an American medical doctor and missionary with that society, gives some indication of the material supplies required to support Western life in Africa.

22. See Francis Galton, *The Art of Travel; or, Shifts and Contrivances Available in Wild Countries* (London: John Murray, 1855). For a fascinating biography of this extremely influential scientist, see Martin Brookes, *Extreme Measures: The Dark Visions and Bright Ideas of Francis Galton* (London: Bloomsbury Publishing, 2004).

that of an equivalent vehicle in North America. Added to this is the price of fuel — in many poor countries running between ten and thirty dollars per gallon. Missionaries are among those who can, and frequently do, drive automobiles.

Attempts to explain the goals, methods, and accomplishments of Western Christian missionary endeavors during the past two hundred years cannot be adequately grasped without some understanding of the much larger social and economic milieu of which they were simply a pious expression. Throughout the nineteenth and well into the twentieth centuries, a powerful confluence of ideological, economic, and political streams issuing from the West flooded much of the globe. True to the nature of floods, this one affected, for good or for ill, everything in its path, and could not be stopped. Some were overwhelmed and destroyed by the torrent; survivors — among them Western missionaries — were swept inexorably along, like bits of flotsam, wherever the raging waters took them. In comparison with the mighty vitality of this rushing tide, even the most energetic attempts at resistance were feeble and, not surprisingly, ineffective.[23]

Among the ideas that influenced missionary theory and practice from the beginning of the modern era, probably none can match the pervasiveness or the power of Western belief in the inevitability of progress. The law of progress was, one historian observed, "the first great lesson that history teaches us."[24] His sentiments resonate with the views of Robert Nisbet, who argues that "No single idea has been more important than, perhaps as important as, the idea of progress in Western civilization.... From at least the early nineteenth century until a few decades ago, belief in the progress of mankind, with Western civilization in the vanguard, was virtually a universal religion on both sides of the Atlantic."[25]

Not only were missionaries convinced of the inevitability of progress, but they saw themselves as its true emissaries. The indolent temperaments or the stubborn conservatism of non-Western peoples might delay progress, but they could not stem the tide, and there could be no doubt about its ultimate triumph. As one veteran missionary explained in the 1897 *Annual Report* of his society, "China...would resist [progress] if she could, but she cannot help herself. There are mighty forces at work pressing China forward, to which she must yield whether she will or no."[26]

---

23. In vol. 4 of his *History of the Expansion of Christianity: The Great Century, A.D. 1800–1914: Europe and the United States of America* (London: Eyre and Spottiswoode, 1941), 9–21, Kenneth Scott Latourette lists thirteen distinguishing characteristics of the nineteenth-century, each influencing to some degree missionary perceptions of the world, of themselves, and of the Christian Gospel.

24. William Samuel Lilly, *Christianity and Modern Civilization: Being Some Chapters in European History with an Introductory Dialogue on the Philosophy of History* (London: Chapman & Hill, 1903), 25. See also Neil Arnott, *A Survey of Human Progress, from the Savage State to the Highest Civilization yet Attained. A Progress as Little Perceived by the Multitude in any Age, as is the Slow Growing of a Tree by the Children who Play under its Shade — but which Is Leading to a New Condition of Mankind on Earth* (London: Longman, Green, Longman, and Roberts, 1861).

25. This quotation is taken from one of the most thorough and masterly studies of its kind, Robert Nisbet's *History of the Idea of Progress* (New York: Basic Books, 1980), 4, 7.

26. John Griffith, *London Missionary Society Annual Report,* 1897, 47. The writer was by then a veteran of more than thirty years as a missionary in China.

Missionary apologists understandably celebrated the dramatic advances made by backward peoples as a direct result of missionary efforts. The most comprehensive of these publications was the massive three-volume study by James Dennis, *Christian Missions and Social Progress.* Written to support the proposition that missions constituted "a supreme force in the social regeneration and elevation of the human race," the evidence marshaled in these volumes promised to be of "striking apologetic import" to readers.[27]

If progress was the destiny of humankind, Western "Christian" civilization was its visible manifestation, a sort of word made flesh, and dwelling among men. There may have been sharp differences of opinion concerning the precise ratio and sequence of those factors that had given rise to Western civilization, but Western missionaries and philosophers, politicians and historians, scientists and dilettantes all regarded the civilizing of the rest of mankind as an almost sacred trust. Even nineteenth-century futurist Winwood Reade, cousin to Charles Darwin and no friend of missionaries, wrote glowingly of a day when, "by means of European conquest . . . the whole earth [would] be as civilized as Europe."[28]

It seemed obvious, furthermore, that Western ideas, values, technology, social and political institutions, military might, and religion "were not only superior to those found in the rest of the world, but were symbols, pointing to what other nations should and would know in due time."[29]

Missionaries were certain that Western civilization had its roots in the Christian Gospel. For proof, they pointed to Britain — once numbered among the most pagan and uncivilized of nations — now "a glowing and graphic picture of the marvelous change which the Gospel accomplishes."[30] Clergymen back home preached the same message. The pastor of the Broadway Tabernacle Church in New York dilated on the theme in an address before the Missionary Societies of Bangor Theological Seminary, Brown and Rochester universities, and Williams College, arguing that neither commerce nor civilization could by themselves or together elevate man. "Christian Missions," he declared, "are the grand reliance for the elevation of mankind in prosperity, in purity, and in happiness."[31]

27. James S. Dennis, *Christian Missions and Social Progress: A Sociological Study of Foreign Missions* 3 vols. (Edinburgh: Oliphant, Anderson and Ferrier, 1898), ix. Similar studies include W. Douglas Mackenzie's *Christianity and the Progress of Man as Illustrated by Modern Missions* (Edinburgh: Oliphant, Anderson and Ferrier, 1898); James Johnston's *A Century of Christian Progress and Its Lessons* (London: James Nisbet & Co., 1888); and the book by James L. Barton, *Human Progress through Missions* (New York: Fleming H. Revell Co., 1912). See also Jonathan J. Bonk, *"Not the Bloom, but the Fruit . . . " Conversion and Its Consequences in Nineteenth-Century Missionary Discourse,* Yale Divinity School Library, Occasional Publication no. 17 (New Haven, CT: Yale Divinity School Library, 2003).

28. W. Winwood Reade, *The Martyrdom of Man* (London: Kegan Paul, Trench, 1909 [1872]), 504, 502.

29. Nisbet, *History of the Idea of Progress,* 308. See also the chapter "The Doctrine of Civilization," 154–200, in A. P. Thornton, *Doctrines of Imperialism* (New York: John Wiley & Sons, 1965).

30. J. Logan Aikman, *Cyclopaedia of Christian Missions: Their Rise, Progress, and Present Position* (London: Richard Griffin and Co., 1860), iv. See also Richard Whately, "On the Origin of Civilization. A Lecture by His Grace the Archbishop of Dublin. To the Young Men's Christian Association" (London, December 1854).

31. Joseph P. Thompson, "Christian Missions Necessary to a True Civilization," *Bibliotheca Sacra* 14, no. 56 (October 1857): 847.

As both emissaries and the embodiments of the civilizational outcome of all true progress, missionaries could scarcely be expected to see personal material advantage vis-à-vis non-Christian peoples as a handicap. Living as civilized Europeans, as conspicuous beacons signaling all that Christianity could and would eventually accomplish in the backward races, was both practically desirable and a God-given duty. Exceptions to this general principle — and there were some, several of whom will be touched upon in the final chapter — were usually regarded as troublesome eccentrics, socially ostracized by the mainstream missionary community.

If talk of "progress" and "civilization" now sounds prosaic, quixotic, and triumphalist, such ideas continue to be at the implicit core of contemporary Western mission agendas — in altered, though not necessarily muted, form. "Cutting edge" mission theory today — in tune with such international financial or political institutions as the International Monetary Fund, the World Bank, and the United Nations — resounds with talk of "development" and "underdevelopment." The West continues to be the standard against which "development" is measured; and Western aid and efforts have, until quite recently, been fueled by the certainty that given enough money, time, and Western expertise, the rest of the world can become what the West now is — "developed." In the popular mind, development is understood to mean movement toward some approximation of Western material and economic standards. Skeptics have been few, and in any case largely disregarded.[32]

It is clear that we are not as far removed from our nineteenth-century roots as some would like to suppose. Those whose "enlightened" criticism creates the illusion of distance between themselves and the triumphalist civilizing efforts of nineteenth-century missionaries should not be surprised if their most telling and subtle attacks frequently rebound upon themselves, as they earnestly seek to advance Western notions of human rights, economic development, and democracy.

Western assumptions concerning progress and civilization are only part of the background against which the relative affluence of missionaries must be seen. The overwhelming racial, material, and political ascendancy of the "Christian" nations was not simply a fact, but — in missionary thinking — a *providential* fact. Missionary racism was of a genre infinitely more benign than that of nineteenth-century scientists. Christian belief in monogenesis required that all human beings, regardless of race, share a common ancestry. Differences between the races derived from extrinsic cultural and religious factors, not from inherent racial capacities. Conversion to Christianity would eventually but inevitably produce cultural outcomes more or less the equivalent of those observed in Western

---

32. Among those who have bravely raised questions about the legitimacy of Western notions of "development," Bob Goudzwaard, author of *Aid for the Overdeveloped West* (Toronto: Wedge Publishing Foundation, 1975), and Ivan Illich, author of *The Church, Change and Development* (Chicago: Urban Training Center Press, 1970), need to be heard. See also the writings of Andrew Greeley, E. F. Schumacher, and Pascal Bruckner.

societies.[33] But in the meanwhile, "The missionary," the well-known foreign Secretary of the London Missionary Society observed, "[belonged] to a race superior in energy and asserting the right to lead and rule, a race whose wealth is evident to the world."[34]

Racial superiority, of course, carried with it the solemn responsibility known as "the white man's burden." "It is on the Anglo-American race that the hopes of the world for liberty and progress rest," David Livingstone had written in the context of a report that was to provoke Western Christians into indignant action on behalf of Africa.[35]

Likewise politically, missionaries by virtue of their citizenship were unavoidably implicated in the subjugation of much of the world by unabashedly imperialist European nations. Western superiority in all things constituted a natural diet for a particularly virulent form of nationalism. No less patriotic than their secular peers, like other nationalists missionaries sometimes, though by no means always, suffered from the myopia so aptly described by George Orwell: "The nationalist," he said, "not only does not disapprove of atrocities committed by his own side, but he has a remarkable capacity for not even hearing about them."[36]

This is not to suggest that missionaries were oblivious to the injustices and hypocrisies inherent in Western global hegemony. On the contrary, their criticism of their own governments sometimes elicited harsh criticism from their more nationalistic countrymen, one of whom accused missionaries of being generally "heedless of [the] great truth ... [that] imperialism is a matter of religion."[37] And Harry Johnston, one of the most famous of the British Colonial administrators, described missionaries as "inconvenient champions of native independence."[38]

On the whole, however, missionaries regarded Western imperialism as both natural and, more significantly, providential in making straight the path for the spread of the Gospel. "A European Colonial government," Johannes Warneck noted in 1909, "cannot fail, as the representative of humanity and enlightenment, to ... prepare the way for the preaching of the Gospel." Western imperialism

---

33. See my article " 'All Things to All Persons' — The Missionary as a Racist-Imperialist, 1860–1910," *Missiology: An International Review* 8, no. 3 (July 1980): 285–306.

34. R. Wardlaw Thompson, "Self Support and Self Government in the Native Church as Affected by Considerations of Race, Previous Religion, and Present Social Conditions," in *Centenary of the London Missionary Society. Proceedings of the Founders' Week Convention, at the City Temple, Holborn Viaduct, London, E.C., September 21st to 27th, 1895. Papers and Speeches in Full* (London: LMS, 1895), 349–50.

35. David Livingstone, *Missionary Travels and Researches in South Africa; Including a Sketch of Sixteen Years Residence in the Interior of Africa, and a Journey from the Cape of Good Hope to Lands on the West Coast; thence across the Continent, down the River Zambesi, to the Eastern Ocean* (London: J. Murray, 1857), 679. See also Andrew F. Walls, "The Legacy of David Livingstone," *International Bulletin of Missionary Research* 11, no. 3 (July 1987): 125–29.

36. George Orwell, "Notes on Nationalism," in *England Your England and Other Essays* (London: Secker & Warburg, 1953), 52.

37. Allan Macdonald, *Trade Politics and Christianity in Africa and the East* (London: Longmans, Green and Co., 1916), 55–56.

38. Harry H. Johnston, *A History of the Colonization of Africa by Alien Races* (Cambridge: Cambridge University Press, 1899), 151.

was, accordingly, best regarded as "one of the powers which God has chosen for bringing the message of salvation to uncivilized peoples."[39]

The extent to which prevailing Western notions about progress, civilization, and power influenced missionary theory and practice is obvious. Just how these same ideas may have affected missionary perceptions of their own relative affluence is more difficult to measure, but no less significant. Affluence was a byproduct of Christian influences upon a civilization. Since missionaries were offering Christianity to any who would have it, and since their own relative affluence in a sense constituted "Exhibit A" in the case for "Christian" civilization, any radical renunciation of their Western affluence would have been tantamount to a betrayal of their mission. As one veteran missionary explained to fellow delegates attending the 1860 Liverpool conference, "The Indian looks upon himself as being of an inferior race; and his desire is to rise as much as possible to the level of the white man.... Civilised men should [therefore] go amongst them, men who [will] be looked up to by them... [and from those lips they will expect] words of wisdom."[40]

An examination of three crucial areas reveals the extent to which nineteenth-century missionary thinking reflected prevailing Eurocentric visions of progress and civilization. In their understanding of the sources and destiny of Western civilization, in their depiction and diagnosis of the maladies of non-Western peoples, and in their flattering perceptions of themselves in relation to non-Europeans, missionaries were simply children of their time.

Who would willfully blind themselves to the obvious ascendancy of Western civilization, and who could resist its inexorable progress worldwide? In the words of an anonymous "French positivist" in an article appearing in a popular missionary magazine, "... the colonial expansion of Christian nations will eventually cover the whole world, and India... will one day spontaneously embrace the faith of her masters and educators, as she has already adopted their arts, industry and commerce."[41]

If missionary anticipation of what we now refer to as globalization seems to have been unclouded by doubt, their view of the source of Western cultural, political, social, economic, and religious superiority was equally clear: European greatness derived ultimately from its close and sustained ties with Christianity. A positive correlation could be observed, according to J. F. T. Hallowes, between the "purity" of a nation's Christianity and the extent of its imperial expansion. "In the providence of God [England] has become the greatest empire of ancient or

---

39. Johannes Warneck, *The Living Forces of the Gospel: Experiences of a Missionary in Animistic Heathendom*. Authorized translation from the 3rd German edition by Neil Buchanan (London: Oliphant, Anderson and Ferrier, 1909), 171, 174. See also "the opinion of an educated African youth" under the title, "Are African Native Races Profited by Foreign Rule?" in *The Illustrated Missionary News* 22 (July 1888): 111.

40. These words were spoken by Fred A. O'Meara, chaplain to the Red Indians on Lake Huron, and superintendent of Indian Missions for the Church of England there. See *Conference on Missions Held in 1860 in Liverpool: The Papers Read, the Conclusions Reached, and a Comprehensive Index, Showing the Various Matters Brought under Review* (London: James Nisbet & Co., 1860), 212–13.

41. W. Garett Horder, "Prophecy of a Positivist," *Chronicle of the London Missionary Society* 59 (November 1886): 455–56.

modern times," explained one missionary-minded clergyman — "Our expansion is directly providential, and links itself with the expansion of another Kingdom, even that Kingdom of Christ...[for] we Britons enshrine the purest form of Christianity current in the world."[42]

Those outside of Christendom did not see things this way, of course. In China, for example, missionaries were constantly frustrated by an obstinate unwillingness to understand "that whatever is best and worthiest in [Western] civilisation is to [Christianity] what the warp is to the woof; that the science, the art, and learning of the West, which the Chinese [coveted], was bound up in a piece with the religion of the West, which they affected to despise."[43]

Chinese refusal to acknowledge the link between Christianity and civilization was lamentable, but understandable, since millions of Europeans likewise lived in willful denial of this fact. Nor were missionaries blind to the evils so painfully evident in the lives of irreligious compatriots who, in ruthless pursuit of economic, military, or more despicable ends, could be found virtually everywhere that missionaries went. Trafficking in opium, liquor, slaves, and coolies, such Europeans constituted a blotch on the escutcheon of Christian civilization, eliciting from missionaries a vast outpouring of outraged condemnation. In addition to perpetrating great injustice upon weaker peoples, these evil compatriots severely compromised missionary testimony since "Every white man is regarded as a Christian...[even] the scum of Europe."[44]

Missionary faith in the core ethical and material superiority of the West was not shaken by the activities of a few unprincipled fellow countrymen, however. Such men were aberrations — cultural Judases who for the sake of lucre betrayed their own heritage — whose reprehensible behavior simply drove missionaries to redouble their own altruistic efforts. The words of "Britain's Mission," a hymn appearing in the centenary hymnal of the London Missionary Society, tell the story:

> Shall Science distant lands explore
> And trade her wealth convey?
> Shall war be heard from shore to shore,
> And sin extend its sway?

---

42. J. F. T. Hallowes, "Our World-Wide Empire," *Chronicle of the London Missionary Society* 59 (October 1894): 225. See also his earlier article, "The Expansion of England in Relation to the Propagation of the Gospel," *Chronicle of the London Missionary Society* 51 (May 1886): 197–200.

43. T. W. Pearce, "Western Civilisation in Relation to Protestant Mission Work," *Chronicle of the London Missionary Society* 55 (August 1890): 239. The point of view expressed by Pearce was a common one. See, for example, Benjamin R. Cowen, *The Miracle of the Nineteenth Century. Do Missions Pay?* (Cincinnati: Cranston and Sons, 1891); Ray Palmer, *The Highest Civilization a Result of Christianity and Christian Learning,* a Discourse Delivered at Norwich, Conn., November 14, 1865, on behalf of The Society for Promoting Collegiate and Theological Education at the West, in Connection with the Annual Meeting of the Board of Directors (Albany: J. Munsell, 1866); or John Cumming, "God in History," in *Lectures Delivered Before the Young Men's Christian Association 1848–1849,* vol. 4 (London: James Nisbet and Co., 1876), 35–78.

44. W. Garrett Horder, "Imperialism and Missions," *Chronicle of the London Missionary Society* 67 (April 1902): 81.

And shall there not be Christians found,
Who will for Christ appear
To spread the Gospel's joyful sound,
And preach redemption there?

Shall Britain's remotest parts
Transmit her sins alone?
And not engage with eager hearts
To make her Saviour known?

O may our dull and languid zeal
Be kindled to a flame;
And burn till all the earth shall feel
The glories of His name.[45]

No less Eurocentric than their convictions regarding Western civilization's essence and Providential destiny were missionary perceptions of the cause and cure for non-Western humankind's troubles. "In estimating the vile, sunk, and wretched moral condition of the heathen," wrote a Scottish missionary in 1863, "it matters not whether we look to China, Japan, Burmah, or Hindoostan, lands in which a barbaric civilization has existed longside of the most childish superstition, or to Africa, whose Negro tribes have, since the days of their father Ham, kept on sinking, from age to age, unaided, until a dreary and bloody fetishism has swallowed up all, and made them the lowest of beings that are called men. Look where we will in heathen lands, we behold the same ghastly scene of death . . . and infidelity . . . and piety."[46]

These words, it must be remembered, were written in the days before the relativism of Western social sciences would drive such candid assessments underground, to be pondered rather than spoken, or to be asserted more obliquely. They were the honest observations — seldom contradicted by those so described — of men and women who were certain not only of their own superiority, but of those obligations resting upon all those providentially wielding such power and privilege.

At the very root of the wretched state to which non-Western life had degenerated lay false religion of one sort or another. Heathen religion, argued the missionary son of the famous Gustav Warneck, was ultimately responsible for the moral ignorance, deception, bondage to fear and fatalism, selfishness, moral perversion, and gross materialism characterizing non-Christian peoples.[47]

Since Western supremacy derived from Christianity, and since the moral depravity and impotence of the rest of the world was traceable to faulty religion, it followed that this world needed the West's religion. Christianity would trans-

---

45. "Britain's Mission," *Centenary Missionary Hymnal,* compiled and ed. Stanley Rogers (London: London Missionary Society, 1895), 75.
46. Alexander Robb, *The Heathen World and the Duty of the Church* (Edinburgh: Andrew Elliott, 1863), 1.
47. Warneck, *Living Forces of the Gospel,* 81–134, passim.

form the world's heathen in much the same way that it had earlier transformed Europe's pagan societies. By means of Christianity, the personal habits, family life, commerce, social institutions, and national character of a people would be transformed. Because the Christian faith was the one "divinely appointed and supremely efficacious ministry to the higher nature of man, embodying the noblest rule of righteousness,"[48] any less dramatic result was impossible, making missionary effort supremely worthwhile.

"When the heathen man becomes a Christian," an Old Calabar missionary had noted fifty years earlier, "he ceases to be the selfish, brutish, earthly being that he was."[49] "Civilization follows so necessarily in the wake of Christianity," argued another contemporary, "that the best way to convey the blessings of the one is to introduce the other, and the more so, because the worst vices of the heathen arise out of their religion, and are perpetrated by it."[50]

There can be no doubt that what these men and others like them said was true. Not only was West Africa the "white man's grave"; it was the grave of tens of thousands of black men as well. Little was idyllic about the Africa of early-nineteenth-century missionary experience. In the Calabar region, for example, floggings, mass executions, and torture of the most indiscriminate kind were the order of the day. Twin babies were routinely dispatched; deceased chiefs were never buried alone, but were accompanied by scores of slaves, wives, subjects, and children — still alive — into the next life; intertribal war was brutal and endemic; married women were chattels, to be disposed of at will; filth, reeking stench, and disease were an integral element of town life. That conversion to the Christian faith brought an amelioration of these conditions in due course was undeniable, and profoundly welcome.[51]

Confidence that true progress was not only rooted in Christianity but that it was inevitable infused mission theory and practice of the day. It was a conviction, furthermore, repeatedly substantiated by actual experience. The wretched conditions in India, Africa, and Asia portrayed in missionary reports and letters are unsparingly graphic. No eyewitness could contest the essential accuracy of their accounts, or gainsay their profound sense of indignation at the cruelty and injustice that they observed. The contemporary Western world likewise registers shock when, as frequently happens, injustice, torture, and atrocities are brought to its attention by such organizations as Amnesty International.

Missionary self-perceptions were profoundly affected by such an outlook and their concomitant experiences. Exploitation of the material and technological

---

48. James S. Dennis, "The Social Influence of Christianity as Illustrated by Foreign Missions," in *Christ and Civilization: A Survey of the Influence of the Christian Religion upon the Course of Civilization,* ed. John Brown Paton, Percy William Bunting, and Alfred Ernest Garvie (London: National Council of Evangelical Free Churches, 1910), 487–88. See my published lecture, *"Not the Bloom, but the Fruit . . ."*

49. Robb, *The Heathen World and the Duty of the Church,* 74.

50. William Pakenham Walsh, *Christian Missions: Six Discourses Delivered before the University of Dublin; Being the Donnellan Lectures for 1861* (Dublin: George Herbert, 1862).

51. For a glimpse of life in Calabar during this time, see James Buchan, *The Expendable Mary Slessor* (Edinburgh: Saint Andrew Press, 1980).

superiority to which their Christian heritage entitled them was both natural and strategically useful. And while at times unwittingly or even deliberately implicated in the less savory aspects of the West's seemingly inexorable and often brutal political, economic, and military hegemony, they often proved to be the most genuine benefactors of vanquished peoples.

In the introduction to *Trade Politics and Christianity in Africa and the East*, Harry H. Johnston confessed an "utter lack of faith or interest in most Christian dogmas."[52] Nevertheless, his years as a colonial administrator had persuaded him that missionary efforts to uplift the weaker races was not, as critics asserted, "a flying in the face of nature." On the contrary, Johnston said that he had been repeatedly impressed with "the splendid work which has been and is being accomplished by all types of Christian missionary amongst the Black, Brown, and Yellow peoples of non-Caucasian race.... "[53]

Missionaries would have been gratified to hear such praise from a man of Johnston's formidable reputation, but hardly surprised, since this had been their understanding from earliest years.[54] Obviously, the standard against which missionary accomplishments were measured was Western civilization itself. To the extent that the heathen adopted Western ideas and values; desired and actively sought Western material culture; meekly emulated Western political, social, and religious institutions; and submitted without murmuring to Western domination, missionary efforts could be judged successful. The overall result was simply another vindication of their Lord's promise to all who would make their priority the search for His Kingdom and His righteousness (Matt. 6:33).

The assassination of Austrian Archduke Franz Ferdinand by teenage members of Black Hand plunged Christian Europe and its colonies into the bloodiest and quite possibly most meaningless conflagration in human history. It also marked the end of innocence for missionary apologists, who, until then, had held up their own societies as evidence of the vitality and virtue of Christian influence.

In his admirable book on the subject, Hew Strachan points out that this European war became known as the First World War because people from all over the world came to fight in the civilized nations' cause. Britain mobilized more than three million troops from her colonies (two million of these from Africa), while France mobilized half-a-million from hers. The war's ultimately pointless savagery sent a shudder through the terra firma on which confidence in the moral,

---

52. In Macdonald, *Trade Politics and Christianity in Africa and the East,* viii.

53. Johnston, *A History of the Colonization of Africa by Alien Races,* 146.

54. See, for example, Thomas Laurie, *The Ely Volume; or, The Contributions of our Foreign Missions to Science and Human Well Being* (Boston: ABCFM, 1881); William Warren, *These for Those: Our Indebtedness to Foreign Missions; or, What We Get for What We Give* (Portland: Hoyt, Fogg and Breed, 1870); John Liggins, *The Great Value and Success of Foreign Missions. Proved by Distinguished Witnesses; Being the Testimony of Diplomatic Ministers, Consuls, Naval Officers, and Scientific and other Travellers in Heathen and Mohammedan Countries; Together With that of English Viceroys, Governors, and Military Officers in India and in the British Colonies; also Leading Facts and Late Statistics of the Missions* (London: James Nisbet & Co., 1889); Robert Young, *The Success of Christian Missions: Testimonies to their Beneficent Results* (London: Hodder & Stoughton, 1890).

social, and political superiority of Western Christendom was based.[55] Missionaries who had confidently proclaimed European civilization to be the natural and inevitable result of societies permeated by Christian values were likewise shaken to their ideological foundations by the war and its aftermath.[56] Commenting on the decline of Chinese interest in mission school education, the Hocking Commission observed that while "By 1920 it had become 'almost the fashion to become a Christian'; since 1922 the tide [had] turned," due, understandably, to "... the disillusionment of the World War and the widespread impression it left that the West did not really believe the Christianity it taught."[57]

This thin edge of British and European self-doubt was driven deeper into the missionary psyche by the shameful pact in 1938 between Hitler and Chamberlain. The subsequent barbarism of the Second World War — with its murder of six million Jews by the world's most "civilized" nation, and its obliteration of an entire city of Japanese civilians by the West's most "Christian" nation — convinced many that the civilization of which they were a part was, after all, a profoundly immoral one. A heretofore unthinkable question now required an answer: was it Africans, Asians, Arabs, and Indians who were walking in darkness? Or was it their would-be civilizers?

Missionary advocacy of *civilization* through *Christian* conversion gradually came to be displaced by secular programs of *development* through *Western* science, education, finance, and political rearrangement. The modus operandi of missions continues to function much as before, since it was embedded in the very warp and woof of Christian missionary identity. But the confident, sometimes breathless, and often patronizing tone of nineteenth-century missionary apologists migrated and is now found almost exclusively in the language and agendas of contemporary nonreligious organizations such as the United Nations, the World Bank, and the International Monetary Fund.

Following the two world wars, the fortunes of British and European Protestantism have been marked by an apparently irreversible, accelerating decline. In Britain and Europe of 1900, affiliated Protestants constituted almost 29 percent of the population. By 1985, this remnant had declined to less than 22 percent, with approximately one out of every 4,355 Protestants opting for an overseas missionary vocation.[58]

While the North American pattern is somewhat different, the trend is likewise unmistakable. As one consequence of the world wars, American perceptions of

---

55. Hew Strachan, *The First World War*, vol. 1, *To Arms* (London: Oxford University Press, 2002); reviewed by Niall Ferguson in the February 13, 2003, issue of the *New York Review of Books*, 21–23. See also Donovan Webster, *Aftermath: The Remnants of War* (New York: Random House, 1996).

56. William Pfaff, *The Wrath of Nations: Civilization and the Furies of Nationalism* (New York: Simon & Schuster, 1993). "The Great War was the most important event of the twentieth century. It was a decisive historical event, a marker" (232–33).

57. William Ernest Hocking, *Re-thinking Missions: A Laymen's Inquiry after One Hundred Years* (New York and London: Harper & Brothers, Publishers, 1932), 154–55.

58. See Robert T. Coote's interpretive essay, "Taking Aim on 2000 AD," 35–80 in *Mission Handbook: North American Protestant Ministries Overseas,* 13th ed. (Monrovia: Missions Advanced Research and Communication Center, 1986), 57, 79–80. My calculations here and below are based on his figures.

their providentially dominant role as savior of the civilized world were reinforced. Americans, enthusiastic heralds of various gospels — science, technology, modern weapons, democracy, and of course, religion — covered the globe. It is only in very recent times that Americans, especially those living abroad, have begun to recognize the self-serving and often immoral nature of their nation's interaction with the rest of the world.[59]

Nevertheless, confident "manifest destiny" thinking continued to exert a profound influence upon both the ends and the means of contemporary Western missionary efforts. Western missionaries, a majority of whom now come from the United States, are nurtured in the ranks of "an almost chosen people,"[60] citizens of a nation still sufficiently rich, powerful, and self-confident to have its own way in the world; a country, furthermore, imbued with a sense of mission — with what one writer referred to as "the Captain America complex."[61]

Many Americans, regarding this nation as the apex of Western civilization and avatar of universal progress, unapologetically pursue their "manifest destiny" of political, cultural, economic, and military hegemony. But to those who look more closely at the why and how of this ascendancy, Western Christendom — born and sustained through violence — has been demystified. Obscured by the noble ideals and economic ideology to which we attribute a way of life that is the envy of the world lies a more sinister history which cannot be legitimately replicated by our would-be emulators: centuries of brutal slavery that emptied Africa of an estimated sixty million of its inhabitants; genocidal conquest of three continents that issued in the obliteration of an estimated 90 percent of their incumbent populations; a two-ocean moat and a century of relatively cheap national defense; maintenance of a privileged position through both the actual and threatened use of nuclear and chemical weapons of mass destruction; such instruments of development are not available to the poor today. While factors such as these do not mitigate the inherent economic and social advantages of a democratic way of life based on law and the protection of private property, they should at the very least induce a profound humility in those of us who consciously serve as exemplars of Christianity or development in the "underdeveloped" populations of our world. It is difficult to imagine what the lands of old Christendom would be like today if virtually the entire populations of the Americas, Australia, and New Zealand — together with large segments of South Africa and Israel — were packed into what is today known as greater Europe.

We are now haunted by distressing indications that for most of our fellow human beings, there neither is nor can there be any possible road to our way of life, with its visions of ever-increasing levels of comfort and consumption. But since the only economic gospel that we Westerners can proclaim is the one that we personally model, we can do little more than keep running on our consumer

---

59. See, for example, Stephen Kinzer, *Overthrow: America's Century of Regime Change from Hawaii to Iraq* (New York: Times Books, 2006).

60. See the book by Walter Nicgorski and Ronald Weber, eds., *An Almost Chosen People: The Moral Aspirations of Americans* (Notre Dame, IN: University of Notre Dame Press, 1976).

61. Robert Jewett, *The Captain America Complex: The Dilemma of Zealous Nationalism* (Philadelphia: Westminster Press, 1973).

treadmills. Quite apart from the factors alluded to above, the stark and brutal truth is that the natural resources of our planet are sufficient to support "developed" life for only a tiny fraction of its human population. Accordingly, emissaries of the Western churches must be prepared as never before to test the truthfulness of their assertion that "Christ is the answer" in the context of personal material want. At the very least, a missionary's personal stake in the most affluent and powerful civilization in the history of our planet needs to be acknowledged and considered when formulating a strategy for Christian mission of any kind.

There are signs that increasing numbers of North American Protestants, including missionaries — perhaps *especially* missionaries — not only feel betrayed, but are experiencing a deep sense of personal shame and even guilt for their country's collusion with and even open support of tyranny and injustice in Central America, Asia, the Middle East, and elsewhere, in a strange perversion of the Great Commission. Contemporary reading of history has, furthermore, raised serious questions about "the good old days," for it is now clear that in her dealings with Indians, African slaves, and their progeny, and in her numerous wars — both economic and military — around the globe, "Christian America" neither was nor is as "civilized" as was once fondly believed. Again and again, America has revealed its Christianity to be at times little more than a nationalistic cult, diametrically opposed to the virtues modeled and advocated by the One whose kingdom was not of this world, bestowing hollow legitimacy to the brutal pursuit of self-interest of the world's most powerful nation.

Incubated socially, politically, and religiously in a powerful, if declining, civilization, most Western missionaries continue to enjoy and employ their relative affluence as a birthright. They are not unaware of the burden of credibility this places upon their personal mission to the world's poor — as will be seen in chapter 4; nor are they blind to the fact that global resources can support consumption on the Western scale for only an elite few. But alternatives to relative personal affluence are both unattractive and unnecessary, in the thinking of most missionaries, for reasons that are outlined in the next chapter where, the text shows, the contemporary missionary rationale for personal affluence echoes that of an earlier era.

Having thus far dwelt mainly upon nineteenth-century influences upon contemporary practices of Christian mission, it remains to touch briefly upon elements of contemporary consumer culture that influence missionary lifestyles and perceptions of "need." There is in North America the widespread belief that perpetual economic growth is possible, desirable, and necessary. In the two decades following World War II, "the expectation of plenty . . . became the reigning assumption of social thought."[62] The word that perhaps best sums up the plethora of secular values which influence all North Americans — including missionaries — from infancy throughout life is *consumerism,* the way of life established upon the principle that the great goal of human life and activity is more things,

---

62. See David E. Shi, *The Simple Life: Plain Living and High Thinking in American Culture* (New York: Oxford University Press, 1985), 248. Chapter 10, "Affluence and Anxiety" is worth reading in this context.

better things, and newer things; in short, that life *does* consist in the abundance of possessions.

Consumerism is — to use Robert Bellah's expression — a "habit" of the heart that affects everything Americans are and do.[63] When combined with the popular equation of "progress" with technological sophistication, and "civilization" with abundance, Western consumerism makes justification of increasingly high standards of missionary living almost inevitable.

Anthropologist Jules Henry noted this preoccupation with consumption in 1963 when he suggested that life in North America could be summed up by two great commandments: "Create more desire" and "Thou shalt consume."[64] American well-being, he argued, rested in the faithful obedience of the majority to these two imperatives.

On the one hand, he pointed out, nothing could be more economically catastrophic than a decline in consumer demand. Should buying lag, economic depression, or at least recession, becomes inevitable. Accordingly, consumers are "daily confronted with a barrage of advertising calculated to frighten or flatter them out of reasonable contentment into the nagging itch for goods and services [they] don't really need."[65]

On the other hand, new consumer cravings had to be discovered and created. Nothing could be more economically destructive than an outbreak of widespread contentment. Were a majority of North Americans to remain content with last year's shoes, hats, clothes, cars, furniture, electronic gadgets, breakfast cereals, detergents, perfumes, hair styles, and houses, the "good life" would sputter to an end. "To bring into being wants that did not previously exist" became the great mission of advertising and salesmanship — a process compared by economist Galbraith to a humanitarian who, while impressing upon would-be donors the urgent need for more hospital facilities, inadvertently overlooks the fact that the local physician is running down pedestrians to keep the hospital fully occupied! As Galbraith laconically comments: "Among the many models of the good society, no one has urged the squirrel wheel."[66] In North America we have come close.

North American missionaries have not been immune to this elemental tendency in their society. True creatures of our times, no sooner does a new product appear than we missionaries discover a plausible reason for putting it into missionary service. Specialized suppliers exist whose "mission" is to ensure that Western missionaries do not become "out of date" in either their personal or missiological effects. Missionaries of today can congratulate themselves that the

---

63. Robert N. Bellah, Richard Madsen, William M. Sullivan, Ann Swidler, and Steven M. Tipton, *Habits of the Heart: Individualism and Commitment in American Life* (Berkeley: University of California Press, 1985).

64. Jules Henry, *Culture Against Man* (New York: Random House, 1963), 19. For a lucid description of the mechanics of this process, see John Kenneth Galbraith, *The Affluent Society,* 3rd ed., rev. (New York: New American Library, 1976), chap. 11.

65. Dorothy Sayers, *Letters to a Post-Christian World: A Selection of Essays,* selected and introduced by Roderick Jellema (Grand Rapids: Wm. B. Eerdmans, 1969), 145.

66. Galbraith, *The Affluent Society,* 124–28.

adjective "missionary" — when applied to wardrobe and equipment — no longer denotes the frumpy obsolescence it once did.

The culture in which most Western missionaries are born and bred has instilled within them the "need" for far more than their nineteenth-century counterparts dreamed possible. Nurtured in and supported by churches which, for the most part, have long since succumbed to the "spirit of the age" that surrounds them, the Western missionary enterprise has not been markedly resistant to the "Laodicean" phenomenon at either personal or institutional levels. Too much criticism of the status quo would undoubtedly cost prophetic missionaries the financial support of a wealthy and self-satisfied church.

In summary, contemporary Western missionaries find it difficult to address the questions surrounding personal affluence for a number of reasons. First, the powerful ideas associated with progress that characterized nineteenth-century Western civilization continue to exert a powerful though often subliminal influence on the theory and practice of missions, making the rationalization of personal affluence possible. Second, missionaries, like everyone else, are susceptible to the enculturation processes by which any society — in their case the *consumer* society — ensures its own economic survival. Third, the churches from which missionaries derive their ethical cues and their financial support virtually ignore biblical teaching on greed and covetousness, elevating both sins to the level of virtue in their espousal of the dominant values that inform North American life.

3

The Rationale
for Missionary Affluence

It is no disgrace to be poor, but it is mighty inconvenient.

— MARK TWAIN

It is no disgrace to be poor. But it is no honor, either.

— YIDDISH PROVERB

*Honest poverty is a gem that even a King might be proud to call his own,
but I wish to sell out. I have sported that kind of jewelry long enough.*

— MARK TWAIN

*Over the centuries, those who have been blessed with wealth have devel-
oped many ingenious and persuasive justifications of their good fortune.*

— JOHN KENNETH GALBRAITH

Missionaries from the West have seldom suffered from the neglect of critics.
From both within and outside mission ranks, there have been those who have —
in their efforts to create general awareness of missionary defects, mistakes, and
misdeeds — demonstrated unstinting and laudably persistent dedication. An early
exemplar of such critics was Canon Sydney Smith, who, with an eye to British
vested interests in the exploitation of India, used the *Edinburgh Review* as a
pulpit from which to disparage missionaries. "Evil," "fanatics," "lunatics," and
"conspirators against common sense," they were not to be trusted.[1] Missionary
attempts to answer these charges elicited from Smith a series of wild fulmina-
tions ridiculing both the objectives and the methods of missions. Railing against
the entire "nest of consecrated cobblers" and their "perilous heap of trash," the
apoplectic canon snorted that "It [was] scarcely possible to reduce the drunken
declamations of Methodism to a point, to grasp the wriggling lubricity of these
cunning animals, [or] to fix them on one position."[2]

Another establishment clergyman, writing eighty years later, was moderately
less vivid in his use of metaphor in decrying foreign missionaries. In two articles

---

1. See Sydney Smith, "Critique," *Edinburgh Review* (January 1808).
2. Sydney Smith "Critique," *Edinburgh Review* (April 1809): 40, 42.

appearing in the *Fortnightly Review,* Canon Isaac Taylor attacked missionary societies for their strategic and pecuniary shortcomings.[3] This unsolicited but sometimes helpful genre of literature continues to thrive.[4]

Although censures of Western missionaries are topically wide-ranging, missionary affluence is a recurring theme. Missionaries have naturally been aware of the misunderstanding that their lifestyles abroad engender. "New missionaries going to the field are often surprised at the general comforts which surround the old missionaries on the field," acknowledged one author in a chapter addressing the issue of "The Missionary and Luxurious Living."[5] Coming to the defense of his missionary friends a few years earlier, Meredith Townsend raised the question "with brutal plainness... Are not missionaries, especially in India, made too comfortable, too like parsons *in partibus* instead of evangelists?"[6] And in New York, smarting from highly censorious accounts of missionary life in the Orient, a prominent missionary began his apology by observing that "It would be difficult to say why it is that the idea of self-immolation has always been somehow connected with this particular enterprise, — why," in his words, "one who enters upon it should be supposed to be indifferent to comfort and to all those things which nine-tenths of the activities of mankind are busied with seeking."[7] More recently, a mission executive explaining to some ministers why a young Canadian couple en route to Zaire should require more than twice the support under his society than would have been the case had they proceeded under the Africa Inter Mennonite Board, declared: "I make no apology for the level of support our mission requires of its missionaries."[8] He then went on to outline the admirably comprehensive support package, which included provision for every thinkable contingency, from maternity to eternity. He was understandably proud of his mission society's responsible approach to the care of its missionaries.

Within the body of missionary apologetic literature, responses to charges of high living can be divided into four broad streams of rationale: economic, domestic, social, and strategic. Defense of the living standards enjoyed by Western missionaries is almost always based upon demonstrably practical, commonsense considerations that must be taken very seriously.

---

3. Isaac Taylor, "The Great Missionary Failure," and "Missionary Finance," in *The Fortnightly Review* 44, New Series (July–December 1888): 488–500, 581–92, respectively.

4. See, for example, Ado K. Tiberondwa's *Missionary Teachers as Agents of Colonialism: A Study of Their Activities in Uganda* (Lusaka: National Educational Company of Zambia, 1978); Soren Hvalkof and Peter Aaby, eds., *Is God An American? An Anthropological Perspective on the Missionary Work of the Summer Institute of Linguistics* (Published jointly by International Work Group for Indigenous Affairs in Copenhagen, Denmark, and Survival International in London, 1981); David Stoll, *Fishers of Men or Founders of Empire? The Wycliffe Bible Translators in Latin America* (London: Zed Press, 1982); or K. P. Yohannan's *The Coming Revolution in World Missions* (Altamonte Springs, FL: Creation House, 1986).

5. J. L. Barton, *The Missionary and His Critics* (New York: Fleming H. Revell Co., 1906), 164.

6. Meredith Townsend, "Cheap Missionaries," *The Contemporary Review* 54 (July 1889): 1.

7. F. F. Ellinwood, "Asceticism in Missions," *The Chinese Recorder and Missionary Journal* 22, no. 1 (January 1891): 1.

8. The meeting took place near Steinbach, Manitoba. Other details must remain anonymous.

Economic Arguments

"The cheapest mission is the mission which can keep its missionaries the longest, and get out of them the best service which they are capable of rendering," concluded the venerable Griffith John, from his vantage point of sixty years of missionary service in Central China. Neither longevity nor effectiveness were possible unless, he said, missionaries were "properly fed and housed, and . . . so provided for that [they are] able to work without distraction."[9] A similar conclusion was drawn by C. C. Thayer, well-known American missionary physician to Turkey: "Missionary economics," he observed, "has to do with the production and conservation of the missionary's vital force."[10] The editor-in-chief of *The Missionary Review of the World* pointed out that many "needless" missionary fatalities could have been avoided by a more careful attention to the plain teaching of the Scriptures on the subject of the health of the human body.[11]

Before Alphonse Laveran identified the cause of malaria in 1880, and Sir Ronald Ross traced the parasite to infected anopheles mosquitoes, the disease-ridden coasts of west and east Africa were referred to as the "white man's grave" or the "burial ground of missionaries." Lions, leopards, poisonous snakes, enraged elephants, and crocodiles were all recognized as menaces to health, as were swamp vapors and indigenous diseases. But the mosquito was simply a pest.

Henry Drummond's travels in Central Africa left a deep impression upon him. The graves of Mrs. Livingstone and Bishop Mackenzie, and the pathetic cemetery at Livingstonia moved him deeply. He saw missionaries prostrated with fever, suffering in solitude often hundreds of miles from their nearest colleague. He was there when he learned of the passing away of James Stewart (1831–1905), and of the painful death of a white mother in childbirth. While he was there, the only two British children to have survived thus far died. "In short," comments his biographer, "Drummond saw all the cruel sacrifices, inseparable from the first heroic assaults of Christianity upon the Dark Continent." "I've been in an atmosphere of death all the time," he said when he returned to Scotland.[12]

Just how dangerous was missionary life abroad? By dividing the number of deaths which occurred in each field by the total number of years which missionaries had spent on the field, Dr. William G. Lennox — then of the Harvard Medical School — calculated missionary mortality rates for the major American societies between 1812 and 1928.[13] His figures (Table 4) show the number

9. Griffith John, *A Voice from China* (London: Religious Tract Society, 1907), 214–15.

10. C. C. Thayer, "Missionary Health Economics," *Missionary Review of the World* 26 (February 1903): 128.

11. A. T. Pierson, "The Needless Sacrifice of Human Life in Mission Work," *The Missionary Review of the World* 27, no. 2 (Old Series) (February 1904): 81.

12. George Adam Smith, *The Life of Henry Drummond* (New York: Doubleday & McClure, 1898), 209–11. See Henry Drummond's own account in his book *Tropical Africa,* 3rd ed. (London: Hodder & Stoughton, 1889), esp. 15–16, 22–23, 41–45.

13. See William G. Lennox, *The Health and Turnover of Missionaries* (New York: Advisory Committee, 1933). The denominations studied included the Presbyterian Church in the United States of America; the Congregational, Methodist, and Episcopal churches; the Northern Baptist Convention; and the Young Women's Christian Association. This valuable study followed his earlier studies, *The Health of Missionary Families in China: A Statistical Study* (Denver: University of Denver

of deaths per thousand in each field.[14] However dangerous missionary life may have been, their death rates never approached those of European troops stationed in Africa. Between 1929 and 1936, British soldiers on the old Coast were devastated by a rate of 483 deaths annually per 1000![15] Furthermore, figures show that after 1869, mortality rates for Presbyterian ministers in the United States were consistently and dramatically higher than for their missionary counterparts in India.[16] Nevertheless, death on any scale was as unpopular among Protestant missionaries then as it is among most groups today.

TABLE 4
American Missionary Deaths per Thousand, 1812–1928

Africa	17.1
Near East	13.2
Malaysia and the Pacific Islands	12.4
India	10.4
North China	9.5
Mexico and Central America	9.4
South China	8.9
Europe	7.6
Japan and Korea	6.6
South America	6.2
Central and West China	5.5

Missionary mortality was only one reason for the termination of missionary service, of course. More frequently, bad health simply invalided a missionary home. Of 3,712 missionary withdrawals from service between 1900 and 1928, 15 percent were due to death, while 31 percent were because of ill health.[17]

Quite apart from the obvious human costs and attendant inconveniences posed by illness or death, from the mission agency's point of view there were strategic costs as well. A missionary's early retirement from active duty, whatever the reason, constituted a staggering economic loss to the sponsoring agency. That a significant percentage (close to 40 percent) of missionary deaths or withdrawals due to ill health occurred during the first term of service was significant.[18] For as a well-known executive member of the American Board of Commissioners for Foreign Missions (ABCFM) explained:

Department of Economics, 1921), and *A Comparative Study of the Health of Missionary Families in Japan and China and a Selected Group in America* (Denver: University of Denver, Department of Economics, 1922).

14. Lennox, *The Health and Turnover of Missionaries,* 120. See also the Frontispiece (Figure 40) of the book, and his entire chapter, "Death Rates," 113–27.

15. Ibid., 120.

16. Ibid., 118.

17. Ibid., 78–79. In his chapter "Reasons for Withdrawal" (77–112), Lennox demonstrates that most of the deaths and illnesses could have been prevented.

18. See ibid., "The Years of Service," 54–76.

For a missionary to become generally useful in the missionary field, and to bear his part of the work, requires from three to six years of preparation. The expense, therefore, of getting a missionary upon the field, apart from the original expense of mental equipment in the schools, is not inconsiderable. . . .

If, during this period, the missionary's health breaks down, and he is compelled to give up the work and return home, all of the money, or most of the money that has been spent on his outfit, traveling expenses, and support, while studying the language and learning the work, is practically thrown away.[19]

The most effective missionary was the living missionary; the most efficient living missionary was the healthy one; the most healthy missionary was the comfortable one; and the most comfortable missionary was the one whose manner of life overseas most closely approximated his or her life back home. Only under such conditions could a missionary's "vital force" be regenerated and sustained over time. Creature comforts and sound health went together. Philip Southon, an American physician in Central Africa who would expire within two years of writing the letter cited below, explained why a comfortable European-style residence was an essential part of a missionary's equipment:

I am now sending my brother an order for things for the home, crockery, glass, cutlery, and lots of little things which really are essential for a residence in this country. For, as you know, I maintain that we should use all reasonable means to make our lives as comfortable as possible under the circumstances, since our health depends largely upon our degree of comfort or discomfort.[20]

As important as domicile was a missionary's diet. Mrs. Gratan Guinness, then honorary secretary of the East London Institute, quotes Henry Stanley with approbation as she explains the high mortality rate of Europeans in the Congo: " . . . the cause of death of so many in African exploring parties," Stanley had written, "is poor food. Feed your Europeans on good English provisions . . . pet and care for him, and he will live; give him only native food, and let him rough it, and he will die."[21]

Modern Western missionaries rarely anticipate disease or early demise as the inevitable price of their vocation. With their fellow clergy, they qualify in the North American insurance industry's actuarial tables for life insurance rates reserved for those whose life expectancy is among the most enviable in the

---

19. Barton, *The Missionary and His Critics,* 162–63. See Lennox, *The Health and Turnover of Missionaries,* "Opportunities for Saving," 181–99.

20. A letter from Southon to Thompson, Urambo, July 12, 1881. See Jonathan J. Bonk, *The Theory and Practice of Missionary Identification, 1860–1920* (Lewiston, NY: Edwin Mellen Press, 1989), 50. See also Daniel Johnson Fleming, *Living as Comrades: A Study of Factors Making for "Community"* (New York: Published for the Foreign Missions Conference of North America by Agricultural Missions, Inc., 1950), 23–24.

21. Mrs. Gratan Guinness, *The New World of Central Africa, With a History of the First Christian Mission on the Congo* (London: Hodder & Stoughton, 1890), 518. Mrs. Guinness was quoting one of Stanley's "Fourteen Rules for Life in Africa."

world.[22] Clearly, Western missionaries have benefited from the tragic experiences of earlier predecessors by steadily improving the conditions and standards of missionary living. According to figures provided by the U.S. Bureau of Economic Analysis in April 2005, disposable personal income per capita in current and constant (2000) dollars increased from $17,108 to $29,404 between 1990 and 2004.[23] Mission agencies have more than kept pace. While the numbers of totally supported U.S. personnel serving overseas between 1992 and 2001 increased by 15.7 percent, financial support for overseas ministries increased by 45 percent, from $2,587,013,186 to $3,199,249,193.[24]

The economic argument in support of missionary affluence is succinctly articulated by James Barton, responding one hundred years ago to the charge that missionary standards of living were unnecessarily extravagant: "Short lives, ordinarily, in the mission field are of little direct value to the work," he reminded his readers, continuing:

> In the ordinary course of events, the missionary who can give the longest life of service to the cause is the one who brings the strongest influence to bear upon the people among whom he lives, and who will produce the largest results by his life. It is the missionary's duty to invest his life in the way that will bring forth the largest and most permanent results, and experience has proved that, as a general thing, these results are not obtained by starving the body or misusing it by unnecessary hardships, or causing it to carry unnecessary burdens, and thus wearing it out early in its career.[25]

While his advice may strike a mildly dissonant chord with those who take literally their Lord's words in Luke 9:24 about saving and losing one's life, it nicely encapsulates the economic sensibility of the modern missionary movement from the West. "Avoidance of fanaticism and folly, and the temptation to run to extremes" was, according to A. T. Pierson, the epitome of common sense where missionary health was concerned. Divine sanction for his point of view, he noted, could be found in the Scriptures themselves: "Be not righteous over much," quotes Pierson approvingly; "neither make thyself over wise; why should'st thou destroy thyself?" (Eccl. 7:16.)[26]

---

22. See, for example, the actuarial tables used by the Presbyterian Ministers' Fund insurance company.

23. U.S. Bureau of Economic Analysis, Survey of Current Business, April 2005. *www.census.gov/compendia/statab/tables/06s0663.xls.*

24. *Mission Handbook 2004–2006,* 13.

25. Barton, *The Missionary and His Critics,* 163–64.

26. Pierson, "The Needless Sacrifice of Human Life in Missionary Work," 84. There have always been Western missionaries who have not heeded this advice, and these have suffered — if not ill health — the censure of their missionary peers. See, for example, Andrew Porter's article, "Evangelical Enthusiasm, Missionary Motivation and West Africa in the Late Nineteenth Century: The Career of G. W. Brooke," in *The Journal of Imperial and Commonwealth History* 6, no. 1 (October 1977): 23–46. From Hudson Taylor and James Gilmour in the nineteenth century, to Bruce Olson and Viv Grigg in the twentieth, missionaries heedless of Solomon's advice have been regarded with deep suspicion.

Domestic Rationale

No rationale for maintaining relatively high living standards can be more compelling than those relating to the care and well-being of a missionary's family. "One of the most difficult questions to be solved in the work of Christian Missions to the heathen is, What should be done for the children of missionaries?" began the anonymous author of an 1855 pamphlet on this most poignant of all married missionary subjects.[27]

The accounts of earlier missionaries who, because of "the great difficulty of bringing them up in a Christian manner amongst a heathen people,"[28] and for want of appropriately Western schools in the lands of their adoption, felt obligated to send their young children to Europe or America for education are heartrending. The resultant emotional and psychological costs to parents and children can only be imagined, although the letters and diaries of mothers do provide some intimation of the extent of their familial distress. The letter below was written in 1842 by Sarah D. Comstock, a Baptist missionary mother, as she contemplates the soon departure of her children:

> Our children are but another name for self. You are right in supposing that I have many anxious thoughts about their future lot; how many and how anxious, no human being can ever know.... From experience and observation, my own as well as others, I am convinced that our children cannot be properly educated and fitted for the greatest usefulness in this country; that I shall wrong my children, seriously wrong them, by suffering them to grow up, inhaling day after day, and year after year, the fatal miasma with which the whole moral atmosphere of this country is so fearfully impregnated. On this point my judgment has long been convinced. Shall we, then, go home with our children, and see them educated under the genial influence of a Christian sky? Or shall we send them away, and commit their best interests, for time and for eternity, to stranger hands, who do not and cannot feel a mother's duties?
>
> As a general rule, I believe a mother's duty to her children is second only to her duty to her Creator. How far missionary mothers may be exempt from this rule, it is difficult to decide. A mother who has spent eight, ten, or twelve of her best years among heathens may be expected to be well acquainted with their language, manners, customs, and habits of thought and feeling. She has proved herself their friend, and gained their confidence and affection. She is, as it were, just prepared for extensive usefulness. At this point shall she go and leave them, with none to tell them of Him who came to ransom their souls from sin and its penalty? Or, if another is raised up to fill her place, it must be years — years during which many precious immortals must go down to a dark, a fearful eternity, ere she is prepared to labor efficiently among them.

---

27. "Remarks on the Provision that Should be Made for the Children of Missionaries" (New York: Anson D. F. Randolph, 1855), 5.
28. Ibid., 15.

I see no other way than for each individual mother prayerfully to consider the subject, and let her own conscience decide as to her duty. As to
my own feelings on this subject, after long, serious, and prayerful consideration, I have come to the conclusion that it is best to send our eldest two
back to America in the course of another year, should a good opportunity
offer. . . . This surely forms the climax of a missionary's sacrifices. . . .

If it were not for the consciousness of doing right, of being in the path
of duty, I could not, no, I could not sustain it. . . . Pray for me; pray for those
dear children who are so soon to be orphans, an age, too, when they most
need the watchful care of parental affection. This thought is at times almost
too much for my aching, bursting heart to endure. Had not my Saviour, yes,
and a compassionate Saviour, added these two words: "and children" to the
list of sacrifices for his sake, I might think it more than was required. . . .

Shall we withhold our Isaac? No; may we rather strive to commit ourselves and our precious offspring in faith to his care, who has said, "Leave
thy fatherless children to me." They are in one sense orphans. But if rendered so by what we feel to be obedience to our heavenly Father's will, will
He not be to them a father and protector? Will He not more than supply
the place of the most affectionate earthly parents?[29]

In time, schools offering a Christian or at least Western cultural environment were established. Today, while missionary parents still sometimes face the
prospect of sending their children to boarding schools, modern air travel and the
availability of international schools on every continent make the requisite sepa-
rations of shorter duration and considerably less painful.[30] Nevertheless, as the
son of missionaries myself, it is only as a father that I could begin to fathom the
muted anguish in my parents' eyes as — year after year — they said their last
goodbyes before surrendering me to the care of the Bingham Academy staff in
Ethiopia.

Missionary children today, with few exceptions, are separated from parents no
more than six to eight weeks at a time. Nevertheless, the distress of separation
together with the inevitable parental cognitive dissonance continue to make the
experience painful for all concerned. Not surprisingly, the care and education

29. Mrs. A. M. Edmond, *Memoir of Mrs. Sarah D. Comstock, Missionary to Arracan* (Philadelphia: American Baptist Publication Society, [1854]), 184–86, as quoted in "Remarks on the Provision
that should be made for the Children of Missionaries," 13–14. Groves S. Comstock and his wife began
service in British-held Arakan in 1835. Both soon died of cholera: she in 1843, and he in 1845. See
Maung She Wa, G. Edwards and E. Edwards, *Burma Baptist Chronicle* (Rangoon, 1963), 106–10.

30. Of particular interest here are three organizations: (1) International Schools Services
(ISS) in Princeton, NJ, "A nonprofit corporation [established in 1955] dedicated to excellence
for children attending overseas schools worldwide . . . the world's leader in providing a comprehensive range of quality educational services for schools, educators, families and corporations"
(*www.iss.edu/index.html*); (2) The Association of Christian Schools International (ACSI), founded
in 1978, "serves over 5,300 member schools in approximately 100 countries with an enrollment
of nearly 1.2 million students" and "strives to enable and equip Christian educators and schools
worldwide to effectively educate young people with the mind of Christ" (*www.acsi.org*); and (3)
Interaction International, founded in 1968, "the world's foremost organization advocating on behalf
of third culture kids of all ages, nations and backgrounds" (*www.tckinteract.net/*).

of missionary children continue to absorb the attention of Western missionary agencies.[31]

Providing a Western education abroad is fiscally expensive. Within the various countries in which schools for missionary children or international schools are located, the number of nonmissionaries who can afford to send their children to these institutions is negligible. In a country in which most of the inhabitants barely subsist, only the very affluent can contemplate spending thousands of dollars per child per year for education.

Any parent will readily appreciate this rationale for missionary affluence. "Even if the cheap missionary could induce a fitting wife to share [his ascetic] lot," explained one writer a century ago,

> ...he will think of the children to come, and perceives from examples all around him what on such an income their fate must be. They will be boys and girls with the white energy who have been bred up as natives — that is, they will, unless exceptional persons, belong to the most hopeless class existing in the world. They cannot be sent home or be kept in the hill schools, or be separated in any way from the perpetual contact of an Asian civilization which eats out of white children their distinctive morale.[32]

Few quibble with the assumption that children of Western missionaries are entitled to the kind of enculturation that will ensure their academic and social survival when they return to North America. Secure in the knowledge that their children are receiving the education and care appropriate to their social station and nationality, parents can focus on their missionary tasks. The psychological and physical well-being of missionary families provides what is probably the single most powerful complex of justifications for the relative affluence and privilege enjoyed by Western missionaries.[33]

Social Justification

In his instructive pamphlet, "Hints for Missionaries Proceeding to Central Africa," Southon's thoughtfully detailed directives on missionary wardrobe — touching upon suits, shirts, collars, undershirts, drawers, socks, scarves, boots, shoes, wading trousers, wading boots, hats, and helmets — are prefaced with these words of sage advice:

> In his travels, the missionary should always present the appearance of a gentleman. There is no necessity for discarding civilised habits because

31. See, for example, David C. Pollock and Ruth E. Van Reken, *The Third Culture Kid Experience: Growing Up among Worlds* (Yarmouth, ME: Intercultural Press, 1999), and Jonathan S. Addleton, "Missionary Kid Memoirs: A Review Essay," in *International Bulletin of Missionary Research* 24, no. 1 (January 2000): 30–34.

32. Townsend, "Cheap Missionaries," 5.

33. See Fleming, *Living as Comrades,* 24; Ellinwood, "Asceticism in Missions," 5; Barton, *The Missionary and His Critics,* 164 and 169; Betty Jo Kenney, *The Missionary Family* (Pasadena, CA: W. Carey Library, 1983). See also Marjorie A. Collins, *Manual for Today's Missionary: From Recruitment to Retirement* (South Pasadena, CA: William Carey Library, 1986), chaps. 22 and 30.

civilisation is left behind; on the contrary, it is for him to carry with him the impress of a society better than that to which he is going; hence, he should always be neat and clean in his appearance, and scrupulously careful that his garb is tidy. An untidy European will surely be criticised by the gentlemanly Arab, if not by natives.[34]

While the particulars of Southon's advice may seem strange to the non-Victorian reader, the underlying rationale is easily appreciated. Personal appropriation of those statuses — together with their accompanying roles — that will best facilitate mission objectives continues to be at the heart of missionary orientation to another culture. Statuses and roles define relationships within any society. Western cross-cultural missionaries are not exempted from this rule.[35]

The historically close connection between missionaries and the highly visible economic, social, and imperial power of the West has made it extremely difficult for them to disassociate themselves from the statuses and roles assigned to the privileged. A century ago, idealistic Church Missionary Society (CMS) missionaries who tried to do so were regarded by skeptical natives as either hypocrites or failed Europeans.[36]

Contemporary missionaries from the West, likewise, usually discover that *because* they are *Western* missionaries, they automatically occupy a high status in most economically poor societies. Missionaries from North America who deliberately choose the path of social-economic asceticism will operate under what Eugene Nida refers to as "a cloud of suspicion . . . since it reverses all the norms of social climbing."[37] Both the incarnation of our Lord and the experience of contemporary missionaries offer proof of the sagacity of Nida's observation. An American missionary writing to me some years ago from Peru confessed that when he and his family had lived in Ecuador, they did "go native, and the local people just thought that we were crazy." As he explained, "They have a conception of 'gringo' and in order to gain their respect, we needed to meet their expectations, build a nice house, get a better vehicle, etc. Too close an identification with native culture diminished our standing in the community, and therefore any message we may have [had] for them."[38] The unpleasant side effects of

---

34. E. J. Southon, "Hints for Missionaries Proceeding to Central Africa" (London: Printed for the Directors of the London Missionary Society by Yates & Alexander, 1880), 2.

35. For a creative explication of missionary roles, see the articles by husband-and-wife team Jacob A. and Anne Loewen, "Role, Self-Image and Missionary Communication," and "The 'Missionary' Role," in *Culture and Human Values: Christian Intervention in Anthropological Perspective: Selections from the Writings of Jacob A. Loewen* (South Pasadena, CA: William Carey Library, 1975), 412–27, and 428–43, respectively. Also stimulating and insightful in this regard are William D. Reyburn's articles on "missionary identification," helpfully reprinted in *Readings in Missionary Anthropology II,* enlarged 1978 ed., ed. William A. Smalley (South Pasadena, CA: William Carey Library, 1978), 746–91.

36. See Thomas O. Beidelman, "Contradictions between the Sacred and the Secular Life: The Church Missionary Society in Ukaguru, Tanzania, East Africa, 1876–1914," in *Comparative Studies in Society and History: An International Quarterly* 23 (1981): 73–95, but especially 89.

37. Eugene Nida, *Message and Mission: The Communication of the Christian Faith* (New York: Harper & Row, 1960), 164–65.

38. Letter of Moore to Bonk, December 11, 1985, Peru.

diminished social standing in a community constitute a powerful rationale for sustaining appropriate levels of Western missionary affluence.

Strategic Validations

The expansion of Christianity over the past two centuries cannot be understood apart from the economic, political, and military ascendancy of the West. As Latourette explains,

> The expansion both of Europe and of Christianity was facilitated by the new mechanical appliances and the mounting wealth associated with the Industrial Revolution. It was machines which produced the outpouring of goods whose sales sent Europeans to the ends of the earth. Machines speeded up transportation and communication and so reduced the size of the earth that it was possible for Europeans, including Christian missionaries, to cover it. The monopoly of the new machines enabled Westerners to gain the mastery of most of the earth's surface and to impose their will upon other peoples. From the machines was derived the wealth, a portion of which, albeit a very small portion, Occidentals devoted to the spread of their faith. It was the exhilaration of the power and the wealth made available and of the doors opened by the machine which accounted in part for that abounding optimism of the 19th century with which the spread of Christianity was so closely associated.[39]

To the economic, domestic, and social benefits accruing to the affluent missionary must be added strategic advantages. The scope, efficiency, and speed of Western missionary strategies bear testimony to both the efficacy and the power of money. While Christian churches in the West are certainly not generous on the basis of per-capita giving to overseas missions,[40] the resulting total is nevertheless impressive when considered in the context of economic resources available to the vast majority of Christians in the Third World. North American Protestant mission agencies reported a total income of just under $4.18 billion for 2001 — an increase of approximately $1.232 billion.[41] Distributed among 690 U.S. and 125 Canadian agencies represented by 45,617 long-term (one year or longer) overseas personnel,[42] the money is used to finance a wide range of mission strategies, including adoption, agriculture, aviation, broadcasting, childcare,

---

39. Kenneth Scott Latourette, *The Unquenchable Light* (London: Eyre and Spottiswoode, 1940), 83.

40. According to figures appearing in the 74th issue of the *Yearbook of American & Canadian Churches, 2006,* ed. Eileen W. Lindner (Nashville: Abingdon Press, 2006), annual per-capita member giving for 2005 was $645.63 in the United States, and $345.67 for Canada. Of this, 15 percent and 18 percent, respectively, were designated as "benevolences," for causes outside of the immediate congregation ("Summary Statistics of Church Finances," 394–95). For a more nuanced and comprehensive analysis of church giving in the United States, see John L. and Sylvia Ronsvalle, *The State of Church Giving through 2002,* 14th ed. (Champaign, IL: Empty Tomb, Inc., 2004).

41. *Mission Handbook 2004–2006,* 13, 39.

42. Ibid., 12–14, 463–98 passim.

church construction, development, education, evangelism, leadership development, linguistics, literature production and distribution, medicine and public health, national church support, relief and rehabilitation, research, technical assistance, translation, youth programs, and so on.[43]

It is hardly necessary to point out that strategies such as these can be initiated and sustained only by those with significant financial resources. Schools, books, hospitals, autoclaves, X-ray machines, vehicles, radio and television sending and receiving equipment, tractors, grain, airplanes, cars, jeeps, trucks, well-drilling machines, computers, scholarships, international conferences and consultations, and the myriad of other vital accoutrements of those mission strategies originating in the West require a scale of affluence seldom available elsewhere in the world.[44] Only relative affluence makes it possible or even conceivable for an estimated one in three American youth to take part in cross-cultural service projects before leaving high school.[45]

Without ample supplies of money, missionary efforts from the West would be severely curtailed, become largely unrecognizable, and possibly cease altogether. Western strategies, beginning with the support of missionaries themselves, are money-intensive. Without funding sufficient to guarantee missionaries a lifestyle roughly equivalent to the one their cultural conditioning has entitled them, obedience to the Great Commission as presently conceived would be no longer conceivable. Obedience thus becomes a rationale for affluence. Western missionary strategies and their concomitant obligations constitute a powerful raison d'être for missionary affluence. "Missionary economics require that the missionary be furnished unto every good work."[46]

---

43. Ibid., 315–45, 501–7.

44. While it is popular to believe that the Western missionary enterprise has been sustained largely by the "widow's mites" of numerous ordinary donors, the financial support of many agencies relies heavily upon the generosity of rich individuals who, by means of purpose-established foundations, trusts, and endowments, have often single-handedly made possible many of the capital-intensive strategies and programs of Western missions. Outstanding among these largely anonymous donors in the nineteenth century were men such as jam manufacturer William Hartley, treasurer of the Primitive Methodist Missionary Society; chemical manufacturers James and John Campbell White, who provided most of the finance necessary for the Free Church of Scotland's Livingstonia Mission; or Robert Arthington, the millionaire largely responsible for both the timing and the strategy used by the several societies instrumental in the missionary occupation of Central Africa. See Brian Stanley, " 'The Miser of Headingly': Robert Arthington and the Baptist Missionary Society, 1877–1900," in *The Church and Wealth: Papers Read at the 1986 Summer Meeting and the 1987 Winter Meeting of the Ecclesiastical History Society,* ed. W. J. Sheils and Diana Wood (Oxford: Published for The Ecclesiastical History Society by Basil Blackwell, 1987), 371–82. See also A. M. Chirgwin, *Arthington's Million: The Romance of the Arthington Trust* (London: Livingstone Press, 1935). The pattern continues. Today, as then, donors remain largely anonymous.

45. According to Robert Wuthnow of Princeton University, about 1.6 million Americans were involved in short-term cross-cultural mission trips in 2005. Each trip was less than two weeks, and cost an average of one thousand dollars. See the article by Greg Latshaw, "Missionaries Make Short Trips to Teach Gospel," in *Pittsburgh Tribune-Review* (June 25, 2006). *www.pittsburghlive.com/x/pittsburghtrib/s_459512.html.* See also G. Jeffrey MacDonald, "Rise of Sunshine Samaritans: On a Mission or Holiday?" *The Christian Science Monitor* (May 25, 2006).

46. C. C. Thayer, "Missionary Economics: Personal Efficiency," *Missionary Review of the World* 26 (July 1903): 517. Thayer served in Turkey under the American Board of Commissioners for Foreign Missions (ABCFM).

At a more personal level, likewise, affluence has proven to be of considerable strategic importance, since it enhances both missionary efficiency and missionary credibility. In the case of the former, no one has better summarized the argument in favor of missionary affluence than Donald McGavran. Between 1933 and 1935, due to the twin influences of Daniel Johnson Fleming at Union Seminary and the Great Depression which was devastating North America, several missionaries in India formed a "Fellowship for Ventures in Simpler Living."[47] As the organization's founding secretary, McGavran and his family attempted to subsist on one rupee (thirty-three cents) a day for food. While it was possible to physically exist on this meager allowance, he quickly found it necessary to temper idealism with realism. As McGavran explained in a letter:

> ... the association for simpler living soon found out that if we were to carry out any effective work and if we were to maintain fellowship with our fellow missionaries in India, we would simply have to accept the level of expenditure which missionaries in general employed.
>
> If they were to do their work, they had to employ servants. If they did not employ servants, they spent most of their time doing the work which the servants did and very little time doing the Lord's work. Furthermore, the existence of such a plan created considerable friction within the missionary body. Missionaries who did not belong to the association were likely to say, "Oh, you're trying to show us up!"
>
> So after two or three years we simply gave up the idea and settled down to doing good solid, hopefully fruitful missionary work.[48]

Second, Western missionaries have discovered in their relative affluence an exceedingly advantageous apologetic element.[49] This manifests itself in several ways. On the one hand, it is Western missionary affluence which, as part of his general novelty, has often gained for him a degree of attention, influence, and power beyond anything that could not have otherwise been achieved. A rich man commands a hearing not because he necessarily has something important to say, but because he is rich. Missionary novelty has frequently been used to *get* the attention of a people; missionary affluence has just as often been the means of *holding* that attention. Something about personal pecuniary advantage inspires great self-confidence in treating with those who are poorer. As a Hindu convert to Christianity observed, "It is easy for Western missionaries to equate *richness* with *rightness,* and *poverty* with *wrongness.*"[50]

---

47. Fleming, who served as a Presbyterian missionary in India for eight years, was professor of missions at Union Theological Seminary in New York. See his *Ventures in Simpler Living* (New York: International Missionary Council, 1933). McGavran did his Ph.D. at Union Seminary and Columbia University under Fleming.

48. Letter of McGavran to Bonk, January 26, 1988, Pasadena.

49. This is the argument of my chapter, "'And They Marveled...': Mammon as Miracle in Western Missionary Encounter," in James R. Krabill, Walter Sawatsky, and Charles E. Van Engen, eds., *Evangelical, Ecumenical, and Anabaptist Missiologies in Conversation: Essays in Honor of Wilbert R. Shenk* (Maryknoll, NY: Orbis Books, 2006), 78–87.

50. Tony Malik, converted in 1975, at the time serving as a missionary with Venture Teams International. These remarks were made in the context of his lecture on "Hinduism," delivered at Winnipeg Theological Seminary in Otterburne, Manitoba, on October 17, 1985.

Historically, the display of missionary affluence played a significant role in the initial impression they made upon non-Westerners. In Central Africa, for example, missionaries of the London Missionary Society were immensely wealthy by indigenous standards, and soon functioned not only as religious teachers, but as employers, chiefs, and magistrates. At first, missionaries were somewhat flattered and amused by the effect that their wealth had upon Africans, most of whom had never seen a white man before. "They come in crowds to see the wagons, and they think us a most wonderful people," wrote one young missionary, adding, "they all seem to have a wholesome dread of us."[51] A nearby missionary, relating his construction of a temporary building a month earlier, described the effect which the sight of a European house had upon the Africans: "Many," he said, "...look in as they pass,...lift their hands in amazement, [and] exclaim 'the white man! the white man!' "[52] For the missionary wishing to be listened to, there is something reassuring about a personal capacity to inspire awe. The material evidences of their affluence were not, it is true, miracles; but their effect upon the African was the same. In some mysterious way, their superior way of life constituted, they thought, irrefutable evidence in favor of the truthfulness and vitality of their gospel. As missionaries well knew, it was often the material aspects of Western life that most attracted the unconverted. "They will watch your house-building and gardening," two CMS missionaries proceeding to the same part of Africa were told, "and see that you are superior to them in knowledge and energy and are worth listening to therefore on all subjects."[53]

Today, wherever Western missionaries are working among a people whose material circumstances are demonstrably poorer than their own, a similar rationale — if required — is frequently produced to quell any doubts, including self doubts, about the propriety of missionary affluence. "While committed to a Peruvian church staffed by Peruvians," one missionary wrote to me several years ago,

> we find that Peruvians will listen to a gringo and give him much more credence than one of their own. So, while we have a few Peruvian members [in our mission], they are less persuasive in dealing with their own people than we, the rich, educated foreigners are![54]

The arguments in favor of Western missionary affluence are strong, sensible, and effective enough to persuade most missionaries that personal affluence, when appropriated and enjoyed with Christian moderation, is — on economic, domestic, social, and strategic grounds — infinitely preferable to the alternative. The next three chapters examine the case for the alternative.

---

51. Letter of Thompson to Mullens, October 1, 1887, Mabisi, as cited in Bonk, *The Theory and Practice of Missionary Identification,* 66.

52. Letter, Jones to Thompson, Fwambo, November 14, 1887, as cited in ibid., 66.

53. Instructions to Dr. E. and Mrs. Baxter, July 31, 1888, as cited by Beidelman in "Contradictions between the Sacred and the Secular Life," 85.

54. Moore to Bonk letter, December 11, 1985, Peru.

Part II

CONSEQUENCES OF WESTERN MISSIONARY AFFLUENCE

Missionary rationale for maintaining and even increasing the economic and material disparity between themselves and those whom they would disciple has tended, not unnaturally, to dwell on the positive advantages of personal health, comfort, security, and efficiency. This was the subject of chapter 3. The three chapters following examine some negative consequences that seem to be an almost inevitable part of the price that missionaries from the West pay for their culturally derived and justified sense of entitlement to relative privilege.

On the surface, there can be no denying that the advantages of affluence far outweigh the disadvantages. The preference for more rather than fewer material accoutrements seems to be universal. To my knowledge, no human society deliberately acculturates its young to strive for personal destitution. The benefits of missionary affluence are obvious, relating largely to comfort, security, and efficiency.[1] *The often overlooked costs, on the other hand, must be calculated in more difficult-to-tally social currencies. How missiologically significant is the virtually unbridgeable economic gulf between Western missionaries and their protégés within the Gospel communication process itself? What effect — if any — does wealth have upon the missionary's personal credibility as communicator and teacher? And what influence does the material privilege of the missionary have on resulting perceptions of just what constitutes the good news? Since Jesus*

---

1. "Efficiency" in the consumer mind is most frequently associated with comfort and velocity. Slow is frustrating; fast is good; faster is better. Discomfort is to be avoided at any cost; comfort is good; more comfort is better. Missionary use of technology increases the speed and the ease with which they carry out their tasks. Technology is expensive, and inaccessible to all but the rich. But speed and ease are thought to justify all. This is well understood by North American church members, whose generosity in funding projects or machines that contribute to logistical "efficiency" is well known.

made it clear that medium and message cannot be separated in matters of faith, answers to such questions will have a direct bearing on Western missionary understanding of themselves and their modus operandi. The following chapters attempt to explore some of the direct and ancillary effects of affluence upon both Western missionaries and their culturally packaged modeling of the Good News.

Western missionaries constitute part of a rich elite whose numbers, relative to the burgeoning populations of poor around the world, constitute a steadily diminishing proportion of the world's total. Furthermore, the economic gulf separating the rich from the poor is widening, despite sincere but essentially desultory efforts on the part of "developed" nations and "development" agencies to reverse the trend. Accordingly, the price that missionaries must pay as personal beneficiaries and exemplars of Western affluence has never been higher. In exchange for the comforts and securities of personal affluence, missionaries sacrifice apostolic effectiveness and credibility. More troubling still is the damage to personal integrity suffered by a rich missionary purporting to represent a Lord who for our sakes became poor.

Failure to recognize and somehow address wealth's insidiously corrosive effects upon its domestic and missionary life will ensure the continued ebb of the Western churches as a Kingdom force. Increasingly mesmerized by the deceitfulness of its own riches and by the cares of its gated, materially secure world, the fruitlessness of the richest church in the world will continue apace, however impressively frenetic or technologically proficient its home and foreign missions (Mark 4:18). Like their first-century Laodicean counterpart, whose spiritual penury seems to have been apparent to everyone but herself, affluent Western churches will become bywords for spiritual sterility (Rev. 3:14–21). As our Christian Scriptures and subsequent history attest, repentance among the secure and the comfortable is exceedingly rare. But it is possible.

The negative dynamics of economic disparity in four overlapping spheres of missionary life and work — relational, communicatory, strategic, and theological — are explored in the following chapters. The relative affluence of missionaries whose ostensible mandate it is to lead the poor of this world in the way of the cross influences each of these spheres in profound if not always immediately obvious ways.

4

Relational Costs
of Missionary Affluence

I have told my missionary friends, "Noble as you are, you have isolated yourselves from the people you want to serve." — GANDHI

The whole biblical teaching is rooted in relationship. Money has ultimate meaning only if it enhances human relationship. — KOSUKE KOYAMA

Unlike so many, we do not peddle the word of God for profit. — ST. PAUL

The social relationships[1] so integral to missionary life and work are most directly and critically affected by the dynamics of interpersonal material and economic inequity. That one's self-identity is to a large degree determined by the people among whom one lives is a truism. A missionary's status — both self-perceived and as perceived by others — is significantly influenced by his or her economic standing within a specific community. Roles — the behavior complexes that are deemed appropriate to a given status — are similarly affected by the relative affluence of the Western missionary.

Western missionary affluence tends to affect interpersonal relationships in at least six ways that are antithetical to the modus operandi modeled and enjoined on his followers by Christ.

Affluence and Missionary Insulation

It is possible to argue that the primary advantage of wealth lies in its capacity to provide goods and services that cushion the wealthy from the harsh vicissitudes of poverty. The survival instinct common to all creatures is, in the case of human beings, supplemented by the desire to proceed from birth to death as comfortably as possible. Compared to the poor, the rich enjoy astounding comfort on their journey through life, while at the same time being able to seemingly postpone or at lease ameliorate the unpleasant end of their journey.

---

1. "Relational" in the chapter title is used in a strictly nontechnical, inclusive sense to refer to both social and psychological aspects of missionary cross-cultural relationships.

The verb "insulate" is thought to have derived from the Late Latin *insulatus* — to make into an island. The word today generally means "to prevent or reduce the transmission of electricity, heat, or sound to or from (a body, device, or region) by surrounding with a nonconducting material."[2] Both the etymology and the definition are instructive in the context of the present discussion, since Western missionaries often inhabit islands in seas of poverty. Their affluence quite literally constitutes the "nonconducting material" that shields them from the "heat" and "sound" of that poverty which is the everyday experience of the people whom they serve.

That insularity to which the privileged assume entitlement manifests itself in virtually every facet of a Western missionary's life. Comfortable, well-furnished residences; closets with several changes of clothing; cupboards stocked with a great variety of nutritious foods; medicine cabinets brimming with efficacious prophylactics and drugs; medical plans to deal with a child's crooked teeth or a parent's failing kidney; insurance policies providing for the well-being of loved ones in the event of an untimely emergency; retirement savings plans which, by taking careful thought of the morrow, are calculated to assist the aged missionary through the final transition between this life and the next; the costly mobility — by means of personal motor vehicles — to which every Westerner feels entitled; resources sufficient for expensive local and international flights to whisk one's own away from danger or to take oneself on a much-needed furlough; for children, educational opportunities unmatched anywhere in the world; fun-filled, exotic vacations for the family; an abundance of ingenious technological aids, each promising and sometimes delivering efficiency in fulfilling personal and professional objectives; such derivatives of personal affluence constitute the "nonconducting material" of which missionary insulation from the "heat" and "sound" of poverty is fashioned.

Such things cannot be hidden from missionary neighbors or national colleagues. In a scathing indictment of American missionaries in Spain, Juan Antonio Monroy cynically observed that "many missionaries arrive in Spain and other countries with the sole intention of taking a vacation in a foreign country." Accordingly, they almost invariably choose to establish themselves in modern cities with comfortable, sunny climates. Worse, they then proceed to "live in a society limited to themselves, and . . . close themselves off in apartment blocks or . . . chalets surrounded by small gardens . . . in order to be alone. They don't seek contact with the people, they are not open to friendship."[3] Such generalized perceptions are probably not entirely fair, but they are the candid observations of a "native" trying to make sense of affluent Western missionary behavior.

---

2. *Collins English Dictionary of the English Language* (London & Glasgow: William Collins Sons, 1979).

3. Juan Antonio Monroy, "Why Do Protestant Missionaries Fail in Spain?" *Milligan Missiogram* 6, no. 3 (Spring 1979): 5, 8. See also the pamphlet by Mavumilusa Makanzu, "The Twentieth-Century Missionaries and the Murmurs of the Africans," *Apophoreta of African Church History* 3 (Aberdeen: Department of Religious Studies, University of Aberdeen, in association with the Scottish Institute of Missionary Studies, 1974).

Affluence and Missionary Isolation

Independence is the state of being free from the control of another. *Segregation* is the practice of creating separate facilities within the same society for the use of minority groups. *Isolation* is a lack of contact, genuine communication, or interaction between persons or groups within a society.

Perhaps nowhere is personal independence — as distinct from interpersonal interdependence — more highly valued than in North America. When he visited the United States almost two centuries ago, Alexis de Tocqueville repeatedly remarked on this quality.[4] Admitting admiration for the "manly independence" of Americans, he noted an ominous side to American pride in self-reliance: profound isolation from the larger human community.[5]

More recent observers support de Tocqueville. The universally human desire for community and interdependence are, according to one sociologist, frustrated in American society by an almost obsessive preoccupation with personal independence, nurtured through education and celebrated in national mythologies. American circumvention of that interdependence upon which all human societies are based is evident in the high regard for personal privacy. In the words of Philip Slater, author of *The Pursuit of Loneliness:*

> We seek a private house, a private means of transportation, a private garden, a private laundry, self-service stores, and do-it-yourself skills of every kind. An enormous technology seems to have set itself the task of making it unnecessary for one human being ever to ask anything of another in the course of going about his daily business. Even within the family Americans are unique in their feeling that each member should have a separate room, and even a separate telephone, television, and car, when economically possible. We seek more and more privacy, and feel more and more alienated and lonely when we get it. What accidental contacts we do have, furthermore, seem more intrusive, not only because they are unsought but because they are unconnected with any familiar pattern of interdependence.[6]

---

4. De Tocqueville was a French nobleman who is today best known for his book *Democracy in America,* containing descriptions and observations made in the course of less than one year of travel in the United States in 1831–32. The book has remained in print ever since, and continues to be cited as an accurate and still useful commentary on the American way of life. Alexis de Tocqueville, *Democracy in America,* 2 vols. (New York: Alfred A. Knopf, 1956 [1835]). De Tocqueville came to America in 1831 and later wrote his famous two-volume study of the American people and their political institutions. Volume 1 appeared in 1835; volume 2 in 1840. *www.tocqueville.org/chap1.htm.* Since that time, countless others have commented on the American love of independence. See, for example, Jules Henry, *Culture Against Man* (New York: Random House, 1963), and Philip Slater, *The Pursuit of Loneliness: American Culture at the Breaking Point* (Boston: Beacon Press, 1970).

5. De Tocqueville, *Democracy in America,* 2:786.

6. Slater, *The Pursuit of Loneliness,* 7. See also Robert D. Putnam, *Bowling Alone: The Collapse and Revival of American Community* (New York: Simon & Schuster, 2000). Putnam, a professor of sociology at Harvard, traces the deterioration of the organized ways in which people relate to one another and partake in civil life in the United States. While 62.8 percent of Americans of voting age participated in the presidential election of 1960, for example, by 1996, the percentage had slipped to

This fierce love of personal independence is not left behind when American missionaries travel abroad. But if independence is expensive in North America, it is much more costly to maintain in other parts of the world.[7] Only the person of considerable means can hope to afford it. Conversely, the person wishing to live an American life in a faraway country must have access to wealth.

Independence is even more costly in nonmonetary terms, however. Not surprisingly, Western missionary communities have usually been marked by a de facto racial segregation, since membership is based upon an economic criterion that can generally only be met by Christians from the lands of old Christendom. This is not to say that all contact with impoverished non-Westerners is avoided. On the contrary, it is often the plight of such poor that will figure most prominently in the vocation and the location of a Western missionary. But particularly in places where there are large concentrations of missionaries among even larger numbers of poor, such contacts have tended to accentuate the missionaries' resolute independence *of* and segregation *from* the poor. This is *isolation.* The specter of a supremely relational gospel being proclaimed by an isolated community of segregated missionaries is at once ironic and tragic.

Details of a report by two of my students who visited one of the largest mission stations in Kenya several years ago sadly confirm that this isolating tendency is no mere vestige of the past. They noticed that Western missionaries on the station were virtually isolated from their closest African neighbors. Africans venturing onto the station were inevitably menials or merchants, tending gardens, doing wash, delivering loads of wood. It was a world apart — a world of privileged, indulged missionary children enjoying the best education that money can buy in that country; a world of industrious, supremely secure white missionaries, spending their lives in worthwhile medical, educational, and developmental programs on behalf of poor Africans; a world of Western families, each with its glowing future; a world viewed by its closest neighbors with no little bitterness, envy, resentment, and sometimes naked hostility.[8] Since biblical faith is above all a relational faith, it is not only sad, but tragically wide of the mark (sinful), when personal possessions and privileges prevent, distort, or destroy missionary relationships with the poor. But this is an almost inevitable price of personal affluence.

48.9 percent. The stable norms of community life have shifted, with 20 percent of Americans moving once a year, and 40 percent moving every five years. The result, according to Putnam, is a society of increasingly isolated, less empathetic individuals. American missionary recruits inevitably mirror, to some degree, the deep currents of their society.

7. This is why the U.S. Department of State issues detailed quarterly tables, "Compensation of American Government Employees in Foreign Countries," taking into account relative costs of living, hardship differentials, and danger (*www.state.gov/m/a/als/qtrpt/*). A number of U.S.-based mission agencies use the data from these tables as a basis for calculating missionary compensation.

8. The observations of youthful visitors are often superficial, it is true. But sadly, in this instance, the report of my students was subsequently corroborated by two Kenyan academic and church leaders whose judgment cannot be so lightly dismissed: the one, an active churchman and departmental chairman in one of Kenya's two major universities; the other, a mission-educated official in the Kenyan Department of Education.

Affluence and Social Gulf

The social gulf described above makes both fraternity and friendship virtually impossible, a phenomenon well documented by Robert Coles in his study of the children of affluent Americans. Responding to the troubled inquiry of her nine-year-old daughter, a wealthy mother's six-word explanation encapsulates everything the rich have ever been able to say about their relationships with the poor: "they are they and we are we."[9]

Perceptive observers of Western missionary social behavior have often noted and commented on the challenge of establishing close friendships with the poor. A friend is an intimate, someone with whom one generally has much in common. In our friendships, we naturally gravitate to those with whom we are not only temperamentally but socially and economically compatible. It is humanly almost impossible for a wealthy family to share a deeply fraternal relationship with a family whose material and economic resources are a pathetic fraction of their own. How does one relate to someone who cannot afford an education for their beloved children beyond minimal literacy, while one's own children take for granted both opportunity and money for education up to the very highest levels? How does one fraternize with a family whose house is a tiny one-room straw or cardboard shack, with no amenities, from the comfort and convenience of a Western-style bungalow, complete with kitchen, bathroom, private bedrooms for each member of the family, carpeted floors, stuffed furniture, closets and bureaus filled with clothes, and personal servants tending to every need? What can a wealthy family — with access to frequently updated motorcycles, cars, jeeps, power-boats, or airplanes — have in common with those who must rely solely upon leg power to get anywhere? What sort of fraternizing can occur between a wealthy vacationing family — enjoying a month of leisurely traveling, sightseeing, swimming, and sunbathing — and their poor counterpart for whom the concept of vacation doesn't even exist?

Between families of widely disparate means and standards of living, friendship is extremely unlikely. With whom does a missionary naturally choose to spend leisure time? With whom is a missionary comfortable enough to share a vacation? Who is likely to listen comprehendingly and sympathetically to a missionary couple in anguish over the peculiar frustrations, burdens, and perplexities of missionary parenting? With whom is a Western missionary likely to go shopping for family birthday or Christmas gifts? Who will be able to commiserate with a missionary on the inadequacy of his or her support level? From whom will a missionary likely seek advice on personal financial matters — investment, banking, or pension? That the poor would or could play any part in these aspects of a missionary's life is extremely doubtful, since the requisite social rapport will be found only among one's social and economic peers. The presence of the poor in such situations would be an embarrassment to any missionary of even moderate sensitivity.

---

9. Robert Coles, *Privileged Ones: The Well-Off and the Rich in America,* vol. 5 of *Children in Crisis* (Boston: Little, Brown, and Company, 1977), 77.

If gross economic disparity poses a virtually insurmountable obstacle to fraternal social reciprocity, it should not be surprising that many Western missionaries
associate with the poor primarily in the context of their official duties. Attempts
by the poor to participate in the social life of missionaries is a recipe for mutual
embarrassment. As long as there is an economic chasm between missionaries
and their converts, social fraternity will be hampered. With economic conditions
within the global community of faith more asymmetrical now than they have ever
been, Bishop Azariah's appeal to the delegates of the 1910 Edinburgh Conference
is more pertinent now than it was a century ago: "Missionaries," he lamented,
"except for a few of the very best, seem to me to fail very largely in getting rid
of an air of patronage and condescension, and in establishing a genuinely brotherly and happy relation as between equals with their Indian flocks.... You have
given your goods to feed the poor. You have given your bodies to be burned. We
also ask for *love*. GIVE US FRIENDS."[10] Western missionary inability to divest
themselves of wealth makes inconceivable any abrogation of what Robert Coles
refers to as "that apartness that goes with wealth."[11]

Economic Disparity and the Illusion of Superiority

As John Kenneth Galbraith wryly observed in a prescient article predicting the
crash of the stock market in 1929, "Nothing so gives the illusion of intelligence
as personal association with large sums of money."[12] Even though the sense of
social superiority concomitant with wealth may at times be denied, the linguistic façade fools nobody. Virtually all known kinds of human power, influence,
and opportunity are directly proportionate to possession of property and wealth.
Conversely, social impotence and economic vulnerability are directly linked to
poverty and material scarcity.

While awareness of personal superiority is still sometimes expressed overtly,
normally the indications are more subtle. It was not always so. One hundred years
ago, Western ascendance was celebrated openly without fear of the censure. The
advice offered by Francis Galton to European would-be explorers and travelers
provides apt illustration of this point. There were occasions, he noted, when a
traveler in Africa must "take the law into his own hands." An African ruler at
his best must be understood as "a savage despot." Accordingly,

> The simple rule, the good old plan, —
> That they should take who have the power,
> And they should keep, who can.

Galton's advice on how best a Western traveler might handle lawless Africans
was harsh, with floggings and penalties based on "the principle of double or treble
restitution." Europeans were urged by Galton to look upon mischievous savages

---

10. *World Missionary Conference, 1910. To Consider Missionary Problems in Relation to the
Non-Christian World* (Edinburgh: Oliphant, Anderson & Ferrier, 1910), 9:309.

11. Coles, *Privileged Ones*, 14.

12. See "The 1929 Parallel," *The Atlantic Monthly* 259, no. 1 (January 1987): 62.

"as you would a kicking mule or a wild animal, whose nature it is to be unruly and vicious, and keep your temper quite unruffled."[13]

While missionaries only occasionally followed his advice literally,[14] consciousness of their own superiority was seldom far beneath the surface. Awareness of the social gulf between themselves and Africans was the basis of the unflattering, ironically humorous accounts of African ways which sprinkled the writings of Western travelers. Henry Drummond, a popular and influential figure in the Student Christian Movement between 1884 and 1894 and a staunch advocate of Christian mission, conducted "a scientific examination" in central southern Africa. The English edition of his published report proved to be immensely popular, selling over thirty-five thousand copies by 1899. "It is a wonderful thing to look at this weird world of human beings — half animal and half children, wholly savage and wholly heathen," he recorded early on his journey. His opinion of African regal attire — evident in his description of a chief — was bitingly burlesque:

> ...in books of travel great chiefs are usually called kings, their wives queens, while their mud-huts are always palaces. But after seeing my first African chief at home, I found I must either change my views of kings or of authors. The regal splendour of Chipitula's court — and Chipitula was a very great chief indeed, and owned all the Shire district — may be judged by the fact that when I paid my respects to his highness his court-dress consisted almost exclusively of a pair of suspenders. I made this king happy for life by the gift of a scarlet tennis cap and a few buttons.[15]

Modern missionaries would never be so brash. But they too, surrounded as they are on every hand with evidence of their economic and social ascendancy, must often fight a losing battle against "secret" feelings of superiority over those who can hardly subsist. Forty years ago this attitude was commonly apparent in what might be referred to as the "Sahib complex" — a condition brought about by the deference that white foreigners were frequently accorded by "the natives." The phenomenon, by no means exclusive to missionaries, is amusingly described by Malcolm Muggeridge as he reminiscences on his Indian teaching experience:

---

13. Francis Galton, *The Art of Travel; or, Shifts and Contrivances Available in Wild Countries* (London: John Murray, 1855), 60–61.

14. Stuart Watt, a Church Missionary Society (CMS) missionary to East Africa in the late nineteenth century, tied up and flogged several porters caught stealing. One of the porters subsequently died. A. M. Mackay, another much-admired Church Missionary Society missionary, shot and wounded several mutinous porters. See Thomas O. Beidelman, "Contradictions between the Sacred and the Secular Life: The Church Missionary Society in Ukaguru, Tanzania, East Africa, 1876–1914," in *Comparative Studies in Society and History: An International Quarterly* 23 no. 1 (January 1981): 80–82. London Missionary Society missionaries in Central Africa during the same period practiced corporal punishment, as I relate in Jonathan Bonk, *The Theory and Practice of Missionary Identification, 1860–1920* (Lewiston, NY: Edwin Mellen Press, 1989), 110–15. Such actions were never sanctioned officially, and drew sharp reprimands from mission administrators.

15. See my article, " 'All Things to All Persons?' — The Missionary as a Racist-Imperialist, 1860–1918," in *Missiology: An International Review* 8, no. 3 (July 1980): 292–93. Henry Drummond, *Tropical Africa,* 3rd ed. (London: Hodder & Stoughton, 1889).

From the moment of landing in Colombo, I was made conscious of my status as a Sahib. It was like suddenly inheriting a peerage and being addressed as My Lord. Just by virtue of being English and white, if you went to buy a ticket at a railway station, people made way for you. Similarly, in a shop. It was very insidious. At first I found it embarrassing and distasteful; then, though I continued to ridicule it, I came to count upon receiving special treatment. Finally, when for some reason it was not accorded, there was an impulse to become sulky and irritated. From that it is but a small step to shouting and insisting, as in the days of the Raj, I saw happen often enough. Our position in India as a ruling race corrupted all concerned; soldiers . . . missionaries, government officials, planters, businessmen, wives and children; everyone. It also corrupted the Indians.[16]

Few Western missionaries working among the poor cannot immediately identify with what Muggeridge describes. Nor are modern missionaries any less susceptible to the corrupting seeds of undeserved deference — the sense of personal entitlement whereby the rich congratulate themselves on their own good fortune and blame the poor for their poverty.[17] This defensive mechanism enables even the most devout among the rich to insist on more than they need, even when surrounded by destitute people who have less than they need — a condition referred to in the Christian Scriptures as "greed, which is idolatry" (Col 3:5).

Contemporary missionaries may find it difficult to identify with the unselfconsciously assumed sense of personal entitlement and intelligence that associate with social and economic superiority. Nevertheless, their obvious affluence and their preference for the company of those who, like themselves, are affluent, incline most to think of themselves as teachers and exemplars, rather than servants, of the poor. It is hard to assume the role of a servant when one is rich and powerful, while those whom one ostensibly serves are mired in poverty and powerlessness. In such situations, the word "service" is usually adapted to mean whatever the powerful condescends to do for the less powerful.

Affluence and Relational Mistrust

Western missionaries are frequently suspected of doing well by doing good. Indeed, it has been observed that when they are no longer doing well — for example, when pressed financially or socially — they cease from doing missionary good and return home where they can do better!

---

16. Malcolm Muggeridge, *Chronicles of Wasted Time. Part I. The Green Stick* (London: Collins, 1972), 100.

17. The "entitlement" mentality is well captured by Fyodor Dostoyevsky's description of Kalganov and his rich friends as they visit a monastery: "It was strange that their arrival did not seem expected, and that they were not received with special honour, though one of them had recently made a donation of a thousand roubles, while another was a very wealthy and highly cultured landowner, upon whom all in the monastery were in a sense dependent. . . . Yet no official personage met them" (from chap. 1 of Book 2, Part 1, of *The Brothers Karamazov*, trans. Constance Garnett [New York: Random House, 1950]).

Of course, human motivation is a complex, sometimes darkly inscrutable phenomenon. That this should be so comes as no surprise to observers of the human predicament, or to those who take the Christian Scriptures seriously: "The heart is deceitful above all things, and desperately wicked, who can know it?" The human capacity to assess the motives of one's fellows is remarkably truncated when turned inward. If missionaries have been reticent to speak of material inducements to their calling, others have been more than willing to do so.

In his superb study of the early British missionaries to India, Stuart Piggin demonstrates that among the many noble considerations involved in a candidate's deciding for or against a missionary vocation were at times included personal quests for economic security, respectability, and honor — each of which was to some degree assured those formally associated with a mission society.[18] While missionaries themselves have naturally stressed the self-giving altruism of their service, outsiders have often regarded the relative affluence, security, and social status enjoyed by missionaries to be a sure sign of darker, essentially self-serving motives. As one typically caustic commentator on Protestant missionary life in China in 1885 observed:

> The missionary business in China is by no means a bad business to run by that class of clergy who occupy that debatable land which is one grade below gentlemanship, and from which the majority of [them]...are recruited. Poverty stricken and without prospects at home, out here they are provided...with an assured and liberal income...[which] is supplemented by liberal contributions from the resident English merchants....The missionary now lives in a condition of affluence which would be unknown to him elsewhere, a luxurious home with luxurious appliances and table, coolies to carry him about, and an ample margin of dollars....In the course of a few years the missionary becomes tired of his work...and hies him back to England....There...he can scarcely fail to gain repute — especially among silly women little apt in weighing evidence — as a noble champion of Christianity, whereby he assumes a social status to which his birth and breeding have by no means entitled him.[19]

However overdrawn Knollys's caricature of missionaries might have been, that missionaries often enjoyed considerable material and social advantages, and that these privileges gave rise to suspicion of their motives cannot be denied.

Missionary lore abounds with examples. In South India, Western missionaries for several years answered to the Indian designation "Dora," taking the term to be simply the linguistic equivalent of "missionary." Investigation soon showed, however, that the word actually meant "rich landlord," a status granted to mis-

---

18. Stuart Piggin, *Making Evangelical Missionaries 1798–1858: The Social Background, Motives and Training of British Protestant Missionaries to India* (London: Sutton Courtenay Press, 1984), especially 124–55.

19. Henry Knollys, *English Life in China* (London: Smith, Elder & Company, 1885). See also the writings of a longtime resident in China, Alexander Michie, especially his *Missionaries in China* (London: Edward Stanford, 1891).

sionaries since, like rich landlords, they were observed to buy land; build walled compounds, houses, schools, temples, and roads for their cars; and keep several wives.[20]

In Central Africa, missionaries reported similar confusion in native minds as to their *real* reasons for being there. Missionaries soon discovered that their presence, while creating little hunger and thirst for righteousness, whetted native appetites for the material benefits enjoyed by the white man. One missionary, haven spoken daily to the people of the "better way," wearily confessed to being confounded by their utter indifference to what he said, and their rapt preoccupation with what he had. He concluded indignantly: "... their only object is just to get what they can out of us."[21] His colleague had earlier been frustrated by the local chief's inability to understand the careful elucidation of his "sole object" in coming to Africa, for his exposition elicited from the chief nothing more than a request for "five or six cloths of different kinds." Concluded the missionary: "It is very difficult to make them understand the nature of our work."[22] The subsequent erosion of goodwill with which their arrival among Central Africans had first been greeted was traced by missionaries themselves to the fact that native expectations of improved material welfare had not been realized, and were apparently unwarranted.[23]

As the foregoing incidents intimate, native misunderstanding and mistrust of missionary motives were, in due course, heartily reciprocated. Missionaries appear to have been unaware of the curious double standard by which they judged themselves and native peoples. Rationalizing the necessity of high material and social standards for themselves, they were deeply suspicious of Africans or Asians who tried to follow their example, labeling them as selfish and worldly minded. Missionaries — earning salaries more than fifty times those of their African colleagues, and enjoying a level of affluence unattainable by most of their converts — expressed disappointment with "worldly minded" native teachers whose "one idea," in the words of one missionary, "seems to be a good education [so]... they can get more money."[24]

In China, likewise, missionaries whose economic and material resources were immense by local standards, and who commanded salaries from thirty to fifty times greater than those of their Christian Chinese counterparts, nevertheless portrayed the Chinese as "... a money-loving people ... [whose] principal divinity is the god of riches, and [whose] one aim is the acquisition of pelf."[25] Such

---

20. Related by Paul Hiebert in his lectures at Overseas Ministries Study Center, October 26–30, 1987. Missionary polygyny was deduced from the presence of single lady missionaries who, if and when a wife died, would take her place as wife of the widower.

21. Shaw to Thompson, March 9, 1885, Urambo, as cited by Bonk, *The Theory and Practice of Missionary Identification*, 61.

22. Jones to Whitehouse, June 24, 1884, Uguha, as cited by Bonk, ibid. Missionary correspondence of this period is checkered with similar complaints.

23. Nutt to Thompson, July 25, 1895, Kambole, as cited by Bonk, ibid., 87.

24. Draper to Thompson, March 26, 1902, Kawimbe, as cited by Bonk, ibid., 88.

25. Griffith John, "North China-Hankow," *The Chronicle of the London Missionary Society* (July 1891): 166.

mutual misunderstanding and mistrust colored social relationships between missionaries and nationals, making genuine friendship at best as difficult as it was unlikely.

One hundred years later, while the economic gulf separating Western missionaries and Third World populations is even wider, the social dynamics of suspicion and mistrust remain the same. To argue otherwise is both foolish and futile. Now, as then, few missionaries would admit that membership in the fraternity of missionaries represented a social step up.[26] In a letter to missionary Murray Rogers, Japanese theologian Kosuke Koyama (after eight years as an Asian missionary in Thailand) confided that speculation on the salaries of American missionaries was "a great pastime," but that all such discussions came to a grinding halt the moment an American missionary appeared. There existed an intuitive understanding that such information was highly classified, and might constitute an acute embarrassment to all parties.[27] It is clear that such a discussion could cause a Western missionary confusion only in the context of inordinate disparity between his income and that of his non-Western colleagues. Such secrecy is the culture in which mistrust, misunderstanding, and suspicion have always bred and proliferated.

As in the nineteenth century, so in the twentieth and twenty-first: the instinctive defensiveness that Western missionaries feel about their privileged status continues to be hidden behind the thin camouflage of concern about native selfishness or worldly mindedness. While this is particularly the case between Western missionaries and indigenous evangelists, it is also a problem in relationships between Western missionaries of widely disparate means themselves. One does not need to travel far or long to realize that there exists on many "mission fields" an economic hierarchy, with American missionaries — often Southern Baptists — on the top; and British missionaries — especially those serving in the more austerely evangelical agencies in the radical tradition of C. T. Studd — deeply suspicious of pleasure. Even within those agencies where care has not been taken to ensure strict economic communism, subtly invidious comparisons are frequently made between the dubious dedication of the missionary whose "ministry" account is running over and that of the involuntary ascetic whose "ministry" account is usually dry.

With the "emergence" of "Third World" missionaries, increasing numbers of whom are either finding placement with Western agencies, or who are working in close cooperation with those agencies, the problems attendant upon inequity within the missionary community are even more complicated. Koyama speaks of

---

26. In my experience, the sort of admission contained in a letter sent to me by a twenty-year veteran missionary from the United States to the Philippines is quite rare. Said he: "Betty and I both come from home backgrounds in Canada and the States respectively where we had sufficient to live on, but were far from the affluence seen even in those days in North America. We then joined [the faith mission] and actually felt we had moved up a step financially (even though [our mission] as you know is far from one of the affluent Missions).... Over the years, we have seen [our mission], including ourselves, move up the economic ladder." See letter of Harrison to Bonk, November 17, 1987, Singapore.

27. *Missionary Service in Asia Today.* A Report on a Consultation Held by the Asia Methodist Advisory Committee, February 18–23, 1971, in cooperation with the Life, Message, Unity Committee of the East Asian Christian Conference (Kuala Lumpur: University of Malaysia, 1971), 132.

the economic division of the missionary community in Thailand into "first class" (Western) and "second class" (Asian) missionaries:

> The gap between us was immense in all areas of life. We tried not to compare ourselves with the 'first class,' and we tried our best, but how could we avoid this comparison? We were living right among them day after day! Once my family was virtually broke...for one week. I finally went to seek 'help' (of 'first-aid-kit' kind) at the office of the 'first class.' I was given a sermon — a good sermon — there. As I came out of that office, feeling like a third class passenger sneaking out of a first class cabin, I met a fellow Western missionary with whom I had studied at the same seminary in the United States, as he drove up in his Volkswagen loaded with items of shopping. He had only been in Thailand a few weeks. Our most 'irritating' problem was our most esteemed Western missionaries![28]

Is the suspicion that Western missionaries do good only to do well warranted? Perhaps the answer to that question will not be known until, or unless, the "all these things" package of support and benefits are for some reason no longer available to would-be apostles from the West, and they have to follow their Lord on the same terms as their poorer brothers and sisters around the world. In such circumstances, how many missionaries will go into all the world from North America? No one knows the answer to such questions as this. What is known is that the social distance that comes with economic disparity constitutes an environment in which mistrust and suspicion thrive, and that this is a part of the relational cost that must be paid by missionaries who cling to their material prerogatives as rich Westerners in a poor world. But there is more besides.

Affluence, Envy, and Hostility

With affluence comes social advantage; with social advantage comes personal security and power — power over those with less, power over one's own destiny, the power of choice.

A frequent side effect of economic and social disparity in close proximity is envy — one of that sinister cluster of sins labeled "deadly" by medieval theologians. Although practice has lagged far behind, mission theory has long advocated the establishment of close personal relationships with the people being proselytized. Ironically, therefore, the closer the social ties between missionaries and their Third World protégés, the greater the likelihood of envy.

Envy is the feeling that besets us when we observe the prosperity or good fortune of those near us. As Galbraith notes, "Envy almost certainly operates efficiently only as regards near neighbors. It is not directed toward the distant rich."[29] Should gross inequity develop within the context of a family, envy is virtually unavoidable. It is hard to rejoice with those who rejoice, particularly if

---

28. *Missionary Service in Asia Today*, 136.
29. Galbraith, *The Affluent Society*, 69.

one is sorrowing. It is painful to see the privileges, advantages, and opportunities that our near neighbors, or brothers and sisters, shower upon their children while ours must experience hunger, privation, and lack of opportunity for betterment. To begrudge the personal and material assets of those who are nearby is a human universal, well documented in personal experience as well as in sociological literature.[30]

The Christian Scriptures, in addition to warning against the sin of envy, contain several examples of its operation. The Philistines, envying Isaac because of his great wealth, filled up all of his wells with dirt (Gen. 26:12–16); Saul, envious of David's military successes and popularity with the people, tried to kill him (1 Sam. 18–26); the plan of Darius to reward Daniel's outstanding abilities by making him his chief administrator so maddened his peers that they plotted to destroy him (Dan. 6).

There can be little doubt that the dynamics which produce envy are present wherever Western missionaries work. As psychologist Marjory Foyle pointed out in an article on missionary relationships, financial disparity within the mission community itself is a significant factor in the creation and perpetuation of bad interpersonal relationships.[31] The pointedly egalitarian financial policies governing a majority of Western mission agencies suggest that this is well understood by missionaries themselves. This being so, to deny that missionary affluence is a significant contributing factor in the tensions and misunderstanding that seem to bedevil relationships between missionaries and the churches they establish is to manifest a willful and dangerous myopia. A professor in one of the more prestigious Christian American graduate schools — a man who worked as a missionary in West Africa, and who now instructs future as well as active missionaries — told me that affluence had not been any problem for him, since his African neighbor owned a better color television than he did!

Not all have chosen to deal with the problem by denying that it exists, however. Koyama's years as an Asian missionary in Asia made apparent to him what Western missionaries have often been curiously reticent to openly address. "The security which some missionaries enjoy in Asia," he writes, "makes many envious, since it is comparable to the fully chaired university professor in the United States." He continues:

> "Threatened life" is the way of life almost universally lived in Thailand and vast areas of South East Asia. I soon began to grapple with the discrepancy between missionary-security and the destiny of the masses without knowing which direction I should take. To my knowledge, this topic has never been

---

30. See especially the brilliant study by Helmut Schoeck, *Envy: A Theory of Social Behaviour* (London: Secker & Warburg, 1969). Schoeck is professor of sociology at the Johannes Gutenberg University, Mainz. His book should be of special interest to missionary theologians, since his sociological model corresponds closely with the Christian doctrine of original sin. For an interesting and open expression of envy, see C. A. Doxiadis, "Three Letters to an American," in *Daedalus: Journal of the American Academy of Arts and Sciences* 101, no. 4 (Fall 1972): 163–83.

31. Marjory Foyle, "Missionary Relationships: Powderkeg or Powerhouse?" *Evangelical Missions Quarterly* 21, no. 4 (October 1985): 346.

taken up at one of those many [closed mission business] meetings as either a sociological or theological one.[32]

The subject continues to elude the agendas of missionary conferences and consultations, at least in evangelical circles.

Ironically, nonmissionary Westerners have no difficulty in discerning the envy and hostility that they elicit because of their affluence. Edward Hoagland, a writer who traveled by himself across the Sudan, relates his embarrassment at parties when, after the normal courtesies were dispelled by drunkenness, the Sudanese would "no longer mask the shock they felt at such a disparity of wealth."[33]

The Economist carried a story in 1985 of a rampage by Chinese soccer fans outside Beijing's Workers' Stadium in which a number of foreigners were attacked. The riot was seen as an expression of resentment against Westerners who have been entering China in increasing numbers since 1979, whose presence is "...a constant reminder to Chinese...of the luxuries not available to them." Only foreigners had access to special shops wherein may be acquired superior local produce as well as imported goods unavailable to ordinary Chinese. Impressive luxury hotels, "...where the occasional local Chinese can slip in to gawk but can never hope to be a paying guest," are likewise the forte of only foreigners. "I can't help looking at the foreigners enjoying nice places to eat," complained a Chinese schoolteacher. "I feel angry that it is our country, but the best is reserved for them."[34]

Brewster's Millions, a comic film released in 1985, is built around the truism that wealth brings isolation, not friendship. A recent visitor to Kenya was shocked to discover just how isolated the residents of a large mission station were. He was even more shocked by the hostility of those Kenyans who were the missionaries' closest neighbors. As the missionary jeep in which he was a passenger drove down the road away from the station, he waved to several children along the way. None of the children returned either his smiles or his friendly gestures: two shook their fists, while a third brandished his walking stick menacingly. He noticed that the farther he traveled from the station, the friendlier the people became.[35]

The sociology and psychology of economic disparity being what they are, the Western church must either grapple seriously with the problem of its affluence, or disappear as a Christian force in the world. Of course, it will continue to send forth committed ambassadors — personal incarnations of the gospel of abundance. But

32. *Missionary Service in Asia Today,* 133.

33. Edward Hoagland, *African Calliope: A Journey to the Sudan* (Harmondsworth: Penguin Books, 1978), 83.

34. Peking Correspondent, "Are You Friend or Foreigner?" *The Economist* 295, no. 7395 (May 25, 1985): 41. The rampage is an apt illustration of the negative, sometimes volatile, dynamics of economic inequity in close social proximity. The problem of gross inequity continues to loom large in China, with acute regional shortages of the basic necessities of life, and with the gulf between rich and poor widening at an alarming rate. See the United Nations Development Programme Press Release: *www.undp.org.cn/modules.php?op=modload&name=News&file=article&catid=14&topic=40&sid=235&mode=thread&order=0&thold=0.* See also George Packer, "When Here Sees There," *New York Times Magazine* (April 21, 2002).

35. Letter of Peters and Nelson to Bonk, November 1, 1987, Nairobi.

these emissaries will find themselves to be generators of envy and hostility, rather than proclaimers of that freedom which is freedom indeed.

The staggeringly high relational price that Western missionaries must pay for their affluence could perhaps be overlooked, or at least endured, were it not for its insidious effects upon the communication process. For medium and message are both significantly affected by the relationship of the missionary to the convert or would-be convert. If the message of the cross consisted simply of a series of theologically correct propositions about God, man, and salvation, then the obligation to preach the Gospel could be fulfilled by means of a series of public announcements over the radio. But the Word must always be made flesh, and dwell among men. And the Way has always best been shown by those who can be accompanied by would-be pilgrims. A missionary is above all a Way-shower, whose life must be imitable by one's converts. The missionary is not simply a voice box, but a pilgrim who invites others to join him or her on the narrow way.

5

Communicatory and Strategic Consequences of Missionary Affluence

You yourselves are our letter, written on our hearts, known and read by everybody. — St. Paul

To live is to communicate! Just as we cannot live without blood, we cannot live without communication. — Kosuke Koyama

Zeal does not ensure the propriety of the means which it employs. We need to recognize that zeal for God is not a guarantee that the means used to express the zeal is divinely inspired. — Roland Allen

When measured in the currency of interpersonal relationships, missionaries pay a high price for their relative affluence vis-à-vis a majority of fellow Christians in the rest of the world — especially when consideration is given to the biblical teaching of brotherly love to which they pay lip service. This was the argument of chapter 4.

Missionary rationale for maintaining and even increasing personal living standards usually includes allusion to communicatory and strategic benefits deriving solely from the availability of ample sums of money. As noted in chapter 3, any contrivance thought to increase missionary efficiency and longevity or that reduces the tedium of missionary tasks not only makes life easier, but is good stewardship. Computers, motor boats, airplanes, cars, jeeps, trucks, durable and comfortable clothing, well-equipped residences, schools for missionary children, and countless other amenities afforded by only the rich make missionary work more efficient, and therefore justifiable. Affluence is a merely one more means to a greater end. Commonly accepted rationalizing, evocative of the military analogy in which the missionary lives simply but utilizes expensive technical means, seldom takes into account the almost inevitable "collateral damage" suffered by the message itself.[1] To the relational costs associated with their economic ascendancy must be added a troubling diminishment of communicatory and strategic effectiveness.

---

1. See, for example, Doris Haley's article, "Ralph and Roberta Winter: A Wartime Lifestyle," *Family Life Today* (March 1983): 29–33.

Communicatory Costs of Missionary Affluence

To communicate is to convey thoughts, feelings, values, and ideas by means of speech, writing, gestures, and lifestyle. The essence of mission is communication — verbal and nonverbal. Like the apostle Paul, contemporary missionaries devote themselves to proclaiming the message of reconciliation. Knowing "what it is to fear the Lord, [they] try to persuade men" (2 Cor. 5:11–21). Whatever the particular strategy, at the very heart of their modus vivendi is telling, proclaiming, preaching, and convincing with the prospect of baptizing and discipling men and women "from every tribe and language and people and nation" (Rev. 5:9). It is ironic, therefore, that the expensive lifestyles and technological means utilized in carrying out this mandate frequently ensure that neither the missionary nor the missionary's good news is understood.

Receptor understanding of the message is powerfully affected by the relative affluence of the communicator. Medium and message, words and deeds, theory and practice, faith and works, cannot be separated in the life of a credible missionary. The quintessential message of the Cross is not composed of theologically correct propositions about God, man, sin, salvation, the church, and eternity. Authentic faith inevitably issues in genuine conversion. It is safe to surmise that the believing demons referred to in James 2:14–26 articulate an admirably correct theology — perhaps akin to that of the foolish builder of Jesus' story in Matthew 7:24–27 — but they make poor missionaries precisely because their lifestyle contradicts their belief. Saying, being, and doing — each is an integral part of the Gospel being communicated by the missionary.

Those who proclaim the good news must practice a faith that is both understandable and imitable. One of the greatest impediments to credible communication of the Gospel is the relative wealth of the evangelist or missionary, since the faith they model can be imitated only by those with correspondingly plentiful material resources.

The relative affluence of missionaries hampers and often distorts communication of the Gospel in several insidious ways. Missionaries have often been the first to observe — with dismay — the spontaneous generation of misunderstanding that their personal wealth engenders in the minds of the poor, both before and after conversion, but they have not been the only ones to comment on the phenomenon. For the past two centuries, missionary efforts have generally flowed from the rich to the poor, providing supporters and detractors alike with ample opportunity to observe the dynamics of economic disparity upon missionary communication of the Gospel. Several recurring themes in mission-related literature suggest a number of conclusions.[2]

1. *Wealthy missionaries cannot identify with the life situations of the poor that their message is intended to address.* Inability to relate more than a theoretical version of the good news to the actual circumstances of the people raises serious

---

2. A number of the issues dealt with in this chapter are more than simply communications problems. Even more fundamentally, they raise theological and ethical questions that any missionary who would avoid hypocrisy must address.

questions about the validity of the good news itself. No matter how plausibly sincere they might appear to be, salespersons who have never tested their own products under adverse conditions — and who are, furthermore, unwilling to do so personally — should be treated with deep skepticism. Similarly, Christianity — when proclaimed by the comfortably secure to the needy poor — is reduced to a series of personally untested and undemonstrated hypotheses. Affluent missionaries specialize in how to abound, but do not know how to be in want. Missionary faith, demonstrably vibrant and self-assured in the context of their own plenty, may in fact not work in the lives of those whose poverty and destitution is endemic. Missionaries model an inversion of the Incarnation depicted in Hebrews 4:15, effectively functioning as comfortable high priests who cannot sympathize with the vulnerabilities of the poor, because they have never personally battled the Furies of poverty. Attempts by idealistic missionaries to imagine themselves in the place of the poor evoke gratitude for material security, rather than efforts to become poor themselves, to see whether the grace of God is in fact as sufficient as they proclaim it to be.

If — as the Bible teaches and communications specialists have affirmed — medium and message are inseparable, it follows that it is not possible to have a contextually relevant Gospel if the missionary is out of context. Not only *what* is said, but *how* and *by whom* it is said are equally integral communicatory elements from the perspective of the person *to whom* a message is directed. To a political conservative, for example, the statement "Revolution is a good thing" can evoke either hearty agreement or vehement denial — depending upon whether it be attributed to Lenin or to Jefferson.[3] That missionaries "communicate to whole men, not simply to souls with ears, [and] . . . whole men communicate — not just souls with mouths. . . ."[4] is obvious. Contrary to the emphases typical of most missiology curriculums, not *communication theory*, but *communicator living*, is the key to incarnational communication.[5]

Commenting on the meager fruits of Western missionary endeavor in China one hundred years ago, Isaac Taylor concluded that unless missionaries were willing " . . . to live among the natives exactly as the natives live," their attempts to communicate the Christian faith would not succeed. "Would a Chinaman," he asked rhetorically, "with his pigtail, feeding on snails, birds' nests, and lizards, have any chance of converting English school boys to Buddhism?" Not likely. It was time, he said, for missionaries to "become brothers of the people . . . give up all European comforts and European society, and cast in their lot with the natives . . . striving to make converts, not by the help of *Paley's Evidences*, but by the great renunciation."[6] Missionaries — who quite rightly drew upon the canon's lack of missionary experience as justification for disdaining his advice —

---

3. See Roger William Brown, *Words and Things* (Glencoe, IL: Free Press, 1958), 321–22.

4. David J. Hesselgrave, *Communicating Christ Cross-Culturally: An Introduction to Missionary Communication* (Grand Rapids: Zondervan, 1978), 91.

5. This theme is more fully elaborated in the concluding chapter. Kosuke Koyama's discussion of the "crucified mind" in his *Waterbuffalo Theology* (Maryknoll, NY: Orbis Books, 1974, 209–24) should be required reading for every North American missiologist and missionary.

6. Canon Isaac Taylor, "The Great Missionary Failure," *The Fortnightly Review* 44 (July–December 1888): 496, 499.

inadvertently proved his point. One veteran, having endured overnight lodgings in a Chinese inn with several squealing pigs, suggested wryly that this might be the ideal place for Canon Taylor to test his theories of mission.[7]

The direct correlation between a missionary's effectiveness as a communicator and his or her level of identification is well known. In the missiological classic *Message and Mission*,[8] Eugene Nida observed that at the **lowest level of communication**, it is not necessary that the source of a message be closely identified with either the message itself or with the receptor of the message. A tourist who is told that his traveler's checks can be cashed in the bank just around the corner will soon know whether the information source is true or not. Nor does such communication require that the source of information be closely identified — psychologically, culturally, socially, economically — with the tourist. The identity and nature of the information source is irrelevant.

The **second level of communication** involves a message which, while making no permanent demands upon the receptor's worldview, has a potential impact on his or her immediate behavior. For example, the woman who urges her neighbor to get out of town to escape an impending flood is not likely to be taken seriously unless the neighbors also see her personally preparing to escape.

Communication at the third level concerns both the immediate behavior and the value system of the receptor. At this level, the source of the message must identify closely not only with his own message, but with the receptors of his message. As Nida explains:

> If . . . someone insists that a man should abandon his carefree way of life, settle down, marry, and raise a family; or if he tries to convince another that he should repent of his sins, become a Christian, and lead an entirely different type of life . . . [then] in addition to identification with his message, he must also demonstrate an identification with the receptors; for the receptor must be convinced that the source understands his, the receptor's, particular background and has respect for his views.[9]

Each successive level of communication requires an increasing degree of identification by the source of the message with the receptors, as illustrated by the diagram on the following page.

The degree to which the source of a credible message must identify with the message itself or with the receptors of that message depends upon the nature of the message being communicated.

Missionaries from the West have succeeded admirably in achieving the level of identification necessary for effective first-level communication, and they have been moderately successful in communicating at the second level. But only rarely

---

7. R. Wardlaw Thompson, *Griffith John: The Story of Fifty Years in China* (London: Religious Tract Society, 1906), 414.

8. See Eugene Nida, *Message and Mission* (New York: Harper & Row, 1960), 164–66 especially, for his discussion of the correlation between degrees of identification and levels of communication. The three communication levels outlined here are an adaptation of the four-level model outlined by Nida.

9. Ibid., 166.

Requisite level of Identification	Level of Communication →		
	1. Information	2. Persuasion	3. Conversion
Minimal identification necessary ————→	"This is an announcement"		
Source must identify closely with the message ————————→		"Let's get out of here! The dam has burst!"	
Sources must identify closely with message and with receptors ——————————————————→			"God understands you, cares for you, and loves you. "Repent! You must be born again!"

have Western missionaries achieved third-level communication with the poor. This failure is popularly attributed to cultural differences or spiritual blindness, rather than to the counterproductive dynamics deriving from the missionary's personal affluence.

The unintended introduction of Islam into Central Africa by LMS missionaries 130 years ago did cause one missionary to muse on a possible link between communicatory failure and affluence, however. Sparked by two utterly fruitless and frustrating years at his station in Uguha, David Picton Jones's letter to the LMS secretary in London is one such rare example:

> It is a remarkable fact that [our Muslim employees from Zanzibar] have far more influence over the natives than we have ever had — in many little things they imitate them, they follow their customs, adopt their ideas, imitate their dress, sing their songs, and...speak their...language. I can only account for this by the fact that [our Muslim employees] live amongst them, in a simple manner like themselves, intermarry with them, and to some extent partake of their notions. Our life, on the other hand...is far above them, and we are surrounded by things entirely beyond their reach. The consequence is, that they despair of trying to follow us, — indeed they *cannot* follow us, as there is here no trade in European goods, with the exception of cheap cloth, beads, etc. I have found by experience that they are exceedingly ready to imitate anything within their power, especially the young, and I feel sure in my own mind, if we were to bring ourselves nearer their own level — as near to it as our health and character as Christians would allow — we would gradually raise them up to a higher standard, and to a more civilised life. As it is they have nothing to lay hold of, they despair or ever becoming like us, they regard us as being of another (if not a higher) order, and they believe that our religion, however well adapted to us, is to them altogether unsuitable. When I talk to them...and tell them that [God] is good and merciful, that we always endeavour to do his will, and that we are his children, they will always answer coolly, pointing to the wonderful things in and about our house — *You* are his children *indeed*.[10]

10. A letter from Jones to Thompson, Uguha, December 2, 1884; see Jonathan J. Bonk, *The Theory and Practice of Missionary Identification*, 54–55. See also Daniel Johnson Fleming, *Living*

Jones dealt with the problem by firing his Muslim employees. He never again — at least in his correspondence — broached the uncomfortable subject of missionaries' affluence as an impediment to the Gospel. But his observations are pertinent in a day when the material gulf between Western missionaries and the world's poor is wider than ever before, and increasing. Wealthy missionaries' inability to identify with the life situations of those for whom their gospel is intended is rendering Western missionary communication of the good news increasingly ineffectual.

2. *There seems to be profound discrepancy between what wealthy missionaries preach and what they personally practice.* This is a second disturbing conclusion to be drawn from the Western missionary record. While theological and ethical dimensions of this issue are dealt with in a later chapter, the discrepancy between missionary teaching and practice is examined here for its impact on missionary communication.

Among the most obviously detrimental effects of an apostolic lifestyle built around wealth is that such a way of life can be imitated only by others with similar means. Not only *can* human beings imitate, they *must* imitate if they are to survive. Children become recognizable members of a culture because of their innate capacity to imitate the behaviors of status and role models within that culture. Similarly, young believers learn the ways of Christ by imitating mature Christians, such as missionaries.[11] In the context of his description of the role of an apostle, St. Paul urged Corinthian believers to "imitate me" (1 Cor. 4:16). Writing on behalf of Silas and Timothy, Paul congratulated the Thessalonians because, he said, in spite of severe suffering, "You became imitators of us and of the Lord...and so you became a model to all the believers in Macedonia and Achaia" (1 Thess. 1:6–7). In addition to questions that poor believers might legitimately raise concerning a Western missionary's disregard for scriptural teaching about the abundance of possessions, there is the fact that Western missionary communication must consist largely of admonitions to "do as we say, not as we do."

An open letter written to a high-ranking mission executive in 1971 accused Western missionaries of being tied...

> ...spiritually, economically, [and] socially, far more firmly to New York and Paris and London than they are to Delhi or Madras or to the Christian Church in [India]...the image of the Church with which people are most familiar is not so much a spiritual movement as a power structure, wealthy and influential, exclusive and sectarian, proudly self-assertive....

---

as Comrades: A Study of Factors Making for "Community" (New York: Published for the Foreign Missions Conference of North America by Agricultural Missions, Inc., 1950), 23–24.

11. The word *mimeomai* (imitate, follow) is found four times in the New Testament (2 Thess. 3:7, 9; Heb. 13:7; 3 John 11); *mimetes* (imitator) six times (1 Cor. 4:16; 11:1; Eph. 5:1; 1 Thess. 1:6; 2:14; Heb. 6:12); and *symmimetes* (fellow imitator) once (Phil. 3:17). In each instance, ethical imperatives associated with a specific kind of Christian conduct are involved. While Christian imitation must ultimately be of Christ, in the New Testament the words are usually applied to actual persons who are obvious living examples of Christ-like living. See W. Bauder's article in vol. 1 of *The New Dictionary of New Testament Theology,* ed. Colin Brown (Grand Rapids: Zondervan, 1975–78), 490–92.

Its offices...centres of social and political power, symbols of prestige and high-roads to Europe and the U.S.A. or privilege and preference in India.[12]

Despite such fine-sounding phrases as "self-reliance," "partnership," and "interdependence" liberally sprinkled throughout missionary writing and speeches, beneath the façade could be observed the silhouette of a less flattering reality. "This is how it still works out," the writer continued: "a Mission board is paying for a foreign missionary couple the rent for an apartment which is as much, or more, monthly than the wages of 20 Indians — and not the poorest at that — who have to support themselves, their wife, their children, from their pay.... So much for pious statements about living alongside, living as partners, etc.!"[13]

Although this description of a phenomenon which is borne of economic disparity was written more than thirty years ago, it as timely now as then. Nor should its application be confined to the older mission establishment, whose denominations are represented in the World Council of Churches. The negative dynamics of wealth and poverty in close proximity is as apparent in Interdenominational Foreign Missions Association [IFMA] member operations or in the Southern Baptist or Evangelical Foreign Missions Association [EFMA] denominations as it is of their more theologically liberal counterparts. One of the most challenging status adjustments that North American missionaries make when they serve abroad involves their metamorphosis. At the very moment when they are most acutely aware of their self-sacrifice, they discover that relative to their new social context, they have metamorphosed into staggeringly rich tycoons. At the end of his frenzied first year in Zaire, one young medical missionary told of his family's struggle with the irony of being considered rich. "By comparison," he wrote, "we seem like the Rockefellers to many Zairians.... We often feel...frustrated because we are seen often as rich 'objects' and some come to us regularly just for the 'things' they want to get from us."[14]

This young doctor's exasperation echoes the experience of thousands of Western missionaries. A full century earlier, not too far away on the same continent, a small contingent of young missionaries who came face to face with the same reality received this scant reassurance from their venerable home secretary:

Native tribes welcome missionaries amongst them, in the first instance because they hope to be enriched by the presence of these white men. When they find that they have got all that is to be obtained their sentiments change, and as they neither understand nor appreciate the real object of

---

12. A letter from C. Murray Rogers to Dr. Taylor-Jones, in *Missionary Service in Asia Today*, a Report on a Consultation Held by the Asia Methodist Advisory Committee, February 18–23, 1971, in cooperation with the Life, Message, Unity Committee of the East Asian Christian Conference (Kuala Lumpur: University of Malaysia, 1971), 126.

13. Ibid., 126–27.

14. Roy Larson, Kinshasa, Zaire, to Trinity Evangelical Free Church, Woodbridge, Connecticut, December 1987.

their presence in the country, they too often may turn around and become unreasonable and bitter opponents of their work.[15]

Western missionary claims of personal sacrifice and privation — however genuine in the context of their pecuniary potential in their own society — can only be greeted with incredulity by a great majority of the world's peoples, many of whom would be rich by local standards if they could but trade places with the missionary for a year, a week, or even a day. That missionary motives and intentions should be questioned in such circumstances is hardly surprising; that they should bridle with indignation at those among their poorer brethren who would imitate them is unfair. For not only is imitation the sincerest form of flattery; it is the quintessence of learning. To know what someone is really teaching, look at his students, rather than at his notes. They are his "letter... known and read by everybody" (2 Cor. 3:2).

3. *The gospel of plenty, persuasively proclaimed in the silent language of missionary lifestyle, frequently overrides or distorts poorer receptor understanding of the Christian Gospel.* This phenomenon is not restricted to the sphere of Western religious proselytizing. Since its inception, the United States has sensed a kind of providential manifest destiny to go into all the world and preach the good news of Jeffersonian "democracy." This mission, assiduously pursued for two hundred years, has been singularly unsuccessful — even at home, where the democratic ideals of the republic are scarcely able to disguise what most observers recognize as entrenched plutocracy. For the American good news embraced by people around the world has not been democracy, but consumption and plenitude, as exemplified by the ubiquitous American entertainment industry and by her citizens abroad — service personnel, diplomats, business people, educators, tourists, and missionaries.[16]

Proclaiming the Gospel of spiritual salvation with their lips, and the gospel of material abundance with their lives, Western missionaries have frequently expressed annoyance with the fact that their presence, while creating little hunger and thirst for righteousness, has stimulated within indigenes' hearty appetites for Western material culture. Converts to the missionary-modeled way of earning a comfortable living from one's religion came to be referred to as "rice Christians," long a source of Western missionary exasperation, as related in chapter 4.

In China, as in Central Africa, LMS missionaries, earning ten times as much as their highest paid Chinese colleagues, and enjoying numerous fringe benefits available only to Western missionaries, were typical of most missionaries.[17] Like their counterparts in Africa, they clearly perceived the materialist mote in Chinese

---

15. Thompson to Jones, July 17, 1885, as cited by Jonathan J. Bonk, *The Theory and Practice of Missionary Identification, 1860–1920,* Studies in the History of Missions, vol. 2 (Lewiston, NY: Edwin Mellen Press, 1989), 54–55.

16. David Potter, *People of Plenty: Economic Abundance and the American Character* (Chicago: University of Chicago Press, 1954), 128–41. See also Gail Kennedy, ed. *Democracy and the Gospel of Wealth* (Boston: D. C. Heath and Company, 1949).

17. Missionaries of the China Inland Mission, founded by the radical Hudson Taylor in 1865, were among the exceptions.

eyes, but failed to notice the beam in their own. The Chinese are "a money loving people," concluded a thirty-year veteran, "[whose] principal divinity is the god of riches, and [whose] one aim is the acquisition of pelf."[18]

Today, the same double standard prevails, on the one hand justifying the growing relative affluence of Western missionaries, and on the other lamenting expressions of similar, albeit more modest, aspirations on the part of poorer Christian brothers and sisters as evidence of worldliness. Profound misgivings about the motives and commitment of non-Westerners who use their training to get economically secure positions outside their countries continue to surface in missionary discourse. While such concerns may well be warranted, the comfortable and economically secure Western missionary is not in a very strong position to credibly raise them.[19]

Whether acknowledged or not, at the root of such concerns lies the affluence of the Western church and her missionaries. While it is true that many whose prospects were limited have bettered themselves economically and socially by taking advantage of opportunities arising out of close association with Western missionaries, it is no less obvious that missionaries themselves have done exceptionally well by most standards, and that missionary motivation is not purely spiritual. What if Western missionary support standards were to be reduced to the level of non-Western colleagues? Is it unduly presumptuous to assume that the missionary force from the West would at the very least shrivel, and perhaps even cease to exist in its present forms? Given widespread mission policies that prevent missionaries from venturing forth until their full support is assured, probably not.

Is it any wonder that Christians from poorer parts of the world — in response to the siren appeal of the gospel of plenty modeled by Western missionaries — respond to the implicit invitation by saying "Yes!" to materialism?[20] We should not be surprised at the discovery that Western missionaries are now credited with being one of the greatest secularizing agencies of the past two centuries.[21]

---

18. Griffith John, "North China-Hankow," in *The Chronicle of the London Missionary Society* 46 (July 1881): 166. See Bonk, *The Theory and Practice of Missionary Identification,* 248–53 for a brief examination of missionary perceptions of non-Western peoples.

19. David Maranz, in *African Friends and Money Matters: Observations from Africa* (Dallas: SIL International, 2001), argues that mutual money-related frustration of missionaries and Africans has to do with different approaches to its use and management. While this is true, it masks a deeper underlying problem of gross economic inequity in close social/ecclesiastical proximity.

20. George M. Foster, *Traditional Societies and Technological Change,* 2nd ed. (New York: Harper & Row, 1973). According to Foster, among the most potent universal stimulants to change are (1) the desire for economic gain, and (2) the desire for prestige. Western missionaries have often been frustrated by native conversions motivated not so much by religious appeal as by a sincere desire to improve economically and socially. Such converts, referred to in missionary literature as "rice Christians," frequently become disillusioned with Christianity's failure to deliver the benefits implicitly implied by the missionaries' lifestyles. "Rice missionaries" produce "rice converts"! The role played by missionary affluence in the generation of modern cargo cults deserves study. The fact that cargo cults are essentially concerned with material rewards suggests that there might be a positive link between them and Western missionary activities.

21. See Elmer S. Miller, "The Christian Missionary: Agent of Secularization," *Missiology: An International Review* 1, no. 1 (January 1973): 99–107. See also Arthur H. Cole, "The Relations of Missionary Activity to Economic Development," *Economic Development and Cultural Change* 9, no. 2 (January 1961): 120–27; and the chapter by Kenneth Scott Latourette, "Christian Missions as

Clearly, any missiological gains associated with affluence must be weighed against the harder-to-measure erosion of missionary effectiveness in communicating the Gospel. Clinging to the prerogatives of personal affluence makes identification with the poor impossible; it creates an irresolvable tension between missionary teaching and missionary living; and it causes the good news to be tainted by the pleasant but ultimately unsatisfying good news of mammon.

The subtle insidiousness of wealth's influence upon those who have it is aptly illustrated in Jacob Loewen's account of a worldview seminar that he conducted for some Indian teachers and their missionary colleagues some years ago. He explained to the group that each culture has at its center an "axle" from which radiate all of the "spokes" that hold the wheel together and help it to perform its appointed tasks smoothly and without undue difficulty. Wondering whether he was getting through to the teachers, he asked them to identify the hub around which their missionaries' way of life revolved. "Money!" was the unhesitating and unanimous response of the group. The missionaries were visibly taken aback.

Asked by the slightly incredulous Loewen how they could be so sure that money was the axle of the missionaries' worldview, the Indian teachers recounted incidents that in their eyes offered clear proof that money was at the core of all material and spiritual aspects of Western missionary life and work.

"What about your fathers and grandfathers before the missionary and the white man came?" Loewen continued to probe. "What was the axle of their way of life?" "War," came the immediate response. Spokesmen explained that their grandfathers had practiced killing because that was the way to get spirit-power. Spirit-power had been, in effect, the integrating hub of their grandfathers' way of life. Had their grandfathers been Christians, the teachers explained to Loewen, the Spirit of God would have been the center of their lives, "because He ... is the most powerful of all spirits."

"And now that all of you are Christians," Loewen persisted, "is the Spirit of God the axle of your Christian way of life, too?"

"No," came the response. "Our axle now is ... money ... because that is what we have learned from the missionaries."[22]

Loewen's story is reminiscent of an observation some two hundred years earlier made by Alexis de Tocqueville who, having traveled extensively through the United States, remarked: "I know of no country ... where the love of money has taken stronger hold on the affections of men."[23] The fifty-one-month journey through America of another famous observer, Frances Trollope, inclined her to concur with the observation of a longtime English resident of the country, who declared that "in following, in meeting, or in overtaking, in the street, on the road, or in the field, at the theatre, the coffee-house, or at home, he had never

---

Mediators of Western Civilization," 83–95 in *Christian Missions in China: Evangelists of What?* ed. Jessie G. Lutz (Boston: D. C. Heath and Company, 1965).

22. Jacob Loewen, *Culture and Human Values: Christian Intervention in Anthropological Perspective* (South Pasadena, CA: William Carey Library, 1975), xi–xii.

23. Alexis de Tocqueville, *Democracy in America,* 2 vols. (New York: Alfred A. Knopf, 1956), 1:51.

overheard Americans conversing without the word DOLLAR being pronounced between them."[24]

Missionaries whose lives and values have been shaped in such a milieu are — although only vaguely, if at all, aware of it themselves — particularly dependent upon and susceptible to the power of mammon. Their mission could not even be contemplated, much less accomplished, without an abundance of money. Both the institutions and the personnel of the Western Christian missionary enterprise bear powerful testimony to the absolute centrality of money. Without money, there would be neither agency nor personnel. The most insidious and detrimental effect that affluence has upon missionary communication is to foster hypocrisy. Wealth can blind missionaries to the great difference between what they think they are communicating, and what their poorer listeners actually see, hear, and believe.

Strategic Costs of Missionary Affluence

The attractive strategic options available to missionaries who have money were outlined in an earlier chapter. The counterproductive dynamics of affluence-based mission strategies are seldom mentioned, much less considered seriously in all of their far-reaching implications. What follows is an attempt to redress that oversight.

Mission strategy is the art or "science" of planning and conducting Christian missions. As the sine qua non of missionary endeavor, most Western missionaries have something to say about it, and have given it considerable thought. Anthropologists, sociologists, development economists, communications experts, theologians, journalists, management specialists, computer programmers, educators, historians, and even marketing consultants — each assured that his or her particular insight provides an indispensable key to more effective mission strategy — engage in what has come to be known as *missiology*. Myriad books, journals, articles, symposiums, consultations, conferences, seminars, seminary and college curriculums, and professional and scholarly associations — all devoted to the development, the delineation, and the implementation of mission strategies to reach this or that hidden or neglected or inadequately evangelized or developed people — reflect the earnest and lively interest of Western Christians in the subject.

The highly publicized pecuniary struggles of institutions such as mission agencies and theological seminaries are now an established part of the Western Christian landscape. It is understandable, therefore, that questions concerning the adverse effects of their affluence upon the strategies that they devise should seldom be raised. Nevertheless, Western missionary strategy increasingly reflects a

---

24. Frances Trollope, *Domestic Manners of the Americans,* ed., with a history of Mrs. Trollope's adventures in America, by Donald Smalley (New York: Alfred A. Knopf, 1949 [1832]), 301. The mother of Anthony Trollope, she traveled in America from December 1827 until July 1831. See also Charles Dickens's book *Dombey and Son.* More recent studies on the theme of the American preoccupation with mammon are so numerous as to make specific mention of any particular book unnecessary.

number of significant inadequacies which are, to a great degree, traceable to the affluence of the Western church.

1. *Western missionary strategy is characterized by dependence upon expensive technology.* As useful as our expensive machines might be in increasing the speed and the comfort with which missionaries accomplish their professional responsibilities and attend to their personal needs, ownership and control of such devices frequently accentuate the distance between missionaries and the people they serve, thus reinforcing that isolation which is the concomitant of independent, technological living. Furthermore, becoming accustomed to doing missions with technology, Western missionaries find it difficult to imagine fulfilling the Great Commission without it.

An airplane crashes, and donors are assured that the Lord's work will suffer irreparable loss unless the more than half a million dollars needed to replace it comes in quickly. "This need could not have come at a worse time and we must act immediately" read a typical appeal letter from a well-known mission agency; "Missionaries are depending on us for flights and the warehouse is full of medical and general supplies waiting to be moved."[25] The keys on a computer keyboard stick, and the anxious and incredibly overworked missionary in Mozambique envisions the closing of Bible school: "If the computer goes out, the seminary closes," he writes, "since most materials are being prepared on a week to week basis on the word processor."[26]

Such appeals do not exaggerate. They are true. The strategies of Western missionaries *are* dependent on technology. Without boats, airplanes, four-wheel-drive vehicles, cars, motorcycles, computers, radios, televisions, refrigerators, electricity, and sometimes air conditioning, missionary work cannot be done — at least not in the way of Western missionaries.

Ironically, the speedier life is lived, the lonelier a person becomes.[27] Technology has enabled Western missionaries to see the big picture as never before. The Joshua Project, whose mission is "to identify and highlight the people groups of the world that have the least exposure to the Gospel and the least Christian presence in their midst," has identified 15,999 distinct people groups, of which 6,705 remain "unreached."[28] But also thanks to technology, fewer and fewer are able to identify with the individual persons behind such numbers. Not wealthy Westerners, but often impoverished "national evangelists" or indigenous catechists end up incarnating Christ in ways that are imitable, thus doing the actual mission work. With mission by remote control, Western strategies become abstract "program" and "people group" oriented. Charts and graphs become a substitute for incarnation and identification. Mobility and speed take precedence over the

---

25. A general appeal sent out on July 31, 1987, by Missionary Aviation Fellowship (MAF), Canada, in the wake of the May 25, 1987, crash, with tragic loss of life, of a Twin Otter in Irian Jaya.

26. Letter of Hardy to Bonk, Fall 1987, Mozambique.

27. See Jacques Ellul's book *The Technological Society,* trans. John Wilkinson (New York: Knopf, 1964), for a sociological and theological analysis of this phenomenon. More recent is the perceptive study by Louise Bernikow, *Alone in America: The Search for Companionship* (New York: Harper & Row, 1986).

28. The Joshua Project Web site [*www.joshuaproject.net/index.php*] was updated on June 28, 2006.

generation-consuming time essential to building personal relationships. As every Western missionary knows, on the field itself — with the exception of modern cities — preoccupation with running and maintaining the technological aids to comfort and efficiency (hence ministry) often so intrude into a missionary's time as to leave him or her scarcely any time to engage in missionary work. This is nothing new, although the problem is worse now than it was a century ago. But even then, the complaint by one missionary that he had been "to some extent interfered with ever since [he] arrived, by an extensive storeroom, management of nails, responsibility of meeting caravans, [etc.]..."[29] was a common one.

Koyama points out that while race horses run at forty-five miles an hour, cars travel comfortably at fifty miles an hour, and jets fly six hundred miles an hour at thirty-five thousand feet above sea level, human beings walk at only three miles an hour. A person's view of the world becomes increasingly detached and superficial in direct proportion to the speed and the altitude which that person is able to achieve. As Koyama explains:

> When we walk (three miles an hour) we see many things, we notice many things, we feel wind, we feel rain, we are warmed by sunshine, we can smell the pleasant aroma as we pass food stalls, we may meet friends or even relatives. We hear children laugh and cry, and see them play. When we walk we see, feel, smell and hear so many interesting things. We are not shut up. We are not rushing at fifty miles an hour. Our pace is three miles an hour on our own feet. That is what makes this seeing, feeling, smelling and hearing possible.[30]

Uncritical utilization of technology in conceiving, designing, and implementing our Western missionary strategies inclines us to forget this most fundamental fact: most persons, whether "reached," or "unreached" still walk — at only three miles per hour. And our incarnate Lord deliberately did also.

2. *Affluence-dependent strategies cannot and should not be imitated by those whom Western missionaries presume to instruct.* The missionary strategies devised by Western agencies and modeled by Western missionaries are too expensive and too technology-dependent to be emulated by any but the richest churches in the non-Western world. Ironically, so closely associated with affluence and technology are popular Western understandings of mission that we do not recognize the missionary activity of poorer churches for what it is. Referring to the exceedingly numerous underpaid and poorly educated missionaries of African, Asian, and South American churches as "native evangelists," Western missiologists reserve the term "missionary" for those with enough money to undertake mission in the Western mode. This means, in effect, that unless a person has enough money to buy a return ticket for an international flight, and

29. From a letter from Jones to Whitehouse, June 24, 1884, Uguha, cited by Bonk, *The Theory and Practice of Missionary Identification,* 61.

30. Kosuke Koyama, *Fifty Meditations* (Maryknoll, NY: Orbis Books, 1979), 149. See also his book *Three Mile an Hour God: Biblical Reflections* (Maryknoll, NY: Orbis Books, 1980), especially the first chapter.

sufficient financial backing to live overseas at the same level as he or she is accustomed to living at home, that person is not a missionary!

Thus, despite the fact that there were an estimated 62,000 Christian foreign missionaries in 1900, a number which by mid-2006 had increased to 448,000,[31] influential Western missiologists generally speak of foreign mission from the Third World as though it were a recent phenomenon. In missiological writing on the subject, the criterion used to define "missionary" renders it impossible to recognize as missionaries any but those associated with societies roughly paralleling Western mission agencies. The thousands of cross-cultural (though not transnational) evangelists on the cutting edge of church growth around the world are not so recognized. The publications of Western mission agencies speak of their evolution into truly international societies, with missionary personnel from Asia or South America joining ranks with Western missionaries. But only the rich need apply. The poor do not and cannot qualify as "real" missionaries, since they can seldom generate the requisite levels of support.

That the earliest Christian missionaries were natives of an obscure, impoverished, foreign-dominated and occupied territory that was little more than a back eddy of the vast imperialist Roman Empire is seldom recalled. Imbedded within the Western Christian psyche seems to be the notion that missions will naturally and most effectively proceed *from* the centers of political, military, and economic power *to* those dominated or impoverished by those same powers. The institutional structures of Western mission agencies so reflect this model of operation that the thought of possibly reversing this modus operandi is regarded as unrealistic. The financial resources are simply not there. Any Christian missions from the poor to the rich are implicitly assumed to be logistically impossible, and in any case, unworkable. Who would listen to an alien missionary distinguished chiefly by personal want?

Further questions concerning Western affluence-based strategies need to be raised. Can affluent missionaries properly model the way in which the local church can and should relate to the indigenous society? The intuitive negative response to this question is supported by at least one study of missionary work in Colombia, Egypt, and South Korea.[32] Or what about the effects of a Western missionary modus operandi that models as its first priority the avoidance of inconvenience, want, or suffering, and which spends prodigious amounts of money and energy to ensure that mission be fulfilled without suffering or inconvenience to the missionary? In such instances, does not the avoidance of personal suffering become a goal to which all other missiological goals are subordinated? Little wonder that those converts whose lives most closely approximate those of Western missionaries are most impotent when it comes to evangelizing their own people.

---

31. David B. Barrett, Todd M. Johnson, and Peter F. Crossing, "Missiometrics 2006: Goals, Resources, Doctrines of the 350 Christian World Communions," *International Bulletin of Missionary Research* 30, no. 1 (January 2006): 28.

32. Bernard E. Quick, "He Who Pays the Piper . . . : A Study of Economic Power and Mission in a Revolutionary World" (unpublished manuscript, Princeton Theological Seminary, n.d.), 56.

3. *Genuinely fraternal strategies in conjunction with poorer churches are usually frustrating and often unworkable from the point of view of both mission agencies and churches.* Money gives power; power results in domination. True partnership between unequals, if not impossible, is extremely unlikely. The slogan of the Whitby Conference of the International Missionary Council in 1947 was *Partnership in Mission.* The reaction of non-Western Christians to the pious goodwill implied in this theme was poignantly expressed by an Indonesian church leader: " 'Partnership in obedience,' yes," he responded to a Dutch delegation, " — the partnership for you; the obedience for us!"[33]

"If you dangle your millions before us, you will make beggars of us and demoralize us," Gandhi warned American missionaries in 1936.[34] His words were both history and prophecy. The relative affluence of Western missionaries has long been and continues to be a key element in seemingly endemic tensions marking the relationship between Western missions and Third World churches. Perhaps no single missiological issue has been so hotly debated or so extensively elaborated. Missionary delegates to the Anglo-American conferences — Liverpool, 1860; London, 1888; New York, 1900; Edinburgh, 1910 — repeatedly but apparently futilely grappled with the tensions arising out of the staggering financial inequities between Western missions and their would-be partners in the poorer part of the world.

Described by Arthur Judson Brown in 1904 as "a serious problem in missions,"[35] it was still problem enough — following the 1928 meeting of the International Missionary Council in Jerusalem — to warrant the establishment of the Department of Social and Economic Research and Counsel, under the directorship of J. Merle Davis. Among the several concerns that this department was to investigate and report on was the question of how the rich Western missionary societies and "Younger [i.e., poor] Churches" could best relate in mutually helpful ways. Although the department produced more than a score of volumes in time for the Tambaram meetings of 1938,[36] anything approaching a solution to the complex problems of relationships between rich missionaries and poor churches was not forthcoming. In 1968 it was still described as "the American

---

33. As quoted by David J. Bosch, "The Missionary: Exemplar or Victim?" *Theologia Evangelica* 17, no. 1 (March 1984): 11.

34. Mohandas K. Gandhi, *The Mahatma and the Missionary: Selected Writings of Mohandas K. Gandhi,* ed. Clifford Manshardt (Chicago: Henry Regnery Company, 1949), 125. The quotation is taken from an article appearing in *Harijan* (December 12, 1936).

35. Arthur Judson Brown, "A Serious Problem in Missions: Salaries and the Increased Cost of Living in Asia," *The Missionary Review of the World* 27 (June 1904): 408–13.

36. See, for example, J. Merle Davis, *The Economic and Social Environment of the Younger Churches: The Report of the Department of Social and Economic Research of the International Missionary Council to the Tambaram Meeting — December 1938* (London: Edinburgh House, 1939). See also his *Mission Finance and the Younger Churches: A Study for the Tambaram Meeting of the International Missionary Council* (Bangalore: Scripture Literature Press, 1938), and the volume edited by him, *The Economic Basis of the Church: Preparatory Studies and Findings, Meeting of the International Missionary Council, at Tambaram, Madras, India, December 12th to 29th, 1938,* vol. 5 of The Madras Series (New York: International Missionary Council, 1939).

missionary problem" in the Philippines.[37] Western-based mission agencies continue to search — without success — for equitable formulas whereby fraternity might be practically expressed by means of equal pay for equal work done by Western missionaries and their non-Western colleagues. The problem bedevils virtually every mission agency with Western missionaries in the Third World, Protestant and Catholic alike.

Evangelicals associated with the Interdenominational Foreign Missions Association and the Evangelical Foreign Missions Association — although our deep suspicion of "liberals" has generally made it difficult for us to learn from the similar and much more thoroughly documented experiences of missionaries whose churches are associated with the World Council of Churches — are likewise confounded by the snarled, multifarious complexity of the relationships governing their economically unequal "partnerships" with the Third World churches in whose orbit they must now move. In 1971, representatives from the Interdenominational Foreign Missions Association and the Evangelical Foreign Missions Association mission societies convened to explore the issue of church-mission tensions.[38] Of the fifteen specific areas of tension identified by the delegates, seven had to do with money.[39] Ironically, non-Western delegates to the conference were conspicuous by their absence, thus providing a mute illustration of the dimensions of the inequity between the sending church/receiving church "partners." The consultation — despite its concern that tensions between two partners be resolved — neglected to invite the weaker partner!

4. *Western affluence results in strategies that cannot effectively reach the poor.* The strategies of Western missions have for the most part bypassed the burgeoning urban poor of the world's great cities — the very people who, if history is in any way instructive, are most likely to prove receptive to the Gospel. Several years ago, a New Zealand missionary well known for his work in Manila slums spent two years of intensive research in eight of the great Asian cities, seeking, in his own words "to know how the great mission surge of the last decades had established the church among the urban poor." He was forced to conclude that "the greatest mission surge in history has entirely missed the greatest migration in history, the migration of Third World rural peasants to great megacities."[40]

---

37. Frederick Dale Bruner, "The American Missionary Problem: An Essay in Conscience," *Christian Century* 85, no. 23 (June 5, 1968): 751–53.

38. For the official report of the Green Lake Conference, see *Missions in Creative Tension,* ed. Vergil Gerber (South Pasadena, CA: William Carey Library, 1971).

39. See Harvie M. Conn's assessment of this conference in his article, "The Money Barrier between Sending and Receiving Churches," *The Evangelical Missions Quarterly* 14, no. 4 (October 1978): 231–39.

40. Viv Grigg, "The Urban Poor: Prime Missionary Target," *Evangelical Review of Theology* 11, no. 3 (July 1987): 261. For a description of his work in Manila, see his book *Companion to the Poor* (Sutherland, NSW, Australia: Albatross Books, 1984). The Roman Catholic church — with its biblical stress upon the necessity of apostolic sharing in the sufferings of Christ, and with its force of missionaries who have taken personal vows of poverty — has not been quite so remiss as has the Protestant. Mother Teresa's Sisters of Charity is but an outstanding example of the outworking of a genre of biblical teaching persistently ignored by Protestants.

Neglect of the world's poorest people by the church's richest missionaries is not a case of simple oversight. The fact is, our affluence makes us uncomfortable in the context of insoluble poverty. The very strategies that ensure Western missionary longevity, efficiency, and comfort make residence among the urban poor unfeasible. Insulation and isolation from the everyday crises of life in the slums reduce missionary proclamation of the "better way" to the "Lord, Lord" language of Matthew 7:22 and 25:44–46. As the founder of L'Arche explained in a recent interview, "Jesus was credible because he did things."[41] Western missionaries, sensing the hypocrisy of ministry without incarnation, but unable to pay the price of identification with the poor, avoid the shantytowns, focusing instead on the somewhat better-off, upwardly mobile elements of city populations. The result is neglect of peoples who have historically been most responsive to the good news. Despite their opposition to moratorium, evangelical missionaries from the West may well be among its chief exemplars when it comes to living and working among the poor.

A second strategic consequence of Western affluence is our evident inability to see the North American continent as a desperately needy mission field. The Christian Scriptures teach that the field is the world, and that every person ever born is born on the mission field. In the words of a well-known Ghanaian theologian, "The idea of one part of the world evangelizing another will not bear scrutiny. Missions are not a movement from the haves to the have-nots, from the educated to the illiterate. They are a movement from the fellowship of faith all over the world to all who stand outside this fellowship, whoever and wherever they may be."[42]

Possibly because of the relative affluence of the West, and because of the close links in the minds of North Americans between the Christian religion and "civilization" — by which is meant consumer capitalism — and because it continues to manifest much of the external and institutional paraphernalia associated with Christendom, Western churches tend to recognize only the rest of the world as "mission field." The fact is that the Western church is a shrinking church, a church that fails two key tests of Christian vitality: the statistical test and the kingdom test. Statistically, the West is one of the least encouraging areas in the world, manifesting neither the burgeoning numerical growth of sub-Saharan African Christianity, nor the dynamic activity of Latin American Christians.[43]

There can be little doubt that personal affluence is one source of this myopia. Perhaps the Laodicean church described in Revelation 3:14–22 — a kind of forerunner of all wealthy churches, including those in North America — was most at ease with theorizing, with the construction of complex sociological models, with patronizing analyses of poorer groups in distant lands, and with proposing

41. Jean Vanier (interview by the editors), "Expert Witness," *U.S. Catholic* 71, no. 8 (August 2006): 18–22.

42. C. G. Baeta, then president of the International Missionary Council, as quoted by D. T. Niles in his book *Upon the Earth: The Mission of God and the Missionary Enterprise of the Churches* (New York: McGraw-Hill, 1962), 194.

43. Andrew F. Walls, "The Voice of One Crying in the Supermarket: The West as the Prime Field for Christian Mission." Unpublished paper received in the fall of 1984 from A. F. Walls, then director of the Scottish Institute of Missionary Studies at New College at the University of Edinburgh.

vicarious strategies that relied upon poorer "native evangelists" who could pay the price for actually implementing such schemes at the grassroots level. We do not know. We are told only that the materially comfortable Laodicean church was oblivious to its own spiritual destitution, and smugly unaware that the Lord of the churches was not in their midst but outside the door, asking to be let in.

There is a third consequence of missionary affluence. By accepting as legitimate the entitlement to affluence which is theirs as Western Christians, missionaries and mission societies forfeit the right to preach a desperately needed prophetic word to a self-satisfied Christian religious establishment, awash with talk about God, but assiduously creative in ensuring that the Christian Scriptures prop up the self-indulgent predisposition of the prevailing culture. Few are in as good a position to see the spiritual deterioration and advancing decay of Western churches as are her missionaries on furlough. But by their complicity and uncritical partaking of her affluence, they relinquish the right to pronounce God's judgment on a decadent, self-absorbed society whose celebrated greed and irresponsibly inflated sense of material entitlement now appear to be holding the entire planet hostage.

It seems doubtful that the recent upsurge of interest in short-term missions on the part of Western young people — as evidenced by student attendance in conferences sponsored by organizations such as InterVarsity Christian Fellowship and Campus Crusade, and in enrollment in the mission studies programs of Christian colleges and seminaries — will be enough to reverse the creeping impotence of the church in North America. In his 2005 *Global Issues Survey,* Robert Wuthnow, director of Princeton University's Center for the Study of Religion, estimates that 1.6 million Americans went on short-term (two weeks or less) mission trips in 2005. This phenomenon is not necessarily a harbinger of North American spiritual renewal, however. For as one journalist shrewdly observed, their "one key stipulation . . . [is that] they expect to get their comfortable lives back a few days later."[44]

Unless young men and women such as these are willing to move beyond the privilege, security, and self-sufficiency that are a hallmark of the North American way of doing mission, there can be no reversal. Expensive, sophisticated, high-tech, highly publicized strategies — designed with a corporate eye to levering maximum measurable results, conceived by comfortable missiologists, administered by well-off mission executives, and implemented by affluent missionaries — will not turn the tide against the "powers of this dark world and against the spiritual forces of evil in the heavenly realms" (Eph. 6:12). Indeed, affluence itself is a frequently preferred sector of that spiritual beachhead referred to in Scripture as "the world" used by the enemy in his most successful invasion of our Western consumer souls.

That the church among the poor is growing both quantitatively and qualitatively around the world — usually in the absence of Western missionaries — while the church in the West continues its comfortable decline is no coincidence.

---

44. Jeffrey MacDonald, "Rise of Sunshine Samaritans: On a Mission or Holiday?" *The Christian Science Monitor* (May 25, 2006). *www.csmonitor.com/2006/0525/p01s01-ussc.html.*

Laodicea was likely a missionary sending church, yet Christ was on the wrong side of the church's door. Philadelphia, on the other hand, without prospects economically, welcomed her Lord, and a great door of opportunity was opened before her (Rev. 3:7–21). God has always preferred human weakness as the vehicle through which to manifest his power.

These, then, are some of the communicatory and strategic costs borne by Western missionaries, making affluence a clearly Faustian bargain from a missiological point of view. It is to the theological and ethical dimensions of missionary life that we now turn, for it is here that wealth exacts its most terrible toll. A missionary who subordinates personal theory and practice to the authority of the Bible deserves a careful hearing, since the Scriptures constitute the supreme rule for life and faith that he or she proclaims. Contrarily, the integrity of anyone whose personal life is in sharp variance with what they profess to believe may be legitimately questioned, according to our Lord:

> [1]Then Jesus said to the crowds and to his disciples: [2]"The teachers of the law and the Pharisees sit in Moses' seat. [3]So you must obey them and do everything they tell you. But do not do what they do, for they do not practice what they preach. [4]They tie up heavy loads and put them on men's shoulders, but they themselves are not willing to lift a finger to move them.
>
> [5]"Everything they do is done for men to see...."
>
> (Matt. 23:1–5a)

This is the subject of the next chapter.

6

Theological, Ethical, and Biblical Considerations on Missionary Affluence

"Woe to you, teachers of the law and Pharisees, you hypocrites! You clean the outside of the cup and dish, but inside are full of greed and self-indulgence.

"Sell your possessions and give to the poor. Provide purses for yourselves that will not wear out, a treasure in heaven that will not be exhausted, where no thief comes near and no moth destroys. For where your treasure is, there your heart will be also.

"But the worries of this life, the deceitfulness of wealth and the desires for other things come in and choke the word, making it unfruitful."

The Pharisees, who loved money, heard all this and were sneering at Jesus. He said to them, "You are the ones who justify yourselves in the eyes of men, but God knows your hearts. What is highly valued among men is detestable in God's sight." — JESUS

"You all know," said the Guide, "that security is mortals' greatest enemy." — C. S. LEWIS

Oh the folly of any mind that would explain God before obeying Him! That would map out the character of God instead of crying, Lord, what wouldst thou have me to do? — GEORGE MACDONALD

Like many other fine things, it lost part of its brilliance when examined too nearly. — FRANCES TROLLOPE

This is the most important chapter of the book. While one might well take issue with the author's opinions on contextual, theoretical, and consequential dimensions of Western missionary affluence in contexts of poverty, the Scriptures must be reckoned with. No matter how inconvenient an injunction or awkward an admonition, the Bible — as God's authoritative revelation of himself and of his will for humankind — is taken seriously by all who try to live by its rule. Missionaries, whose vocation it is to proclaim the revealed precepts of God in both word and deed, can be expected to evince close harmony between what they teach and how they live. As our Lord's brother cautioned would-be teachers two millennia ago, "Not many of you should presume to be teachers, my brothers, because you know that we who teach will be judged more strictly" (James 3:1).

This chapter is comprised of two major sections. In the first part, theological and ethical issues that emerge as a natural result of personal affluence in a context of poverty are considered. In the second part, an overview of biblical teaching on the subject of wealth and poverty is undertaken, with special application to the life and work of affluent missionaries. Essays by Christopher J. H. Wright and Justo L. Gonzalez are intended to supplement and support the material.

Theological and Ethical Considerations

Each relational, communicatory, and strategic consequence of missionary affluence discussed in the foregoing chapters carries ethical and theological corollaries. It is clear that permeating all of the complex and variegated social and physical dimensions constituting "human being" is a core, enduring theological reality: human beings are made in the image of God, and play a significant role in the quintessentially moral drama of their Creator's universe. Accordingly, no facet of life or thought does not in some way both reflect and affect one's theology.

For this reason, missionary social insulation, isolation, independence, and segregation from the poor — seemingly inevitable and, on the surface, relatively insignificant *relational consequences* of missionary affluence — become profoundly troubling when they characterize those who represent a Lord who emptied himself in order to enter fully into the pathos of humankind — "[making] himself nothing, taking the very nature of a servant" — and who instructed his followers to do the same (Phil. 2:1–11). Ethical questions also arise from the great gulf between the public profession and private practice of men and women whose special calling is to *communicate* the Gospel in both word and deed. Asymmetry between the profession of faith and the life of faith is in the New Testament referred to as *hypocrisy*. What follows is no more than a bare sketch of the wide range and complex nature of theological and ethical questions raised by the affluence of those who proclaim the Gospel.

Since personal affluence in contexts of poverty raises troubling doubts about a missionary's willingness to obey and qualifications to teach the whole counsel of God on mammon, three questions merit careful consideration:

1. Is Western missionary preoccupation with material things — "with a continual lust for more" — no more than an innocently acquired trait of their consumer culture?[1] As I tried to show in chapter 2, acculturation in a society committed to and structured around the proposition that life consists in the abundance of possessions does have a significant bearing upon a missionary's orientation to life. The Western missionary is the product of a society that devotes

---

1. This phrase was employed by St. Paul in Eph. 4:17–19 when he contrasted the futile way of Gentile thinking to that characterizing the children of light. Those preoccupied with earthly things never have enough. The title of Peter C. Whybrow's recent book captures the restless absorption with material acquisitiveness characterizing the societies in which Western missionaries are incubated: *American Mania: When More Is Not Enough* (New York: W. W. Norton, 2005).

more of its collective resources to security than to any other needs.[2] This great preoccupation with financial security is faithfully reflected in the policies of most Western mission agencies — policies for which missionaries are quite rightly deeply grateful. But such security cannot be had without certain costs.

First, actual missionary work is often severely curtailed by the complicated challenge of living up to the standards of consumer culture entitlement in the non-Western world. This was the complaint of Jamaican Charles Hemans, a young missionary who worked in central southern Africa toward the end of the nineteenth century. Responding to his young charge by drawing upon several decades of mission-related experience, LMS Home Secretary Ralph Wardlaw Thompson could offer scant comfort. "One of the greatest hindrances to the spiritual progress of our missions," he wrote, "is in the demands made upon the missionary for purely material things. One is so occupied and constantly worried in the process of attending to house and garden, and directing the labours of ignorant and incompetent people . . . that the mind becomes pre-occupied; attention to spiritual duties is hurried and unsatisfactory, and even the time for personal spiritual improvement is entirely absorbed."[3]

More serious than the problem of wasted time, however, are troubling issues bearing directly upon the theological integrity of a Christian teacher. Can an economically secure and comfortably accoutred missionary teach the poor — with any degree of credibility — about simplicity, generosity, contentment, or the costly sacrifice entailed in all genuine discipleship? A missionary must teach these things, for they are themes that permeate the Christian Scriptures. And what about the frequently overriding "thought for the morrow" reflected in a missionary's practical need to maintain and increase his or her family's personal comfort and ongoing security? How can missionaries, who in countless ways insist on a spectacularly good life in the here and now, reassure their poverty-stricken disciples about the great hope of the life to come? Is it possible to maintain both credibility and an affluent lifestyle when teaching the poor what God says about the stewardship of possessions? Biblical answers to questions such as these suggest that emissaries of affluent Western churches dare not excuse their materialist preoccupations by simply blaming their culture.

A second question is equally important:

2. Is the sin of greed less deadly for affluent missionaries than for the poor among whom they live? The answer must surely be no. If — as I am often reminded by my missionary friends — poverty and wealth are *relative* concepts, making it possible for the same person to be poor in North America but rich in Africa, then it must be conceded that a life of pecuniary modesty in one society may well be regarded as extravagant in another.

It did not take a theologian to discern that in North America the seven deadly sins — with the exception of sloth — were early transformed into positive virtues,

---

2. Philip Slater, *The Pursuit of Loneliness: American Culture at the Breaking Point* (Boston: Beacon Press, 1970), 1.

3. A letter from Thompson to Hemans, December 24, 1898, as cited by Jonathan Bonk, *The Theory and Practice of Missionary Identification, 1860–1920* (Lewiston, NY: Edwin Mellen Press, 1989), 60.

with "Greed, avarice, envy, gluttony, luxury, and pride [becoming] the driving force of the new economy."[4] Of vital concern to Western missionaries must be the question of how and to what degree they unconsciously manifest this unabashed inversion of biblical values. Can it be that even the most pious and esteemed representatives of Western churches have inherited the ethical deformity that lies at the heart of what we call "consumerism"? Does the cultural DNA that gives rise to an American acquisitiveness so obsessive that more is never enough affect missionaries? The rapidity with which even marginally technological "breakthroughs" mutate into "necessities" in Western mission practice hints at how this question must be answered.[5]

If *greed* be defined as the insistence on more than enough in a social context made up of those who have less than enough, then many missionaries who journey from North American shores will be surprised to discover themselves numbered among the greedy.

Among the most awkward challenges faced by North American missionaries abroad is the necessity of explaining to the truly needy why they not only "need" to be staggeringly wealthy by the standards of those around them, but why they will "need" more next year, and still more the year after that. To the poor, even the most ordinary Western missionary exhibits two behavior traits which, according to St. Paul, disqualify a person from holding office in a church: a lover of money (1 Tim. 3:3) and embracer of great gain (1 Tim. 6:5–11). According to the apostle, furthermore, a prime trait of "the children of darkness" is their broad-spectrum self-indulgence, and an accompanying "continual lust for more" (Eph. 4:19). "But among you," St. Paul continues, "there must not be even a *hint* [emphasis mine] . . . of greed. . . . For of this you can be sure: . . . no greedy person . . . has any inheritance in the kingdom of Christ and of God" (Eph. 5:3–5). Such words make sober reading for those of us who — despite being surrounded by the truly needy — assume and sometimes demand steady improvement in our already high standard of living, even if — in the case of the Western economies — it must be at the expense of those who barely subsist.

The third question relates to the affluent missionary's relationship to the one he or she refers to as "Lord."

3. Can a comfortably secure, independent missionary have any genuine sense of dependence upon God? In the Old Testament record of relationships between God and his people, prosperity almost inevitably gave rise to a spiritually fatal sense of independence. "When you have eaten and are satisfied . . . be careful

---

4. Lewis Mumford, *The Transformations of Man,* cited by David E. Shi, *The Simple Life: Plain Living and High Thinking in American Culture* (New York: Oxford University Press, 1985), 250.

5. For a perceptive description and diagnosis of American "mania" for things, see Whybrow, *American Mania,* referred to earlier. Also helpful, but written from the perspective of a Christian economist, is Henry Rempel, *A High Price for Abundant Living: The Story of Capitalism* (Waterloo, Ontario: Herald Press, 2003). Churches mirror the broader cultural phenomenon, as Vincent J. Miller demonstrates in *Consuming Religion: Christian Faith and Practice in a Consumer Culture* (New York: Continuum, 2005). See also Skye Jethani, "From Christ's Church to iChurch: How Consumerism Undermines Our Faith and Community," posted on the LeadershipJournal.net Web site of *Christianity Today: www.christianitytoday.com/leaders/newsletter/2006/cln60710.html.* This article is an abridgment of his full-length article "All We Like Sheep" appearing in the Summer 2006 issue of *Leadership.*

that you do not forget the Lord your God" was the oft-repeated warning as his slave nation prepared to occupy the land flowing with milk and honey (Deut. 6:11–12; 8:10–11; 32:15; Ezek. 28:4–5; Hos. 13:6).

Independence from God was not expressed by inattention to prescribed religious services, it should be pointed out. On the contrary, it was frequently when Israel's relationship with God was at its lowest ebb that its apparent worship evinced a most enviable finesse and enthusiasm. Independence was a matter of the heart (Ezek. 33:31–32; 34:25). God could see it; his prophets preached against it; the poor were made cynical by it; while rich worshipers were, apparently, oblivious of it.

One subtle manifestation of this independence-from-God prevalent in affluent Western churches is evident in the widespread agnosticism or practical skepticism regarding the actual value of prayer. The pious clichés are there among evangelicals, of course, and these are matched by the elegantly phrased set prayers of their more liturgical counterparts. But *can* the secure and independent missionary really pray? Does he or she need to?[6] Agnosticism concerning prayer is one consequence of plenty. Trust in money becomes embarrassingly evident when — as frequently happens — missionary "prayer" letters come to be little more than thinly veiled appeals for financial support for one project or another.

The secret misgivings that Western missionaries have about prayer is sometimes obvious to their less affluent brothers and sisters in other lands. Jacob Loewen illustrates this in a story from the Choco Church in Panama, where he and another missionary were attending a leadership conference hosted by an Indian pastor whose wife was very ill with malaria. Pastor Aureliano, with access to only small fragments of the Bible in his own language, was overjoyed to hear Loewen's translation of James 5:14–15, assuring the sick of healing if prayer offered on their behalf were offered by elders with requisite faith. After double checking, just to make sure the Bible really did make such a promise, the pastor asked why prayer should not be offered for his wife.

This has been the outcome most feared by Jacob Loewen. Aureliano was, after all, a simple man, inclined to take the Bible as literal truth. He lacked the Western hermeneutical sophistication necessary to understand that much of what one read in the Bible did not actually mean what the author seemed to be saying. Nevertheless, in order to adequately fulfill their role expectations as respected Christian leaders (how could they *not* have faith?!), the missionaries agreed — albeit with profound misgivings about the outcome. What, they wondered, would happen to the touchingly naïve faith of these Indian Christians if, as would in all probability be the case, the sick woman was not healed? But appearing to have more faith than in fact was the case, they joined with Indian leaders to offer prayer. To Loewen's immense relief, the woman's condition seemed marginally improved. But she soon suffered a relapse. Later, Loewen observed Pastor Aureliano and

---

6. The results of a survey of 390 missionaries working in thirty-two countries and representing thirty-seven different mission societies indicated that 60 percent pray between eleven and thirty minutes daily, while 11 percent pray an average of less than five minutes a day. See Phil Parshall's article, "How Spiritual Are Missionaries?" *Evangelical Missions Quarterly* 23, no. 1 (January 1987): 10.

the Indian leaders gather once again — this time without the missionaries — to pray for the ailing woman. She was healed, and spent the rest of the day cooking for the conference attendees.

Later that evening, discreetly inquiring why he and his fellow missionary had been excluded from the prayer circle, Loewen was smitten by Pastor Aureliano's reply: "No," he said, "we could not take you along because you two do not believe."[7]

Western subliminal agnosticism is not deliberate, but seemingly the human default mode of material and physical security. We try hard to believe, to the extent that some devotees — none more than our missionaries — even attend prayer meetings. But our affluence makes God necessary in only an ontological or religious sense. Prayer, as a biblical study of the subject quickly reveals, is not the activity of people who are in reasonable control of their lives. It is the resort of weak, overwrought, desperate people whose life circumstances call for resources beyond their own. And herein lies the problem: A "good" missionary society will take every possible step — by means of elaborate medical, financial, educational, and logistical support systems — to ensure that all aspects of a missionary's life are cared for. This is a natural, commendable, and — humanly speaking — desirable course to follow. But it apparently leaves God with very little to actually do in our lives.[8]

Sadly, it is evident that Western missionaries — true sons and daughters of their churches back home — find it as difficult as any other North American to deliberately lose all things for the sake of Jesus Christ. Far from being, in Paul's words, "rubbish" (Phil. 3:7–8), the material symbols of affluence are thought to be indispensable to mission. Christ's teaching on the abundance of possessions cannot be taught by Western Christian leaders, because it will be all too evident that it is not being practiced. From this issues a second theological/ethical conundrum for most North American missions: their strategies and statuses, contingent on money and power, contradict the very core Christian mission as prescribed in the New Testament — the Incarnation itself.

The Incarnation and the Cross are models for all distinctively Christian apostolic life and ministry. Although the implications of the Incarnation for mission are explored further in the concluding chapter, it is appropriate to raise certain related questions with those who cling to their Western prerogatives of privilege. One unsurprising conclusion emerging from the 1978 *Willowbank Consultation on the Gospel and Culture* was that the Incarnation is a model for Christian witness. Applied to Christian missionary endeavor this meant, the authors of the *Report* went on to explain, a threefold renunciation of status, independence, and immunity.[9] The practical difficulty arises from the fact that most "progressive"

---

7. Jacob Loewen, "Missions and the Problems of Cultural Background," in *The Church in Mission: A Sixtieth Anniversary Tribute to J. B. Toews,* ed. A. J. Klassen (Fresno, CA: Board of Christian Literature, Mennonite Brethren Church, 1967), 290–92.

8. The chapter "The Question of Finance" in Watchman Nee's book *Concerning Our Missions* (Shanghai: Gospel Book Room, 1939), 192–222, should be read by every missionary, mission executive, and missiologist.

9. Lausanne Committee for World Evangelization, Occasional Paper no. 2, *The Willowbank Report*. Report of a Consultation on Gospel and Culture held at Willowbank, Somerset Bridge,

Western missions labor to demonstrate the institutional reversal of this pattern: the missionary vocation becomes a distinguished career, longevity of tenure ensuring a pleasant retirement in Florida, and perhaps even the status of "statesman"; a rich variety of home-based support infrastructures reduce local dependence to a minimum; financial, logistical, and medical contingencies are anticipated and dealt with in such a way as to guarantee the missionary immunity from the dire straits of those among whom he or she works. We save ourselves, the reasoning goes, so that we can save others.

The affluence-based mission of the Western church — in contrast to the Incarnation-based mission of her Lord — most naturally serves as an ecclesiastical springboard for moving up, not down. Her independently secure missionaries find lording both more natural and more immediately effective than serving, although many possess sufficient ingenuity to convince themselves that their particular kind of domination *is* service. The great marvel of living in the technological age is that mission can be and even should be accelerated and undertaken in comfort, rather than — as in the case of Christ — slowing down and finally coming to a complete halt on the cross. We have discovered that prolonging one's comfortably secure life is not only personally gratifying but, to our immense relief, it is a demonstrably superior way of marketing the good news than, say, suffering and dying. The Gospel is thus reduced to assertions about the One who was rich but for our sakes became poor, and who personally demonstrated what has proven to be true ever since: that spiritual vitality comes to full potency only through weakness (1 Cor. 12:9–10).

By abandoning the Incarnation as a model for its own life and mission, the affluent church has assured its fundamental spiritual impotence. For as theologian Trevor Verryn reminds us, "Only the truly strong are able to lay aside their power in an act of self-emptying and assume a position of powerlessness."[10] The strategy of the cross that has always marked the true servant of God is nowhere more accurately — if only inadvertently — summarized than in the sardonic words of the religious leaders who, satisfied that they had rid themselves of a tiresome troublemaker by disposing of Jesus, scornfully pointed out, "He saved others, but he can't save himself!"[11] Alas for religious teachers of that day and this! In saving themselves, both they and those over whom they wield authority are doomed.

Added to the self-preservation impulses of affluent missions, which leave as little room as possible for that weakness in which God is said to delight, a third deeply theological problem must be mentioned: Biblical instruction on wealth

Bermuda, from 6th to 13th January 1978. Sponsored by the Lausanne Theology and Education Group (Wheaton, IL: Lausanne Committee for World Evangelization, 1978), 17–18.

10. Trevor D. Verryn, "Outside the Camp: A Study of Religious Authority and Conversion" (unpublished D.Th. thesis, University of South Africa), as cited by David Bosch in his article "The Missionary: Exemplar or Victim?" *Theologia Evangelica* 17, no. 1 (March 1984): 14.

11. Mark 15:31. See Kosuke Koyama's chapter, "Theology of the Cross" in his book *Mount Fuji and Mount Sinai: A Critique of Idols* (Maryknoll, NY: Orbis Books, 1985), 240–61, for a thought-provoking development of this theme. See also the article by Catholic theologian William B. Frazier, "Where Mission Begins: A Foundational Probe," *International Bulletin of Missionary Research* 11, no. 4 (October 1987): 146–56.

and poverty must necessarily be truncated when the teacher is himself or herself comfortably well off. No missionary can credibly challenge converts to a way of life that he or she is manifestly unwilling to live. This is a centuries-old problem that almost inevitably recurs when Western missionaries work among the materially poor.

Africans, for example, had great difficulty comprehending the religious motives underlying the missionary presence among them a century ago. A young British missionary, describing Africans as "most friendly...to us...and [possessing] liberal notions of friendship," went on to explain: "They consider it their duty to supply their friends with food or any such thing as may be acceptable to him."[12] Africans were unimpressed by reciprocal missionary notions of generosity, however. When missionaries celebrated Christmas a few years later by giving each mission employee and neighboring chief a colored cloth, they found their supply of milk cut off by disgruntled chiefs who regarded the size of the gift, when considered as a proportion of missionary wealth, as perversely and inappropriately parsimonious. "The African," concluded one badly ruffled missionary, "has very little idea of gratitude,"[13] a sentiment that the chiefs must have heartily reciprocated. Several years later another chief, observing the missionary's great wealth, and in accordance with his own customs, made known his request for a small portion. Not only was his request denied outright, but he entered the annals of missionary disapproval. Even such a "great" chief as Chungu, recorded the indignant missionary, "is not free from the weakness prevalent among African chieftains — a begging propensity. I gave him a good talking to about this, and I hope it will do him good."[14]

The meager wages paid by missionaries to their employees has been and continues to be a chronic source of misunderstanding and tension.[15] Western missionaries — except for a notable few — have studiously overlooked the curious double standard by which they govern themselves and their nonmissionary colleagues. Rationalizing the necessity of relatively high economic and social standards for themselves, they have frequently evinced a deep suspicion *of* and profound disappointment *with* converts who try to follow the missionary example. Such converts, they conclude, are selfish and worldly minded.

---

12. Hutley to Whitehouse, April 23, 1880, Uguha, as cited by Bonk, *The Theory and Practice of Missionary Identification,* 61.

13. Jones to Thompson, January 6, 1888, Fwambo, ibid., 87.

14. Jones to Thompson, March 26, 1895, Kambole, ibid. Confusion arising from mutual misunderstanding of sharing customs on the part of missionaries and their nonmissionary hosts is a frequent subject in missionary writing. See, for example, the article by Donald E. Douglas, "On Sharing Wealth Philippine Style," in *Readings in Missionary Anthropology II,* enlarged 1978 ed., ed. William A. Smalley (South Pasadena, CA: William Carey Library, 1978), 800–806.

15. Choan-seng Song, voicing the frustrations of many non-Western Christians, speaks of "the system called mission boards" as symbolizing injustice in the eyes of many Third World Christians: "A mission board is paying for a foreign missionary couple the rent for an apartment which is as much, or more, monthly than the wages of twenty Indians who have to support themselves, their wives, their children from their pay. The system has encouraged division among Christians and missionaries." From an unpublished paper, "The System, Missionaries and the Future of the Christian Mission" [ca. 1971] located in the Yale Divinity School Pamphlet Collection, Box 359, Folder 2465. Professor Choan-seng Song, author of *Third-Eye Theology* (Maryknoll, NY: Orbis Books, 1979), served at the time as secretary for Asian ministries with the Reformed Church in America.

The irony of missionary rationale for the low wages is captured by Herman Melville in his portrayal of Bildad, the miserly, Quaker ship owner. Having begun as a cabin boy, he is now in a position to negotiate wages for crew members on his own ship. Young Ishmael stands before him, hoping to be given a berth as cabin boy aboard the whaling ship:

> [He] went on mumbling to himself out of his book. "*Lay* not up for yourselves treasures upon earth, where moth — "
>
> "Well, Captain Bildad," interrupted Peleg, "what d'ye say, what lay[16] shall we give this young man?"
>
> "Thou knowest best," was the sepulchral reply, "the seven hundred and seventy-seventh wouldn't be too much, would it? ... 'where moth and rust do corrupt, but *lay....* ' "
>
> *Lay*, indeed, thought I, and such a lay! The seven hundred and seventy-seventh! Well, old Bildad, you are determined that I, or one, shall not *lay* up many *lays* here below, where moth and rust do corrupt.
>
> "Why, blast your eyes, Bildad," cried Peleg, "thou dost not want to swindle this young man! He must have more than that."
>
> "Seven hundred and seventy-seven," again said Bildad, without lifting his eyes; and then went on mumbling — "for where your treasure is, there will your heart be also."
>
> "Thou, Bildad!" roared Peleg, starting up and clattering about the cabin. "Blast ye, Captain Bildad, if I had followed thy advice in these matters, I would afore now had a conscience to lug about that would be heavy enough to founder the largest ship that ever sailed round Cape Horn."[17]

In summary, missionary affluence is the human culture in which three profoundly theological/ethical problems most naturally thrive: (1) preoccupation with possessions, (2) preferred reliance upon power-based statuses and strategies, and (3) ethical double standards. As will become more apparent in the rest of this chapter, a large proportion of the Christian revelation revolves around the proposition that "a man's life does not consist in the abundance of his possessions," and that one of the hardest-to-achieve but most essential spiritual victories is against the notion that it does.

What follows is an attempt to outline biblical teaching on wealth and poverty. At one level, no missionary can be unfamiliar with this important strand of revelation. Yet this teaching has been virtually neglected in those institutions, agencies, and churches most actively involved in the preparation and commissioning of missionaries. Not only are missionaries accountable for this teaching, but as teachers, they will "be judged more strictly" (James 3:1). Like any other Christian, so missionaries must give careful attention to the ways in which they *explain* biblical teaching on wealth, poverty, and the God-ordained patterns of reciprocity that are to mark the relationships between rich and poor; furthermore,

---

16. A "lay" was a portion of the catch of profits from a whaling expedition. Typically, the cabin boy could fairly expect a lay of at least one five-hundredth.

17. Herman Melville, *Moby Dick or The White Whale* (New York: Dodd, Mead and Company, 1922), 70–71.

they must either *apply and model* this teaching in their personal lives, or at least be prepared to explain whey they do not.

An Outline of Biblical Teaching on Wealth and Poverty[18]

Biblical teaching on wealth, poverty, and related issues is abundant and — from the standpoint of the privileged at least — painfully clear. When Jim Wallis was a fellow seminarian at Trinity Evangelical Divinity School in the early 1970s, he and several of his "radical" friends read through the Bible to see what and how much it had to say about the poor. They discovered that next to idolatry, it was the most recurring theme. Furthermore, the two themes were often related. By their estimate, one out of every sixteen verses in the New Testament had something to do with wealth and poverty, a ratio that is an even more striking one to ten in the first three Gospels, and one to seven in the Gospel of Luke. One of his friends took a pair of scissors and went through the Bible, from Genesis to Revelation, snipping out all references to wealth and poverty, the rich and the poor. In Wallis's own words, "It took him a long time. By the time he was finished the Prophets were decimated, the Psalms were destroyed, the Gospels were ripped to shreds and the Epistles turned to tattered rags. The Bible was full of holes."[19]

When within a given social context we are rich, it follows that what the Bible says *to* and *about* the rich, it says *to* and *about* us. Missionaries are not an exception to this rule. While gross material inequity in close social proximity poses profound relational, communicatory, and strategic challenges for missionaries, as argued above, more fundamental are the complex questions of ethical integrity that challenge any wealthy follower of Jesus moving in contexts of profound poverty. Among those who make their living by speaking *for* God and *about* God, Christian missionaries — perhaps more than any other professional religious group — are acutely aware of the need for consistency between what they say they believe and how they actually live.

In both the Old Testament and the New, there is a modest stream of teaching that is of some consolation to those who, by whatever means, find themselves in the happy state of relative comfort and affluence: the sanctity of private property, the association of wealth with happiness, prosperity as a reward for righteousness, and the sometimes close link between personal behavior and poverty. A judiciously selective reading of these texts might even allow for a measure of modest self-congratulation, while affording opportunity to give thanks to God, the true source of our personal good fortune.

But any soothing theological reverie into which the materially blessed might blissfully retreat is more than counteracted by the less flattering and painfully

---

18. I have deliberately organized the material in outline form to facilitate its use for personal or group study. For the most part, aside from actually classifying and citing the references, my comments are kept to a minimum. All scriptural quotations are from the New International Version of the Bible. Readers are advised to study the essays by Christopher Wright, "The Righteous Rich in the Old Testament," and by Justo González, "New Testament *Koinonía* and Wealth" and "Wealth in the Subapostolic Church" (chaps. 8–10 of this volume).

19. Jim Wallis, "A Bible Full of Holes," *The Mennonite* (November 21, 2000): 6.

didactic portrayal of the rich that permeates the Bible from start to finish. This teaching, woven into the warp and woof of God's directives about what is good and appropriate for his people, is calculated to make those of us who are rich much less sanguine about our good fortune. For they make it abundantly clear that it will not be enough to simply sit back and "praise God from whom all blessings flow," but to biblically reassess both ourselves and the self-flattering national myths and self-serving ideologies that define Westerners and our culturally diluted Christianity.

I recall a story related by a missionary-linguist from my denomination (Evangelical Mennonite Church) who, with his wife and children, lived and worked for several decades among the Siamoo in Burkina Faso. As one of eight children born to the village cobbler in a small Mennonite community in southern Manitoba, he recalled the shame of having to go to school in hand-me-down clothes and shoes, with a simple lunch of lard and bread sandwiches. A naturally shy boy, among his better memories was the thrill of hearing his minister expound on biblical texts that stressed God's concern for the poor, and the frightful judgment in store for the rich.

He and his family settled in the largest village of Siamoo-speaking people — a community of some eight hundred persons. The most powerful man was the chief, whose prestige was marked by his possession of an old bicycle — in a state of fatal disrepair — parked conspicuously by the entrance to the chief's compound. As the missionary began the work of Bible translation, the passages from which he had derived consolation as a poor boy now made him uncomfortable; the tables had been turned. Exposed by the glare of God's word as a rich man in his African context, the status he now occupied left him and his family embarrassingly exposed, raising deep questions about their integrity. The material in this chapter will show why.

From a didactic, literary, or historical point of view, the Bible is a somewhat awkward, sprawling book, evincing the unvarnished marks of diverse authors with markedly different personalities, intellectual aptitudes, and literary styles, writing and speaking in different languages across a several-millennia range of cultural, social, and political contexts. Accordingly, any attempt to organize material topically is a necessarily arbitrary and somewhat unsatisfactory exercise. Nevertheless, it is instructive to observe the revelatory attention and significance assigned to issues of wealth and poverty, and to relationships between rich and poor, powerful and weak, across the gamut of several thousand years of biblical revelation.

My handling of the biblical text is straightforward and nontechnical. I am not unaware of the strand of biblical teaching that treats wealth as a sign of divine blessing — especially in Deuteronomy — and touch on that below. The earliest Christian missionaries were often supported by wealthy patrons (e.g., the women who followed Jesus [Luke 8:1–31]; Gaius, whose hospitality extended to Paul and the whole Corinthian church [Rom. 16:23]; etc.). The socioeconomic milieu in which the early church existed was inevitably reflected in the sociology of the church itself. Some have gone so far as to suggest that Paul's missionary strategy produced churches whose membership comprised predominantly urban, middle-class, even wealthy, converts.[20] I have no quarrel with this, but would argue that the relationship of wealthy converts to their wealth was [ideally] necessarily transformed. Theirs was a wealth sanctified — to God rather than to self. In chapter 7 I attempt to explain what this might mean, in practical terms, for the North American missionary.

In working through the ensuing synthesis of biblical teaching, it is important that the reader keep in mind the several points established earlier in the book: (1) The West is rich; (2) the church in the West is rich; (3) missionaries sent by the Western church are rich; (4) most of the peoples among whom Western missionaries live and work are poor; (5) what the Bible says about the rich and the poor has a direct bearing on the Western church generally, and on Western missionaries specifically. My approach has been, whenever possible, to cite select representative biblical passages in full, providing supporting corresponding text references in the footnotes.

Old Testament Teaching That the Wealthy Find Reassuring

1. Private property is not wrong. The Bible's encouragement of generosity and its prohibition of theft assume the sanctity of personal ownership. Injunctions against stealing and covetousness, on the one hand, and provision for the protection of one's possessions, on the other, make sense only if ownership is presumed.

You shall not steal. (Exod. 20:15; cf. Deut. 5:19)

You shall not covet your neighbor's house. You shall not covet your neighbor's wife, or his manservant or maidservant, his ox or donkey, or anything that belongs to your neighbor. (Exod. 20:17; cf. Deut. 5:21)

[1]If a man steals an ox or a sheep and slaughters it or sells it, he must pay back five head of cattle for the ox and four sheep for the sheep. [2]If a thief is caught breaking in and is struck so that he dies, the defender is not guilty of bloodshed; [3]but if it happens after sunrise, he is guilty of bloodshed. A thief must certainly make restitution, but if he has nothing, he must be sold to pay for his theft. [4]If the stolen animal is found alive in his possession — whether ox or donkey or sheep — he must pay back double. [5]If a man grazes his livestock in a field or vineyard and lets them stray and they graze in another man's field, he must make restitution from the best of his own field or vineyard. [6]If a fire breaks out and spreads into thornbushes so that it burns shocks of grain or standing grain or the whole field, the one who started the fire must make restitution. [7]If a man gives his neighbor silver or goods for safekeeping and they are stolen from the

---

20. Among the many worthy participants in the ongoing discussion, Frederick Norris, Robert H. Smith, George Buchanan, Wolfgang Stegemann, and Claus Westermann are particularly helpful.

neighbor's house, the thief, if he is caught, must pay back double. [8]But if the thief is not found, the owner of the house must appear before the judges to determine whether he has laid his hands on the other man's property. [9]In all cases of illegal possession of an ox, a donkey, a sheep, a garment, or any other lost property about which somebody says, 'This is mine,' both parties are to bring their cases before the judges. The one whom the judges declare guilty must pay back double to his neighbor. [10]If a man gives a donkey, an ox, a sheep or any other animal to his neighbor for safekeeping and it dies or is injured or is taken away while no one is looking, [11]the issue between them will be settled by the taking of an oath before the LORD that the neighbor did not lay hands on the other person's property. The owner is to accept this, and no restitution is required. [12]But if the animal was stolen from the neighbor, he must make restitution to the owner. [13]If it was torn to pieces by a wild animal, he shall bring in the remains as evidence and he will not be required to pay for the torn animal. [14]If a man borrows an animal from his neighbor and it is injured or dies while the owner is not present, he must make restitution. [15]But if the owner is with the animal, the borrower will not have to pay. If the animal was hired, the money paid for the hire covers the loss. (Exod. 22:1–15)

2. Wealth can bring happiness. Although personal or systemic envy may incline to the comforting notion that the wealthy are miserable, in fact they are often supremely happy, secure in the present and unworried about the future.

[19]Moreover, when God gives any man wealth and possessions, and enables him to enjoy them, to accept his lot and be happy in his work — this is a gift of God. [20]He seldom reflects on the days of his life, because God keeps him occupied with gladness of heart. (Eccles. 5:19–20)

3. The righteous prosper. While it is true that some fail to prosper precisely because of their righteousness, there is a current of commonsense teaching in the Old Testament that promises tangible rewards to right-living people.

[1]Blessed are all who fear the LORD, who walk in his ways. [2]You will eat the fruit of your labor; blessings and prosperity will be yours. [3]Your wife will be like a fruitful vine within your house; your sons will be like olive shoots around your table. [4]Thus is the man blessed who fears the LORD. [5]May the LORD bless you from Zion all the days of your life; may you see the prosperity of Jerusalem, [6]and may you live to see your children's children. Peace be upon Israel. (Ps. 128:1–6)

[9]Honor the LORD with your wealth, with the firstfruits of all your crops; [10]then your barns will be filled to overflowing, and your vats will brim over with new wine. (Prov. 3:9–10)[21]

---

21. See also Prov. 10:22; 11:24–28; 22:9; 28:22, 27.

4. The poor are sometimes to blame for their own poverty.

6Go to the ant, you sluggard; consider its ways and be wise! **7**It has no commander, no overseer or ruler, **8**yet it stores its provisions in summer and gathers its food at harvest.

9How long will you lie there, you sluggard? When will you get up from your sleep?

10A little sleep, a little slumber, a little folding of the hands to rest — **11**and poverty will come on you like a bandit and scarcity like an armed man. (Prov. 6:6–11)[22]

5. Poverty and the impoverished must not be romanticized. There are obvious advantages to wealth over poverty. Descriptions of famine in 2 Kings 6–7 and Jeremiah 52 make it clear that extreme poverty is something to be avoided.

20The poor are shunned even by their neighbors, but the rich have many friends. (Prov. 14:20)[23]

9Those killed by the sword are better off than those who die of famine; racked with hunger, they waste away for lack of food from the field. **10**With their own hands compassionate women have cooked their own children, who became their food when my people were destroyed. (Lam. 4:9–10)

It should be noted that those parts of the Bible that the rich find most reassuring were, for the most part, written by wealthy royalty, the most famous of whom was Solomon, a man whose wealth boggled the imagination of his day:

13The weight of the gold that Solomon received yearly was 666 talents, **14**not including the revenues brought in by merchants and traders. Also all the kings of Arabia and the governors of the land brought gold and silver to Solomon. **15**King Solomon made two hundred large shields of hammered gold; six hundred bekas of hammered gold went into each shield. **16**He also made three hundred small shields of hammered gold, with three hundred bekas of gold in each shield. The king put them in the Palace of the Forest of Lebanon.

17Then the king made a great throne inlaid with ivory and overlaid with pure gold. **18**The throne had six steps, and a footstool of gold was attached to it. On both sides of the seat were armrests, with a lion standing beside each of them. **19**Twelve lions stood on the six steps, one at either end of each step. Nothing like it had ever been made for any other kingdom. **20**All King Solomon's goblets were gold, and all the household articles in the Palace of the Forest of Lebanon were pure gold. Nothing was made of silver, because silver was considered of little value in Solomon's day. **21**The king had a

---

22. See also Prov. 10:4; 13:4, 11; 20:4, 13; 1:5, 6; 28:19–20.
23. See also Prov. 13:23; 22:7; 19:4, 7; Eccles. 4:1–2; Isa. 32:7; 41:17.

fleet of trading ships manned by Hiram's men. Once every three years it returned, carrying gold, silver and ivory, and apes and baboons.

22King Solomon was greater in riches and wisdom than all the other kings of the earth. 23All the kings of the earth sought audience with Solomon to hear the wisdom God had put in his heart. 24Year after year, everyone who came brought a gift — articles of silver and gold, and robes, weapons and spices, and horses and mules.

25Solomon had four thousand stalls for horses and chariots, and twelve thousand horses, which he kept in the chariot cities and also with him in Jerusalem. 26He ruled over all the kings from the River to the land of the Philistines, as far as the border of Egypt. 27The king made silver as common in Jerusalem as stones, and cedar as plentiful as sycamore-fig trees in the foothills. 28Solomon's horses were imported from Egypt and from all other countries. (2 Chron. 9:13–28)

Solomon's personal fortune was vast and ostentatiously displayed. But more significantly, it represented a brazen disregard for the divine regulations which were to have governed the kings of God's people.

14When you enter the land the LORD your God is giving you and have taken possession of it and settled in it, and you say, "Let us set a king over us like all the nations around us," 15be sure to appoint over you the king the LORD your God chooses. He must be from among your own brothers. Do not place a foreigner over you, one who is not a brother Israelite. 16The king, moreover, must not acquire great numbers of horses for himself or make the people return to Egypt to get more of them, for the LORD has told you, "You are not to go back that way again." 17He must not take many wives, or his heart will be led astray. He must not accumulate large amounts of silver and gold.

18When he takes the throne of his kingdom, he is to write for himself on a scroll a copy of this law, taken from that of the priests, who are Levites. 19It is to be with him, and he is to read it all the days of his life so that he may learn to revere the LORD his God and follow carefully all the words of this law and these decrees 20and not consider himself better than his brothers and turn from the law to the right or to the left. Then he and his descendants will reign a long time over his kingdom in Israel. (Deut. 17:14–20)

Solomon began well, but his growing self-absorption would eventually tyrannize and virtually enslave his own people. Rehoboam's foolish decision to continue his father's disastrously oppressive policies permanently divided and would eventually destroy the kingdom.

1Rehoboam went to Shechem, for all the Israelites had gone there to make him king. 2When Jeroboam son of Nebat heard this (he was in Egypt, where he had fled from King Solomon), he returned from Egypt. 3So they sent for Jeroboam, and he and all Israel went to Rehoboam and said to him:

4"Your father put a heavy yoke on us, but now lighten the harsh labor and the heavy yoke he put on us, and we will serve you."

5Rehoboam answered, "Come back to me in three days." So the people went away. 6Then King Rehoboam consulted the elders who had served his father Solomon during his lifetime. "How would you advise me to answer these people?" he asked. 7They replied, "If you will be kind to these people and please them and give them a favorable answer, they will always be your servants."

8But Rehoboam rejected the advice the elders gave him and consulted the young men who had grown up with him and were serving him. 9He asked them, "What is your advice? How should we answer these people who say to me, 'Lighten the yoke your father put on us'?" 10The young men who had grown up with him replied, "Tell the people who have said to you, 'Your father put a heavy yoke on us, but make our yoke lighter' — tell them, 'My little finger is thicker than my father's waist. 11My father laid on you a heavy yoke; I will make it even heavier. My father scourged you with whips; I will scourge you with scorpions.'"

12Three days later Jeroboam and all the people returned to Rehoboam, as the king had said, "Come back to me in three days." 13The king answered them harshly. Rejecting the advice of the elders, 14he followed the advice of the young men and said, "My father made your yoke heavy; I will make it even heavier. My father scourged you with whips; I will scourge you with scorpions." 15So the king did not listen to the people, for this turn of events was from God, to fulfill the word the LORD had spoken to Jeroboam son of Nebat through Ahijah the Shilonite.

16When all Israel saw that the king refused to listen to them, they answered the king: "What share do we have in David, what part in Jesse's son? To your tents, O Israel! Look after your own house, O David!"

So all the Israelites went home. 17But as for the Israelites who were living in the towns of Judah, Rehoboam still ruled over them. 18King Rehoboam sent out Adoniram, who was in charge of forced labor, but the Israelites stoned him to death. King Rehoboam, however, managed to get into his chariot and escape to Jerusalem. 19So Israel has been in rebellion against the house of David to this day. (2 Chron. 10:1–19)

Solomon ignored Mosaic teaching concerning wealth, and contradicted most of his own advice. "Better a little with righteousness than much gain with injustice," he had sagely observed (Prov. 16:8), even though his name became a byword for oppression. The collapse of his kingdom shortly after he died proved the veracity of his famous adages, "The Lord tears down the proud man's house. . . . [and] A greedy man brings trouble to his family" (Prov. 15:25, 27). As a religiously informed rich man who didn't practice what he preached, Solomon is one of the most sobering examples in Scripture.

New Testament Teaching That the Wealthy Find Reassuring

In the New Testament there is a corresponding strand of teaching that can somewhat ameliorate the conscience pangs of a rich person living in contexts of poverty.

1. Private property is legitimate. As in the Old Testament, so in the New, a strong case for private property can be adduced. The followers of Jesus were encouraged to loan freely to the poor — an action that presupposes ownership — although the terms that he prescribes are not necessarily conducive to personal wealth creation.

> [34]And if you lend to those from whom you expect repayment, what credit is that to you? Even "sinners" lend to "sinners," expecting to be repaid in full. [35]But love your enemies, do good to them, and lend to them without expecting to get anything back. Then your reward will be great, and you will be sons of the Most High, because he is kind to the ungrateful and wicked. (Matt. 5:42; cf. Luke 6:34–35)

Similarly, Jesus urges his followers to give to the poor. Since giving away what belongs to someone else is theft, the legitimacy of property ownership can be presumed.

> [2]"So when you give to the needy, do not announce it with trumpets, as the hypocrites do in the synagogues and on the streets, to be honored by men. I tell you the truth, they have received their reward in full. [3]But when you give to the needy, do not let your left hand know what your right hand is doing, [4]so that your giving may be in secret. Then your Father, who sees what is done in secret, will reward you. (Matt. 6:2–4; cf. Luke 6:30)

Simon owned a house in which his friend Jesus was a frequent guest; there is no record that Jesus disapproved of private ownership of a house.

> [29]As soon as they left the synagogue, they went with James and John to the home of Simon and Andrew. (Mark 1:29)

> [38]Jesus left the synagogue and went to the home of Simon. Now Simon's mother-in-law was suffering from a high fever, and they asked Jesus to help her. (Luke 4:38)

The legitimacy of private property is also implied in numerous parables — for example, in Jesus' parable of the talents (Matt. 25:14–30), the unjust steward (Luke 16:1–8), and the pounds (Luke 19:12–27) — all of which feature the use of money without any suggestion that it is intrinsically evil.

In those instances where Jesus challenges people such as the *rich young ruler* to part with personal wealth, he is not denying the right of his followers to own property per se. On the contrary, he challenges these aspiring disciples to forego this right for his sake — presenting them with a moral choice, rather than establishing a biblical principle (Matt. 19:21; Luke 12:33; 14:33; 18:22).

2. Jesus' followers included some who were wealthy. The *Magi,* for instance, were among the earliest to acknowledge and worship Jesus as the Christ (Matt. 2:1–12); *Nicodemus,* a member of the Jewish ruling council, was a person of some means (John 3:1; 19:39); and *Joseph of Arimathea* was the rich disciple who made arrangements to bury Jesus in his own new tomb (Matt. 27:57–60).

3. Jesus' parables sometimes featured astute businessmen who are commended for their profitable investments. Best known among these is the famous parable of the talents, in which the two investors willing to take risks in order to increase their master's wealth are commended and rewarded, while their hapless colleague is condemned and punished for his fiscal conservatism:

> [14]"Again, it will be like a man going on a journey, who called his servants and entrusted his property to them. [15]To one he gave five talents of money, to another two talents, and to another one talent, each according to his ability. Then he went on his journey. [16]The man who had received the five talents went at once and put his money to work and gained five more. [17]So also, the one with the two talents gained two more. [18]But the man who had received the one talent went off, dug a hole in the ground and hid his master's money.
>
> [19]"After a long time the master of those servants returned and settled accounts with them. [20]The man who had received the five talents brought the other five. 'Master,' he said, 'you entrusted me with five talents. See, I have gained five more.'
>
> [21]"His master replied, 'Well done, good and faithful servant! You have been faithful with a few things; I will put you in charge of many things. Come and share your master's happiness!'
>
> [22]"The man with the two talents also came. 'Master,' he said, 'you entrusted me with two talents; see, I have gained two more.'
>
> [23]"His master replied, 'Well done, good and faithful servant! You have been faithful with a few things; I will put you in charge of many things. Come and share your master's happiness!'
>
> [24]"Then the man who had received the one talent came. 'Master,' he said, 'I knew that you are a hard man, harvesting where you have not sown and gathering where you have not scattered seed. [25]So I was afraid and went out and hid your talent in the ground. See, here is what belongs to you.'
>
> [26]"His master replied, 'You wicked, lazy servant! So you knew that I harvest where I have not sown and gather where I have not scattered seed? [27]Well then, you should have put my money on deposit with the bankers, so that when I returned I would have received it back with interest.
>
> [28]" 'Take the talent from him and give it to the one who has the ten talents. [29]For everyone who has will be given more, and he will have an abundance. Whoever does not have, even what he has will be taken from him. [30]And throw that worthless servant outside, into the darkness, where

there will be weeping and gnashing of teeth.' " (Matt. 25:14–30; cf. Luke 19:12–27)

We now turn to the much broader, deeper, and more treacherously swirling channel of biblical teaching that every Christian must negotiate. These texts, which lie at the heart of this book, make very uncomfortable reading for the rich, particularly those who live and work as missionaries often do among those who are poor ... whose material resources constitute only a tiny fraction of the missionary's, and whose economic prospects are negligible.

Old Testament Teaching That the Wealthy Find Troubling

1. Material possessions and their concomitant comfort and security are not to be a primary goal of life. The great purpose of life — contrary to the false notions that are bred into the bone and tissue of North American consumers — is not to move from birth to death as comfortably as possible. In the words of Jesus, **A person's life does *not* consist in the abundance of possessions.**[24]

> [3]He humbled you, causing you to hunger and then feeding you with manna, which neither you nor your fathers had known, to teach you that man does not live on bread alone but on every word that comes from the mouth of the LORD. [4]Your clothes did not wear out and your feet did not swell during these forty years. [5]Know then in your heart that as a man disciplines his son, so the LORD your God disciplines you. (Deut. 8:3–5)

> [10]I denied myself nothing my eyes desired; I refused my heart no pleasure.
>   My heart took delight in all my work, and this was the reward for all my labor.
> [11]Yet when I surveyed all that my hands had done and what I had toiled to achieve,
>   everything was meaningless, a chasing after the wind; nothing was gained under the sun. (Eccles. 2:10–11; cf. 4:13)

> > [23]This is what the LORD says:
> >   "Let not the wise man boast of his wisdom
> >   or the strong man boast of his strength
> >   or the rich man boast of his riches,
> > [24]but let him who boasts boast about this:
> >   that he understands and knows me,
> >   that I am the LORD, who exercises kindness,
> >   justice and righteousness on earth,
> > for in these I delight,"
> >
> >   declares the LORD.
> >   (Jer. 9:23–24)

---

24. In addition to the texts cited, see also Job 1:21; Ps. 37:16; 39:5–11; 49:12–13, 16–20; 68:5–6, 10; Prov. 11:4; 15:16–17; 16:8, 16, 19; 17:1; 22:1; 23:45; 28:3, 6.

2. For the people of God, the rights associated with personal property and possessions are not absolute because:

a. God is Lord of all creation and all creatures (Gen. 1–3). God's followers are frequently and necessarily reminded of this fact and its attendant implications. "The foundations of the earth are the Lord's," humbly grateful Hannah acknowledged in her moving dedication of Samuel, her firstborn son (1 Sam. 2:8b). As Moses descended with the tablets the second time, he reminded the chastened Israelites that obedience was the only sensible response to the One who had "set his affection on [their] forefathers and loved them," for "To the Lord your God belong the heavens . . . the earth and everything in it" (Deut. 10:14–15).[25] As creator and Lord of all things, God has established the ground rules that most fairly govern the acquiring and use of property and possessions by his people, rich and poor alike.

b. For the people of God, any rights associated with the acquiring, the use, or the disposal of personal wealth are in principle subordinated to an obligation to care for poorer, weaker members of society. That this was a primary concern in the Old Testament is evident in the regulations that were to govern the community life of God's people.

(i) The Year of Jubilee. The Jubilee year seems to have been designed to have a leveling effect. Its practice meant that whatever economic advantage, momentum, or mass which might for any reason — luck, good management or mismanagement, ability or lack of ability — have been gained by one person over another could not be legitimately sustained indefinitely. Jubilee was a time of fresh beginnings for the land and for the personal economic prospects of the unfortunate. It made the endless accumulation of properties impossible, as the Leviticus text below shows.

> [8]" 'Count off seven sabbaths of years — seven times seven years — so that the seven sabbaths of years amount to a period of forty-nine years. [9]Then have the trumpet sounded everywhere on the tenth day of the seventh month; on the Day of Atonement sound the trumpet throughout your land. [10]Consecrate the fiftieth year and proclaim liberty throughout the land to all its inhabitants. It shall be a jubilee for you; each one of you is to return to his family property and each to his own clan. [11]The fiftieth year shall be a jubilee for you; do not sow and do not reap what grows of itself or harvest the untended vines. [12]For it is a jubilee and is to be holy for you; eat only what is taken directly from the fields.
>
> [13]" 'In this Year of Jubilee everyone is to return to his own property.
>
> [14]" 'If you sell land to one of your countrymen or buy any from him, do not take advantage of each other. [15]You are to buy from your countryman on the basis of the number of years since the Jubilee. And he is to sell to you on the basis of the number of years left for harvesting crops. [16]When the years are many, you are to increase the price, and when the years are

---

25. See also Deut. 10:1–22; 1 Chron. 29:14–19; Job 41:11; Ps. 24:1–2; Prov. 22:2.

few, you are to decrease the price, because what he is really selling you is the number of crops. ¹⁷Do not take advantage of each other, but fear your God. I am the LORD your God.

¹⁸" 'Follow my decrees and be careful to obey my laws, and you will live safely in the land. ¹⁹Then the land will yield its fruit, and you will eat your fill and live there in safety. ²⁰You may ask, "What will we eat in the seventh year if we do not plant or harvest our crops?" ²¹I will send you such a blessing in the sixth year that the land will yield enough for three years. ²²While you plant during the eighth year, you will eat from the old crop and will continue to eat from it until the harvest of the ninth year comes in.

²³" 'The land must not be sold permanently, because the land is mine and you are but aliens and my tenants. ²⁴Throughout the country that you hold as a possession, you must provide for the redemption of the land.

²⁵" 'If one of your countrymen becomes poor and sells some of his property, his nearest relative is to come and redeem what his countryman has sold. ²⁶If, however, a man has no one to redeem it for him but he himself prospers and acquires sufficient means to redeem it, ²⁷he is to determine the value for the years since he sold it and refund the balance to the man to whom he sold it; he can then go back to his own property. ²⁸But if he does not acquire the means to repay him, what he sold will remain in the possession of the buyer until the Year of Jubilee. It will be returned in the Jubilee, and he can then go back to his property.

²⁹" 'If a man sells a house in a walled city, he retains the right of redemption a full year after its sale. During that time he may redeem it. ³⁰If it is not redeemed before a full year has passed, the house in the walled city shall belong permanently to the buyer and his descendants. It is not to be returned in the Jubilee. ³¹But houses in villages without walls around them are to be considered as open country. They can be redeemed, and they are to be returned in the Jubilee.

³²" 'The Levites always have the right to redeem their houses in the Levitical towns, which they possess. ³³So the property of the Levites is redeemable — that is, a house sold in any town they hold — and is to be returned in the Jubilee, because the houses in the towns of the Levites are their property among the Israelites. ³⁴But the pastureland belonging to their towns must not be sold; it is their permanent possession.

³⁵" 'If one of your countrymen becomes poor and is unable to support himself among you, help him as you would an alien or a temporary resident, so he can continue to live among you. ³⁶Do not take interest of any kind from him, but fear your God, so that your countryman may continue to live among you. ³⁷You must not lend him money at interest or sell him food at a profit. ³⁸I am the LORD your God, who brought you out of Egypt to give you the land of Canaan and to be your God.

³⁹" 'If one of your countrymen becomes poor among you and sells himself to you, do not make him work as a slave. ⁴⁰He is to be treated as a hired worker or a temporary resident among you; he is to work for you until the

Year of Jubilee. [41]Then he and his children are to be released, and he will
go back to his own clan and to the property of his forefathers. [42]Because
the Israelites are my servants, whom I brought out of Egypt, they must not
be sold as slaves. [43]Do not rule over them ruthlessly, but fear your God.' "
(Lev. 25:8–43)

(ii) **The Sabbatical Year.** The sabbatical was intended for the well-being of
the poor, the wild animals, and the land itself. Debts were to be canceled, to give
the unfortunate poor recurring opportunity for a fresh beginning.

[1]At the end of every seven years you must cancel debts. [2]This is how it is
to be done: Every creditor shall cancel the loan he has made to his fellow
Israelite. He shall not require payment from his fellow Israelite or brother,
because the LORD's time for canceling debts has been proclaimed. [3]You
may require payment from a foreigner, but you must cancel any debt your
brother owes you. [4]However, there should be no poor among you, for in
the land the LORD your God is giving you to possess as your inheritance,
he will richly bless you, [5]if only you fully obey the LORD your God and
are careful to follow all these commands I am giving you today. [6]For the
LORD your God will bless you as he has promised, and you will lend to
many nations but will borrow from none. You will rule over many nations
but none will rule over you.

[7]If there is a poor man among your brothers in any of the towns of
the land that the LORD your God is giving you, do not be hardhearted
or tightfisted toward your poor brother. [8]Rather be openhanded and freely
lend him whatever he needs. [9]Be careful not to harbor this wicked thought:
"The seventh year, the year for canceling debts, is near," so that you do not
show ill will toward your needy brother and give him nothing. He may then
appeal to the LORD against you, and you will be found guilty of sin. [10]Give
generously to him and do so without a grudging heart; then because of this
the LORD your God will bless you in all your work and in everything you
put your hand to. [11]There will always be poor people in the land. Therefore
I command you to be openhanded toward your brothers and toward the
poor and needy in your land. (Deut. 15:1–11)[26]

A reading of the prophets makes one quickly aware that the rich, then as now,
quickly discovered ingenious ways to annul or at least circumvent any provision
that impinged upon their presumed entitlements. This is not surprising, given
that its literal application would have made it difficult for anyone wishing to
lever temporary economic advantage into permanent, cross-generational family
or clan privilege, whatever the cost to the poor. Interestingly, chronic failure to
implement these sabbatical provisions resulted in the demise and exile of an entire
nation. This, at least, seems to have been the understanding of the chronicler as
he recounts the sad details of the fall of Jerusalem:

---

26. See also Exod. 23:10–11; Lev. 25:1–7.

¹⁵The Lord, the God of their fathers, sent word to them through his messengers again and again, because he had pity on his people and on his dwelling place. ¹⁶But they mocked God's messengers, despised his words and scoffed at his prophets until the wrath of the Lord was aroused against his people and there was no remedy. ¹⁷He brought up against them the king of the Babylonians, who killed their young men with the sword in the sanctuary, and spared neither young man nor young woman, old man or aged. God handed all of them over to Nebuchadnezzar. ¹⁸He carried to Babylon all the articles from the temple of God, both large and small, and the treasures of the Lord's temple and the treasures of the king and his officials.

¹⁹They set fire to God's temple and broke down the wall of Jerusalem; they burned all the palaces and destroyed everything of value there.

²⁰He carried into exile to Babylon the remnant, who escaped from the sword, and they became servants to him and his sons until the kingdom of Persia came to power. ²¹The land enjoyed its Sabbath rests; all the time of its desolation it rested, until the seventy years were completed in fulfillment of the word of the Lord spoken by Jeremiah. (2 Chron. 36:15–21)

(iii) **Tithing.** The tithe that was gathered every three years was to be centrally stored for the use of aliens, fatherless, widows, and Levites. In effect, giving to God and giving to the poor were inseparable. It is a worthwhile exercise to compare Old Testament guidelines for the allocation of tithes to those pertaining in North American churches.

¹When you have entered the land the Lord your God is giving you as an inheritance and have taken possession of it and settled in it, ²take some of the firstfruits of all that you produce from the soil of the land the Lord your God is giving you and put them in a basket. Then go to the place the Lord your God will choose as a dwelling for his Name ³and say to the priest in office at the time, "I declare today to the Lord your God that I have come to the land the Lord swore to our forefathers to give us." ⁴The priest shall take the basket from your hands and set it down in front of the altar of the Lord your God.

⁵Then you shall declare before the Lord your God: "My father was a wandering Aramean, and he went down into Egypt with a few people and lived there and became a great nation, powerful and numerous. ⁶But the Egyptians mistreated us and made us suffer, putting us to hard labor. ⁷Then we cried out to the Lord, the God of our fathers, and the Lord heard our voice and saw our misery, toil and oppression. ⁸So the Lord brought us out of Egypt with a mighty hand and an outstretched arm, with great terror and with miraculous signs and wonders. ⁹He brought us to this place and gave us this land, a land flowing with milk and honey; ¹⁰and now I bring the firstfruits of the soil that you, O Lord, have given me." Place the basket before the Lord your God and bow down before him. ¹¹And you and the Levites and the aliens among you shall rejoice in all the good things the Lord your God has given to you and your household.

[12]When you have finished setting aside a tenth of all your produce in the third year, the year of the tithe, you shall give it to the Levite, the alien, the fatherless and the widow, so that they may eat in your towns and be satisfied. [13]Then say to the LORD your God: "I have removed from my house the sacred portion and have given it to the Levite, the alien, the fatherless and the widow, according to all you commanded. I have not turned aside from your commands nor have I forgotten any of them. [14]I have not eaten any of the sacred portion while I was in mourning, nor have I removed any of it while I was unclean, nor have I offered any of it to the dead. I have obeyed the LORD my God; I have done everything you commanded me. [15]Look down from heaven, your holy dwelling place, and bless your people Israel and the land you have given us as you promised on oath to our forefathers, a land flowing with milk and honey." (Deut. 26:1–15)[27]

(iv) Loans, Interest, and Collateral. Any benefits accruing from the lending of money were strictly curtailed for the people of God. Interest could not be charged on money loaned to the needy fellow Israelite. Even the rules governing loan collateral were deliberately designed to protect the borrower, rather than benefit the lender.

[25]If you lend money to one of my people among you who is needy, do not be like a moneylender; charge him no interest. [26]If you take your neighbor's cloak as a pledge, return it to him by sunset, [27]because his cloak is the only covering he has for his body. What else will he sleep in? When he cries out to me, I will hear, for I am compassionate. (Exod. 22:25–27)

[6]Do not take a pair of millstones — not even the upper one — as security for a debt, because that would be taking a man's livelihood as security. . . .

[10]When you make a loan of any kind to your neighbor, do not go into his house to get what he is offering as a pledge. [11]Stay outside and let the man to whom you are making the loan bring the pledge out to you. [12]If the man is poor, do not go to sleep with his pledge in your possession. [13]Return his cloak to him by sunset so that he may sleep in it. Then he will thank you, and it will be regarded as a righteous act in the sight of the LORD your God. . . .

[17]Do not deprive the alien or the fatherless of justice, or take the cloak of the widow as a pledge.

[18]Remember that you were slaves in Egypt and the LORD your God redeemed you from there. That is why I command you to do this. (Deut. 24:6, 10–13, 17–18)[28]

(v) Gleaning. Harvesting was not to be so efficient as to leave nothing behind for the poor. The story of Ruth and Boaz in the book of Ruth (2:2, 3, 7, 16, 17) provides a moving example of gleaning laws in practice.

---

27. See also Exod. 22:29–30; 23:19; and Deut. 14:22–29.

28. See also Lev. 25:35–38; Deut. 15:1–11 (What we would consider a sound business principle — refusal to lend money to someone who in all likelihood never repay it — God calls a "wicked thought" in v. 9!); and Deut. 23:19–20.

[19]When you are harvesting in your field and you overlook a sheaf, do not go back to get it. Leave it for the alien, the fatherless and the widow, so that the LORD your God may bless you in all the work of your hands. [20]When you beat the olives from your trees, do not go over the branches a second time. Leave what remains for the alien, the fatherless and the widow. (Deut. 24:19–20)[29]

(vi) Repayment of Debts. As already mentioned above (Deut. 15:1–11), debts were to be canceled at the end of every seven-year cycle. "There should be no poor among you," said the Lord (v. 4). Such laws were meant to ensure that among the people of God, neither poverty nor its opposite would ever become a reified, intergenerational phenomenon.

(vii) Treatment of Employees. No employer was to take advantage of the poor employee. He or she was to be paid "each day before sunset."

[14]Do not take advantage of a hired man who is poor and needy, whether he is a brother Israelite or an alien living in one of your towns. [15]Pay him his wages each day before sunset, because he is poor and is counting on it. Otherwise he may cry to the LORD against you, and you will be guilty of sin. (Deut. 24:14–15)[30]

(viii) Strictures on the Wealth of Kings. The wealth that a king could legitimately acquire was to be strictly curtailed. He was not allowed to "accumulate large amounts of silver and gold." Sadly, Solomon's magnificent disregard of this command resulted in the oppression of the poor and in the division of his kingdom. It took him seven years to complete work on the temple, what at the time was a magnificent edifice. But his far more grandiose personal palace dwarfed the temple, and as the chronicler is at pains to show (1 Kings 6–7), took thirteen years to finish.

[14]When you enter the land the LORD your God is giving you and have taken possession of it and settled in it, and you say, "Let us set a king over us like all the nations around us," [15]be sure to appoint over you the king the LORD your God chooses. He must be from among your own brothers. Do not place a foreigner over you, one who is not a brother Israelite. [16]The king, moreover, must not acquire great numbers of horses for himself or make the people return to Egypt to get more of them, for the LORD has told you, "You are not to go back that way again." [17]He must not take many wives, or his heart will be led astray. He must not accumulate large amounts of silver and gold. (Deut. 17:14–17)

[2]The temple that King Solomon built for the LORD was sixty cubits long, twenty wide and thirty high. [3]The portico at the front of the main hall of the temple extended the width of the temple, that is twenty cubits, and projected ten cubits from the front of the temple. [4]He made narrow clerestory

---

29. See also Lev. 19:9–10; 23:22.
30. See also Lev. 25:35–43; Deut. 15:12–18; Prov. 14:31; 19:17.

windows in the temple. ⁵Against the walls of the main hall and inner sanctuary he built a structure around the building, in which there were side
rooms. ⁶The lowest floor was five cubits wide, the middle floor six cubits
and the third floor seven. He made offset ledges around the outside of the
temple so that nothing would be inserted into the temple walls. (1 Kings
6:2–6)

¹It took Solomon thirteen years, however, to complete the construction of
his palace. ²He built the Palace of the Forest of Lebanon a hundred cubits
long, fifty wide and thirty high, with four rows of cedar columns supporting
trimmed cedar beams. ³It was roofed with cedar above the beams that
rested on the columns — forty-five beams, fifteen to a row. ⁴Its windows
were placed high in sets of three, facing each other. ⁵All the doorways
had rectangular frames; they were in the front part in sets of three, facing
each other.
    ⁶He made a colonnade fifty cubits long and thirty wide. In front of it
was a portico, and in front of that were pillars and an overhanging roof.
⁷He built the throne hall, the Hall of Justice, where he was to judge, and
he covered it with cedar from floor to ceiling. ⁸And the palace in which he
was to live, set farther back, was similar in design. Solomon also made a
palace like this hall for Pharaoh's daughter, whom he had married.
    ⁹All these structures, from the outside to the great courtyard and from
foundation to eaves, were made of blocks of high-grade stone cut to size
and trimmed with a saw on their inner and outer faces. ¹⁰The foundations
were laid with large stones of good quality, some measuring ten cubits and
some eight.
    ¹¹Above were high-grade stones, cut to size, and cedar beams. ¹²The
great courtyard was surrounded by a wall of three courses of dressed stone
and one course of trimmed cedar beams, as was the inner courtyard of the
temple of the LORD with its portico. (1 Kings 7:1–12)

¹King Solomon, however, loved many foreign women besides Pharaoh's
daughter — Moabites, Ammonites, Edomites, Sidonians and Hittites. ²They
were from nations about which the LORD had told the Israelites, "You must
not intermarry with them, because they will surely turn your hearts after
their gods." Nevertheless, Solomon held fast to them in love. ³He had seven
hundred wives of royal birth and three hundred concubines, and his wives
led him astray. ⁴As Solomon grew old, his wives turned his heart after other
gods, and his heart was not fully devoted to the LORD his God, as the heart
of David his father had been. ⁵He followed Ashtoreth the goddess of the
Sidonians, and Molech the detestable god of the Ammonites. ⁶So Solomon
did evil in the eyes of the LORD; he did not follow the LORD completely,
as David his father had done. (1 Kings 11:1–6)

If, as is popularly thought, Solomon is the author of Ecclesiastes, it is little
wonder that he should have concluded that everything is meaningless. Having
begun his reign so auspiciously, with the full blessing of God, and with prodigious

intellectual and administrative abilities, a lifetime of disregard for godly practice left him a cynical old man, with his kingdom on the verge of disintegration. A profound sense of regret at a lifetime of squandered opportunities are evident in his words, "Better a poor but wise youth than an old but foolish king who no longer knows how to take a warning" (Eccles. 4:13).

3. Wealth and prosperity are inherently dangerous spiritually. As the story of Solomon demonstrates, and as the King Midas legend reminds us, wealth is dangerous because of its power to dehumanize the wealthy. "Great wealth sears the soul, dries up the wellsprings of the heart, thickens the skin, cauterizes the nerve ends, and dulls the sensibilities to the pains and groans of all — save its own."[31] While the author of this tract may sound somewhat frenzied, his outburst nevertheless touches upon a universally observable fact. But in the Scriptures, the sweeping range of wealth's risks is spelled out with pitiless clarity for those of us who are wealthy and who have ears to hear.

a. Wealth and security make God redundant and unnecessary, and tempt man to conveniently forget, ignore, or even defy God.

[1]Be careful to follow every command I am giving you today, so that you may live and increase and may enter and possess the land that the LORD promised on oath to your forefathers. [2]Remember how the LORD your God led you all the way in the desert these forty years, to humble you and to test you in order to know what was in your heart, whether or not you would keep his commands. [3]He humbled you, causing you to hunger and then feeding you with manna, which neither you nor your fathers had known, to teach you that man does not live on bread alone but on every word that comes from the mouth of the LORD. [4]Your clothes did not wear out and your feet did not swell during these forty years. [5]Know then in your heart that as a man disciplines his son, so the LORD your God disciplines you.

[6]Observe the commands of the LORD your God, walking in his ways and revering him. [7]For the LORD your God is bringing you into a good land — a land with streams and pools of water, with springs flowing in the valleys and hills; [8a]land with wheat and barley, vines and fig trees, pomegranates, olive oil and honey; [9a]land where bread will not be scarce and you will lack nothing; a land where the rocks are iron and you can dig copper out of the hills.

[10]When you have eaten and are satisfied, praise the LORD your God for the good land he has given you.

[11]Be careful that you do not forget the LORD your God, failing to observe his commands, his laws and his decrees that I am giving you this day. [12]Otherwise, when you eat and are satisfied, when you build fine houses and settle down, [13]and when your herds and flocks grow large and your silver and gold increase and all you have is multiplied, [14]then your heart will become proud and you will forget the LORD your God, who brought

---

31. From a 1914 pamphlet quoted by Robert L. Heilbroner in *The Quest for Wealth: A Study of Acquisitive Man* (New York: Simon and Schuster, 1956), 238.

you out of Egypt, out of the land of slavery. [15]He led you through the vast and dreadful desert, that thirsty and waterless land, with its venomous snakes and scorpions. He brought you water out of hard rock. [16]He gave you manna to eat in the desert, something your fathers had never known, to humble and to test you so that in the end it might go well with you. [17]You may say to yourself, "My power and the strength of my hands have produced this wealth for me." [18]But remember the LORD your God, for it is he who gives you the ability to produce wealth, and so confirms his covenant, which he swore to your forefathers, as it is today.

[19]If you ever forget the LORD your God and follow other gods and worship and bow down to them, I testify against you today that you will surely be destroyed. [20]Like the nations the LORD destroyed before you, so you will be destroyed for not obeying the LORD your God. (Deut. 8:1–20)[32]

b. Wealth fosters a false sense of security.

[6]"When I felt secure," I said, "I will never be shaken." (Ps. 30:6)

[11]"The wealth of the rich is their fortified city; they imagine it an unscalable wall.
    [12]"Before his downfall a man's heart is proud, but humility comes before honor." (Prov. 18:11–12)

[10]Israel's watchmen are blind, they all lack knowledge; they are all mute dogs, they cannot bark;
    they lie around and dream, they love to sleep.
[11]They are dogs with mighty appetites; they never have enough.
    They are shepherds who lack understanding; they all turn to their own way, each seeks his own gain.
[12]"Come," each one cries, "let me get wine! Let us drink our fill of beer!
    And tomorrow will be like today, or even far better." (Isa. 56:9–12)[33]

c. Wealth and security often spawn pride in one's imagined personal accomplishments or entitlements. Wealth and security are enemies of humility and meekness.

[23]This is what the LORD says: "Let not the wise man boast of his wisdom or the strong man boast of his strength or the rich man boast of his riches, [24]but let him who boasts boast about this: that he understands and knows me, that I am the LORD, who exercises kindness, justice and righteousness on earth, for in these I delight," declares the LORD. (Jer. 9:23–24)

[4]By your wisdom and understanding you have gained wealth for yourself and amassed gold and silver in your treasuries. [5]By your great skill in trading you have increased your wealth, and because of your wealth your heart has grown proud. (Ezek. 28:4–5)

---

32. See also Deut. 9:4–6; 31:19–20; 32:15; 1 Kings 6–7; 11:1–13; Ps. 119:36–37; Ezek. 28:4–5; 13:31–32; Hos. 13:6.
33. See also Ps. 49:5–6; Prov. 10:15; Prov. 11:28; Jer. 17:11; 49:4–5.

d. The independence, imagined security, and pride that usually accompany wealth result in profound self-delusion and dangerously distorted judgment.

¹¹A rich man may be wise in his own eyes, but a poor man who has discernment sees through him. (Prov. 28:11)

⁸If you see the poor oppressed in a district, and justice and rights denied, do not be surprised at such things; for one official is eyed by a higher one, and over them both are others higher still. ⁹The increase from the land is taken by all; the king himself profits from the fields. ¹⁰Whoever loves money never has money enough; whoever loves wealth is never satisfied with his income. This too is meaningless. ¹¹As goods increase, so do those who consume them. And what benefit are they to the owner except to feast his eyes on them? ¹²The sleep of a laborer is sweet, whether he eats little or much, but the abundance of a rich man permits him no sleep. ¹³I have seen a grievous evil under the sun: wealth hoarded to the harm of its owner, ¹⁴or wealth lost through some misfortune, so that when he has a son there is nothing left for him. ¹⁵Naked a man comes from his mother's womb, and as he comes, so he departs. He takes nothing from his labor that he can carry in his hand. (Eccles. 5:8–15)³⁴

e. Repentance can be distorted or derailed by wealth.

¹²The Lord, the LORD Almighty, called you on that day to weep and to wail, to tear out your hair and put on sackcloth. ¹³But see, there is joy and revelry, slaughtering of cattle and killing of sheep, eating of meat and drinking of wine! "Let us eat and drink," you say, "for tomorrow we die!" (Isa. 22:12–13)

f. The rich are particularly susceptible to certain sins:

(i) Wealth is almost inevitably associated with overindulgence, gluttony, and greed. As noted above (2.viii), Solomon's greed and his blatant lack of self-control set in irreversible motion a set of events that would result in the obliteration of his kingdom. One of the grandest and most famous despots of ancient times, he flouted his own vaunted wisdom, ending his reign as a tragic old hypocrite.³⁵ Insofar as Ecclesiastes is autobiographical, it well conveys a sense of the futility of a possessions-absorbed life.

(ii) The wealthy frequently — in the scriptural record, usually — abuse personal power by their mistreatment of the weak and their contempt for the poor.³⁶

---

34. See also Isa. 30:9–11; Jer. 6:13–15; 8:10–11; Hos. 2:8; 9:7; 12:6–8.
35. See 1 Kings 6–7; 10:14–29; cf. 1 Kings 11:1–6; 12:1–24.
36. This is the record of numerous kings in the scriptural record. See 2 Samuel 11–12 (David and Uriah); 1 Kings 10:14–29, cf. 1 Kings 12:1–24 (Solomon and Rehoboam); 1 Kings 21:1–16 (Ahab and Naboth).

"Men at ease have contempt for misfortune as the fate of those whose feet are slipping." (Job 12:5)

"Do not deny justice to your poor people in their lawsuits." (Exod. 23:6)

" 'Now this was the sin of your sister Sodom: She and her daughters were arrogant, overfed and unconcerned; they did not help the poor and needy." (Ezek. 16:49)

(iii) Mesmerized by wealth and possessions, the priorities and orientations of the rich are often fatally misguided. The prayer of the prophet is apt:

[7]The vineyard of the LORD Almighty is the house of Israel, and the men of Judah are the garden of his delight. And he looked for justice, but saw bloodshed; for righteousness, but heard cries of distress.
     [8]Woe to you who add house to house and join field to field till no space is left and you live alone in the land. [9]The LORD Almighty has declared in my hearing: "Surely the great houses will become desolate, the fine mansions left without occupants. [10]A ten-acre vineyard will produce only a bath of wine, a homer of seed only an ephah of grain."
     [11]Woe to those who rise early in the morning to run after their drinks, who stay up late at night till they are inflamed with wine. [12]They have harps and lyres at their banquets, tambourines and flutes and wine, but they have no regard for the deeds of the LORD, no respect for the work of his hands.
     [13]Therefore my people will go into exile for lack of understanding; their men of rank will die of hunger and their masses will be parched with thirst. [14]Therefore the grave enlarges its appetite and opens its mouth without limit; into it will descend their nobles and masses with all their brawlers and revelers. [15]So man will be brought low and mankind humbled, the eyes of the arrogant humbled. [16]But the LORD Almighty will be exalted by his justice, and the holy God will show himself holy by his righteousness. [17]Then sheep will graze as in their own pasture; lambs will feed among the ruins of the rich.
     [18]Woe to those who draw sin along with cords of deceit, and wickedness as with cart ropes, [19]to those who say, "Let God hurry, let him hasten his work so we may see it. Let it approach, let the plan of the Holy One of Israel come, so we may know it."
     [20]Woe to those who call evil good and good evil, who put darkness for light and light for darkness, who put bitter for sweet and sweet for bitter. [21]Woe to those who are wise in their own eyes and clever in their own sight. [22]Woe to those who are heroes at drinking wine and champions at mixing drinks, [23]who acquit the guilty for a bribe, but deny justice to the innocent. (Isa. 5:7–23)

> [36]Turn my heart toward your statutes and not toward selfish gain.
> [37]Turn my eyes away from worthless things; preserve my life
>   according to your word. (Ps. 119:36–37)

g. Greed, gluttony, and covetousness — sins that have been labeled virtues by our society — are ethically and morally disastrous at every level of human life — individual, family, community, and nation, both secular and religious. Recognizing this, Christian theologians early included these among the "deadly" or "root" sins.[37]

> [21]You shall not covet your neighbor's wife. You shall not set your desire on your neighbor's house or land, his manservant or maidservant, his ox or donkey, or anything that belongs to your neighbor. (Deut. 5:21; cf. Exod. 20:17)[38]

h. Godliness with contentment, on the other hand, is great gain. Discontent with one's lot is at the root of the overindulgence that we sanction as "consumerism." God's people are to be content with enough, even if that is only a little. The story of Israel's response to a major security crisis and to subsequent critical shortages of food and water as Moses led them out of Egypt is revealing (Exodus 14–17). Who among us could possibly deny the legitimacy of their complaints? What would be done to any contemporary political leader whose misguided decisions might result in the absence of such basic necessities as personal safety, water, and food? Under such circumstances, complaining would be the entirely legitimate mildest possible response open to American consumers. But that is not God's assessment:

> [10]For forty years I was angry with that generation; I said, "They are a people whose hearts go astray, and they have not known my ways." [11]So I declared on oath in my anger, "They shall never enter my rest." (Ps. 95:10–11)

i. Personal overindulgence and craven respect for the wealthy compromise the integrity of those who claim to speak for God.
The one who pays the fiddler calls the tune. Preachers paid to do the job often gear the message to the tastes of the largest donor. The rich have the resources to pay for any message they may wish to hear concerning themselves and their relationship to people and possessions, thus confirming their dangerous but comforting self-delusion.[39]

> [9]These are rebellious people, deceitful children, children unwilling to listen to the LORD's instruction.
> [10]They say to the seers, "See no more visions!" and to the prophets, "Give us no more visions of what is right! Tell us pleasant things, prophesy

---

37. In the introduction to her translation of volume 2 (Purgatory) of Dante's *Divine Comedy*, Dorothy Sayers explains that the "seven deadly sins" of medieval theology are more properly understood as the "Seven Capital Sins" (Latin: *caput* = head; "the head or font of offending"), or as the Seven Roots of Sinfulness. "These," she points out, "are the fundamental bad habits of mind recognized and defined by the Church as the well-heads from which all sinful behaviour ultimately springs" (p. 65).

38. See also Prov. 30:11–14; Isa. 57:17–21.

39. One of the more blatant examples is Balaam, paid by Balak to curse Israel (see Numbers 22, esp. v. 15).

illusions. [11]Leave this way, get off this path, and stop confronting us with the Holy One of Israel!" (Isa. 30:9–11)

[13]"From the least to the greatest, all are greedy for gain; prophets and priests alike, all practice deceit. [14]They dress the wound of my people as though it were not serious. 'Peace, peace,' they say, when there is no peace. [15]Are they ashamed of their loathsome conduct? No, they have no shame at all; they do not even know how to blush. So they will fall among the fallen; they will be brought down when I punish them," says the LORD. (Jer. 6:13–15)

[1]Then I said, "Listen, you leaders of Jacob, you rulers of the house of Israel. Should you not know justice, [2]you who hate good and love evil; who tear the skin from my people and the flesh from their bones; [3]who eat my people's flesh, strip off their skin and break their bones in pieces; who chop them up like meat for the pan, like flesh for the pot?" [4]Then they will cry out to the LORD, but he will not answer them. At that time he will hide his face from them because of the evil they have done.

[5]This is what the LORD says: "As for the prophets who lead my people astray, if one feeds them, they proclaim 'peace'; if he does not, they prepare to wage war against him. [6]Therefore night will come over you, without visions, and darkness, without divination. The sun will set for the prophets, and the day will go dark for them. [7]The seers will be ashamed and the diviners disgraced. They will all cover their faces because there is no answer from God." [8]But as for me, I am filled with power, with the Spirit of the LORD, and with justice and might, to declare to Jacob his transgression, to Israel his sin.

[9]Hear this, you leaders of the house of Jacob, you rulers of the house of Israel, who despise justice and distort all that is right; [10]who build Zion with bloodshed, and Jerusalem with wickedness. [11]Her leaders judge for a bribe, her priests teach for a price, and her prophets tell fortunes for money. Yet they lean upon the LORD and say, "Is not the LORD among us? No disaster will come upon us." (Mic. 3:1–11)[40]

4. In the Old Testament, wealth and prosperity are most frequently tangible symbols of brutality, disobedience, and endemic injustice, rather than signs of God's blessing as a reward for personal or national righteousness.

The prosperity of Egypt was built on slavery. The inhabitants of Canaan, a land flowing with milk and honey, were notoriously wicked (compare Num. 13:26–29 with Lev. 18:24–28; 20:23–24). Sodom and Gomorrah, now bywords for decadence of the most appalling kind, were affluent (Gen. 13:13; 18:16–29; Ezek. 16:49). Many kings of Israel and Judah were materially and politically prosperous yet notoriously wicked: Baasha (1 Kings 15:33–16:7); Omri (1 Kings 16:21–28); Ahab (1 Kings 16:29; 22:40); Jehoram (2 Kings 8:16–24); Ahaziah (2 Kings 8:25–29); Jehoahaz (2 Kings 13:1–9); Jehoash (2 Kings 13:10–25);

---

40. See also Jer. 8:10–11; 14:14–16; 23:14–17, 25–32; Ezek. 34:1–5, 17–24; Mic. 2:6–11; 7:1–3.

Jeroboam II (2 Kings 14:23–29); Menahem (2 Kings 15:17–22); Pekah (2 Kings 5:27–31); Ahaz (2 Kings 16:1–20); Manasseh (2 Kings 21:1–18); Amon (2 Kings 21:19–26); Jehoahaz (2 Kings 23:31–35). While our Scriptures make it clear that the short-sighted behavior of these and other kings resulted in the eventual destruction of both Israel and Judah, yet individually they and their peers enjoyed personal wealth and comfort.[41]

One of the most perennially perplexing theological conundrums facing human-kind is the question of how — given that God is both omnipotent and absolutely just — the righteous suffer and the wicked prosper.

> [7]Why do the wicked live on, growing old and increasing in power? [8]They see their children established around them, their offspring before their eyes. [9]Their homes are safe and free from fear; the rod of God is not upon them. [10]Their bulls never fail to breed; their cows calve and do not miscarry. [11]They send forth their children as a flock; their little ones dance about. [12]They sing to the music of tambourine and harp; they make merry to the sound of the flute. [13]They spend their years in prosperity and go down to the grave in peace. [14]Yet they say to God, "Leave us alone! We have no desire to know your ways." (Job 21:7–14)

> [2]In his arrogance the wicked man hunts down the weak, who are caught in the schemes he devises. [3]He boasts of the cravings of his heart; he blesses the greedy and reviles the LORD. [4]In his pride the wicked does not seek him; in all his thoughts there is no room for God. [5]His ways are always prosperous; he is haughty and your laws are far from him; he sneers at all his enemies. [6]He says to himself, "Nothing will shake me; I'll always be happy and never have trouble." (Ps. 10:2–6)[42]

b. The rich and the powerful are often to blame for the plight of the poor, either by their actions or by their failure to act. "A poor man's field may produce abundant food, but injustice sweeps it away," Solomon observed — and probably exemplified personally (Prov. 13:23).[43]

c. It is possible not only to have too little, but too much.

> [8]Keep falsehood and lies far from me; give me neither poverty nor riches, but give me only my daily bread.
> [9]Otherwise, I may have too much and disown you and say, "Who is the LORD?" Or I may become poor and steal, and so dishonor the name of my God. (Prov. 30:8–9)

---

41. The biblical text remarks on both the prosperity and the wickedness of Noah's contemporaries (Gen. 6:1–8) and of the Tower of Babel builders (Gen. 11:1–9).

42. Numerous biblical texts wrestling with this theme include: Ps. 37:14–17; 52:7; 73:2–17; 92:7; 109:1–16; Prov. 11:16; Eccles. 5:8–15; Isa. 1:10–23; 2:6–9; 3:15–24; 5:7–8; 56:9–12; Jer. 2:34; 5:26–29; 12:1–4; 17:11; 22:13–19; 44:15–18; Hos. 10:1–2; 12:6–8; Amos 5:4–7, 11–15, 21–24; 6:4–7; 8:4–7; Hab. 2:4–12; Zech. 11:4–6.

43. See also Eccles. 5:8–15; Isa. 32:7.

d. Preoccupation with personal material advancement and personal security is a sign of spiritual bankruptcy. It renders public professions of faith a hollow sham to one's immediate family.

Lot's fatal decision to choose the best for himself displayed his fundamentally hedonistic orientation to life. No wonder his sons thought he was joking when at the last moment he took seriously the angels' warning of pending doom (Gen. 13:10–11; 19:14). Eli, another tragic example of someone who made obedience to God a secondary concern, forfeited both his sons and his posterity as a result (1 Sam. 2:12–36).

e. Religious orthodoxy without a passion for justice is a hollow sham. Oppression or neglect of the poor leads inevitably to judgment. Solidarity with the poor leads just as inevitably to reward.

[10]Hear the word of the LORD, you rulers of Sodom; listen to the law of our God, you people of Gomorrah!

[11]"The multitude of your sacrifices — what are they to me?" says the LORD. "I have more than enough of burnt offerings, of rams and the fat of fattened animals; I have no pleasure in the blood of bulls and lambs and goats. [12]When you come to appear before me, who has asked this of you, this trampling of my courts?

[13]"Stop bringing meaningless offerings! Your incense is detestable to me. New Moons, Sabbaths and convocations — I cannot bear your evil assemblies. [14]Your New Moon festivals and your appointed feasts my soul hates. They have become a burden to me; I am weary of bearing them. [15]When you spread out your hands in prayer, I will hide my eyes from you; even if you offer many prayers, I will not listen. Your hands are full of blood; [16]wash and make yourselves clean. Take your evil deeds out of my sight! Stop doing wrong, [17]learn to do right! Seek justice, encourage the oppressed. Defend the cause of the fatherless, plead the case of the widow.

[18]"Come now, let us reason together," says the LORD. "Though your sins are like scarlet, they shall be as white as snow; though they are red as crimson, they shall be like wool. [19]If you are willing and obedient, you will eat the best from the land; [20]but if you resist and rebel, you will be devoured by the sword." For the mouth of the LORD has spoken. (Isa. 1:10–20)

[1]Woe to those who make unjust laws, to those who issue oppressive decrees, [2]to deprive the poor of their rights and withhold justice from the oppressed of my people, making widows their prey and robbing the fatherless. [3]What will you do on the day of reckoning, when disaster comes from afar? To whom will you run for help? Where will you leave your riches? [4]Nothing will remain but to cringe among the captives or fall among the slain. Yet for all this, his anger is not turned away, his hand is still upraised. (Isa. 10:1–4)[44]

44. See also Prov. 29:14; 2 Chron. 36:15–21; Prov. 28:22–27; Isa. 3:15–24; Jer. 7:3–7; 14:11–16; 22:13–23; Mic. 2:1–2; Hab. 2:6–12; Zech. 7:8–14.

5. God deliberately, consistently, and proactively aligns himself with the poor, the needy, and the oppressed. This is a theme reiterated again and again in the story of his chosen people, beginning with their exodus from Egypt, when they were oppressed themselves, and throughout their history when the rich among them in turn became oppressors of their own people. The Messiah would identify with the poor, the needy, the oppressed, coming not only *for* them but as *one of* them.[45] It is little wonder, then, that God's true children always actively identified with the poor, the needy, and the oppressed. Biblical good was never simply a matter of passive restraint from doing harm to another. It was always enjoined and described as initiative-taking goodwill toward others. The godly rich related to both their personal possessions and to the poor in accordance with God's principles of justice, spelled out and illustrated in the biblical narrative.

The biblical record is unsparing in its criticism of those who either oppress or simply neglect the poor. Any claim such a person might make to some special affiliation with God is treated as either an outright lie or as evidence of self-delusion. Job, portrayed as righteous rich exemplar par excellence in the Old Testament narrative, professed to taking an active interest in the well-being of the poor around him.

[11]"Whoever heard me spoke well of me, and those who saw me commended me,
[12]because I rescued the poor who cried for help, and the fatherless who had none to assist him.
[13]The man who was dying blessed me; I made the widow's heart sing.
[14]I put on righteousness as my clothing; justice was my robe and my turban.
[15]I was eyes to the blind and feet to the lame.
[16]I was a father to the needy; I took up the case of the stranger.
[17]I broke the fangs of the wicked and snatched the victims from their teeth." (Job 29:11–17)

[24]"Surely no one lays a hand on a broken man when he cries for help in his distress.
[25]Have I not wept for those in trouble? Has not my soul grieved for the poor?" (Job 30:24–25)

[13]"If I have denied justice to my menservants and maidservants when they had a grievance against me, [14]what will I do when God confronts me? What will I answer when called to account? [15]Did not he who made me in the womb make them? Did not the same one form us both within our mothers?

[16]"If I have denied the desires of the poor or let the eyes of the widow grow weary, [17]if I have kept my bread to myself, not sharing it with the

45. Exod. 22:21–27; Lev. 25:39–43; Deut. 10:14–20; 15:7–18; 27:19; Job 5:8–27; Ps. 9:9, 12, 18; 10:17–18; 12:5; 18:27; 22; 35:10; 37:10–11; 68:4–6; 72:2–4, 12–14; 103:6; 107:9; 109:31; 112:9; 113:7–8; 136; 138:6; 140:12; 146:7–9; 147:6; Prov. 14:31; 15:25, 27; 16:8; 17:5; 19:17; 21:13, 17; 10:1–4; Isa. 11:1–4; 26:3–6; 29:13–21; 41:17–20; 53:1–12; 57:15; 61:1–8; Jer. 20:13; 49:11; Hos. 14:3.

fatherless — [18]but from my youth I reared him as would a father, and from my birth I guided the widow — [19]if I have seen anyone perishing for lack of clothing, or a needy man without a garment, [20]and his heart did not bless me for warming him with the fleece from my sheep, [21]if I have raised my hand against the fatherless, knowing that I had influence in court, [22]then let my arm fall from the shoulder, let it be broken off at the joint. [23]For I dreaded destruction from God, and for fear of his splendor I could not do such things.

[24]"If I have put my trust in gold or said to pure gold, 'You are my security,' [25]if I have rejoiced over my great wealth, the fortune my hands had gained, [26]if I have regarded the sun in its radiance or the moon moving in splendor, [27]so that my heart was secretly enticed and my hand offered them a kiss of homage, [28]then these also would be sins to be judged, for I would have been unfaithful to God on high." (Job 31:26–28)[46]

6. Righteousness (justice) always expresses itself in an obedience that concerns itself with the well-being of the poor, and is never content with mere conformity to religious rites and the mouthing of pious platitudes.

[4]Hear this, you who trample the needy and do away with the poor of the land, [5]saying, "When will the New Moon be over that we may sell grain, and the Sabbath be ended that we may market wheat?" — skimping the measure, boosting the price and cheating with dishonest scales, [6]buying the poor with silver and the needy for a pair of sandals, selling even the sweepings with the wheat.

[7]The LORD has sworn by the Pride of Jacob: "I will never forget anything they have done." (Amos 8:4–7)

[8]And the word of the LORD came again to Zechariah: [9]"This is what the LORD Almighty says: 'Administer true justice; show mercy and compassion to one another. [10]Do not oppress the widow or the fatherless, the alien or the poor. In your hearts do not think evil of each other.' " (Zech. 7:8–10)[47]

a. God meets the needs of the poor through the actions and interventions of his obedient people. This was the intent of the laws dealing with the treatment of the poor by the rich, and finds rare illustration in the story of Nehemiah and the impoverished fellow countrymen who were rebuilding the wall of Jerusalem.

[1]Now the men and their wives raised a great outcry against their Jewish brothers. [2]Some were saying, "We and our sons and daughters are numerous; in order for us to eat and stay alive, we must get grain."

---

46. Ps. 37:21–28; 41:1–3; 74:21; 94:1, 3, 6; 112:5; Prov. 25:21; 31:8–9; 31:18–20; Jer. 22:3, 16–17.

47. See also Exod. 23:6–7; 1 Sam. 15:22–23; Job 30:24–25; 31:16–28; Ps. 40:6–8; Prov. 3:27–28; Isa. 1:10–23; 29:13–21; 58:1–11; Jer. 7:3–7, 21–23; 21:11–14; 22:3; Ezek. 16:49; 33:31–32; Amos 5:4–24; 6:4–7.

³Others were saying, "We are mortgaging our fields, our vineyards and our homes to get grain during the famine."

⁴Still others were saying, "We have had to borrow money to pay the king's tax on our fields and vineyards. ⁵Although we are of the same flesh and blood as our countrymen and though our sons are as good as theirs, yet we have to subject our sons and daughters to slavery. Some of our daughters have already been enslaved, but we are powerless, because our fields and our vineyards belong to others."

⁶When I heard their outcry and these charges, I was very angry. ⁷I pondered them in my mind and then accused the nobles and officials. I told them, "You are exacting usury from your own countrymen!" So I called together a large meeting to deal with them ⁸and said: "As far as possible, we have bought back our Jewish brothers who were sold to the Gentiles. Now you are selling your brothers, only for them to be sold back to us!" They kept quiet, because they could find nothing to say.

⁹So I continued, "What you are doing is not right. Shouldn't you walk in the fear of our God to avoid the reproach of our Gentile enemies? ¹⁰I and my brothers and my men are also lending the people money and grain. But let the exacting of usury stop! ¹¹Give back to them immediately their fields, vineyards, olive groves and houses, and also the usury you are charging them — the hundredth part of the money, grain, new wine and oil."

¹²"We will give it back," they said. "And we will not demand anything more from them. We will do as you say."

Then I summoned the priests and made the nobles and officials take an oath to do what they had promised. ¹³I also shook out the folds of my robe and said, "In this way may God shake out of his house and possessions every man who does not keep this promise. So may such a man be shaken out and emptied!"

At this the whole assembly said, "Amen," and praised the LORD. And the people did as they had promised. (Neh. 5:1–13)

b. True giving to God involves that which we genuinely value — not just our surplus or discards. It is easy to be a cheerful giver when we give away what we neither need nor want. The warm, inner feeling of self-congratulations is very gratifying. But to give what we will really miss — a kind of giving which in the Bible is called sacrifice, and which has always characterized the giving of God's true children — is the giving with which God is pleased. It is an interesting fact that while there is a great volume of criticism in the Scriptures leveled against those whose aid for the poor is either inadequate or nonexistent, there is no instance of prophetic preaching against giving too much.

⁶"A son honors his father, and a servant his master. If I am a father, where is the honor due me? If I am a master, where is the respect due me?" says the LORD Almighty. "It is you, O priests, who show contempt for my name.

"But you ask, 'How have we shown contempt for your name?'

⁷"You place defiled food on my altar.

"But you ask, 'How have we defiled you?'

"By saying that the Lᴏʀᴅ's table is contemptible. [8]When you bring blind animals for sacrifice, is that not wrong? When you sacrifice crippled or diseased animals, is that not wrong? Try offering them to your governor! Would he be pleased with you? Would he accept you?" says the Lᴏʀᴅ Almighty.

[9]"Now implore God to be gracious to us. With such offerings from your hands, will he accept you?" — says the Lᴏʀᴅ Almighty.

[10]"Oh, that one of you would shut the temple doors, so that you would not light useless fires on my altar! I am not pleased with you," says the Lᴏʀᴅ Almighty, "and I will accept no offering from your hands. [11]My name will be great among the nations, from the rising to the setting of the sun. In every place incense and pure offerings will be brought to my name, because my name will be great among the nations," says the Lᴏʀᴅ Almighty.

[12]"But you profane it by saying of the Lᴏʀᴅ's table, 'It is defiled,' and of its food, 'It is contemptible.' [13]And you say, 'What a burden!' and you sniff at it contemptuously," says the Lᴏʀᴅ Almighty. "When you bring injured, crippled or diseased animals and offer them as sacrifices, should I accept them from your hands?" says the Lᴏʀᴅ. [14]"Cursed is the cheat who has an acceptable male in his flock and vows to give it, but then sacrifices a blemished animal to the Lord. For I am a great king," says the Lᴏʀᴅ Almighty, "and my name is to be feared among the nations." (Mal. 1:6–14)[48]

7. True repentance and spiritual vitality involve economic reformation and justice. Repentance without the fruit of repentance is meaningless.

[1]"Shout it aloud, do not hold back. Raise your voice like a trumpet. Declare to my people their rebellion and to the house of Jacob their sins. [2]For day after day they seek me out; they seem eager to know my ways, as if they were a nation that does what is right and has not forsaken the commands of its God. They ask me for just decisions and seem eager for God to come near them.

[3]" 'Why have we fasted,' they say, 'and you have not seen it? Why have we humbled ourselves, and you have not noticed?' "Yet on the day of your fasting, you do as you please and exploit all your workers.

[4]"Your fasting ends in quarreling and strife, and in striking each other with wicked fists. You cannot fast as you do today and expect your voice to be heard on high.

[5]"Is this the kind of fast I have chosen, only a day for a man to humble himself? Is it only for bowing one's head like a reed and for lying on sackcloth and ashes? Is that what you call a fast, a day acceptable to the Lᴏʀᴅ?

[6]"Is not this the kind of fasting I have chosen: to loose the chains of injustice and untie the cords of the yoke, to set the oppressed free and break every yoke? [7]Is it not to share your food with the hungry and to provide

---

48. Compare Lev. 1:3, 10; 2:1, 4; 3:1, 6; 27:1–33; Deut. 17:1; 2 Sam. 24:18–25.

the poor wanderer with shelter — when you see the naked, to clothe him, and not to turn away from your own flesh and blood?

[8]"Then your light will break forth like the dawn, and your healing will quickly appear; then your righteousness will go before you, and the glory of the LORD will be your rear guard. [9]Then you will call, and the LORD will answer; you will cry for help, and he will say: Here am I.

"If you do away with the yoke of oppression, with the pointing finger and malicious talk, [10]and if you spend yourselves in behalf of the hungry and satisfy the needs of the oppressed, then your light will rise in the darkness, and your night will become like the noonday. [11]The LORD will guide you always; he will satisfy your needs in a sun-scorched land and will strengthen your frame. You will be like a well-watered garden, like a spring whose waters never fail." (Isa. 58:1–11)[49]

8. Economic repentance is costly, and therefore very rare. But it is possible. The powerful and wealthy usually deal with prophetic preaching by doing away with the preacher, and hiring someone with a more tolerant appreciation for their excesses, and for the unjust means whereby wealthy advantage is gained, maintained, and exploited (e.g., Isa. 30:9–11; Ezek. 18:5–23). A rare Old Testament account of economic repentance by the powerful is found in Nehemiah 5:1–12. Another is found in the book of Jonah. But most wealthy or powerful people, including the professionally religious ones, do not repent.

New Testament Teaching That the Wealthy Find Troubling

In the New Testament, as in the Old, most of the economic teaching is annoying, meddlesome, unpopular, or distressing to those who are rich. Instruction to Christ's followers concerning the use of their personal resources is both abundant and painfully clear. As members of the best-fed, best-clothed, best-housed society in the world, Western missionaries need desperately to apply this teaching to themselves. New Testament teaching on wealth and poverty may be organized according to the following principles:

1. In the New Testament as in the Old, wealth and possessions, together with the comfort, security, and efficiency that they can provide, are subordinate goods, and neither their pursuit nor their accumulation can ever be regarded as intrinsically worthwhile goals in life. Western consumer societies, including its religious expressions, "fix their eyes on what is seen, for what is seen is the stuff of a comfortable and secure lifestyle, while what is unseen is pie in the sky," thus inverting St. Paul's teaching in 2 Corinthians 4:7–18.

It is ironic that while the conservative evangelical church in the West is quick to share what it claims is most valuable — the good news — it is often less willing to share its professedly unimportant material possessions, thus demonstrating the truth of Christ's dictum, "Where your treasure is, there will your heart be also"

---

49. See also Neh. 5:1–12; Isa. 1:10–23; Jer. 7:3–7, 21–23; Hos. 4:7; 8:2; Mic. 6:6–16; Zech. 7:8–10.

(Luke 12:34). Few Christian leaders today, including missionaries, could claim with St. Paul that as followers of Christ they "consider everything a loss compared to the surpassing greatness of knowing Christ Jesus [their] Lord, for whose sake [they] have lost all things [considering them] rubbish" (Phil. 3:8). Such texts can be legitimately construed this way by the poor among whom wealthy missionaries live and work.

2. The personal possessions of Christ's followers are regarded as a trust, to be used for the good of others. Possessions and wealth are of positive value only when they promote his purposes. To be possessive of one's possessions is extremely ill advised, given what we read in the New Testament. Sharing of possessions was one of the significant characteristics of the earliest community of believers. Freedom from love of money and contentment with one's possessions are absolutely essential for the believer. But can the wealthy believer credibly teach this precept to impoverished brothers and sisters?[50]

> [42]Give to the one who asks you, and do not turn away from the one who wants to borrow from you. (Matt. 5:42)

> [34]Then he called the crowd to him along with his disciples and said: "If anyone would come after me, he must deny himself and take up his cross and follow me. [35]For whoever wants to save his life will lose it, but whoever loses his life for me and for the gospel will save it. [36]What good is it for a man to gain the whole world, yet forfeit his soul? [37]Or what can a man give in exchange for his soul? [38]If anyone is ashamed of me and my words in this adulterous and sinful generation, the Son of Man will be ashamed of him when he comes in his Father's glory with the holy angels." (Mark 8:34–38)

> [12]Then Jesus said to his host, "When you give a luncheon or dinner, do not invite your friends, your brothers or relatives, or your rich neighbors; if you do, they may invite you back and so you will be repaid. [13]But when you give a banquet, invite the poor, the crippled, the lame, the blind, [14]and you will be blessed. Although they cannot repay you, you will be repaid at the resurrection of the righteous." (Luke 14:12–14)

> [32]All the believers were one in heart and mind. No one claimed that any of his possessions was his own, but they shared everything they had. [33]With great power the apostles continued to testify to the resurrection of the Lord Jesus, and much grace was upon them all. [34]There were no needy persons among them. For from time to time those who owned lands or houses sold them, brought the money from the sales [35]and put it at the apostles' feet, and it was distributed to anyone as he had need. (Acts 4:32–35)

3. Wealth and prosperity are not signs of righteousness, but of greed; conversely, poverty and hardship are not indications of God's displeasure, but often the inevitable consequence of obedience. St. Paul's hardship, like that

---

50. In addition to the references cited, see also Luke 6:27–36; 10:25–37; 16:19–31.

of his Lord, was directly attributable to his persistent obedience to his calling as a follower of Jesus and an apostle of the good news.

> [16]I repeat: Let no one take me for a fool. But if you do, then receive me just as you would a fool, so that I may do a little boasting. [17]In this self-confident boasting I am not talking as the Lord would, but as a fool. [18]Since many are boasting in the way the world does, I too will boast. [19]You gladly put up with fools since you are so wise! [20]In fact, you even put up with anyone who enslaves you or exploits you or takes advantage of you or pushes himself forward or slaps you in the face. [21]To my shame I admit that we were too weak for that!
>
> What anyone else dares to boast about — I am speaking as a fool — I also dare to boast about. [22]Are they Hebrews? So am I. Are they Israelites? So am I. Are they Abraham's descendants? So am I. [23]Are they servants of Christ? (I am out of my mind to talk like this.) I am more. I have worked much harder, been in prison more frequently, been flogged more severely, and been exposed to death again and again. [24]Five times I received from the Jews the forty lashes minus one. [25]Three times I was beaten with rods, once I was stoned, three times I was shipwrecked, I spent a night and a day in the open sea, [26]I have been constantly on the move. I have been in danger from rivers, in danger from bandits, in danger from my own countrymen, in danger from Gentiles; in danger in the city, in danger in the country, in danger at sea; and in danger from false brothers. [27]I have labored and toiled and have often gone without sleep; I have known hunger and thirst and have often gone without food; I have been cold and naked. [28]Besides everything else, I face daily the pressure of my concern for all the churches. [29]Who is weak, and I do not feel weak? Who is led into sin, and I do not inwardly burn?
>
> [30]If I must boast, I will boast of the things that show my weakness. [31]The God and Father of the Lord Jesus, who is to be praised forever, knows that I am not lying. [32]In Damascus the governor under King Aretas had the city of the Damascenes guarded in order to arrest me. [33]But I was lowered in a basket from a window in the wall and slipped through his hands. (2 Cor. 11:16–33)
>
> [1]I must go on boasting. Although there is nothing to be gained, I will go on to visions and revelations from the Lord. [2]I know a man in Christ who fourteen years ago was caught up to the third heaven. Whether it was in the body or out of the body I do not know — God knows. [3]And I know that this man — whether in the body or apart from the body I do not know, but God knows — [4]was caught up to paradise. He heard inexpressible things, things that man is not permitted to tell. [5]I will boast about a man like that, but I will not boast about myself, except about my weaknesses. [6]Even if I should choose to boast, I would not be a fool, because I would be speaking the truth. But I refrain, so no one will think more of me than is warranted by what I do or say.

[7]To keep me from becoming conceited because of these surpassingly great revelations, there was given me a thorn in my flesh, a messenger of Satan, to torment me. [8]Three times I pleaded with the Lord to take it away from me. [9]But he said to me, "My grace is sufficient for you, for my power is made perfect in weakness." Therefore I will boast all the more gladly about my weaknesses, so that Christ's power may rest on me. [10]That is why, for Christ's sake, I delight in weaknesses, in insults, in hardships, in persecutions, in difficulties. For when I am weak, then I am strong. (2 Cor. 12:1–10)[51]

Throughout the New Testament, as in the Old, personal affluence generally represents dissonance with Kingdom values, and is closely associated with mistreatment of the poor, preoccupation with self, and spiritual impotence. Thus, for example, Zacchaeus was wealthy not because he was a righteous man, but because he was corrupt (Luke 19:1–10). His repentance involved giving away half of his possessions, and making fourfold restitution to anyone he had cheated.

a. Christ pronounced woes on the wealthy, emphatically insisting that it was virtually impossible for a rich person to inherit eternal life. To be both "wealthy" and a "disciple" seemed, with rare exceptions, to have been a virtual oxymoron. Freedom from the love of money and contentment with what one has were defining marks of Christ's true followers. In the Sermon on the Mount, it is the poor who are blessed. For those whose who are rich, discipleship on Jesus' terms is especially costly (Luke 14:25–33).

[16]Now a man came up to Jesus and asked, "Teacher, what good thing must I do to get eternal life?"

[17]"Why do you ask me about what is good?" Jesus replied. "There is only One who is good. If you want to enter life, obey the commandments."

[18]"Which ones?" the man inquired.

Jesus replied, " 'Do not murder, do not commit adultery, do not steal, do not give false testimony, [19]honor your father and mother,' and 'love your neighbor as yourself.' "

[20]"All these I have kept," the young man said. "What do I still lack?"

[21]Jesus answered, "If you want to be perfect, go, sell your possessions and give to the poor, and you will have treasure in heaven. Then come, follow me."

[22]When the young man heard this, he went away sad, because he had great wealth.

[23]Then Jesus said to his disciples, "I tell you the truth, it is hard for a rich man to enter the kingdom of heaven. [24]Again I tell you, it is easier for a camel to go through the eye of a needle than for a rich man to enter the kingdom of God." (Matt. 19:16–24; cf. Mark 10:17–31)

[5]Keep your lives free from the love of money and be content with what you have, because God has said, "Never will I leave you; never will I forsake

---

51. See also 1 Cor. 4:1–17; 2 Cor. 4:1–18; Acts 20:22–24; 21:10–14; 2 Cor. 8:9.

you." ⁶So we say with confidence, "The Lord is my helper; I will not be afraid. What can man do to me?" (Heb. 13:5–6)

> ²⁰Looking at his disciples, he said:
> "Blessed are you who are poor,
>   for yours is the kingdom of God.
> ²¹Blessed are you who hunger now,
>   for you will be satisfied.
> Blessed are you who weep now,
>   for you will laugh.
> ²²Blessed are you when men hate you,
>   when they exclude you and insult you
>   and reject your name as evil,
>   because of the Son of Man.

²³"Rejoice in that day and leap for joy, because great is your reward in heaven. For that is how their fathers treated the prophets."

> ²⁴"But woe to you who are rich,
>   for you have already received your comfort.
> ²⁵Woe to you who are well fed now,
>   for you will go hungry.
> Woe to you who laugh now,
>   for you will mourn and weep.
> ²⁶Woe to you when all men speak well of you,
>   for that is how their fathers treated the false prophets."
>   (Luke 6:20–26; cf. Matt. 5:1–12)

b. Sins to which the rich are especially prone — greed (the desire for more than you need even at the expense of those who have less than they need), gluttony, and callous disregard of the poor — are closely associated with idolatry, impurity, and immorality. Even in a son's seemingly legitimate desire to share in the family inheritance Jesus detected greed, warning his followers to be on guard against "all kinds of greed" (Luke 12:13–21). Paul urged Corinthian believers to be as wary of the greedy as they were of swindlers:

> ⁹I have written you in my letter not to associate with sexually immoral people — ¹⁰not at all meaning the people of this world who are immoral, or the greedy and swindlers, or idolaters. In that case you would have to leave this world. ¹¹But now I am writing you that you must not associate with anyone who calls himself a brother but is sexually immoral or greedy, an idolater or a slanderer, a drunkard or a swindler. With such a man do not even eat. (1 Cor. 5:9–11)

Present economic relationships in the church worldwide are equally scandalous. What if Christian congregations in the overindulged and overweight West were to refrain from the Lord's Supper until all their poor brothers and sisters elsewhere in the world had enough to eat?

²⁰When you come together, it is not the Lord's Supper you eat, ²¹for as you eat, each of you goes ahead without waiting for anybody else. One remains hungry, another gets drunk. ²²Don't you have homes to eat and drink in? Or do you despise the church of God and humiliate those who have nothing? What shall I say to you? Shall I praise you for this? Certainly not! (1 Cor. 11:20–22)

St. Paul describes greed — the insistence of more than enough in contexts where brothers and sisters have less than enough — as idolatry, part of the futile way of thinking that characterizes godless societies. For Western missionaries, representing "continual lust for more" consumer societies, with their vision of infinite, expanding good as the God-given entitlement of all patriotic Americans, these sobering words need to be carefully pondered.

¹⁷So I tell you this, and insist on it in the Lord, that you must no longer live as the Gentiles do, in the futility of their thinking. ¹⁸They are darkened in their understanding and separated from the life of God because of the ignorance that is in them due to the hardening of their hearts. ¹⁹Having lost all sensitivity, they have given themselves over to sensuality so as to indulge in every kind of impurity, with a continual lust for more.

²⁰You, however, did not come to know Christ that way. ²¹Surely you heard of him and were taught in him in accordance with the truth that is in Jesus. ²²You were taught, with regard to your former way of life, to put off your old self, which is being corrupted by its deceitful desires; ²³to be made new in the attitude of your minds; ²⁴and to put on the new self, created to be like God in true righteousness and holiness.

²⁵Therefore each of you must put off falsehood and speak truthfully to his neighbor, for we are all members of one body. ²⁶"In your anger do not sin": Do not let the sun go down while you are still angry, ²⁷and do not give the devil a foothold. ²⁸He who has been stealing must steal no longer, but must work, doing something useful with his own hands, that he may have something to share with those in need.

²⁹Do not let any unwholesome talk come out of your mouths, but only what is helpful for building others up according to their needs, that it may benefit those who listen. ³⁰And do not grieve the Holy Spirit of God, with whom you were sealed for the day of redemption. ³¹Get rid of all bitterness, rage and anger, brawling and slander, along with every form of malice. ³²Be kind and compassionate to one another, forgiving each other, just as in Christ God forgave you. (Eph. 4:17–32)

¹Be imitators of God, therefore, as dearly loved children ²and live a life of love, just as Christ loved us and gave himself up for us as a fragrant offering and sacrifice to God.

³But among you there must not be even a hint of sexual immorality, or of any kind of impurity, or of greed, because these are improper for God's holy people. ⁴Nor should there be obscenity, foolish talk or coarse joking, which are out of place, but rather thanksgiving. ⁵For of this you can be sure:

No immoral, impure or greedy person — such a man is an idolater — has any inheritance in the kingdom of Christ and of God. [6]Let no one deceive you with empty words, for because of such things God's wrath comes on those who are disobedient. [7]Therefore do not be partners with them. (Eph. 5:1–7)[52]

c. **"Where your treasure is, there your heart will be also."** This is a difficult precept for a rich missionary to teach to the poor. If only Christ had reversed the order — "Where your heart is, there your treasure will be" — he could have made it so much easier for his wealthy followers to save appearances!

[32]Do not be afraid, little flock, for your Father has been pleased to give you the kingdom. [33]Sell your possessions and give to the poor. Provide purses for yourselves that will not wear out, a treasure in heaven that will not be exhausted, where no thief comes near and no moth destroys. [34]For where your treasure is, there your heart will be also. (Luke 12:32–34)

d. **Christ's followers are to be in the world but not of it; but the advantages of personal wealth ensure that they are of it, but not in it.**

[16]They are not of the world, even as I am not of it. [17]Sanctify them by the truth; your word is truth. [18]As you sent me into the world, I have sent them into the world. [19]For them I sanctify myself, that they too may be truly sanctified. (John 17:16–19)

e. **Preoccupation with self, money, and pleasure is an indication of a way of life on the brink of destruction . . . a "last days" way of life.**

[1]But mark this: There will be terrible times in the last days. [2]People will be lovers of themselves, lovers of money, boastful, proud, abusive, disobedient to their parents, ungrateful, unholy, [3]without love, unforgiving, slanderous, without self-control, brutal, not lovers of the good, [4]treacherous, rash, conceited, lovers of pleasure rather than lovers of God — [5]having a form of godliness but denying its power. Have nothing to do with them. (2 Tim. 3:1–5)

4. **Wealth and prosperity are inherently dangerous spiritually.** Most wealthy Christians simply do not believe New Testament teaching about the seductive power of wealth in their own lives. There are many missionary stories detailing the shipwreck of their converts on the treacherous shoals of even modest economic ambition, but scarcely a word on the personal and institutional manifestations of similar economic preoccupation in Western missions and missionaries. Both credibility and integrity require that any teaching on mammon that is applied to the poor must surely apply to their wealthy exemplars and instructors!

---

52. Compare Gal. 5:16–25 and Col. 3:1–6.

a. Wealth is the natural culture in which pride and a self-deluding sense of security seem inevitably to flourish. It is fatal to the virtues of humility and meekness.

[6]But godliness with contentment is great gain. [7]For we brought nothing into the world, and we can take nothing out of it. [8]But if we have food and clothing, we will be content with that. [9]People who want to get rich fall into temptation and a trap and into many foolish and harmful desires that plunge men into ruin and destruction. [10]For the love of money is a root of all kinds of evil. Some people, eager for money, have wandered from the faith and pierced themselves with many griefs.

[11]But you, man of God, flee from all this, and pursue righteousness, godliness, faith, love, endurance and gentleness. [12]Fight the good fight of the faith. Take hold of the eternal life to which you were called when you made your good confession in the presence of many witnesses. [13]In the sight of God, who gives life to everything, and of Christ Jesus, who while testifying before Pontius Pilate made the good confession, I charge you [14]to keep this command without spot or blame until the appearing of our Lord Jesus Christ, [15]which God will bring about in his own time — God, the blessed and only Ruler, the King of kings and Lord of lords, [16]who alone is immortal and who lives in unapproachable light, whom no one has seen or can see. To him be honor and might forever. Amen.

[17]Command those who are rich in this present world not to be arrogant nor to put their hope in wealth, which is so uncertain, but to put their hope in God, who richly provides us with everything for our enjoyment. [18]Command them to do good, to be rich in good deeds, and to be generous and willing to share. [19]In this way they will lay up treasure for themselves as a firm foundation for the coming age, so that they may take hold of the life that is truly life. (1 Tim. 6:6–19)

b. Wealth deludes both the person and those around that person concerning his or her real worth and expertise. It colors and distorts a person's perspective on life itself. The New Testament, borne out by personal experience and observation, confirms Galbraith in his wry observation that "Nothing so gives the illusion of intelligence as personal association with large sums of money."[53] Wealth as a stumbling block to either ourselves or to those under our missionary or pastoral care calls for drastic measures.

[1]At that time the disciples came to Jesus and asked, "Who is the greatest in the kingdom of heaven?"

[2]He called a little child and had him stand among them. [3]And he said: "I tell you the truth, unless you change and become like little children, you will never enter the kingdom of heaven. [4]Therefore, whoever humbles himself like this child is the greatest in the kingdom of heaven.

---

53. John Kenneth Galbraith, "The 1929 Parallel," *The Atlantic* 259, no. 1 (January 1987): 62.

[5]"And whoever welcomes a little child like this in my name welcomes me. [6]But if anyone causes one of these little ones who believe in me to sin, it would be better for him to have a large millstone hung around his neck and to be drowned in the depths of the sea.

[7]"Woe to the world because of the things that cause people to sin! Such things must come, but woe to the man through whom they come! [8]If your hand or your foot causes you to sin, cut it off and throw it away. It is better for you to enter life maimed or crippled than to have two hands or two feet and be thrown into eternal fire. [9]And if your eye causes you to sin, gouge it out and throw it away. It is better for you to enter life with one eye than to have two eyes and be thrown into the fire of hell." (Matt. 18:1–9)

Despite our Lord's repeated insistence that there is little room in his Kingdom for the great and the powerful of this world (Luke 22:24–30), we humans are mesmerized by power, like moths attracted to a burning candle. We tend to favor the rich with our attention and respect — intuiting close association with them as a possible means of self-advancement — despite the fact that the greatest injustices and violence can be traced directly to the greed of those who already have more than enough. As our Lord himself taught us, not personal ambition, but the needs of others, should be each Christian's preoccupation (Phil. 2:1–4).

[1]My brothers, as believers in our glorious Lord Jesus Christ, don't show favoritism. [2]Suppose a man comes into your meeting wearing a gold ring and fine clothes, and a poor man in shabby clothes also comes in. [3]If you show special attention to the man wearing fine clothes and say, "Here's a good seat for you," but say to the poor man, "You stand there" or "Sit on the floor by my feet," [4]have you not discriminated among yourselves and become judges with evil thoughts?

[5]Listen, my dear brothers: Has not God chosen those who are poor in the eyes of the world to be rich in faith and to inherit the kingdom he promised those who love him? [6]But you have insulted the poor. Is it not the rich who are exploiting you? Are they not the ones who are dragging you into court? [7]Are they not the ones who are slandering the noble name of him to whom you belong? (James 2:1–7)

[1]Now listen, you rich people, weep and wail because of the misery that is coming upon you. [2]Your wealth has rotted, and moths have eaten your clothes. [3]Your gold and silver are corroded. Their corrosion will testify against you and eat your flesh like fire. You have hoarded wealth in the last days. [4]Look! The wages you failed to pay the workmen who mowed your fields are crying out against you. The cries of the harvesters have reached the ears of the Lord Almighty. [5]You have lived on earth in luxury and self-indulgence. You have fattened yourselves in the day of slaughter. [6]You have condemned and murdered innocent men, who were not opposing you. (James 5:1–6)

c. Wealth, with its concomitant preoccupations, dulls the sense of personal spiritual need and fosters alienation from God. The rich are often so busy that they have no time to respond obediently to God's invitation, or they are completely unaware that they have a need. The Laodicean church thought it lacked nothing. In fact, it lacked that which is the very essence of the church — Christ himself.

> 22The one who received the seed that fell among the thorns is the man who hears the word, but the worries of this life and the deceitfulness of wealth choke it, making it unfruitful. (Matt. 13:22)

> 13Someone in the crowd said to him, "Teacher, tell my brother to divide the inheritance with me."
> 14Jesus replied, "Man, who appointed me a judge or an arbiter between you?" 15Then he said to them, "Watch out! Be on your guard against all kinds of greed; a man's life does not consist in the abundance of his possessions."
> 16And he told them this parable: "The ground of a certain rich man produced a good crop. 17He thought to himself, 'What shall I do? I have no place to store my crops.'
> 18"Then he said, 'This is what I'll do. I will tear down my barns and build bigger ones, and there I will store all my grain and my goods. 19And I'll say to myself, "You have plenty of good things laid up for many years. Take life easy; eat, drink and be merry." '
> 20"But God said to him, 'You fool! This very night your life will be demanded from you. Then who will get what you have prepared for yourself?'
> 21"This is how it will be with anyone who stores up things for himself but is not rich toward God." (Luke 12:13–21)

> 14"To the angel of the church in Laodicea write:
> These are the words of the Amen, the faithful and true witness, the ruler of God's creation. 15I know your deeds, that you are neither cold nor hot. I wish you were either one or the other! 16So, because you are lukewarm — neither hot nor cold — I am about to spit you out of my mouth. 17You say, 'I am rich; I have acquired wealth and do not need a thing.' But you do not realize that you are wretched, pitiful, poor, blind and naked. 18I counsel you to buy from me gold refined in the fire, so you can become rich; and white clothes to wear, so you can cover your shameful nakedness; and salve to put on your eyes, so you can see.
> 19Those whom I love I rebuke and discipline. So be earnest, and repent. 20Here I am! I stand at the door and knock. If anyone hears my voice and opens the door, I will come in and eat with him, and he with me. 21To him who overcomes, I will give the right to sit with me on my throne, just as I overcame and sat down with my Father on his throne. (Rev. 3:14–21)[54]

d. Since prayer is not the natural activity of comfortable, secure people, but the spontaneous outcry of desperate people whose life circumstances are

---

54. See also Luke 16:19–31; 2 Tim. 6:6–19; James 5:1–6; 1 John 2:15–17.

out of their own control, wealth makes genuine prayer difficult. Synonyms for "prayer" in the New Testament (request, ask, bow down before, fall prostrate before, kneel before, beseech, beg, implore, plead, petition, entreat) can hardly be used to describe the pious clichés mouthed by the comfortably well-off. Self-sufficiency and security are the enemies of prayer, as are materialism and secularism.

    e. Wealth almost inevitably comes into conflict with the demands of the Kingdom of God, as far as the Gospel record is concerned. Western missionaries often appear to be doing well by doing good. The cost of discipleship, while relatively simple to teach verbally, is difficult for a wealthy person to teach by modeling. In response to the implausible financial advice from someone as parochial as Jesus, the Pharisees — many of them comfortably well-established — sneered. This highly impractical man was obviously out of touch with reality.

[17]As Jesus started on his way, a man ran up to him and fell on his knees before him. "Good teacher," he asked, "what must I do to inherit eternal life?"
    [18]"Why do you call me good?" Jesus answered. "No one is good — except God alone. [19]You know the commandments: 'Do not murder, do not commit adultery, do not steal, do not give false testimony, do not defraud, honor your father and mother.'"
    [20]"Teacher," he declared, "all these I have kept since I was a boy."
    [21]Jesus looked at him and loved him. "One thing you lack," he said. "Go, sell everything you have and give to the poor, and you will have treasure in heaven. Then come, follow me."
    [22]At this the man's face fell. He went away sad, because he had great wealth.
    [23]Jesus looked around and said to his disciples, "How hard it is for the rich to enter the kingdom of God!"
    [24]The disciples were amazed at his words. But Jesus said again, "Children, how hard it is to enter the kingdom of God! [25]It is easier for a camel to go through the eye of a needle than for a rich man to enter the kingdom of God."
    [26]The disciples were even more amazed, and said to each other, "Who then can be saved?"
    [27]Jesus looked at them and said, "With man this is impossible, but not with God; all things are possible with God."
    [28]Peter said to him, "We have left everything to follow you!"
    [29]"I tell you the truth," Jesus replied, "no one who has left home or brothers or sisters or mother or father or children or fields for me and the gospel [30]will fail to receive a hundred times as much in this present age (homes, brothers, sisters, mothers, children and fields — and with them, persecutions) and in the age to come, eternal life. [31]But many who are first will be last, and the last first." (Mark 10:17–31)

[13]"No servant can serve two masters. Either he will hate the one and love the other, or he will be devoted to the one and despise the other. You cannot serve both God and Money."

[14]The Pharisees, who loved money, heard all this and were sneering at Jesus. [15]He said to them, "You are the ones who justify yourselves in the eyes of men, but God knows your hearts. What is highly valued among men is detestable in God's sight." (Luke 16:13–15)[55]

f. The New Testament has little good to say about wealth, and holds out scant hope that some select group of disciples from the West might one day be resistant to its baneful effects. Wealth tends to produce alienation from one's fellow human beings (1 Cor. 11:17–34; James 2:1–13; 5:1–6). It easily assumes the role of a deity in human behavior (Matt. 6:19–24; Luke 16:13), but ultimately never satisfies. Wealth breeds covetousness and greed, with an insatiable desire for more. Jesus wrapped up his instruction on the signs of the end of the age by cautioning his disciples:

[34]"Be careful, or your hearts will be weighed down with dissipation, drunkenness and the anxieties of life, and that day will close on you unexpectedly like a trap. [35]For it will come upon all those who live on the face of the whole earth. [36]Be always on the watch, and pray that you may be able to escape all that is about to happen, and that you may be able to stand before the Son of Man." (Luke 21:34–36)[56]

"Dissipation" is unrestrained indulgence and the pursuit of pleasure, an apt portrayal of our consumer society, dedicated to the pursuit of pleasure, and constitutionally guaranteeing every citizen that inalienable right. To what extent can men and women reared in such an environment practice obedience in settings that throw into sharp relief their utter reliance on the consumer way of life?

g. Wealth chokes the Word, resulting in spiritual sterility. Like the Sirens of Greek mythology, wealth's allure is almost irresistible, and when heeded, always fatal. The Gospel narrators all agree, suggesting that this must have been a commonly reiterated theme in Jesus' teaching.

[22]The one who received the seed that fell among the thorns is the man who hears the word, but the worries of this life and the deceitfulness of wealth choke it, making it unfruitful. (Matt. 13:22)

[18]Still others, like seed sown among thorns, hear the word; [19]but the worries of this life, the deceitfulness of wealth and the desires for other things come in and choke the word, making it unfruitful. (Mark 4:18–19)

[14]The seed that fell among thorns stands for those who hear, but as they go on their way they are choked by life's worries, riches and pleasures, and they do not mature. (Luke 8:14)

55. See also Matt. 10:5–10; 10:37–39; 13:44–46; 16:24–28; 19:16–24; Luke 14:15–35; 17:32; 18:18–30; 1 John 2:15–17.
56. Compare Eph. 4:17–19 and Col. 3:1–17 with American consumer culture.

j. Love for the better things in life tempts us to betray Jesus. In the case of Judas, the price was thirty silver coins (Matt. 26:14–16). In the case of Ananias and Sapphira, the concern was to appear more devoted to God than was actually the case — a common phenomenon among the wealthy, including those who earn a good living by being religious teachers and missionaries.

> [1]Now a man named Ananias, together with his wife Sapphira, also sold a piece of property. [2]With his wife's full knowledge he kept back part of the money for himself, but brought the rest and put it at the apostles' feet.
>
> [3]Then Peter said, "Ananias, how is it that Satan has so filled your heart that you have lied to the Holy Spirit and have kept for yourself some of the money you received for the land? [4]Didn't it belong to you before it was sold? And after it was sold, wasn't the money at your disposal? What made you think of doing such a thing? You have not lied to men but to God."
>
> [5]When Ananias heard this, he fell down and died. And great fear seized all who heard what had happened. [6]Then the young men came forward, wrapped up his body, and carried him out and buried him.
>
> [7]About three hours later his wife came in, not knowing what had happened. [8]Peter asked her, "Tell me, is this the price you and Ananias got for the land?"
>
> "Yes," she said, "that is the price."
>
> [9]Peter said to her, "How could you agree to test the Spirit of the Lord? Look! The feet of the men who buried your husband are at the door, and they will carry you out also."
>
> [10]At that moment she fell down at his feet and died. Then the young men came in and, finding her dead, carried her out and buried her beside her husband. (Acts 5:1–10)

5. Christ identified with the poor, coming for the poor and as one of the poor. Jesus' first recorded public words related to the poor (Luke 4:18–30). He made it clear that God's Kingdom was not intended for the rich, but for the poor. While it can be argued that he came to liberate both rich and poor, nevertheless it was as a poor man — born in a stable (Luke 2), out of wedlock, beholden to the pedigreed rich, and subject to Roman political and military power — that he identified himself with the human race. Judging from the circumstances of his presentation at the Temple, his parents were poor, a fact reflected by their humble offering.

> [22]When the time of their purification according to the Law of Moses had been completed, Joseph and Mary took him to Jerusalem to present him to the Lord [23](as it is written in the Law of the Lord, "Every firstborn male is to be consecrated to the Lord"), [24]and to offer a sacrifice in keeping with what is said in the Law of the Lord: "a pair of doves or two young pigeons." (Luke 2:22–24)

> [1]The LORD said to Moses, [2]"Say to the Israelites: 'A woman who becomes pregnant and gives birth to a son will be ceremonially unclean for seven days, just as she is unclean during her monthly period. [3]On the eighth day

the boy is to be circumcised. [4]Then the woman must wait thirty-three days to be purified from her bleeding. She must not touch anything sacred or go to the sanctuary until the days of her purification are over. [5]If she gives birth to a daughter, for two weeks the woman will be unclean, as during her period. Then she must wait sixty-six days to be purified from her bleeding.

[6]" 'When the days of her purification for a son or daughter are over, she is to bring to the priest at the entrance to the Tent of Meeting a year-old lamb for a burnt offering and a young pigeon or a dove for a sin offering. [7]He shall offer them before the Lord to make atonement for her, and then she will be ceremonially clean from her flow of blood.

" 'These are the regulations for the woman who gives birth to a boy or a girl. [8]If she cannot afford a lamb, she is to bring two doves or two young pigeons, one for a burnt offering and the other for a sin offering. In this way the priest will make atonement for her, and she will be clean.' " (Lev. 12:1–8)

Not surprisingly, and as predicted by the prophet Isaiah, his mission was to the poor, not to the rich.

[16]He went to Nazareth, where he had been brought up, and on the Sabbath day he went into the synagogue, as was his custom. And he stood up to read. [17]The scroll of the prophet Isaiah was handed to him. Unrolling it, he found the place where it is written:

> [18]"The Spirit of the Lord is on me,
>   because he has anointed me
>   to preach good news to the poor.
> He has sent me to proclaim freedom for the prisoners
>   and recovery of sight for the blind,
>   to release the oppressed,
> [19]to proclaim the year of the Lord's favor." (Luke 4:16–19)

> [1]The Spirit of the Sovereign Lord is on me,
>   because the Lord has anointed me
>   to preach good news to the poor.
> He has sent me to bind up the brokenhearted,
>   to proclaim freedom for the captives
>   and release from darkness for the prisoners,
> [2]to proclaim the year of the Lord's favor
>   and the day of vengeance of our God,
> to comfort all who mourn,
>   [3]and provide for those who grieve in Zion —
> to bestow on them a crown of beauty
>   instead of ashes,
> the oil of gladness
>   instead of mourning,
> and a garment of praise
>   instead of a spirit of despair.

> They will be called oaks of righteousness,
>   a planting of the LORD
>   for the display of his splendor. (Isa. 61:1–3)[57]

Strategically speaking, it would have made much more sense to enter human society at the top, in the manner of a spectacularly provisioned Western missionary from a powerful country with all of the prestige and efficiency that money can provide. But entering the world — a tiny bit of the moral universe that he had created and whose operations he well understood — he resisted the temptation to adopt the more commonsense approach that would have given him political and economic power (Luke 4).

His followers should not be surprised, then, if mission today is least effective when it is not carried out with the trappings of power and money. Evangelists and catechists, on the other hand, well down the missionary's economic and social ladder, have been powerfully effective, as indicated in my second chapter.[58]

a. Christ's followers identify with the poor in practical, costly ways. Those who neglect the poor cannot regard themselves, nor should they be regarded, as Christ's disciples — no matter how orthodox their creeds and confessions, and no matter how enthusiastic their pious rituals. Identification with the needy was a matter of paramount importance for Christ himself, and is a mark of all authentic followers. Lack of active practical involvement in ameliorating the plight of the poor is a sure indication of spiritual infidelity, or worse.

> [31]"When the Son of Man comes in his glory, and all the angels with him, he will sit on his throne in heavenly glory. [32]All the nations will be gathered before him, and he will separate the people one from another as a shepherd separates the sheep from the goats. [33]He will put the sheep on his right and the goats on his left.
>
> [34]"Then the King will say to those on his right, 'Come, you who are blessed by my Father; take your inheritance, the kingdom prepared for you since the creation of the world. [35]For I was hungry and you gave me something to eat, I was thirsty and you gave me something to drink, I was a stranger and you invited me in, [36]I needed clothes and you clothed me, I was sick and you looked after me, I was in prison and you came to visit me.'
>
> [37]"Then the righteous will answer him, 'Lord, when did we see you hungry and feed you, or thirsty and give you something to drink? [38]When did we see you a stranger and invite you in, or needing clothes and clothe you? [39]When did we see you sick or in prison and go to visit you?'
>
> [40]"The King will reply, 'I tell you the truth, whatever you did for one of the least of these brothers of mine, you did for me.'

---

57. All of Isa. 58 and 61 need to be read, to get a better sense of what Jesus was saying.

58. It is in the poor that we see and minister to Christ (Matt. 25:31–46); the poor are blessed, and the rich are damned (Luke 1:46–56; 6:20–26; 14:12–14; 16:19–31; Matt. 8:2, 18–20); Jesus became poor for our sakes (2 Cor. 8:9); for our sakes Jesus became nothing, a servant, humbly obedient to the point of death; and his followers are to be like him (Phil. 2:1–11).

41"Then he will say to those on his left, 'Depart from me, you who are cursed, into the eternal fire prepared for the devil and his angels. **42**For I was hungry and you gave me nothing to eat, I was thirsty and you gave me nothing to drink, **43**I was a stranger and you did not invite me in, I needed clothes and you did not clothe me, I was sick and in prison and you did not look after me.'

44"They also will answer, 'Lord, when did we see you hungry or thirsty or a stranger or needing clothes or sick or in prison, and did not help you?'

45"He will reply, 'I tell you the truth, whatever you did not do for one of the least of these, you did not do for me.'

46"Then they will go away to eternal punishment, but the righteous to eternal life." (Matt. 25:31–46)

Our Lord's earliest followers well understood this, and exemplified their risen Lord's concern for the poor. This concern manifested itself in such remarkably practical ways that they "had everything in common," and "there were no needy persons among them." Sharing our resources is a sacrifice with which God is pleased (Heb. 13:16). It is no wonder that early believers were not called Christians, but followers of "the Way."[59]

42They devoted themselves to the apostles' teaching and to the fellowship, to the breaking of bread and to prayer. **43**Everyone was filled with awe, and many wonders and miraculous signs were done by the apostles. **44**All the believers were together and had everything in common. **45**Selling their possessions and goods, they gave to anyone as he had need. **46**Every day they continued to meet together in the temple courts. They broke bread in their homes and ate together with glad and sincere hearts, **47**praising God and enjoying the favor of all the people. And the Lord added to their number daily those who were being saved. (Acts 2:42–47)

32All the believers were one in heart and mind. No one claimed that any of his possessions was his own, but they shared everything they had. **33**With great power the apostles continued to testify to the resurrection of the Lord Jesus, and much grace was upon them all. **34**There were no needy persons among them. For from time to time those who owned lands or houses sold them, brought the money from the sales **35**and put it at the apostles' feet, and it was distributed to anyone as he had need. (Acts 4:32–35)

The New Testament record is replete with this theme. Paul worked hard to help the weak, reminding the sorrowing Ephesian elders as he bid them a final farewell that they should do the same (Acts 20:17–38); the impoverished congregations of Macedonia pleaded for the privilege of sharing with the needy (2 Cor. 8:1–15); and the church in Philippi contributed to the needs of Paul (Phil. 4:14–19).[60]

---

59. See Acts 9:2; 19:9, 23; 22:4; 24:14, 22.
60. See also Luke 14:12–14; Acts 11:27–42; 2 Cor. 9:1–15 (We reap not only *what* we sow; we reap *more* than we sow. God loves a cheerful giver); Gal. 2:10/Acts 21:17ff.; Gal. 6:7–10.

In everything I did, I showed you that by this kind of hard work we must help the weak, remembering the words the Lord Jesus himself said: "It is more blessed to give than to receive." (Acts 20:35)

¹And now, brothers, we want you to know about the grace that God has given the Macedonian churches. ²Out of the most severe trial, their over-flowing joy and their extreme poverty welled up in rich generosity. ³For I testify that they gave as much as they were able, and even beyond their ability. Entirely on their own, ⁴they urgently pleaded with us for the privilege of sharing in this service to the saints. ⁵And they did not do as we expected, but they gave themselves first to the Lord and then to us in keeping with God's will. ⁶So we urged Titus, since he had earlier made a beginning, to bring also to completion this act of grace on your part. ⁷But just as you excel in everything — in faith, in speech, in knowledge, in complete earnestness and in your love for us — see that you also excel in this grace of giving.

⁸I am not commanding you, but I want to test the sincerity of your love by comparing it with the earnestness of others. ⁹For you know the grace of our Lord Jesus Christ, that though he was rich, yet for your sakes he became poor, so that you through his poverty might become rich.

¹⁰And here is my advice about what is best for you in this matter: Last year you were the first not only to give but also to have the desire to do so. ¹¹Now finish the work, so that your eager willingness to do it may be matched by your completion of it, according to your means. ¹²For if the willingness is there, the gift is acceptable according to what one has, not according to what he does not have.

¹³Our desire is not that others might be relieved while you are hard pressed, but that there might be equality. ¹⁴At the present time your plenty will supply what they need, so that in turn their plenty will supply what you need. Then there will be equality, ¹⁵as it is written: "He who gathered much did not have too much, and he who gathered little did not have too little." (2 Cor. 8:1–15)

¹⁴Yet it was good of you to share in my troubles. ¹⁵Moreover, as you Philip-pians know, in the early days of your acquaintance with the gospel, when I set out from Macedonia, not one church shared with me in the matter of giving and receiving, except you only; ¹⁶for even when I was in Thessa-lonica, you sent me aid again and again when I was in need. ¹⁷Not that I am looking for a gift, but I am looking for what may be credited to your ac-count. ¹⁸I have received full payment and even more; I am amply supplied, now that I have received from Epaphroditus the gifts you sent. They are a fragrant offering, an acceptable sacrifice, pleasing to God. ¹⁹And my God will meet all your needs according to his glorious riches in Christ Jesus. (Phil. 4:14–19)

¹⁶And do not forget to do good and to share with others, for with such sacrifices God is pleased. (Heb. 13:16)

[27]Religion that God our Father accepts as pure and faultless is this: to look after orphans and widows in their distress and to keep oneself from being polluted by the world. (James 1:27)

Significantly, assurance of salvation for John rests not upon the recollection of some altar call experience in the past, or the presentation of an infant baptismal certificate, but on one's relationship with his possessions and with the needy. In the words of James 2:19, "the demons believe," that is, insofar as orthodoxy is a matter of mental assent to a series of propositions about God, Jesus, the Holy Spirit, and so forth, the demons are believers! But their "belief" does not produce conversion. Only the converted are God's children.

[7]Dear children, do not let anyone lead you astray. He who does what is right is righteous, just as he is righteous. [8]He who does what is sinful is of the devil, because the devil has been sinning from the beginning. The reason the Son of God appeared was to destroy the devil's work. [9]No one who is born of God will continue to sin, because God's seed remains in him; he cannot go on sinning, because he has been born of God. [10]This is how we know who the children of God are and who the children of the devil are: Anyone who does not do what is right is not a child of God; nor is anyone who does not love his brother.

[11]This is the message you heard from the beginning: We should love one another. [12]Do not be like Cain, who belonged to the evil one and murdered his brother. And why did he murder him? Because his own actions were evil and his brother's were righteous. [13]Do not be surprised, my brothers, if the world hates you. [14]We know that we have passed from death to life, because we love our brothers. Anyone who does not love remains in death. [15]Anyone who hates his brother is a murderer, and you know that no murderer has eternal life in him.

[16]This is how we know what love is: Jesus Christ laid down his life for us. And we ought to lay down our lives for our brothers. [17]If anyone has material possessions and sees his brother in need but has no pity on him, how can the love of God be in him? [18]Dear children, let us not love with words or tongue but with actions and in truth. [19]This then is how we know that we belong to the truth, and how we set our hearts at rest in his presence [20]whenever our hearts condemn us. For God is greater than our hearts, and he knows everything. (1 John 3:7–20)

b. God deliberately does his work through the poor and the weak rather than through the rich and the strong.[61] Mary, the humble fiancée of Joseph, a carpenter, was chosen to bear, nurture, and train the incarnate Son of God. The cost to her was not only her reputation and the lifelong stigma of conceiving a child out of wedlock in a shame-and-guilt culture, but a life of distress and misunderstanding as the earthly mother of a man who so irritated the respectable

---

61. The churches described in the first three chapters of Revelation illustrate this: Smyrna — poor but deemed rich (2:8–11); Philadelphia — weak, yet deemed strong (3:7–13); Laodicea — rich, yet deemed impoverished (3:14–21).

guardians of Jewish orthodoxy that he drove them to murder him. This is a part of the human cost of obedience and divine favor.

> [5]Listen, my dear brothers: Has not God chosen those who are poor in the eyes of the world to be rich in faith and to inherit the kingdom he promised those who love him? (James 2:5)

> [18]This is how the birth of Jesus Christ came about: His mother Mary was pledged to be married to Joseph, but before they came together, she was found to be with child through the Holy Spirit. [19]Because Joseph her husband was a righteous man and did not want to expose her to public disgrace, he had in mind to divorce her quietly.

> [20]But after he had considered this, an angel of the Lord appeared to him in a dream and said, "Joseph son of David, do not be afraid to take Mary home as your wife, because what is conceived in her is from the Holy Spirit. [21]She will give birth to a son, and you are to give him the name Jesus, because he will save his people from their sins." (Matt 1:18–21; cf. Luke 1:26–38)

> [18]For the message of the cross is foolishness to those who are perishing, but to us who are being saved it is the power of God. [19]For it is written:

> "I will destroy the wisdom of the wise;
> the intelligence of the intelligent I will frustrate."

> [20]Where is the wise man? Where is the scholar? Where is the philosopher of this age? Has not God made foolish the wisdom of the world? [21]For since in the wisdom of God the world through its wisdom did not know him, God was pleased through the foolishness of what was preached to save those who believe. [22]Jews demand miraculous signs and Greeks look for wisdom, [23]but we preach Christ crucified: a stumbling block to Jews and foolishness to Gentiles, [24]but to those whom God has called, both Jews and Greeks, Christ is the power of God and the wisdom of God. [25]For the foolishness of God is wiser than man's wisdom, and the weakness of God is stronger than man's strength.

> [26]Brothers, think of what you were when you were called. Not many of you were wise by human standards; not many were influential; not many were of noble birth. [27]But God chose the foolish things of the world to shame the wise; God chose the weak things of the world to shame the strong. [28]He chose the lowly things of this world and the despised things — and the things that are not — to nullify the things that are, [29]so that no one may boast before him. [30]It is because of him that you are in Christ Jesus, who has become for us wisdom from God — that is, our righteousness, holiness and redemption. [31]Therefore, as it is written: "Let him who boasts boast in the Lord." (1 Cor. 1:16–31)

> [7]To keep me from becoming conceited because of these surpassingly great revelations, there was given me a thorn in my flesh, a messenger of Satan, to torment me. [8]Three times I pleaded with the Lord to take it away from

me. ⁹But he said to me, "My grace is sufficient for you, for my power is made perfect in weakness." Therefore I will boast all the more gladly about my weaknesses, so that Christ's power may rest on me. ¹⁰That is why, for Christ's sake, I delight in weaknesses, in insults, in hardships, in persecutions, in difficulties. For when I am weak, then I am strong. (2 Cor. 12:7–10)

c. Not religious orthodoxy, but one's relationship with the needy, is the true indicator of a person's standing with God. That is an emphasis in Jesus' teaching on the final judgment of the nations, when sheep and goats are differentiated purely on the basis of how they treated the poor (Matt. 25:3–46), and in the story of the good Samaritan, where someone whose theology is wrong inherits eternal life because of his proactive concern for a wounded enemy.

²⁵On one occasion an expert in the law stood up to test Jesus. "Teacher," he asked, "what must I do to inherit eternal life?"

²⁶"What is written in the Law?" he replied. "How do you read it?"

²⁷He answered: " 'Love the Lord your God with all your heart and with all your soul and with all your strength and with all your mind'; and, 'Love your neighbor as yourself.' "

²⁸"You have answered correctly," Jesus replied. "Do this and you will live."

²⁹But he wanted to justify himself, so he asked Jesus, "And who is my neighbor?"

³⁰In reply Jesus said: "A man was going down from Jerusalem to Jericho, when he fell into the hands of robbers. They stripped him of his clothes, beat him and went away, leaving him half dead. ³¹A priest happened to be going down the same road, and when he saw the man, he passed by on the other side. ³²So too, a Levite, when he came to the place and saw him, passed by on the other side. ³³But a Samaritan, as he traveled, came where the man was; and when he saw him, he took pity on him. ³⁴He went to him and bandaged his wounds, pouring on oil and wine. Then he put the man on his own donkey, took him to an inn and took care of him. ³⁵The next day he took out two silver coins and gave them to the innkeeper. 'Look after him,' he said, 'and when I return, I will reimburse you for any extra expense you may have.'

³⁶"Which of these three do you think was a neighbor to the man who fell into the hands of robbers?"

³⁷The expert in the law replied, "The one who had mercy on him." Jesus told him, "Go and do likewise." (Luke 10:25–37)

d. Identification with the poor in the New Testament involves relating to *specific persons*, **rather than to an abstract sociological class.** To commiserate with "the poor" as a class necessitates little more than pious hand-wringing, giving some money to charitable causes, and indulging in the satisfying exercise of haranguing those who don't measure up to even our conspicuously low standards. It costs almost nothing, while yielding gratifying self-satisfaction. But to come alongside actual human beings who are poor, in all of the frustrating complexity of their life situations and personalities, requires the substantial investment of personal resources, time, and agenda. And it is this kind of identification that marks the true follower of our Lord. To have the former without the latter is simple hypocrisy. To have the latter — however inchoate our verbal profession — is a basic requirement of every disciple. Only this provides a disciple with the moral foundation and the ethical credibility to speak boldly against the powerful political, economic, and social vested interests that are so often implicated in the impoverishment of millions. For Christians born and bred in a culture that all too blithely substitutes legality for justice, and consumption for fulfillment, and acquisition for happiness, living as "people of the Way" will not come naturally or easily. But it is, nevertheless, essential.

6. Genuine repentance is always marked by genuine giving, which is always sacrificial. God honors giving that involves the sacrifice of things of value to us — not merely a ritual dumping of surpluses and discards. True worship involves sacrificing that which is most dear to us. At the most basic level, Christ's followers are enjoined to present their bodies as living sacrifices unto God (Rom. 12:1–21). That this is no mere mental exercise, but a matter of profound reorientation of oneself vis-à-vis others, becomes clear as one reads the chapter. Cultural conformity, mental conditioning, and life orientation — each is affected, with profound implications for those of us conditioned to a life of escalating plenty in a consumer society that will even resort to violence against civilian populations to protect and expand its imagined entitlement to the lion's share of global markets and resources. This is the nature of all peoples. But it is not permitted to the citizens of God's kingdom. Our loyalties lie elsewhere, and our mission is accomplished through giving.

> [1]Therefore, I urge you, brothers, in view of God's mercy, to offer your bodies as living sacrifices, holy and pleasing to God — this is your spiritual act of worship. [2]Do not conform any longer to the pattern of this world, but be transformed by the renewing of your mind. Then you will be able to test and approve what God's will is — his good, pleasing and perfect will.
>
> [3]For by the grace given me I say to every one of you: Do not think of yourself more highly than you ought, but rather think of yourself with sober judgment, in accordance with the measure of faith God has given you. [4]Just as each of us has one body with many members, and these members do not all have the same function, [5]so in Christ we who are many form one body, and each member belongs to all the others. [6]We have different gifts, according to the grace given us. If a man's gift is prophesying, let him use it in proportion to his faith. [7]If it is serving, let him serve; if it is teaching, let him teach; [8]if it is encouraging, let him encourage; if it is contributing to the needs of others, let him give generously; if it is leadership, let him govern diligently; if it is showing mercy, let him do it cheerfully.
>
> [9]Love must be sincere. Hate what is evil; cling to what is good. [10]Be devoted to one another in brotherly love. Honor one another above yourselves. [11]Never be lacking in zeal, but keep your spiritual fervor, serving

the Lord. [12]Be joyful in hope, patient in affliction, faithful in prayer. [13]Share with God's people who are in need. Practice hospitality.

[14]Bless those who persecute you; bless and do not curse. [15]Rejoice with those who rejoice; mourn with those who mourn. [16]Live in harmony with one another. Do not be proud, but be willing to associate with people of low position. Do not be conceited.

[17]Do not repay anyone evil for evil. Be careful to do what is right in the eyes of everybody. [18]If it is possible, as far as it depends on you, live at peace with everyone. [19]Do not take revenge, my friends, but leave room for God's wrath, for it is written: "It is mine to avenge; I will repay," says the Lord. [20]On the contrary:

> "If your enemy is hungry, feed him;
> if he is thirsty, give him something to drink.
> In doing this, you will heap burning coals on his head."

[21]Do not be overcome by evil, but overcome evil with good. (Rom. 12: 1–21)

The poor widow's two copper coins — worth only a fraction of a penny — were of much greater significance than the large donations of the rich. It is interesting to note that Jesus does not appear to have been unduly concerned with whether the recipient of the gift was worthy or not. In this case, the widow gave all that she had to a corrupt Temple regime. Jesus did not regard this as waste, since he was more concerned with the widow's motives than with the relative merits of the recipient.

[41]Jesus sat down opposite the place where the offerings were put and watched the crowd putting their money into the temple treasury. Many rich people threw in large amounts. [42]But a poor widow came and put in two very small copper coins, worth only a fraction of a penny.

[43]Calling his disciples to him, Jesus said, "I tell you the truth, this poor widow has put more into the treasury than all the others. [44]They all gave out of their wealth; but she, out of her poverty, put in everything — all she had to live on." (Mark 12:41–44)[62]

a. Christ's followers are not called to self-fulfillment, but to self-denial. As an ultimate goal, self-fulfillment is an elusive, ever-receding horizon. For the Christian, self-fulfillment, like happiness, is a byproduct of a life lived on behalf of others. To live a self-indulgent life is to fritter away eternal opportunity. Peter, rebuking Jesus for his determination to suffer, was disconcerted to hear that his understandable concern for his Lord's well-being was not merely inappropriate, but positively Satanic: "Out of my sight, Satan!" Jesus said. "You do not have in mind the things of God, but the things of men."

---

62. Cf. Mark 14:1–9 and John 12:1–8, the story of Mary who "wasted" the expensive perfume on Jesus' feet.

[31]He then began to teach them that the Son of Man must suffer many things and be rejected by the elders, chief priests and teachers of the law, and that he must be killed and after three days rise again. [32]He spoke plainly about this, and Peter took him aside and began to rebuke him.

[33]But when Jesus turned and looked at his disciples, he rebuked Peter. "Get behind me, Satan!" he said. "You do not have in mind the things of God, but the things of men."

[34]Then he called the crowd to him along with his disciples and said: "If anyone would come after me, he must deny himself and take up his cross and follow me. [35]For whoever wants to save his life will lose it, but whoever loses his life for me and for the gospel will save it. [36]What good is it for a man to gain the whole world, yet forfeit his soul? [37]Or what can a man give in exchange for his soul? [38]If anyone is ashamed of me and my words in this adulterous and sinful generation, the Son of Man will be ashamed of him when he comes in his Father's glory with the holy angels." (Mark 8:31–38)

As they encouraged fellow believers in Lystra, Iconium, and Antioch, Paul and Barnabas explained that the path of obedience for disciples often leads through extraordinary hardships. Indeed, "God has put us apostles [missionaries] on display at the end of the procession, like men condemned to die in the arena," Paul declared, invoking an image that would have been familiar throughout the brutal Roman Empire, with its insatiable lust for bloody gladiatorial spectacles (1 Cor. 4:9).

[19]Then some Jews came from Antioch and Iconium and won the crowd over. They stoned Paul and dragged him outside the city, thinking he was dead. [20]But after the disciples had gathered around him, he got up and went back into the city. The next day he and Barnabas left for Derbe.

[21]They preached the good news in that city and won a large number of disciples. Then they returned to Lystra, Iconium and Antioch, [22]strengthening the disciples and encouraging them to remain true to the faith. "We must go through many hardships to enter the kingdom of God," they said. (Acts 14:19–22)

[1]So then, men ought to regard us as servants of Christ and as those entrusted with the secret things of God. [2]Now it is required that those who have been given a trust must prove faithful. [3]I care very little if I am judged by you or by any human court; indeed, I do not even judge myself. [4]My conscience is clear, but that does not make me innocent. It is the Lord who judges me. [5]Therefore judge nothing before the appointed time; wait till the Lord comes. He will bring to light what is hidden in darkness and will expose the motives of men's hearts. At that time each will receive his praise from God.

[6]Now, brothers, I have applied these things to myself and Apollos for your benefit, so that you may learn from us the meaning of the saying, "Do not go beyond what is written." Then you will not take pride in one man over against another. [7]For who makes you different from anyone else?

What do you have that you did not receive? And if you did receive it, why do you boast as though you did not? ⁸Already you have all you want! Already you have become rich! You have become kings — and that without us! How I wish that you really had become kings so that we might be kings with you! ⁹For it seems to me that God has put us apostles on display at the end of the procession, like men condemned to die in the arena. We have been made a spectacle to the whole universe, to angels as well as to men. ¹⁰We are fools for Christ, but you are so wise in Christ! We are weak, but you are strong! You are honored, we are dishonored! ¹¹To this very hour we go hungry and thirsty, we are in rags, we are brutally treated, we are homeless. ¹²We work hard with our own hands. When we are cursed, we bless; when we are persecuted, we endure it; ¹³when we are slandered, we answer kindly. Up to this moment we have become the scum of the earth, the refuse of the world.

¹⁴I am not writing this to shame you, but to warn you, as my dear children. ¹⁵Even though you have ten thousand guardians in Christ, you do not have many fathers, for in Christ Jesus I became your father through the gospel. ¹⁶Therefore I urge you to imitate me. (1 Cor. 4:1–16)

Christ's followers — and especially those called to be missionaries — are not called to be first, but last; not masters, but servants. This is a constant refrain of both Jesus and Paul, borne out in their lives, and held out as an example to follow. For the wealthy person living among the poor, this goes absolutely contrary to natural practice, necessitating a redefinition of "service" so that the ruler sees himself as the servant of the ruled.[63]

b. The generosity of Christ's follower is to be uncalculating, and should extend even — or especially — to one's undeserving enemies.

³⁸"You have heard that it was said, 'Eye for eye, and tooth for tooth.' ³⁹But I tell you, Do not resist an evil person. If someone strikes you on the right cheek, turn to him the other also. ⁴⁰And if someone wants to sue you and take your tunic, let him have your cloak as well. ⁴¹If someone forces you to go one mile, go with him two miles. ⁴²Give to the one who asks you, and do not turn away from the one who wants to borrow from you.

⁴³"You have heard that it was said, 'Love your neighbor and hate your enemy.' ⁴⁴But I tell you: Love your enemies and pray for those who persecute you, ⁴⁵that you may be sons of your Father in heaven. He causes his sun to rise on the evil and the good, and sends rain on the righteous and the unrighteous. ⁴⁶If you love those who love you, what reward will you get? Are not even the tax collectors doing that? ⁴⁷And if you greet only your brothers, what are you doing more than others? Do not even pagans do that? ⁴⁸Be perfect, therefore, as your heavenly Father is perfect." (Matt. 5:38–48)[64]

---

63. See also Rom. 8:18–39; 1 Cor. 4:9–16; 2 Cor. 4:1–18; 6:3–10; 11:16–12:10; Mark 9:33–37; Luke 13:22–29.

64. See also Luke 6:27–36; Rom. 12:17–21.

c. Genuine repentance for the wealthy always contains a practical, economic dimension. It is important to note that the "fruit in keeping with repentance" to which John the Baptist called his listeners involved economic relationships. And Luke makes the point that when Zacchaeus repented, he not only paid back four times as much as he had extorted, but gave half of his possessions to the poor. "Today," Jesus said, "salvation has come to this house" (Luke 19:1–9).[65]

> [7]John said to the crowds coming out to be baptized by him, "You brood of vipers! Who warned you to flee from the coming wrath? [8]Produce fruit in keeping with repentance. And do not begin to say to yourselves, 'We have Abraham as our father.' For I tell you that out of these stones God can raise up children for Abraham. [9]The axe is already at the root of the trees, and every tree that does not produce good fruit will be cut down and thrown into the fire."
>
> [10]"What should we do then?" the crowd asked.
>
> [11]John answered, "The man with two tunics should share with him who has none, and the one who has food should do the same."
>
> [12]Tax collectors also came to be baptized. "Teacher," they asked, "what should we do?"
>
> [13]"Don't collect any more than you are required to," he told them.
>
> [14]Then some soldiers asked him, "And what should we do?"
>
> He replied, "Don't extort money and don't accuse people falsely — be content with your pay." (Luke 3:7–14)

Wide-scale repentance in North America would undoubtedly have severe economic and political repercussions. Nothing could more quickly undermine our way of life than an outbreak of widespread contentment, or conversion to our Lord's teaching on mammon and the poor. Even men and women with modest vested economic interests — such as those in the United States whose livelihoods depend upon the invention, manufacture, sale, and use of military weapons — make repentance too costly for most to contemplate. For this reason, those who stand to lose economically are usually and understandably resistant to the Gospel.

> [23]About that time there arose a great disturbance about the Way. [24]A silversmith named Demetrius, who made silver shrines of Artemis, brought in no little business for the craftsmen. [25]He called them together, along with the workmen in related trades, and said: "Men, you know we receive a good income from this business. [26]And you see and hear how this fellow Paul has convinced and led astray large numbers of people here in Ephesus and in practically the whole province of Asia. He says that man-made gods are no gods at all. [27]There is danger not only that our trade will lose its good name, but also that the temple of the great goddess Artemis will be discredited, and the goddess herself, who is worshiped throughout the province of Asia and the world, will be robbed of her divine majesty."

---

65. Compare also Acts 2:42–47; 4:32–5:1; and 10:2, where Cornelius is deemed to be a righteous man because he "gave generously to those in need."

²⁸When they heard this, they were furious and began shouting: "Great is Artemis of the Ephesians!" (Acts 19:23–28ff)

7. Repentance by the rich is rare, but possible. There can be no doubt that Jesus had many dealings with the rich. What, then, was he trying to say to them? Their situation did not have to remain as it was. They could be converted. Conversion would result in the fruit of repentance. Repentance would involve them in radically new relationships to their wealth and to the poor. Although the rich young ruler did not repent (Luke 18:18–30), and only few Pharisees — such as the apostle Paul — became followers, the joyful repentance of Zacchaeus holds out hope for the rich (Luke 19:1–9).

Those within the church who are rich — and this applies to a majority of North American missionaries when they go abroad — are commanded "not to be arrogant nor to put their hope in wealth... to do good, to be rich in good deeds, and to be generous and willing to share." One can only imagine how difficult it must have been for Timothy to follow this advice. Had he been rich himself, he would have needed to teach by example. This is the only option open to wealthy missionaries, should they venture to teach a passage such as this one.

> ¹⁷Command those who are rich in this present world not to be arrogant nor to put their hope in wealth, which is so uncertain, but to put their hope in God, who richly provides us with everything for our enjoyment. ¹⁸Command them to do good, to be rich in good deeds, and to be generous and willing to share. ¹⁹In this way they will lay up treasure for themselves as a firm foundation for the coming age, so that they may take hold of the life that is truly life. (1 Tim. 6:17–19)

8. Many religious leaders and missionaries in New Testament times, as now, loved money. In admirable anticipation of free-market capitalism, they made a good living out of their religion, "peddling the word of God for profit" (2 Cor. 2:17). Insofar as Western Christianity still regards itself (subliminally) as the theological and ecclesiastical standard against which to gauge orthodoxy or viability, and to which the rest of world Christianity aspires, our missionaries and church leaders are in a position not unlike that of the Pharisees of Christ's day. Jesus, who in Matthew 23 exposes the ugly reality behind their pious façade of self-justification and professional religiosity, describes them as "full of greed and self-indulgence" (Matt. 23:25).

Religious teachers, since they are to be judged by a standard more rigorous than that applied to others, need to work hard at ensuring consistency between what they teach and how they live.

> ¹Not many of you should presume to be teachers, my brothers, because you know that we who teach will be judged more strictly. (James 3:1)⁶⁶

Personal affluence places Christian teachers or missionaries in great jeopardy, since they must practice what they preach. Failure to do so compromises their

---

66. Compare Matt. 7:1–5; Rom. 2:21–24.

credibility as exemplary followers of the Lord whose teachings and way of life they represent. "My mother and my brothers are those who hear God's word and put it into practice," Jesus said (Luke 8:21; cf. Matt. 7:21–27; Luke 6:46; 11:28; James 1:22–27). Paul is emphatic about it: the one who loves money is disqualified from spiritual leadership positions in the church (1 Tim. 3:3).[67] Those whose lives, priorities, and preoccupations revolve around personal security are living as "enemies of the cross" (Phil. 3:17–21). "Godliness" can be lucrative (1 Tim. 6:3–5). Some who claim to follow Christ do well by doing good. Such religious leaders, while not genuinely interested in the poor, find in them a way for personal advancement of one sort or another. Judas, for example, was not really interested in the poor, but cleverly invoked their cause as a way to supplement his own purse (John 12:1–8).[68] To those of us whose livelihood and very identity derives from our close association with the poor, such teaching strikes close to home, and deserves our utmost careful attention.

[7]Dear children, do not let anyone lead you astray. He who does what is right is righteous, just as he is righteous. [8]He who does what is sinful is of the devil, because the devil has been sinning from the beginning. The reason the Son of God appeared was to destroy the devil's work. [9]No one who is born of God will continue to sin, because God's seed remains in him; he cannot go on sinning, because he has been born of God. [10]This is how we know who the children of God are and who the children of the devil are: Anyone who does not do what is right is not a child of God; nor is anyone who does not love his brother....

[16]This is how we know what love is: Jesus Christ laid down his life for us. And we ought to lay down our lives for our brothers. [17]If anyone has material possessions and sees his brother in need but has no pity on him, how can the love of God be in him? [18]Dear children, let us not love with words or tongue but with actions and in truth. [19]This then is how we know that we belong to the truth, and how we set our hearts at rest in his presence [20]whenever our hearts condemn us. For God is greater than our hearts, and he knows everything. (1 John 3:7–10, 16–20)

[14]What good is it, my brothers, if a man claims to have faith but has no deeds? Can such faith save him? [15]Suppose a brother or sister is without clothes and daily food. [16]If one of you says to him, "Go, I wish you well; keep warm and well fed," but does nothing about his physical needs, what good is it? [17]In the same way, faith by itself, if it is not accompanied by action, is dead. (James 2:14–17)

9. Obedience, not theological orthodoxy, distinguishes the true follower of Jesus from the fraud. Echoing Habakkuk and Paul, the author of the letter to

---

67. It is hard to disguise one's true motives when one is peddling the word of God for profit (2 Cor. 2:17; 2 Pet. 2:1–3; Jude 3:16; 1 Thess. 2:5).

68. Jorgen Lissner speaks to this in his *The Politics of Altruism: A Study of the Political Behaviour of Voluntary Development Agencies* (Geneva: Lutheran World Federation, Department of Studies, 1977), as does Redmond Mullin in his *Present Alms: On the Corruption of Philanthropy* (Birmingham: Phlogiston Publishing Ltd., 1980).

the Hebrews reminds us that the righteous person *lives* by faith. In many church circles, faith has been understood to be primarily a matter of mental assent to a series of correct theological propositions. While it is good to be right theologically, the New Testament understanding of faith is emphatically on practice, not theory. That is the argument of what is perhaps the most well-known passage on the subject, Hebrews 10:19–12:12, portions of which are quoted below. In order to highlight the natural stress on practice, as the inevitable concomitant to theory in all genuine faith, the tangible evidence of faith in each instance below is in bold, italicized print.

[38]"But my righteous one will *live* by faith. And if he shrinks back, I will not be pleased with him." [39]But we are not of those who shrink back and are destroyed, but of those who believe and are saved. (Heb. 10:38–39)

[1]Now faith is being sure of what we hope for and certain of what we do not see. [2]This is what the ancients were commended for.

[3]*By faith we understand* that the universe was formed at God's command, so that what is seen was not made out of what was visible. [4]*By faith Abel offered* God a better sacrifice than Cain did. By faith he was commended as a righteous man, when God spoke well of his offerings. And by faith he still speaks, even though he is dead.

[5]*By faith Enoch* was taken from this life, so that he did not experience death; he could not be found, because God had taken him away. For before he was taken, he *was commended as one who pleased God*....

[7]*By faith Noah*, when warned about things not yet seen, in holy fear *built an ark* to save his family. By his faith he condemned the world and became heir of the righteousness that comes by faith.

[8]*By faith Abraham*, when called to go to a place he would later receive as his inheritance, *obeyed and went,* even though he did not know where he was going. [9]*By faith he made his home in the promised land like a stranger in a foreign country;* he *lived in tents, as did Isaac and Jacob,* who were heirs with him of the same promise. [10]For he was looking forward to the city with foundations, whose architect and builder is God....

[17]*By faith Abraham*, when God tested him, *offered Isaac as a sacrifice.* [20]By faith Isaac blessed Jacob and Esau in regard to their future....

[22]*By faith Joseph*, when his end was near, *spoke about the exodus* of the Israelites from Egypt and *gave instructions about his bones*.

[23]*By faith Moses' parents hid him* for three months after he was born, because they saw he was no ordinary child, and they were not afraid of the king's edict.

[24]*By faith Moses*, when he had grown up, *refused to be known as the son of Pharaoh's daughter.* [25]He *chose to be mistreated* along with the people of God rather than to enjoy the pleasures of sin for a short time. [26]He regarded disgrace for the sake of Christ as of greater value than the treasures of Egypt, because he was looking ahead to his reward. [27]*By faith he left Egypt,* not fearing the king's anger; he persevered because he saw him who is invisible. [28]*By faith he kept the Passover* and the sprinkling of

blood, so that the destroyer of the firstborn would not touch the firstborn of Israel.

²⁹*By faith the people passed through the Red Sea* as on dry land; but when the Egyptians tried to do so, they were drowned.

³⁰By faith the walls of Jericho fell, after the people had marched around them for seven days.

³¹*By faith the prostitute Rahab*, because she *welcomed the spies,* was not killed with those who were disobedient.

³²And what more shall I say? I do not have time to tell about Gideon, Barak, Samson, Jephthah, David, Samuel and the prophets, **³³**who through faith conquered kingdoms, administered justice, and gained what was promised; who shut the mouths of lions, **³⁴**quenched the fury of the flames, and escaped the edge of the sword; whose weakness was turned to strength; and who became powerful in battle and routed foreign armies. **³⁵**Women received back their dead, raised to life again. Others were tortured and refused to be released, so that they might gain a better resurrection. **³⁶**Some faced jeers and flogging, while still others were chained and put in prison. **³⁷**They were stoned; they were sawed in two; they were put to death by the sword. They went about in sheepskins and goatskins, destitute, persecuted and mistreated — **³⁸**the world was not worthy of them. They wandered in deserts and mountains, and in caves and holes in the ground.

³⁹These were all commended for their faith, yet none of them received what had been promised. **⁴⁰**God had planned something better for us so that only together with us would they be made perfect. (Heb. 11:1–40)

The faith for which the ancients were commended was sufficiently authentic as to produce correspondingly appropriate conduct, no matter how odd or counterintuitive such behavior must have seemed at the time. So it must be with the faith of Christian missionaries in contexts of poverty today. The only real difference between the faith of demons and the faith of Christ's followers, according to James, lies in the accompanying behavior.

¹⁴What good is it, my brothers, if a man claims to have faith but has no deeds? Can such faith save him?

¹⁵Suppose a brother or sister is without clothes and daily food. **¹⁶**If one of you says to him, "Go, I wish you well; keep warm and well fed," but does nothing about his physical needs, what good is it? **¹⁷**In the same way, faith by itself, if it is not accompanied by action, is dead.

¹⁸But someone will say, "You have faith; I have deeds."

Show me your faith without deeds, and I will show you my faith by what I do.

¹⁹You believe that there is one God. Good! Even the demons believe that — and shudder.

²⁰You foolish man, do you want evidence that faith without deeds is useless? **²¹**Was not our ancestor Abraham considered righteous for what he did when he offered his son Isaac on the altar? **²²**You see that his faith and his actions were working together, and his faith was made complete by what he did. [23]And the scripture was fulfilled that says, "Abraham believed God, and it was credited to him as righteousness," and he was called God's friend. [24]You see that a person is justified by what he does and not by faith alone.

[25]In the same way, was not even Rahab the prostitute considered righteous for what she did when she gave lodging to the spies and sent them off in a different direction? [26]As the body without the spirit is dead, so faith without deeds is dead. (James 2:14–26)[69]

Conclusion

Let no one think that possession of wealth is a sin, or that only the wealthy sin. *All* sin and fall short of the glory of God. The poor have sins to which they are particularly susceptible. But wealth is the context in which the faith of the rich is tested. The Gospel is for the rich, as well as for the poor — although we rich might at times not recognize the "good news" as *good* when it is focused so painfully on our pleasantly desperate plight.

It is clear that Christianity was never designed to make people comfortably at ease with wealth and power. Nor, predictably, has genuine discipleship ever been widely popular among the rich. Wealth on any wide scale has never been the norm in human experience. Subsistence, rather than abundance, has been the distinguishing mark of most societies. The modern missionary movement from the West, coinciding as it has with the economic and military hegemony of the West and the relatively widely distributed affluence of those traditionally missionary-sending nations, is now confronted with theological and ethical dilemmas engendered by its own affluence.

In view of the fact that Western missionaries must often number themselves among the rich of this world, the teaching of the Old and New Testaments on the subject of the wealthy and the poor makes very uncomfortable reading. Furthermore, for those who live privileged lives among the poor, it becomes difficult if not impossible to teach. This is perhaps one reason that missionaries to the world's great cities focus on those sectors of the population with prospects of upward mobility, and have *little to say to* and even *less to do with* the inhabitants of the slums.[70] This may be one reason that the door of opportunity in Christian mission today is not open before the wealthy Laodicean church, but before the impoverished Philadelphian church. Affluent missions are becoming increasingly marginalized in the great spiritual mission of the church.

Even the least self-examined person cannot but feel uncomfortable when confronted with the Scripture's plain teaching on these matters. One is left with recourse to one of three possible options: (1) ignore the teaching altogether, (2) employ a self-justification hermeneutic that satisfactorily explains why such uncomfortable teaching cannot apply to one's personal situation, or (3) repent and be converted.

---

69. Compare Hab. 2:3–4; Rom. 1:16–17; Acts 6:7; 7:53.

70. This is part of the message of the Report of the Consultation of World Evangelization Mini-Consultation on Reaching the Urban Poor, *The Thailand Report on the Urban Poor,* held in Pattaya, Thailand, June 16–27, 1980 (Wheaton, IL: Lausanne Committee for World Evangelization, 1980).

Part III

THE CHALLENGE OF
WESTERN MISSIONARY
AFFLUENCE

*"But how can God bring this about in me?"... Let Him do it and perhaps
you will know.*
— George MacDonald

*There is a profound sense in which my concluding chapter can never be finished,
at least not in the pages of a book. Most of what remains to be said needs to be
written in the flesh and blood of everyday life. Some readers will, no doubt, be
frustrated by the discovery that while I have taken them some way beyond the
conclusions reached in the first edition of the book, I still have not spelled out
the precise details of that repentance which leads to conversion, and to which
the Scriptures clearly call us. As I said in the earlier edition, no one can write a
discipleship agenda for someone else. Each disciple is called from a particular
place, at a particular time, to a particular obedience, by a personal Savior and
Lord. Nevertheless, I hope that readers — in particular, missionaries and those
who train or administer missionaries — will find me more helpfully suggestive
in this chapter than I was able to be when I first wrote the book almost twenty
years ago.*

*As Western Christians we rightly regard the poverty of our fellow human
beings as a gigantic problem about which we seem able to do very little; we have
proven less willing to view our personal affluence as an equally perplexing and,
in many ways, a more immediately perplexing problem ethically. Global poverty
is an acute material challenge, no doubt; but Western affluence is a profoundly
spiritual one. It is at least as difficult for affluent Christians to surmount the
spiritual challenges of our affluence as it is for our poverty-stricken brothers and
sisters in the rest of the world to survive their poverty.*

Unless we come to see our world through the eyes of Jesus and the writers of our Scriptures, we will continue to excuse the personal and collective covetousness and greed that have made us "great," and above the locked door to the heart of the richest church in the world will be written — in splendid gilt lettering — the word "ICHABOD," for her Savior will remain on the outside (Rev. 3:17–20).

7

Toward a Missiology
of the Righteous Rich

*If anyone would come after me, he must deny himself and take up his cross
and follow me. For whoever wants to save his life will lose it, but whoever
loses his life for me and for the Gospel will save it.*   — JESUS

*Heroes, being men of marked character, are deemed by the vulgar herd
to be eccentric: their very superiority prevents their being estimated. The
circumstances of their death shakes weak Faith, but the true Christian
through Death to Life sees clearly, how God of seeming evil works lasting
good. To die for one's country is a great gain: to die for one's Saviour, to fill
up what remains of His sufferings, is sweeter.*   — ROBERT NEEDHAM CUST

*There are two kinds of Christianity — success-Christianity and failure-
Christianity. Jesus said, "Unless I fail, my work will be useless."*
                                                       — TOYOHIKO KAGAWA

*She had not learned that the look of things as you go, is not their look when
you turn to go back... Nature is like a lobster pot: she lets you easily go
on, but not easily return.*   — GEORGE MACDONALD

We come now to the most difficult part of the book. For mission communities in which most members enjoy access to the minimal material entitlements
thought to be essential to North American families, scriptural teaching on wealth
and poverty is vaguely, though not poignantly, disquieting. Of course, we North
Americans are well aware that this planet is home to vast numbers of impoverished and even destitute peoples, and that some of these can be found in our
inner cities. But any niggling disquiet of conscience that we might feel — usually
sparked by fleetingly surreal images on our flat-screen television sets — is easily
quelled or at least controlled. What, after all, do such people have to do with
us? Our very helplessness in the face of endemic human tragedy is, in its own
way, mercifully reassuring. But when the spiritual teachers and exemplars of an
impoverished church are the only people enjoying a relatively lavish standard
of living, biblical teaching becomes more difficult to either explain or model, a
point that is most problematic for the wealthy missionary.

The argument of the book thus far has been this: missionaries from North America are often relatively wealthy within their ministry contexts, due often to factors which cannot be replicated in the non-Western world. Since this is so, I argued, what the Bible says *to* and *about* the wealthy, it says to and about the missionaries themselves. In chapters 2 and 3, I examined aspects of the cultural and social milieu that make it possible for Western missionaries to uncritically accept, expect, and justify their own rising material expectations and standards of living in a world populated by a growing majority of impoverished inhabitants. These three chapters together served as introduction to the dynamic social and economic context in which the theory and practice of Western Christian missions are conceived and implemented.

In chapters 4 through 6, attention was focused on some troublesome consequences of missionary affluence in a world increasingly polarized between the rich few and the impoverished many. Since our faith is above all a relational faith, lived out in actual social and cultural contexts, the verbalization of "the real Gospel" is potentially contradicted, obscured, or subverted by the good news of plenty, of which a missionary himself or herself often constitutes "Exhibit A." The quality of missionary relationships with the poor, the clarity of their communication of the good news to the poor, and the credibility of their life and teaching among the poor, it was argued, have been and continue to be deeply affected — sometimes in profoundly negative ways — by their steadily growing affluence vis-à-vis the people among whom they live and work.

In addition to multifaceted communicatory, strategic, and relational consequences issuing from a missionary's relative affluence, fundamental questions having to do with his or her ethical integrity emerge as a direct result of scriptural teaching on the relationship between rich and poor, and between God's people and their possessions. This was the burden of chapter 6. When a missionary is "rich" in contexts of poverty, what the Bible says to and about the wealthy it says about the missionary. In light of all this, what should or can a wealthy missionary do?

Western missionaries, long uneasy about their relative affluence, have tended to adopt (slip into) one or some combination of four possible responses to this state of affairs: (1) associate primarily with those of approximately equal social and economic privilege; (2) assume a simple lifestyle that belies the extent of their privilege, while surreptitiously maintaining the benefits of Western entitlement in critical areas such as medical care, transportation, education of children, and retirement; (3) shift the debate from the moral/ethical dimensions of missionary affluence to the realm of mission strategy, focusing on the relative advantages of church independence as compared to dependence or interdependence; and, finally, (4) adopt a radically incarnational lifestyle, genuinely forfeiting privilege and living as those among whom they minister. While each of these approaches can be sufficiently beneficial as to be defensible, later in this chapter I propose a fifth alternative: assumption of a biblically informed and contextually delineated status of "righteous rich."

If knowledge and virtue were synonymous, this book could end here. But since they are not, it remains to return to that acutely practical question which is the inevitable corollary of all that has been said so far: what should or can a wealthy missionary do? Is it really true, as Ivan Illich insisted almost forty years ago, that "There is no exit" from a way of life built on large and ever-increasing amounts of money?[1] The last two decades of Western missionary experience seem to support his pessimism. But are change, repentance, conversion — the stock-in-trade of missionary evangelism — possible only for nonmissionaries?

The narrow path of discipleship has never been popular among those whose numerous and bulky possessions make passage through the narrow gate and negotiation of the narrow way virtually impossible. Our Lord insisted that it is easier for the poor than for the rich to enter the kingdom of Heaven — in spite of the fact that the rich with their ingenious hermeneutics of self-justification are well-prepared and splendidly equipped to expound at length upon eternal verities. But did not some of Christ's first followers come from the ranks of the then-wealthy? The rich young ruler found it impractical to give up all that he had to be Christ's disciple, it is true (Luke 18:18–25); but Levi must have been a man of considerable economic means, and he repented (Luke 5:27–30). His story, along with those of Zacchaeus, Barnabas, Paul, Luke, and others, suggests that Illich's conclusion may be overly pessimistic, for such exemplars show us that there *is* an exit from our blatantly materialistic way of life!

It is obvious that as North Americans, missionaries are affected by the press and pull of a social ethos which, if examined closely, is shaped, inspired, and animated by the deep assumption that life — in consonance with the economic logic of any consumer economy — consists in the abundance of possessions, especially more, better, and up-to-date possessions. In a more innocent age, it was possible for missionaries to believe that their comfortable way of life was the inevitable outcome of national life organized in a Christian way, and that, given enough time and sufficient conversions, the poorer peoples of the world would enjoy the good life. Not only were Christianity and civilization inseparable, but, in the sober judgment of some of the best of the West's nineteenth-century Christian minds, no one could "become a Christian in the true sense of the term, however savage [they] may have been before, without becoming...civilised."[2] Well after the dawn of the twentieth century, with the "civilised" nations in the throes of one of the most bloody and pointless struggles in the pathetically war-strewn record of humankind, it was still bravely asserted that:

> The civilisation which is called Western is the slowly developed product of religion... [and has] surged forward to its present high water by means of the internal pressure of its inner Christian elan,... an impulse which is but the expression of a Christian principle of life moving within.[3]

---

1. Ivan Illich, *Celebration of Awareness: A Call for Institutional Revolution* (Garden City, NY: Doubleday, 1970), 27.
   2. David Jonathan East, *Western Africa: Its Condition, and Christianity the Means of Its Recovery* (London: Houlston & Stoneman, 1844), 243.
   3. Allan J. M. Macdonald, *Trade Politics and Christianity in Africa and the East* (London: Longmans, Green and Co., 1916), 54.

We have gradually come to recognize that this is false. The West has been demystified.[4] We know with terrifying certainty that for nine out of ten of our fellow human beings, there is no possible road to our way of life in the foreseeable future. The stark and brutal truth is that the natural resources of our planet are sufficient to support "civilized" life for only a tiny fraction of its human population. As Tim Flannery noted in an essay appearing in *The New York Review of Books,* given the sorry condition of our environment, consumerism as a model of development is a dead-end model. Referring to a table in the 2004 edition of the World Wildlife Fund's *Living Planet Report* charting human impacts on our planet from 1961 to 2001,[5] Flannery, whose publications on the global environment are well-known and respected,[6] wrote:

> In 1961 there were three billion people, and they were using around half of the total resources of food, water, energy, and arable land that our global ecosystem could sustainably provide. By 1986 there were five billion of us, and such was our thirst for resources that we had already reached Earth's carrying capacity, that is, its ability to maintain its natural resources at levels that will make them available to future generations. Ever since 1986 we have been running the environmental equivalent of a budget deficit, which can only be sustained by plundering the capital made available in the natural world. That plundering takes the form of overexploiting fisheries, overusing and overfertilizing farmland, destroying forests, and polluting our oceans and atmosphere.
>
> By 2001 the environmental deficit had ballooned to 20 percent more than Earth's sustainable yield, and our population to over six billion. By 2050, when the population is expected to be around nine billion, human beings will be using — if they can still be found — nearly two planets' worth of resources. The inevitable conclusion is that our species has entered a crisis that will last for much of the twenty-first century.[7]

Surely, Western missionaries of all peoples must be prepared as never before to test the truthfulness of their assertion that "Christ is the answer" in the context of personal material want.

But there is another point that we overlook at our peril. Wealth is not a prerequisite for undertaking the work of God. The North American experience of wealth on a wide scale is, in terms of historical precedence, an anomaly. As Galbraith points out, "the experience of nations with well-being is exceedingly brief. Nearly all, throughout all history, have been very poor. The exception, almost insignificant in the whole span of human existence, has been the last

---

4. See chap. 2 above.

5. World Wide Fund for Nature, *Living Planet Report 2004* (Gland, Switzerland: WWF, 2004), *www.assets.panda.org/downloads/lpr2004.pdf.*

6. Tim Flannery, *The Weather Makers: How Man Is Changing the Climate and What It Means for Life on Earth* (New York: Grove/Atlantic, 2006). See also his earlier book *The Eternal Frontier: An Ecological History of North America and Its Peoples* (Melbourne, Australia: Text Publishing, 2001). No North American should fail to see the compelling feature-film documentary by Al Gore, *An Inconvenient Truth,* based on his book by the same title, published by Rodale in 2006.

7. Tim Flannery, "Endgame," in *The New York Review of Books* 52, no. 13 (August 11, 2005): 29.

few generations in the comparatively small corner of the world populated by Europeans."[8]

As I pointed out in chapter 1, when the "modern missionary movement" was in its infancy at the turn of the nineteenth century, the per-capita gross national products of the developed and nondeveloped worlds were separated by a factor of less than two; by 1913, the ratio stood at three-to-one, widening to seven-to-one by 1970.[9] The gap has continued to grow at an accelerating rate, reaching a staggering seventy-two-to-one in 1992.

The thought of viable Christian mission without vast financial resources or an elite corps of highly paid professional Western missionaries is not a merely theoretical possibility, it must be remembered, since this has characterized missionaries for most of the church's existence. Now, as the twenty-first century dawns, it is recognized even by Westerners that the most effective missionary endeavor has been, is being, and must continue to be undertaken by missionaries from the poorer churches.[10] One of the most difficult but unavoidable lessons the Western church will be compelled to learn is, according to theologian David Bosch, "how to become again what it originally was and was always supposed to be: the church without privileges, the church of the catacombs rather than of the halls of fame and power and wealth."[11]

It is appropriate to speak of sinful social structures, since evil — a parasite on all that is good — infuses every dimension of human expression. Yet it is vain to imagine that by changing a given social, economic, or political environment a new, more virtuous human being will somehow emerge. This was the conceit of Western societies to which the first and second world wars dealt a mortal blow. A cathedral constructed of flawed bricks will be structurally unsound, no matter what its architectural design. Accordingly, the emphasis in this chapter is on personal change, that is, on the "bricks" of Western missions. The culture that shapes us, the laws that govern us, the education that conditions us, and the institutions that employ us, while significantly influential, are not absolutely determinative. On the other hand, it would be foolish to imagine that a Western missionary, no matter how disagreeable the selfish excesses of his or her own society, can emerge unscathed by its baneful influences. To borrow Trevor Verryn's apt metaphor, "[The Western missionary] cannot help but carry something of [the West's] atmosphere with him, like the smell of stale cigarettes clinging to the clothes of a non-smoker who has been in a room full of people smoking."[12]

---

8. John Kenneth Galbraith, *The Affluent Society,* 3rd ed., rev. (New York: New American Library, 1976), 1.

9. See E. J. Hobsbawm, *The Age of Empire, 1875–1914* (New York: Pantheon Books, 1987), 15.

10. According to David B. Barrett, Todd M. Johnson, and Peter F. Crossing, in "Missiometrics 2006: Goals, Resources, Doctrines of the 350 World Communions," *International Bulletin of Missionary Research* 30, no. 1 (January 2006): 27–30, there are now an estimated 448,000 foreign missionaries and 4,410 foreign mission sending agencies. Most of these, in all cases, are non-Western and, by Western standards, poor.

11. David J. Bosch, "Vision for Mission," *International Review of Mission* 76, no. 301 (January 1987), 15.

12. Trevor D. Verryn, "What Is Communication? Searching for a Missiological Model," *Missionalia* 11, no. 1 (April 1983): 25.

When it comes to transforming international or national political, social, economic, or religious institutions, the efforts of one person must seem comically inadequate. We yearn for "structural change" in which to cocoon personal change, making it easier. In the colorful words of the once editor of the *Edinburgh Review,* we feel "like flies on the chariot wheel; perched upon a question of which we can neither see the diameter, nor control the motion, nor influence the moving force."[13] But fatalism has never been a forte of Christian missionaries. Like the apostle Paul (Rom. 7:14–25), they well know that the line between good and evil cannot be drawn between opposing political or economic ideologies, or along racial, social, national, or even religious lines. The "axis of evil" is within the heart of every one of us. They affirm, furthermore, that the goal of a Christian's life is not the creation and maintenance of a personal utopia. Cultivating the fruit of the Spirit in a less-than-perfect social or material environment is an approach that is both more worthwhile and more authentically Christian in a creation that groans "as in the pains of childbirth right up to the present time" (Rom. 8:22).

Setting the Direction

And so the missionary is urged to begin his or her lifelong wrestling with affluence, not with family, church, denomination, mission society, or nation, but with himself or herself. For Jesus never encourages his disciples to a life of conformity to each other, but to himself. Not *revolution,* but *repentance* is the theme of the Christian Scriptures. This is significant. Revolving wheels and social revolutions have much in common: In the case of the former, one full revolution leaves the tire slightly further down the road, a little worn, perhaps, but otherwise the same. The parts of the tire relative to each other remain unchanged. Thousands of such revolutions simply wear the tire out. Human revolutions have proven similarly ineffective in transforming the human predicament. Repentance, on the other hand, means a deliberate change in direction, leading to genuine conversion. A much more radical concept than is revolution, it is profoundly Christian.

Repentance is a hopeful term, because — unlike revolution — it does not suggest that turning and transformation occur simultaneously. A change in one's direction is not synonymous with arrival at one's ultimate destination. Change in direction is simply an essential beginning, making the prospect of reaching a specific goal realizable. When issued to Western mission, the call to repentance is simply a call to begin moving in a new direction — the direction pointed to by the Incarnation, by the cross, and by the paradox of weakness.

Of course, to the unrepentant, talk of repentance has never been popular. Indeed, it is safe to say that had early Christians refrained from insisting upon this aspect of the "good news," not only would their message have been more palatable to unbelievers, their lives would have been spared.

---

13. W. E. Russell, *Sydney Smith* (London: Macmillan & Co., 1905), 107.

A Place to Begin: Toward a Missiology of the "Righteous Rich"[14]

Formidable as the many barriers to repentance might be — and some of these are addressed later in this chapter — a beginning must be made in attempting to surmount them. The suggestions following are merely that — suggestions. To prescribe any uniform pattern of discipleship is to ensure Pharisaism. The disciple is not called to *look* good, but to *be* good. This is the essence of Christian integrity. Obedience is a matter of the heart, and its external patterns cannot be legislated or institutionalized.

In a world that is even more economically polarized than it was when I wrote the book, the relative affluence of Western missionaries continues to be a major problem. Little has changed. What has changed has been my understanding of how best to respond. When I wrote the first edition of my book while on sabbatical in 1987–1988, my concluding chapter — bravely titled "Grappling with Affluence" — made vague calls to bring missionary lifestyles and strategies into conformity with New Testament teaching on the *Incarnation* — as both theologically descriptive and strategically prescriptive; the *cross* — as both symbol of the atonement and prescription for the only way of life promised to the followers of Jesus; and *weakness* — as channel of God's transforming power. While this call continues to be imperative, to the extent that it reflects the mind of Christ, at the time I was unable to specify just what this change might entail. I invited readers to become part of an ill-defined, inchoate "Fellowship of Venturers in Simpler Living,"[15] and to this day receive a trickle of letters — one as recently as July 2006 — from idealistic, conscience-stricken Western missionaries wrestling with complex personal questions concerning lifestyle, sharing, tithing, children's education, health care, and retirement.

To the extent that my thinking on these matters has moved toward a more constructive and helpful conclusion — and I cannot be the judge of that — I am indebted to both the writings and the example of Jacob A. Loewen and his wife, Anne, venerable Christian pilgrims, missionaries, linguists, and anthropologists.[16]

Each individual in any society is defined by a series of statuses, acknowledged and recognized by other members of that society. It is understood that each status carries with it certain roles and their associated behavioral expectations, which

---

14. I am deeply indebted to Christopher J. H. Wright for his original contribution to this book, "The Righteous Rich in the Old Testament" (chap. 8), and to Justo L. González for allowing me to use two chapters from his now out-of-print book *Faith and Wealth: A History of Early Christian Ideas on the Origin and Significance, and Use of Money* (San Francisco: Harper & Row, 1990): "New Testament *Koinonía* and Wealth" and "Wealth in the Subapostolic Church" (chaps. 9 and 10).

15. Jonathan J. Bonk, *Missions and Money: The Role of Affluence in the Christian Missionary Enterprise from the West* (Maryknoll, NY: Orbis Books, 1991), 111–32, passim.

16. Jacob A. Loewen, one of the most self-transparent missionaries it was ever my privilege to meet, wrestled in deeply insightful ways about missionary roles. Particularly helpful is his essay, "Missions and the Problems of Cultural Background," in *The Church in Mission: A Sixtieth Anniversary Tribute to J. B. Toews,* ed. A. J. Klassen (Fresno, CA: Mennonite Brethren Church, 1967), 286–318. See also two articles coauthored with his wife, Anne Loewen, "Role, Self-Image and Missionary Communication," and "The 'Missionary' Role," appearing in *Culture and Human Values: Christian Intervention in Anthropological Perspective. Selections from the Writings of Jacob A. Loewen* (South Pasadena, CA: William Carey Library, 1975), 412–27, 428–43.

vary with the social context. Human identities and relationships are shaped by the complex interplay of recognized statuses, roles, and self-images that make up the society. In the words of Loewen:

> Roles are the traditional ways people act in given situations. They are learned within the cultural setting. Very frequently the missionary is quite unconscious of this inventory of roles which he brings with him, and so never questions their legitimacy. But we must point out that even the very role of a missionary — a person paid by a foreign source to live in a strange country and to preach a new religion — is quite difficult for most people to understand.[17]

For a missionary's communication of the Gospel to be effective, teaching must be accompanied by personal behavioral and character traits that are consistent with what is being taught. Role sincerity is absolutely crucial to missionary integrity. Those who make a living by being religious are often tempted to act and speak as if all the points they make are personal convictions. When this happens, *role insincerity* functions as a contradicting para-message.[18] As the old adage notes, "What you are speaks so loud that the world can't hear what you say."

Loewen points out that until a newcomer has been duly incorporated into the established network of relationships, members of a society will not know how to act toward him or her. This is why early explorers and traders in North America often found it necessary to become blood brothers to individual tribesmen. Once such a link had been established, the whole group knew how to behave toward the newcomer, even though the newcomer might not yet know what was expected of him. While most societies allow for a period of trial and error for newcomers to learn to play their roles appropriately, if a newcomer persists in unpredictable or inappropriate behavior beyond the allowed limit, he or she will be judged to be unreliable at best, perhaps even false.

A related problem arises from "roles" appropriated by a new missionary. He or she behaves in ways which, in that society — unbeknownst to the missionary — mark him or her as belonging to a given status. When the missionary fulfills only a part of expected behavior associated with the status and its accompanying roles, there are problems, and people can feel deeply betrayed or angry. For example, many missionaries, in an effort to help people economically, have unwittingly assumed the role of patron or feudal master. When they then refuse to fulfill the obligations associated with that role, people are confused, frustrated, and even angry. They question the sincerity and honesty of that missionary.[19]

---

17. Jacob A. Loewen, "Missions and the Problems of Cultural Background," 291.

18. Loewen relates the story of the healing of Pastor Aureliano's wife, who was ill with malaria. The missionaries "pretended" to believe James 5:14–15 — *"Is any one of you sick? He should call the elders of the church to pray over him and anoint him with oil in the name of the Lord. And the prayer offered in faith will make the sick person well..."* — but their prayer for her was not effectual. Later, the Indian pastors prayed for her healing, this time with the desired result. When the missionaries asked why they had not been invited to participate in the prayer, Pastor Aureliano explained that it had been evident that they did not really believe, and that according to the text itself, their prayers would be ineffective. See Jacob A. Loewen, "Missions and the Problems of Cultural Background," 289–92.

19. Jacob A. Loewen and Anne Loewen, "Role, Self-Image and Missionary Communication," 426–27, passim.

I would like to propose that Western Christians generally, including mission-aries — whenever they either anticipate or discover that their way of life and its entitlements make them rich by the standards of those around them — embrace the status of "righteous rich" and learn to play its associated roles in ways that are both culturally appropriate and biblically disciplined. Expectations vary from culture to culture, of course, but in every instance, it is probable that people make a clear distinction between rich people who are good and rich people who are bad. Missionaries should be on the good end of the continuum, culturally speak-ing. In turn, these culturally defined ideal statuses and their accompanying roles need to be informed biblically, to ensure that the missionary's life measures up to his or her teaching.

Chapter 6 makes it clear that the Christian Scriptures portray sharp behavioral distinctions between the righteous and unrighteous rich, and that these differences are conspicuously manifest in their respective relationships to the poor. It would seem absolutely vital for Western missionaries to make the biblical study of this subject an essential aspect of both their preparation for mission and throughout their missionary careers.

Representative of this ubiquitous genre of scriptural teaching — already al-luded to in the previous chapter — are below representative texts from five books of the Bible — three from the Old Testament and two from the New Testament: Job 29:11–17; 31:16–28; Deuteronomy 5:1–11; Nehemiah 5:1–12; 1 John 3:16–20; and 1 Timothy 6:6–10, 17–19. From texts such as these one can discern habits of behavior which, in God's eyes, signal the righteousness of a rich person. West-ern missionaries would do well to memorize such texts for ready meditation in the complexities and pressures of their lives as rich foreigners living as Christians in contexts of poverty. They are cited in full, below.

Job 29:11–17

[11]Whoever heard me spoke well of me, and those who saw me commended me, [12]because I rescued the poor who cried for help, and the fatherless who had none to assist him. [13]The man who was dying blessed me; I made the widow's heart sing. [14]I put on righteousness as my clothing; justice was my robe and my turban. [15]I was eyes to the blind and feet to the lame. [16]I was a father to the needy; I took up the case of the stranger. [17]I broke the fangs of the wicked and snatched the victims from their teeth.

Job 31:16–28

[16]"If I have denied the desires of the poor or let the eyes of the widow grow weary, [17]if I have kept my bread to myself, not sharing it with the fatherless — [18]but from my youth I reared him as would a father, and from my birth I guided the widow — [19]if I have seen anyone perishing for lack of clothing, or a needy man without a garment, [20]and his heart did not bless me for warming him with the fleece from my sheep, [21]if I have raised my hand against the fatherless, knowing that I had influence in court, [22]then

let my arm fall from the shoulder, let it be broken off at the joint. ²³For I dreaded destruction from God, and for fear of his splendor I could not do such things. ²⁴"If I have put my trust in gold or said to pure gold, 'You are my security,' ²⁵if I have rejoiced over my great wealth, the fortune my hands had gained, ²⁶if I have regarded the sun in its radiance or the moon moving in splendor, ²⁷so that my heart was secretly enticed and my hand offered them a kiss of homage, ²⁸then these also would be sins to be judged, for I would have been unfaithful to God on high."

Whether one subscribes to the "hidden hand of the market" as the source of all good things, or whether one detects in the regional, national, and global marketplace the not-so-hidden hand of the economically and politically powerful, it is clear that Job understood himself to be personally responsible for playing a proactive role in the material well-being of poor people in his orbit, and that this is the way God wanted him to be. At the very least, a wealthy missionary will need to be prepared to explain why God-fearing Western missionaries should be considered exempt from this ancient standard, and whether God has changed His mind since Adam Smith provided an intellectually plausible framework for capitalism, thereby — in laissez-faire economic thinking — rectifying the muddled idealism of apparently untenable Mosaic economics.

Deuteronomy 15:1–11

¹At the end of every seven years you must cancel debts. ²This is how it is to be done: Every creditor shall cancel the loan he has made to his fellow Israelite. He shall not require payment from his fellow Israelite or brother, because the LORD's time for canceling debts has been proclaimed. ³You may require payment from a foreigner, but you must cancel any debt your brother owes you. ⁴However, there should be no poor among you, for in the land the LORD your God is giving you to possess as your inheritance, he will richly bless you, ⁵if only you fully obey the LORD your God and are careful to follow all these commands I am giving you today. ⁶For the LORD your God will bless you as he has promised, and you will lend to many nations but will borrow from none. You will rule over many nations but none will rule over you.

⁷If there is a poor man among your brothers in any of the towns of the land that the LORD your God is giving you, do not be hardhearted or tightfisted toward your poor brother. ⁸Rather be openhanded and freely lend him whatever he needs. ⁹Be careful not to harbor this wicked thought: "The seventh year, the year for canceling debts, is near," so that you do not show ill will toward your needy brother and give him nothing. He may then appeal to the LORD against you, and you will be found guilty of sin. ¹⁰Give generously to him and do so without a grudging heart; then because of this the LORD your God will bless you in all your work and in everything you put your hand to. ¹¹There will always be poor people in the land. Therefore

I command you to be openhanded toward your brothers and toward the poor and needy in your land.

If the principles, ideals, and objectives outlined in Deuteronomy 15:1–11 (cf. Lev. 25:8–17) have any kind of legitimacy across time and cultures, one may well ask whether any nation today — on the basis of its treatment of its poor — could pass this biblical litmus test for righteousness. Whatever the shortcoming of Western nations — descended from a Christendom that *was* and *is* far from *Christian* — the people of God, especially missionaries, must explain how the relationship between rich and poor is to be addressed similarly — in culturally appropriate and practical ways — today.

Nehemiah 5:1–12

[1]Now the men and their wives raised a great outcry against their Jewish brothers. [2]Some were saying, "We and our sons and daughters are numerous; in order for us to eat and stay alive, we must get grain." [3]Others were saying, "We are mortgaging our fields, our vineyards and our homes to get grain during the famine." [4]Still others were saying, "We have had to borrow money to pay the king's tax on our fields and vineyards. [5]Although we are of the same flesh and blood as our countrymen and though our sons are as good as theirs, yet we have to subject our sons and daughters to slavery. Some of our daughters have already been enslaved, but we are powerless, because our fields and our vineyards belong to others."

[6]When I heard their outcry and these charges, I was very angry. [7]I pondered them in my mind and then accused the nobles and officials. I told them, "You are exacting usury from your own countrymen!" So I called together a large meeting to deal with them [8]and said: "As far as possible, we have bought back our Jewish brothers who were sold to the Gentiles. Now you are selling your brothers, only for them to be sold back to us!" They kept quiet, because they could find nothing to say.

[9]So I continued, "What you are doing is not right. Shouldn't you walk in the fear of our God to avoid the reproach of our Gentile enemies? [10]I and my brothers and my men are also lending the people money and grain. But let the exacting of usury stop! [11]Give back to them immediately their fields, vineyards, olive groves and houses, and also the usury you are charging them — the hundredth part of the money, grain, new wine and oil." [12]"We will give it back," they said. "And we will not demand anything more from them. We will do as you say." Then I summoned the priests and made the nobles and officials take an oath to do what they had promised.

For those of us who are wealthy, it is sobering to find in the Scriptures scarcely any record of repentance on the part of the rich. Here in Nehemiah is one heartening instance, a reminder that no matter how complicated the issues or how deeply entrenched and personally vested the self-interests, it is possible to repent. What would repentance look like from the vantage point of powerful mission organizations in contexts of poverty? That is difficult to say, since the righteous rich missionary or mission agency, while informed biblically, must be defined contextually.

What can be observed in this account is the difference between mere *legality* (the privileged were not breaking their own laws) and *justice* (what God required of them). This is an important distinction for Christians to make, since the laws of any nation — including the United States — are often framed or evolve to protect the vested interests of the powerful. But while the law is almost always on the side of the rich and the powerful, God's standards of justice frequently rule against them.

1 John 3:16–20

[16]This is how we know what love is: Jesus Christ laid down his life for us. And we ought to lay down our lives for our brothers. [17]If anyone has material possessions and sees his brother in need but has no pity on him, how can the love of God be in him? [18]Dear children, let us not love with words or tongue but with actions and in truth. [19]This then is how we know that we belong to the truth, and how we set our hearts at rest in his presence [20]whenever our hearts condemn us. For God is greater than our hearts, and he knows everything.

This passage, and many others like it, makes acutely uncomfortable public reading when wealthy missionaries serve in contexts of dire poverty. Clearly, rich Christians are called upon to be generously and energetically proactive in their concerns for the poor. In an age of mass media, none of us can escape the blunt fact that we are wealthy, and that as followers of Jesus we dare not be mere passive observers, piously giving thanks that our predicament is not as harrowing as theirs.

1 Timothy 6:6–10, 17–19

[6]But godliness with contentment is great gain. [7]For we brought nothing into the world, and we can take nothing out of it. [8]But if we have food and clothing, we will be content with that. [9]People who want to get rich fall into temptation and a trap and into many foolish and harmful desires that plunge men into ruin and destruction. [10]For the love of money is a root of all kinds of evil. Some people, eager for money, have wandered from the faith and pierced themselves with many griefs....

[17]Command those who are rich in this present world not to be arrogant nor to put their hope in wealth, which is so uncertain, but to put their hope in God, who richly provides us with everything for our enjoyment. [18]Command them to do good, to be rich in good deeds, and to be generous and willing to share. [19]In this way they will lay up treasure for themselves as a firm foundation for the coming age, so that they may take hold of the life that is truly life.

Texts such as this one are damning to the rich, and difficult for Christian teachers to obey. It is clear that from the perspective of the poor among whom a wealthy person lives that this text needs careful rationalizing by most rich people hoping to escape its censure.

Such texts are only suggestive and are supplemented by the more careful studies of the righteous rich provided in the essays by Christopher J. H. Wright and Justo L. González. But contained in these texts are the minimal guidelines — "righteous rich templates," in a manner of speaking — that should guide and characterize the righteous rich, whatever their time or place. That such texts will be applied to wealthy missionaries by the poor among whom they live and work is both a certainty and a divine necessity. The challenge for any wealthy missionary will be to make sure that he or she is perceived as righteous according to the standards of the group in which he or she lives and works, and above all, in ways that consistently reflect the mind of Christ whom he or she represents.

I have been involved in the training and nurturing of missionaries for much of my adult life. For the past ten years, it has been my extraordinary privilege to serve Christian leaders and missionaries from around the world here at the Overseas Ministries Study Center, assisting them in their quest for spiritual, professional, and intellectual renewal through our community life and programs. It is natural, then, that I should propose that the Western missionary training and retraining curricula and on-field orientations should include courses and forums for serious, sustained discussion of this troublesome issue. To my knowledge, systematic exploration of the dynamics and missiological implications of economic inequity in close social proximity is not usually a part of missionary training, on-field orientation, or postgraduate mission studies. Included in every mission studies curriculum should be at least one seminar exploring biblical teaching on wealth and poverty, the rich and the poor, with implications drawn and applications made for Christian missions and missionaries.[20]

A missiology of the righteous rich is, at its core, no more than a willingness to be useful in terms defined by the local contexts and people. For this there can be no better exemplar than our Lord himself. With a mission more sweeping in scope and magnitude than those of even the most daring mission strategists, his commission was to save the world. Oddly, by the standards of Western missions, he spent his life as a laughably parochial figure, never venturing in his actual ministry beyond the borders of his own foreign-occupied country. By the standards of even the most forgiving mission administrators, he proved to be frustratingly deficient when it came to actually fulfilling his mission. His major difficulty seemed to have been the interruptions that intruded into his larger plans for the world.

---

20. Most Western seminaries offering graduate training for missionaries do not address this issue to any significant degree, and those that do tend to use my book. Sometimes — for example, at Gordon-Conwell Seminary — I am invited each year to come and engage in dialogue with D.Min. and M.Div. students who have read my book. Other seminaries, such as Trinity Evangelical Divinity School, have invited me to facilitate "missions and money" seminars in their D.Miss. program. While I welcome such opportunities, teaching on the subject should begin much earlier, at the undergraduate level. It is this, more than anything else, which has prodded me into issuing this second edition of the book that first appeared in 1991.

Almost everything written in the Gospel accounts of his life relates directly or indirectly to the wrenching, but strategically petty, personal agendas of the ordinary men and women who pressed in on him on all sides during the few short years of his ministry. The Creator God incarnate, bent on saving the whole world, allowed himself to be interrupted by the sick, the lame, the blind, the withered, the bereaved, the outcasts, the pariahs, the deaf, the demon-possessed, the grieving. Whatever he may have been doing at the time, he seemed never too busy or tired to stop and pay close attention to their agendas.

How understandable it would have been for Jesus to regretfully turn away the ordinary people who constantly sought his attention, reminding them that as Creator of their planet, now charged with redeeming it, he simply did not have time to give attention to the personal details of their everyday lives. Instead, he demonstrated that any proclamation of the good news that does not intersect with the actual needs of ordinary people is not good news, but mere religious propaganda. On this issue he was at distinct odds with the Pharisees, as his followers today should be.

It is trite to remind ourselves that it was his willingness to yield to one final, fatal interruption on a hill just outside Jerusalem that accomplished our redemption. It is this interruption that lies at the heart of the Gospel that takes missionaries to the ends of the earth.

We Western missionaries have a lot to learn from our Lord. Defined and driven by corporate and ecclesiastical agendas that are the product of organizations and well-meaning church leaders often thousands of miles away, we sometimes have no time to serve people on their own terms, thereby implicitly denying both that we are servants, at the beck and call of those among whom we minister, and that *they,* rather than we, ultimately determine our usefulness.

Were the role of "righteous rich" to be widely appropriated by Western missionaries, it is safe to assume that the missionary enterprise would be transformed. We would at once become more Christ-like — not merely comfortably accoutred promulgators of admirably correct propositions about God and inherited notions of ecclesiology — righteous rich followers of Jesus, whose immense good fortune is put at the disposal of the neighbors among whom God places us.

Practical Steps

Within the context of missionary ministry, affluence and its contextually defined and biblically refined derivative statuses and roles need to be explored and addressed from four practical perspectives: individual, family, mission agencies, and training institutions/sending churches.

1. Individual

We instinctively long for the security of conformity. We do not mind paying the price of discipleship — provided the sacrifice can be made in the company of similarly sacrificing and approving peers. Peter, upon hearing of the fate awaiting him, was curious about what lay ahead for John. Jesus' words to Peter are his words to all of us whose personal obedience is contingent upon the obedience of the group: "If I want him to remain alive until I return, what is it to you? You must follow me" (John 21:18–22).

While the call to follow Jesus in self-denial is a profoundly personal matter, the fact that self-denial can never be lived in isolation from others means that it can easily degenerate into a display of self-righteousness, or into an insistence that others conform to the same external standards. The individual who senses the urging of the Spirit to personal repentance must guard diligently against the sin of pride, and must be prepared to be misunderstood by his or her peers. As Koyama notes, "If we go we must be prepared to go the way of self denial. We want to go, but we do not want to be mocked. Bishops, theologians and church leaders are prepared to go as long as their spiritual, intellectual and ecclesiastical prestige is safely protected."[21]

Each missionary must, furthermore, come to grips with the fact that many of the underlying values which have shaped and which continue to power Western societies are not godly, but godless. Thinking it no longer "worthwhile to retain the knowledge of God," Western societies display increasing evidence that "God [has given] them over to a depraved mind, to do what ought not to be done" (Rom. 1:28). Sadly, at all levels, even in its expression of mission, the Western church appears to be more comfortable with "the mind of the West" than with "the mind of Christ."

Simpler personal lifestyles are necessary. The missionary is not, after all, a saint living in the Millennium, but a soldier engaged in a cosmic conflict in which no treaty is possible — only defeat or victory. Traveling lightly is absolutely essential. The disciple is not the owner, but the steward of those material possessions and personal talents entrusted to him or her. These talents are not to be wasted by burying them in the ground of self-indulgence.

"Needs" must not be defined by Western standards, but by local conditions. Real renunciation — not just the appearance of renunciation — must be practiced (Acts 5:1–11). It is sometimes necessary to sell our personal possessions so that those who have real needs may be helped (Acts 2:45). Our human tendency has ever been to accumulate possessions — even at the cost of indebtedness — and then excuse ourselves from giving on the grounds that we have no money to give. There is nothing very notable about a willingness to part with spare cash for the sake of the needy. It is only when a Christian, for the sake of others, willingly parts with dearest possessions that the mind of Christ is manifest.

2. Family

The family has perhaps been the most frequent resort of those who explain their unwillingness to obey Christ's economic instructions. "I will follow you," Christ is often told by conscripts and volunteers, "but first . . . [my family]" (Luke 9:57–62). But is obedience in this crucial area possible only for those without a family? The children of Western missionaries are, like their parents, privileged beyond the wildest prospects of the majority of children who have ever lived. I

---

21. Kosuke Koyama, *Three Mile an Hour God: Biblical Reflections* (Maryknoll, NY: Orbis Books, 1980), 53.

write as the son of missionaries — as a beneficiary of the costly privileges and special environment so lovingly provided for all such children abroad.

In an age of growing want, the services and privileges accorded to the children of Western missionaries are by no means being curtailed. On the contrary, every effort is being made to enhance current programs and to provide new ones. Naturally, we want "the best" for *our* children. Books, articles, and consultations on "missionary family" and "missionary kids" take relative affluence as a given. The possibility of voluntary poverty at the family level is never raised. This reinforces the idea that Western missionary families need not question the status quo. Nor are the issues facing the children of the tens of thousands of poor non-Western missionaries ever broached. Although numerically a majority, and strategically at the cutting edge, it is as though they didn't exist.[22] Even the curriculums of those schools catering to the children of Western missionaries pointedly exclude incorporation of the language, perspectives, or content of indigenous educational systems. Third World missionary parents and their children must do the best they can with their negligible resources, while the children of affluent Western missionaries look forward as a matter of course to special facilities, special care, special education, and a special place among the world's elite.

There is a singular lack of critical sensitivity to the impact of schools for missionaries' children — often conspicuously exclusive enclaves of Western culture and values, bastions of privilege that the poor can only see from outside — upon missionary children themselves and upon the people from whom they are so carefully insulated and isolated. Many children of Western missionaries take up the vocation of their parents. There can be little doubt that enculturation to the entitlements of privilege make it difficult for them to operate along lines of genuine sharing, fraternity, and mutuality with non-Western Christians. That missionary children, when they become missionaries themselves, should perpetuate within the Western missionary enterprise a modus operandi that is increasingly suspect, and which has for decades been relatively impotent, is not surprising. But it is sad.

As to those non-Western peoples in a position to observe most closely the privilege accorded to Western missionaries and their children, does not such institutionalized privilege serve to confirm in their minds that the *real* good news is the good news of *plenty?*

As parents, we need to heed the lesson of Old Testament parents who put their children first. Lot and Eli come to mind as examples of parents who made their children's well-being a priority. Lot, choosing to put his own economic security before that of his uncle, did exceedingly well materially (Gen. 13). This may have been the beginning of a steady erosion of his spiritual integrity, for

---

22. See, for example, the compendium of the "International Conference on Missionary Kids" held in Manila, Philippines, November 5–9, 1984: *New Directions in Missions: Implications for MKs,* ed. Beth A. Tetzel and Patricia Mortenson (West Battleboro, VT: International Conference on Missionary Kids [ICMK], 1986). There is absolutely no mention made of the children of poor missionaries. An Overseas Ministries Study Center (OMSC)–sponsored "Study Group on Mission Issues" featuring the topic "Resolving the Crisis in MK Education" (December 4–5, 1987) manifested a similar myopia, although a Filipino pastor and his wife who had been invited to attend expressed amazement at the notion that the children of Western missionaries were anything but privileged.

he offers his virgin daughters in an attempt to stave off the threatening mob at his door (19:8), and when he later warned his sons-in-law about Sodom's impending doom, "his sons-in-law thought he was joking" (Gen. 19:14). Eli is another example of one who put his sons before his obedience to the Lord (1 Sam. 2:1–36, especially v. 29), with similarly dire consequences. By his indulgence, he unwittingly doomed his beloved sons. Elkinah and Hannah, on the other hand, are examples of parents for whom the well-being of a firstborn son was of less importance than obedience. Samuel was their son of promise. In accordance with her vow, Hannah took her small, just-weaned son to the temple, where he was to be raised by Eli — a man who had already demonstrated his paternal incompetence by ruining his own sons (1 Sam. 1–3).

Is it more harmful for children to share the experiences of the rich or the experiences of the poor? If the teaching of the Bible is taken seriously, the answer to this question must be obvious. To quote John Woolman,

> In our present condition, to love our children is needful; but except this love proceeds from the true heavenly principle which sees beyond earthly treasures, it will rather be injurious than of any real advantage to them. Where the fountain is corrupt, the streams must necessarily be impure.[23]

3. Mission Agencies

Mission boards and agencies cannot insist that member missionaries lower their standard of living. But they can try to provide a milieu in which those who choose to do so are given understanding, acceptance, and encouragement. Change, apart from radical conversion or catastrophe, comes slowly to an institution. But why should not the problems associated with missionary affluence be grappled with frankly and regularly at mission conferences and consultations? Although the subject does not appear on the agendas of many missiologists or administrators, it frequently troubles individual missionaries, especially those in their first term of service. The candor with which agencies and denominations share their needs for more money is well known. Could not the other side of the equation be dealt with as well — not in "missionary only" gatherings, but in meetings in which the poor themselves are invited to share their perceptions of Western missionary economics?

Several years ago, in answering the question "How does a missionary function and relate in today's Asia?" Renuka Somesakhar offered some practical suggestions to Western missionaries serious about overcoming the handicap of their affluence. "In the past," he pointed out,

> those missionaries endeared themselves most to the people, who lived within the economic framework of those with and among whom they worked. To persons coming from affluent countries acceptance of "lower wages" seems like a big sacrifice. But it is lower in comparison with which

---

23. John Woolman, *The Journal and Major Essays of John Woolman,* ed. Phillips P. Moulton (New York: Oxford University Press, 1971), 199.

standard.... Mission boards and missionaries themselves have done considerable amount of discussion on this point. Unfortunately, seldom, if ever, is the host country consulted on this extremely important matter which, in the last analysis, does influence greatly the function and relationship of a missionary to Asians.[24]

It may be that societies of a new kind will need to be generated.[25] Protestants can learn much from Catholic orders of missionaries who — like our Savior — choose poverty or parity rather than wealth as a basis for missionary service. Is there no room in Western evangelical missionary circles for a "great renunciation"? The Moravians, the Salvation Army, the Oxford Brethren at Calcutta, the Universities' Mission to Eastern Africa, and the China Inland Mission — like the Jesuit fathers — operated on principles of apostolic simplicity, austerity, and self-denial. They provide proof that Evangelical societies need not be organized around the principles of plenty. Catholic missionary orders have long, often effectively, practiced it; missionaries sent by the Confessional churches continue to spend time and money discussing and writing about it; Evangelicals — alas — have in recent years virtually ignored it, at least in practice.[26]

Must we conclude that this kind of obedience is impossible for evangelical missionaries? Is it heresy to suggest that the One whose grace is sufficient for the weakness and poverty of Catholic or non-Western missionaries is inadequate in the case of evangelical Western missionaries? Only those who will answer "No" to these questions with their lives need consider missionary service. For all others, mission must remain simply a career.

---

24. *Missionary Service in Asia Today.* A Report on a Consultation Held by the Asia Methodist Advisory Committee, February 18–23, 1971, in cooperation with the Life, Message, Unity Committee of the East Asian Christian Conference (Kuala Lumpur: University of Malayasia, 1971), 94.

25. Some recently established agencies have avoided the question of the legitimacy of Western missionary affluence, instead encouraging Westerners to support bargain-basement "national" missionaries from Western coffers at one-thirtieth of the cost of a North American. An example of this approach would include the "Gospel for Asia" organization, whose founding president, K. P. Yohannan, spells out his vision in his book *The Coming Revolution in World Missions* (Altamonte Springs, FL: Creation House, 1986). While a very good case can be made for this practice on economic grounds, it does not address the problem of why Western missionaries should not be able, when challenged, to follow their Savior among the poor. Another such agency is the "Christian Nationals Evangelism Commission," founded by Allen Finley. His book (co-authored by Lorry Lutz), *The Family Tie* (Nashville: Thomas Nelson Publishers, 1983), outlines what on the cover is described as "an exciting approach that could revolutionize world missions." Christian Aid Mission (201 Stanton St., Fort Erie, Ontario L2A 3N8) has released the film (available on video) *The Hidden Missionaries,* which argues that the need for Western missionaries is past. Recently founded by John and Lynn Samaan, Servants Among the Poor is a rare example of a Western evangelical agency committed to serving the urban poor in slums of Third World megacities, "incarnationally and holistically by covenanting together to live a simple and devotional lifestyle...." (from their brochure, available by writing to the organization at: 691 E. Howard St., Pasadena, CA 91104).

26. There are some notable exceptions, of course. The writings of Viv Grigg, Ron Sider, and Harvie Conn are a rich, but missiologically neglected source. Likewise, the Lausanne Committee for World Evangelization's Thailand Report no. 22, *The Thailand Report on the Urban Poor,* subtitled "Report of the Consultation of World Evangelization Mini-Consultation on Reaching the Urban Poor," held in Pattaya, Thailand, June 16–27, 1980, is highly commendable. But its recommendations have yet to be acted upon by those responsible for designing and implementing the policies of Western-based missions.

4. Training Institutions and Sending Churches

Can secure, rich clergy in their pinstriped suits, or tenured seminary professors operating out of their comfortable and well-equipped environments credibly challenge Western missionaries to consider the "crucified mind" strategy in matters of personal and family privilege? Can congregations of churches that have deliberately moved into the comfortable suburbs in order to avoid the inconvenience, frustration, and hopelessness of being surrounded by the poor of our inner cities insist that their missionaries follow a more radically biblical pattern? I think not. Kipling's verse captures the incongruity of those who might be insensitive enough to try:

> The toad beneath the harrows knows,
> Exactly where each tooth point goes;
> The butterfly upon the road,
> Preaches contentment to that toad.

As long as we North American Christians and leaders demonstrate that we have learned only to abound, it will be hypocritical to insist that missionaries from among us should learn how to be in want. The Laodicean church cannot inspire its members to great sacrifice for the sake of Christ. Only a community of believers who themselves have chosen to reject the materialist spirit of the age can stir its members to pursue genuine self-sacrifice abroad. A wealthy church is bound by the rules of propriety to support its missionaries according to its own ever-inflating notions of adequacy. On the other hand, missionaries so supported are not morally obligated to conform to Western standards of consumption and privilege. They are free — indeed morally obligated as Christ's followers — to practice stewardship of these resources according to the dictates of their consciences.

Nor are those North American training institutions busily engaged in the preparation of missionaries in a morally strong position to admonish missionary graduates to choose the narrow way of self-denial. The embarrassingly brazen trumpeting of their own imagined superiority over other institutions, together with an unblushing willingness to make the convenience and comfort of their facilities and services a selling point, smack of the competitive spirit of the age, and not of Christ. That such practices are the rule rather than the exception in North America makes it clear that the humility which is a prerequisite of self-denial is simply not there. Such self-promoting ecclesiastical and academic environments will — except by the accident of a "genetic throwback" to the church's ancient root — produce their own kind of offspring. Soldiers of Jesus Christ emerging from such a milieu will be prepared to expect comfort, rather than to endure hardness (2 Tim. 2:3).

But a beginning can be made. A number of seminaries and colleges are offering courses designed to grapple with the complexities of being rich Christians in an age of hunger. Some are becoming more critically aware of the evil that the Bible calls greed, but which is sanctified and legitimized by the term "consumerism" in Western society. A number of them have incorporated this element into their mission curriculums. At Fuller Theological Seminary School of World Mission, for example, Elizabeth Brewster teaches a course entitled "Incarnation & Mission Among the World's Urban Poor," in which an effort is made "to gain a Scriptural and experiential perspective for mission outreach among Third World Poor...[on the] assumption...that the incarnation of Christ provides a Biblical model for ministry."[27]

At the school where I once taught, two courses required of all students in the department of mission studies dealt directly with the challenge of doing missions out of affluence. One of these, "Rich and Poor: The Problem of Affluence in Mission," surveys and applies scriptural teaching regarding ethical and practical aspects of issues growing out of wealth and poverty in proximity. A second course, "Missionary Identification," explores the significance and implications of the Incarnation as a normative model for Christian ministry. Where mission courses touch upon strategy, cognizance is taken of the implications of the Western missionary's relative affluence upon the effectual implementation of a given strategy.

More can be done. All students, but especially those contemplating foreign missionary service, should be given every encouragement to familiarize themselves with the great cloud of witnesses for whom the Incarnation and the cross of our Lord have been not only the means of salvation, but models for mission. We need models — heroes, if you will — who can inspire us to move beyond the expectations of convention. Not forgetting Jesus and Paul, the lives and the writings of men and women such as Roberto de Nobili, Henry Martyn, Allen Gardiner, Coleridge Patteson, John Williams, Mary Slessor, Hudson Taylor, James Gilmour, Dan Crawford, Malla Moe, Toyohiko Kagawa, Daniel Johnson Fleming, Bruce Olson, Mother Teresa, Ron Sider, Stephan Kovalski, Viv Grigg, Niall O'Brien, and others too numerous to mention — people much admired but seldom emulated — must be studied and imitated. Those who have struggled notably with the lethal materialism that Western Christians have so heartily embraced must be introduced to the next generation of Western missionaries. Students preparing for missionary service must be inspired to make Kagawa's conversion prayer *their* lifelong prayer: "Oh God," he prayed, "make me like Christ."[28] His prayer was answered.

We need also to hear the stories of godly missionaries and evangelists who, because they are poor, and in many cases scarcely literate, are largely unknown to us. Too often, these men and women, responsible for most of the growth of the church around the world, are known — if at all — only as characters in a story told by a Western missionary. Cannot they tell their own stories? Listening to them, one is both inspired and humbled: *inspired* because God's Spirit is not restricted to working through affluent Western missionaries; *humbled* because the role of Western missionaries in these stories is often so incidental.[29]

---

27. From the 1987 syllabus, "Incarnation & Mission Among the World's Urban Poor — MB595," Fuller Theological Seminary, 135 N. Oakland #91, Pasadena, CA 91182.

28. Cyril J. Davey, *Kagawa of Japan* (Nashville: Abingdon Press, 1960), 18.

29. An example of what I have in mind is the mimeographed, 176-page book produced in 1985 by Brian Fargher (then a missionary with SIM International), *Philip: An Ethiopian Evangelist* (Ethiopia:

Needless to say, teachers and leaders of missionaries should themselves model simplicity in lifestyle and contentment in personal ambition if they are to help their students to do the same. Physical facilities likewise should — in the midst of a society that makes of fun and comfort supreme values to which all other considerations are subjected — model plainness, not ostentation. Better far to err on the side of austerity than luxury!

Obstacles to Repentance

As suggested above, obstacles to repentance are almost inevitably rooted in the practicalities of our everyday lives as men and women living in a particular time and a particular place as part of a particular people. Since it is within specific social milieus that one must repent, those who contemplate embarking upon a new direction in mission do well to remind themselves of the sort of obstacles that they will invariably encounter. Humankind has ever evinced a remarkable capacity to make ridiculous that which threatens personal privilege. The missionary choosing to part direction with more pragmatic peers will find that practical problems, thoughtful objections, and complex relational considerations will most certainly abound at all levels — institutional, family, and individual.

At the *institutional* level, that stabilizing inertia which is built into policies can hardly be avoided. Nonconformists within any organization are rightly perceived to be dangerously centrifugal. Christian obedience has never been successfully legislated. The institution, as the abstract yet tangible expression of the collective identity of its members, is more than the sum of its parts, for its life will extend well beyond the years allotted to any of its particular members. In addition to providing its members with an accredited religious and social identity, it also serves to both define and legitimate their personal ends and means. It is exceedingly difficult for an institution to engage in the sort of self-criticism that can lead to repentance. Nor can an institution repent on behalf of its members. Troublesome questions concerning policies and practices are, therefore, frequently dealt with by ostracizing or dismissing the one who raises them. Reformers — whether they be politicians, theologians, or missionaries — are to their institutions what prophets are to their home countries: embarrassing blots on the institutional escutcheon, they are not welcome (Luke 4:24). The self-justification mechanism that is an attribute of all institutions will be one of the most difficult challenges faced by the person or the family wishing to grapple with the challenge of Western missionary affluence.

Addis Ababa, 1985). The book is essentially a transcription of the Ethiopian missionary's recorded autobiography. Philip (not his real name), who has struggled with tuberculosis all his life, played the key role in the planting of numerous churches. A good proportion of his missionary career was spent in prison. He was almost always destitute. What is humbling in this story is the relatively insignificant role played by Western missionaries in the life of the Ethiopian Church. It is good to see ourselves as we are seen, and to humbly serve those who are better able than we to pay the price of effective apostolic ministry. My students have been deeply challenged by this simple story. Would that more of these unsung heroes could tell their story to us!

Why should this be so? John Woolman's comments on the complacency with which high-placed Christians of his day regarded personal complicity in the economically complex question of slavery seem to apply equally to the unwillingness of many Western missionaries to deal with the problem of affluence: "Customs generally approved and opinions received by youth from their superiors become like the natural produce of a soil, especially when they are suited to favourite inclinations," he observed.[30]

When Christian leaders of high reputation themselves engage in culturally acceptable but dubious practices, similar behavior at the individual level is easily rationalized. However natural this tendency might be, personal accountability to God is by no means thereby abrogated. "For as justice remains justice," Woolman warns,

> so many people of reputation in the world joining with wrong things do not excuse others in joining with them nor make the consequences of their proceedings less dreadful in the final issue than it would be otherwise.
>
> Where unrighteousness is justified from one age to another, it is like dark matter gathering into clouds over us. We may know that this gloom will remain till the cause be removed by a reformation or change of times and may feel a desire . . . to speak on the occasion; yet where error is so strong that it may not be spoken against without some prospect of inconvenience to the speaker, this difficulty is likely to operate on our weakness and quench the good desires in us, except we dwell so steadily under the weight of it as to be made willing to endure hardness on that account.[31]

The power of the institution over the individual can hardly be overemphasized. Missionaries can and must be critical about their institutions where these come into conflict with personal obedience. Testimony against Western missionary affluence will be a lonely and costly task. Nonconformity arouses fierce resistance against it, even in pious missionary circles. James Gilmour's ascetic adaptation to Chinese life one hundred years ago was regarded by his colleagues with hostility because of its implicit criticism of their way of life.[32] The little band of Western missionaries to India who, under Donald McGavran's leadership, formed the "Fellowship of Venturers in Simpler Living" in the 1930s soon lost heart due in large part to "the considerable friction in the missionary body" which "the existence of such a plan created."[33] To have invidious comparisons drawn between

---

30. Woolman, *The Journal and Major Essays of John Woolman,* 198.

31. Ibid., 212. These words were first published in 1761.

32. See Richard Lovett, *James Gilmour of Mongolia: His Diaries, Letters and Reports* (London: Religious Tract Society, 1893), 211, 203. See also my article, "The Role of Affluence in the Christian Missionary Enterprise from the West," *Missiology: An International Review* 14, no. 4 (October 1986): 444.

33. Letter of McGavran to Bonk, January 26, 1988, Pasadena. In the first edition of this book (131), I proposed the resurrection — in slightly modified form — of this "Fellowship of Ventures in Simpler Living" founded by Donald McGavran. I conceived of it as an international forum in which problems, examples, ideas, and proposals relating to the topic of missionary affluence could be discussed and debated. At the time I envisaged a modest publication — to be issued at least once a year to fellowship members — a kind of ongoing, open discussion in which members might freely

one's own comfortable way of life and that of an apparently more dedicated colleague is always distressing, and stirs the self-justification instinct to vigorous action. Sydney Smith's explanation of the collective ire of English clergy against social reformer Elizabeth Fry rings true: "She is very unpopular with the clergy," Smith explained, "[because] examples of living, active virtue disturb our repose, and give rise to distressing comparisons: we long to burn her alive."[34]

A number of Western mission agencies, while not addressing the problem of their affluence by renouncing it, have recognized the morally questionable pattern of relationships that have long characterized and bedeviled Western missions and non-Western churches. They have begun to move away from the traditional Western stresses on *independence, autonomy,* and *self-sufficiency,* restructuring along lines more consistent with biblical teaching on the church as the Body of Christ. In these societies, the emphasis is on the *interdependence* of Western and non-Western churches and institutions. An the institutional level, this has resulted in structures which — in terms of power, policies, and personnel — are becoming more genuinely international. This is a hopeful sign, and if pursued, will be the salvation of Western missions abroad.[35]

Little more needs to be said here concerning *family* and *personal* obstacles to simpler missionary living. As was pointed out in chapter 3, humanly speaking there is much to be lost, and little to be gained from pursuit of a deliberate policy of economic austerity. At the family level, children, spouses, parents, and in-laws complicate obedience to some of Christ's more extreme commands (e.g., Luke 9:57–62; Matt. 10:34–39). Despite all that Christ said about the danger of riches, we believe — at least where our families are concerned — that poverty is even more dangerous. To risk the misunderstanding of our next of kin is a heavy price to pay for what they will doubtless regard as foolhardy economic eccentricity. The necessity of preparing our children to "fit" into the materialistic culture of the West makes privilege abroad absolutely essential. Excusing personal participation in the Western love affair with mammon on the grounds that our materialist excess is simply "cultural" is too strong a temptation for most of us to resist. The

---

share their problems, questions, observations, visions, and insights with one another. Initial membership was to have been restricted to those who wrote to me concerning some aspect of the challenge of doing mission out of affluence. Professors, missionary supporters, missionaries, administrators, church leaders, students, observers, and others with a personal interest in the subject — Westerners and non-Westerners alike — were invited to use this as a means of encouraging, guiding, inspiring, and admonishing each other "toward love and good deeds" (Heb. 10:24). Although I received scores of letters, the most recent of which arrived in July 2006, due to my own inertia arising from preoccupation with many other responsibilities, the fellowship never got off the ground.

34. See Russell, *Sydney Smith,* 85 n.

35. Conciliar Protestant churches have long led the way in searching for alternatives to the old pattern of "sending church–receiving church" relationships. While independent and even denominational Evangelical agencies have, for a variety of reasons, been slower to move away from the nineteenth-century stress of Rufus Anderson, Henry Venn, and Roland Allen on the "indigenous church," there is evidence that this is changing. Overseas Missionary Fellowship (OMF), Wycliffe Bible Translators, Communauté Evangelique d'Action Apostolique (CEVAA), Community of Latin American Evangelical Ministries (CLAEM), and Pengutusan Injil dan Pelayanan Kasih (PIPKA) are notable examples. See Wilbert R. Shenk's excellent study, "God's New Economy: Interdependence and Mission" (Elkhart, IN: Mission Focus, 1988).

powerlessness and loss of personal influence that must inevitably accompany renunciation of affluence-based status is too great a price to pay.

Back to Our Foundation: Theological Moorings

It is appropriate that this chapter should end by returning to the very well-springs of our Christian faith. Among the richly varied theological motifs running through the pages of the New Testament, three are of such broad significance as to touch upon every other facet of Christian faith and practice: the Incarnation, the cross, and weakness as power.

The Incarnation

The Incarnation is the very heart of the Christian faith. "In the beginning was the Word," John wrote, and "The Word became flesh and lived for a while among us" (John 1:1, 14). Paul, echoing this most elementary of Christian teachings, reminded the churches in Galatia that "When the time had fully come, God sent his Son, born of a woman, born under law, to redeem those under law" (Gal. 4:4–5). Western missionaries have been among those most committed to the proclamation of this good news. Growing personal affluence and temporal security have made it increasingly difficult to regard the Incarnation as a model for personal action. For much of Western evangelicalism, *Incarnation* is merely a *theologically descriptive*, rather than a *strategically prescriptive*, term (Phil. 2:1–11). It is from the Incarnation, rather than from Marshall McLuhan, that missionary communicators learn that the *medium is the message*. The Living Word must always be made vulnerable flesh.

The Incarnation teaches us that power, speed, mobility, comprehensiveness, efficiency, and success are not the measure of missionary strategy. God so loved the world that he gave his only Son; that Son came into the world — not with an impressive show of force, but as the powerless, vulnerable, "illegitimate" child of a peasant mother. All the creative and sustaining power in heaven and on earth was his (Col. 1:15–17), yet he willingly entered his own creation as a helpless, dependent, suckling infant, occupying only one or two square feet in the bottom of a manger, needing to learn obedience and grow in wisdom. The Word made flesh grew up poor, lived his life surrounded by and in sympathy with the poor, and died poor. In carrying out his mission to save the world, he walked about Palestine for three years, often delayed by crowds and hampered by the religious establishment. Coming in the "fullness of time," he was to all practical purposes unaware of unreached people groups in the world next door. Had his Father miscalculated?

Could not his credibility have been enhanced had he come as the privileged, gifted, well-bred, highly educated, cultured heir apparent to the throne of some powerful, affluent kingdom? Would it not have been better for him to postpone his debut until the age of the global village — with its jets, computers, telecommunications networks, mass media, public health programs, and human rights organizations at his disposal, to make the accomplishing of his mission more realistic? Was the life of Christ really the preposterously naïve, ill-conceived, amateurish fiasco that it appears to have been by modern missiological standards of strategic planning and performance?

The answer, of course, is clear. There *were* more appropriate ways for him to authenticate his claims to being the Son of God. There *were* more effective ways of inaugurating the Kingdom of God. Even then, in the absence of motor vehicles, airplanes, computers, and highly technical communications media, there *were* more efficient ways of proclaiming the good news. Despite the absence of marketing consultants and advertising specialists, surely there *were* practical means available for the packaging and selling to the general public of the Word made flesh.

The fact is, the Messianic modus operandi was not accidental, but deliberate. The temptation to prove his sonship and fulfill his mission by means of demonstrations of and association with power was deliberately and utterly rejected (Matt. 4:1–11; Luke 4:1–13). His mission would — because it should — unfold in poverty, weakness, and obscurity. The inspiration behind Peter's subsequent suggestion that Christ's mission should be carried out by a more attractive means was traced to Satan himself, when Jesus' scathing rebuke could scarcely have been harsher: "Out of my sight, Satan!" Jesus said to Peter (Mark 8:31–33).

The missiological lessons of the Incarnation are clear. "As you have sent me into the world, I have sent [those whom you gave me] into the world," Christ prayed as he pled with his Father for those who, like him, were "not of the world" (John 17:16, 17). "Your attitude should be the same as that of Christ Jesus," Paul reminded believers at Philippi, whose methods for achieving personal objectives appear to have been only too natural (Phil. 2:5). At the very least, the Incarnation means giving up the power, privilege, and social position that are our natural due. Christ's mission in Christ's way must always begin, proceed, and end with the great renunciation. And this sacrifice is made not merely with reference to "what could have been" back home, but by the standards of the people among whom the missionary is called to incarnate the Gospel. This does not leave much room for the power-generating, status-inflating, career-building, self-protecting affluence to which emissaries of the Western churches have become accustomed.

There are those who have suggested that a Western missionary should not try to identify too literally with a lower group if, in the eyes of this lower group, he has an ascribed right to a higher status. Such a course of action, it is argued, will not only be misunderstood by people, "since it reverses all norms of social climbing"; it will surround the missionary with "a cloud of suspicion."[36]

That misunderstanding and suspicion are among the penalties paid by all who go against the social norms of a society cannot be denied. But that this should be regarded as sufficient reason to continue to enjoy the privileges of affluence is more than doubtful; it is wrong. Jesus, in lowering himself and becoming of no reputation, *did* suffer lifelong misunderstanding, suspicion, and eventual death —

---

36. See Eugene A. Nida, *Message and Mission: The Communication of the Christian Faith* (New York: Harper & Row, 1960), 164–65.

because he did not operate according to the social expectations associated in the Jewish mind with the role of Messiah. Much that is distinctive in his good news runs dangerously contrary to human conventions, and sounds suspiciously like bad news! Those who love their enemies, bless their persecutors, refuse to store up treasure on earth, give way before others, and surrender their lives in selfless service are frequently, quite rightly, regarded as a threat to the status quo. This is not the behavior of natural man, but of those whose King is not of this world. God's wisdom has always seemed, to fallen man, foolishness.

Western mission agencies — if they wish to be truly Christian — must return to this "foolishness" of their Lord. No matter how enlightened the technique, how massive the budget, how sophisticated the technology, or how numerous the well-qualified personnel, nothing but God's strategy revealed in the Incarnation will prevail against either "the powers of this dark world" or "the spiritual forces of evil in heavenly realms." However strange or inappropriate our spiritual weapons may seem to the natural man, they are the only ones that work in the spiritual battle.

The Cross

The cross, likewise, is not merely a symbol of the atonement, but a prescription for the only way of life promised to all who would follow Jesus. The New Testament attaches tremendous importance to the crucifixion of Christ. It is the very heart of apostolic teaching. Our Savior's death on this diabolical instrument of suffering was the central act in the drama which brings salvation to humankind. In his death, Christ made himself one with sinners, absorbing our richly deserved punishment. "He is the atoning sacrifice for our sins," John assured his readers (1 John 2:2; 4:10); and Paul, addressing the self-righteous Galatians, reminded them of the central fact of the Gospel: "Christ redeemed us from the curse of the law by becoming a curse for us" (Gal. 3:13). This is good news indeed!

But there is a disturbing, and therefore often ignored, thread of truth in New Testament teaching about the cross. Those who would follow Christ look forward not only to the comforting prospect of "pie in the sky in the sweet by and by," but to suffering and death in the here and now. For Jesus deliberately chose to make the fellowship of the cross an integral part of what he offers each would-be disciple. "Anyone," he said, "who does not take up his cross and follow me is not worthy of me" (Matt. 10:38). These words were spoken in the context of the natural tendency of his followers, then as now, to put family concerns before obedience to God.

As Jesus approached his own terrible, mortal suffering, Mark records that he called the crowds to him along with his disciples, and said, "If anyone would come after me, he must deny himself and take up his cross and follow me" (Mark 8:34). In this instance, his unvarnished account of the rejection and suffering that lay just ahead for him earned him Peter's love-inspired remonstrance. "You do not have in mind the things of God, but the things of men," was Jesus' response to a suggestion which, if followed, would have put him in collusion with the forces of darkness (Mark 8:31–33).

Do not these words constitute a serious challenge to the Western way of doing mission? The cross, that instrument of dreadful suffering and shame, not only results in our salvation, but prescribes the way of life for all who follow Christ! The cross not only gives life, it takes it. The cross achieves reconciliation between God and humankind, it is true; but it also divides, separating those whose kingdom is not of this world from those at home with the spirit of their age. For Christ's followers, the cross is not only the power of God unto salvation; it is the guarantee of misunderstanding, persecution, and suffering at the hands of those to whom it is a foolish and obnoxious stumbling block (1 Cor. 1:17–18; Gal. 6:12–14). There is nothing attractive, easy, secure, comfortable, convenient, strategically efficient, economical, or self-fulfilling about taking up a cross.

Many, regarding themselves as Christ's disciples because they have accepted, at a superficial level, what Christ offers through the cross, are in actual fact nothing of the sort. Encountering such "believers" in Philippi, Paul tearfully acknowledged that "many live as enemies of the cross of Christ... [for] their mind is on earthly things." The fellowship of the cross was foreign to these church members. They were not conformed to Christ's death. "Their destiny is destruction," was Paul's sorrowful conclusion (Phil. 3:17–20).

For such people, the cross means judgment. Their lives, shaped, directed, and consumed by self-gratification, are a mute but effective denial of the Christ whom they profess to follow. Horrified at the prospect of a personal cross, they choose the security of surrender to the enemy of their souls rather than the foolishly painful cross of the lover of their souls. Living out their lives in pleasant, self-fulfilling ways, according to the wisdom of their particular world, like kernels of wheat that refuse to fall into the ground and die, the potential for multiplying life is never realized.

In the highly competitive drive to meet increasingly expensive institutional commitments and expand (or at least maintain) membership ranks, personnel recruitment by Western churches and mission agencies does not often dwell upon the call to the fellowship of the cross. Great care is taken to show the extent to which the agency or denomination is prepared to attend to the needs and wants of its missionaries; comprehensive support packages ensure that no needless suffering will be incurred on the part of either the missionary or the missionary's family. The enlightened strategies of the mission are duly elaborated, replete with success testimonials calculated to convince the potential still-wavering recruit that this is the mission society for him or her. New Testament teaching on self-denial is reinterpreted to mean little more than a comfortable life abroad. There are exceptions, of course. But, like the affluent churches it represents, much that the West calls "mission" is no longer an example of participation in the sufferings of Christ. "He saved others; he cannot save himself" has been conspicuously rewritten in missionary flesh to read, "Western Christians save themselves and their children; perhaps if we are fortunate they will save a few of us too."

The Western church is invited to join the fellowship of the cross. Western mission structures, policies, strategies, and personnel need to reflect the way of the cross. Of the many responses to the controversial "Laymen's Foreign Mission

Inquiry" of 1932,[37] the most theologically apposite criticism was that of Japanese reformer Toyohiko Kagawa: "Can Christianity exist without the Cross?" he asked. " 'Re-Thinking Missions' tries to interpret to us Christ without the Cross as Christianity ... nothing is said about the inevitability of paying the price of the Cross in order to bring in the Kingdom of God."[38] His words apply equally to more contemporary, evangelical missions from the West. Mission that does not operate according to the principles of the cross cannot be *Christian* mission.

Weakness

The third paradoxical element characterizing mission done in the New Testament way is *weakness*. Humankind has always been awed and cowed by power. Power of various kinds — military, political, social, economic, ecclesiastical — is avidly sought and clung to in the natural course of human affairs. We Westerners are a privileged people; privileges require protecting; protection requires power — in the case of missions, the power of money, excellent organization, well-educated missionaries, and skillful strategies.

According to the New Testament, on the other hand, obedient followers are not to either strive for or maintain personal power and privilege; all that they do is marked by personal vulnerability and self-giving. The mission that truly serves its Head never looks for ways of gaining and wielding power, but for ways of subjecting itself on behalf of others. No other pattern is consistent with incarnational or cross-bearing mission.

The power of God unto salvation began with the powerlessness of a poor infant, in the presence of an assortment of peasants, shepherds, and common barnyard animals. The mortal struggle against the terrible forces of evil in our universe (Eph. 6:12) pitted all the violent power of which Satan was capable against the pathetic weakness of a newborn infant.

The infant survived, and grew, but came to a tragic and early end. Unable to answer charges of political insurrection brought against him by the people he had come to save, he died. Unable to defend either himself or his followers, he hung — helpless, pain-racked in body and spirit, a victim of trumped-up charges — on a cross between two thieves. His mother, tearful witness to her firstborn's death agonies, must have recalled with bitter irony the joyful outpouring of hopes and expectations with which she had greeted the news that this child would liberate Israel (Luke 1:46–55). How naive she had been then! How differently her son's life had unfolded before her: he had not brought down rulers from their thrones — they had brought him down instead; he had tried to lift the humble, but had been trampled by them in return; he had on occasion filled the hungry with good

---

37. William Ernest Hocking, *Re-thinking Missions: A Laymen's Inquiry after One Hundred Years* (New York: Harper & Brothers, 1932).

38. Kagawa's ten-point critique of the Report was published under the title "A Significant Word from Asia, Giving Dr. Toyohiko Kagawa's Clarion-call to the Church of Christ" (Bombay: Printed by F. Borton for G. Claridge & Co., published by Bishop B. T. Badley, n.d.). This quotation is from p. 8. His thinking on the cross is further developed in his book *Meditations on the Cross*, trans. Helen F. Topping and Marion R. Draper (Chicago: Willett, Clark & Co., 1935).

things, and sent the rich way empty, but the rich now had their revenge. Her son's weakness was no match for their power. Of course, we now know that not the crucifiers, but the Crucified, manifested the mighty power of God which transformed persons, nations, and the course of history.

The apostle Paul's Damascus Road conversion — from power to weakness — made him the most effective of the earliest missionaries. Having understood the futile incongruity of utilizing worldly power in carrying out Christ's mission, in his letters to the Corinthian church Paul repeatedly returns to the theme.[39] "God chose the weak things of the world to shame the strong," he reminded the quarreling church (1 Cor. 1:27). He made it clear that to be a missionary (an apostle) meant, in God's mysterious strategy, to be "on display at the end of the procession" (1 Cor. 4:9), least among the prisoners of war, condemned to a public death. He was a spectacle, yes, but not the spectacle of affluence, efficiency, and comfort modeled by many of his Western apostolic counterparts.

"It seems to me," said Paul, "that God has put us apostles on display." What was it that people watching the procession would notice about these missionaries? Not their strength, but their weakness; not their honor, but their dishonor; not their healthy bodies, fine wardrobes, and comfortable homes, but their poverty, rags, and homelessness; not the flattering accolades of the powerful, but curses, slander, and persecution at the hands of everyone. In short, to be a missionary meant to become "the scum of the earth, the refuse of the world" (1 Cor. 4:8– 13)! Like his Savior's before him, Paul's life did not have a happy ending, a "missionary statesman" surrounded by devoted supporters and fellow veterans in a Christian retirement village somewhere on the Mediterranean. He spent his last days almost alone, in a Roman dungeon, a frail old man whose life was finally snuffed out by executioners at the behest of a powerful state. It is hard to imagine a weaker, more vulnerable person than this. Yet, as Japanese theologian Kosuke Koyama observes, "Through Paul who was imprisoned, beaten, stoned, shipwrecked, threatened by all kinds of people, hungry, thirsty, cold and exposed, God touched the foundation of history, and he let Paul touch it too."[40]

What is the significance of these three themes for the Western mission today? Any mission strategy worthy to be called "Christian" must be consistent with biblical teaching on the Incarnation, the cross, and weakness. A strategy conceived and generated from afar — within the protected confines of an American church or educational institution — is not an incarnational strategy. A strategy that guarantees security, comfort, and privilege for its practitioners knows nothing of the cross; a powerful, all-encompassing, grandiose plan calling for the mobilization of tens of thousands of North Americans and the expenditure of millions of dollars to support them cannot possibly express itself in that weakness which is, according to the Bible and supported by the facts, the only vehicle whereby God's power may be made perfect.

---

39. Cf. 1 Cor. 1:18–31; 2:1–5; 4:1–16; 2 Cor. 3:7–11; 4:1–18; 11:7–33; 12:7–10.
40. Kosuke Koyama, *No Handle on the Cross: An Asian Meditation on the Crucified Mind* (London: SCM, 1976), 77.

For the affluent Western Christian mission, grappling with its economic power at the theological level will mean subjecting all personal, family, ecclesiastical, and strategic plans, policies, practices, or considerations to these three questions: (1) Does it reflect the Incarnation, or is it essentially self-serving? (2) Is the cross both the message and the method, or is self-preservation the bottom line? (3) Are people more impressed by its stability and strength or by its weakness? The answer to each of these questions will determine the "Christian-ness" of both the missions and the missionaries of the Western churches.

In the final analysis, Christian stewardship is not something we do, but something we become. Not a technique but a way of living. Two ways in which a missionary may resist the mesmerizing pull of Western materialism are well illustrated in the encounters of two Greek heroes, Odysseus and Jason. Odysseus having heard of the deadly but irresistibly appealing call of the Sirens, was determined to experience the pull without succumbing to its effects. Accordingly, he had himself bound to the mast of his ship, and the ears of his oarsmen plugged with beeswax, after issuing firm instructions that he was not under any circumstances to be released until the ship had sailed well past the island inhabited by the Sirens. As the boat approached the island, Odysseus began to hear the song of the Sirens, gradually, inexorably, succumbing to its spell until at last he writhed and struggled in his bonds, begging his crew to let him heed the deadly song, and cursing them for ignoring his frenzied appeals. As the boat drew past the island, and the voices of the Sirens faded into silence, Odysseus was able to assert self-control once again, and reflected on his desire to rush to what must have been certain death. His method of resistance illustrates the way of bonds and restrictions. It is not pleasant, but it can be effective in saving us from our own desires.

Jason and his Argonauts faced a similar peril, as — approaching the island whose shores were lined with the bleaching bones of thousands of sailors who had been unable to resist the appeal of the Sirens — they began to lose the will to resist the Sirens' deadly pull. Fortunately, as the story goes, Princess Medea had the presence of mind to urge Orpheus (Greek god of music) to counter the Sirens' song with the music of the gods. This he did so effectively that the music of heaven drowned out the sound of the Sirens, thus neutralizing its mesmerizing effects, and saving the lives of all on board.

As evangelical missionaries, we can choose to respond to the appeals of mammon in three ways: (1) we can give in to its deadly appeal; (2) we can bind ourselves by rules and regulations that make it impossible for us to respond as we would like; (3) or we can drown out the Sirens' invitation to death by listening instead to the music of the Spirit, and by learning to sing God's song.

"...And the things of earth will grow strangely dim in the light of his glory and grace."

Part IV

FAITH AND WEALTH
IN THE HEBREW SCRIPTURES
AND THE EARLY CHURCH

In the dynamic and often controversial judicial and legislative processes of the United States, there is one document to which constant reference is made. Those who generate new laws or who challenge, interpret, apply and enforce existing laws are obliged to prove that what they are doing is consistent with either the letter or the intent of the Constitution of the founding fathers of their country. We followers of Christ similarly attempt to ensure that as individuals, families, and faith communities there is a recognizable correspondence between what the Bible teaches on the one hand, and our ethical, relational, and material lives, on the other. For this reason, nothing in this book is more important that its invitation to bring correspondence between what missionaries believe and how missionaries live. In chapter 6, detailed consideration was given to theological, ethical, and biblical teaching on mammon, and to the implications of such teaching for missionaries. But as the author of that chapter, I am acutely aware of my limitations. I am neither a biblical scholar nor a theologian. Accordingly, when a second, expanded edition of this book was in the making, I was deeply gratified when two highly respected biblical scholars — Christopher J. H. Wright and Justo L. González — responded enthusiastically to my invitation to contribute chapters that would strengthen the book's theological underpinnings.

Christopher J. H. Wright, International Ministry Director of Langham Partnership International, is a well-known evangelical Old Testament scholar whose published works include Eye for Eye: the Place of Old Testament Ethics Today *(IVP, 1983), and* God's People in God's Land: Family, Land, and Property in the Old Testament *(Eerdmans, 1990), a commentary on Deuteronomy (Paternoster, 1996), and — most recently —* The Mission of God: Unlocking the Bible's Grand

Narrative *(IVP, 2006). His chapter "Faith and Wealth: The Righteous Rich in the Old Testament" was written especially for this book.*

Justo L. González, the editor of Apuntes, *a journal of Hispanic theology, and of* Comentario Bíblico Hispanoamericano, *directs the Hispanic Summer Seminary Program of the Fund for Theological Education in Decatur, Georgia. A highly respected church historian among whose scores of publications is the highly acclaimed three-volume* A History of Christian Thought *(Abingdon, 1970–75),* González had already published the material that I wanted to include in his Faith and Wealth: A History of Early Christian Ideas on the Origin, Significance, and Use of Money *(Harper & Row, 1990). He generously gave his permission to publish the requested chapters — "The New Testament Koinonia" and "The Subapostolic Church" — which appear in this section.*

Since the Scriptures transcend time and culture, these three chapters may well be the book's most enduring contribution to missiological theory and practice, and without doubt are foundational to what I have attempted to say.

8

The Righteous Rich
in the Old Testament

Christopher J. H. Wright

Much is written and preached about the problem of poverty from a biblical perspective, and much of what is written and preached acknowledges the fact that most poverty does not just happen — it is caused. There are, of course, those who are poor for reasons that have little or no human or moral causation (e.g., as a result of devastating weather, or disabling illness or disastrous bereavement, or the aftermath of locusts or blight), but it is still the case, and probably always has been, that the greatest cause of poverty is to be found in the wide range of direct or indirect forms of oppression, greed, and injustice by which those who are not poor sustain their advantageous position. In other words, in most discussions of wealth and poverty, the rich are the bad guys. And in scholarly discussions about poverty in the Bible, that is also frequently the case.

So it is refreshing to look at the matter from the more unusual angle of our title, which may seem somewhat oxymoronic to those immersed in the kind of writing and preaching mentioned above. Righteous and rich are words not often found in each other's company. Perhaps it is to the familiar rhetoric of Amos that we owe the dominance of the reverse word association. For it was Amos who challenged a culture in which the rich may well have been using a distorted Deuteronomic logic to claim that their wealth was a proof of their status of righteousness and blessing before God. On the contrary, thundered Amos, it was the oppressed poor who were "the righteous." This did not mean that the poor were morally perfect or not sinners like the rest of us, but that they were the ones whom the divine judge's verdict deemed to be "in the right," in a situation where the wealthy, by their oppressive actions, were clearly "in the wrong" — that is, "the wicked." Amos used the terms in a forensic sense, but the association had an enduring moral flavor summed up in a deceptively simple and familiar binary alternative: the righteous poor and the wicked rich.

Yet clearly the Old Testament has a lot more to say on the subject than we can glean from the prophetic monochrome of Amos. It does not assert that *all* wealth

Christopher J. H. Wright is director of Langham Trust International and has authored numerous books and articles, including *Old Testament Ethics for the People of God* (Leicester and Downers Grove: IVP and InterVarsity, 2004), and *God's People in God's Land* (Carlisle: Paternoster, 1990).

must have been gained through wickedness. To paraphrase Shakespeare, some
are born rich, some achieve riches, and others have riches thrust upon them; to
which the Old Testament would doubtless add, some are blessed by God with
riches within the framework of covenant obedience.

My plan in what follows is first of all to make a canonical survey — observing
some texts relevant to the title in each of the major genres of Old Testament
literature; and then second, and more briefly, to make a thematic summary —
drawing the threads together in a way which, it is hoped, can be fruitfully applied
in different contexts by different readers.

A Canonical Survey[1]

The Narratives

Abraham

The foundational story of Abraham combines wealth with righteousness and
put both under the sign of God's blessing. "Abram had become very wealthy in
livestock and in silver and gold" (Gen. 13:2); "Abram believed the LORD, and he
credited it to him as righteousness" (Gen. 15:6). Both of these texts come after the
original word of God to Abram (Gen. 12:1–3), in which God promised not only
to bless Abram, but also that he would be a blessing. Indeed, the verb in the last
line of Genesis 12:2 is actually imperative, matching the imperatives of v. 1. The
thrust of the whole word is thus: "Go . . . Be a blessing . . . and all peoples on earth
will be blessed through you."[2] Abraham is thus the one who receives blessing and
is the means of blessing others. This is the context in which his wealth is to be set.
It is, in fact, the very first context in which wealth is mentioned at all in the Bible,
and its strong connection with the blessing of God is apparent. The connection is
even more explicit in the case of Isaac. Following hard on the reminder of God's
promise to bless the world through Abraham because of his obedience (Gen.
26:4–5) comes the record of Isaac's enrichment under God's blessing (26:12–
13), which even a foreigner acknowledges (26:29). The patriarchal narratives
thus portray the righteous rich as those who receive their wealth from God as a
token of his blessing, respond in risky faith and costly obedience (cf. Gen. 22),
and participate in God's mission of blessing others. Since, as we have said, this is
the first substantial appearance of wealth in the Bible, it is important to note that
it is set in a very wholesome light — in companionship with covenant, blessing,
obedience, and mission.

Boaz

Boaz is not actually described as wealthy, but as "a man of standing" — a
person of substance in the local community (Ruth 2:1). However, the axis of

---

1. I have chosen to follow the loose order of the English Bible rather than the stricter order of
the Hebrew canon — Law, Prophets, and Writings.

2. God's command to Abraham has as much claim to the phrase the "Great Commission" as
the end of Matthew's Gospel. It launches the history of the mission of God (to bless the nations),
through the mission of God's people (to be blessed and to be the means of blessing).

the story of the book of Ruth is that he is certainly wealthy *in comparison with* Ruth and Naomi in their need. He possesses land, servants, good harvests, and the spare cash to redeem Elimelech's land. Nor is Boaz described specifically as righteous, but the character that emerges from the story shows all the marks associated with righteousness in the Old Testament. He acts with kindness to one who was an alien and a widow (one of the commonest exhortations in Israel's law); he respects her decision to move to the land of Israel and take refuge under the wings of the God of Israel (thus aligning himself with the Abrahamic stance of being a blessing to the nations); he acts with committed and sacrificial faithfulness (*hesed*) towards his deceased relative Elimelech, by redeeming the land of Naomi and taking his widowed daughter-in-law Ruth with a view to raising a son to inherit Elimelech's line rather than his own. He thus fulfills the role of kinsman-redeemer (*go'el*), and is warmly commended by the local community and blessed by God in the birth of a son who became the ancestor of David, and eventually of the Messiah, Jesus. Boaz, in using his wealth with risky generosity, stands in contrast to the nearer but nameless kinsman who declines to do his duty for the family for fear of spoiling his own inheritance (4:6; i.e., by having to spend money on raising a potential son who would not inherit in his own line).

David

The most significant context in which the wealth of King David is discussed is his provision for the building of the temple by his son Solomon in 1 Chronicles 28–29. One might have to set to one side at this point questions regarding the *sources* of David's personal wealth, some of which at least certainly came from tribute imposed upon nations he defeated in his many wars (ironically, the very reason that he was not allowed to build the temple himself; 28:3). The stance of the narrator seems to be that this particular use of David's wealth, however it was accumulated, was worthy and exemplary. Certainly, his example of putting his personal wealth into the temple project (29:2–5) motivated the rest of the leaders to do the same (29:6–8), which seems to have motivated the rest of the people in turn (29:9). The whole act of national giving is then followed by an exemplary prayer in which David acknowledges the true source of all wealth (God himself), and the comparative unworthiness of all human giving, which is merely giving back to God what already belongs to him.

Insofar as this could be characterized as an example of "righteous riches" (or at least riches put to the service of righteousness), it is marked by willingness, wholeheartedness, and joy (29:9), along with God-honoring worship, humility, integrity, and honest intent (29:10–17).

Solomon

There is much greater ambivalence about the riches of Solomon, which were legendary even in his own day. In one sense, he just stepped into them as the heir of his father David (though the succession was marked with excesses of conspiracy and violence), and by continuing his policy of exacting tribute from the many nations under his rule (1 Kings 4:21). To this he added a trading genius that was highly lucrative but of very questionable legitimacy (1 Kings 10:26–29; contrast Deut. 17:16–17). So the riches of Solomon are set under a moral question mark, and yet the narrator affirms that he received them also as an unasked-for gift from God, because Solomon had asked for wisdom to rule his people justly (1 Kings 3:9–14). So again, insofar as the wealth of Solomon had any tinge of righteousness, it lay in its early connection with his desire to do justice, and his express prioritizing of wisdom over wealth in itself. Sadly, the later Solomon was tinged with everything but righteousness, and his wealth came to constitute a symbol of oppression and an enduring snare to his successors.

Nehemiah

Nehemiah 5 records an incident of public protest against a range of unjust and oppressive economic practices in the postexilic community, of which Nehemiah was governor, and the actions that Nehemiah took in righteous anger to rectify them. In the public arena, Nehemiah's action turned around a situation that was "not right" (Neh. 5:9). But Nehemiah goes on to record his own personal example in handling his finances. Whether his self-commendation is quite to our taste or not, we would concede that his refusal to exploit his political office for private gain, or to allow his entourage to live in burdensome luxury and excess, is a token of righteousness in his handling of the wealth to which his position gave him access (Neh. 5:14–19).

The Law

Since so much of Israel's law in the Pentateuch is oriented toward life in the land, economic relationships, principles, and practices are prominent. This is not the place for a survey of the wide range of such material.[3] We may consider just a few texts that specifically refer to the righteous (or otherwise) use of personal wealth.

The Old Testament regards it as a fundamental duty of those who have wealth to be willing to lend to the poor. Lending is not in itself associated with exploitation, but is a mark of righteousness. However, the key distinction between righteous and unrighteous lending is the matter of interest. Among the marks of the one who is "blameless" and "righteous" is that he lends his money, but does so without demanding interest (Ps. 15:2, 5). To lend is to prioritize the need of the poor person by making one's wealth available to him. To demand interest to is to prioritize one's personal profit by exploiting the poor person's need.

Leviticus 25:35–38

Set within a whole raft of legislation designed to address the threat of impoverishment, this paragraph puts a responsibility on the better-off kinsman to provide practical support to the kinsman who is sinking into poverty. Interest-free loans are the recommended method at this stage. As throughout the chapter, this

---

3. I have, however, tried to cover it fairly thoroughly in *Old Testament Ethics for the People of God* and *God's People in God's Land.*

action is motivated by a sense of vertical obligation to the God who delivered them from Egypt. Righteousness in the OT includes a right response to the saving action of God; part of that right response is generous care for the poor.

Deuteronomy 24:6, 10–13

Lending was a duty in OT Israel, but it was also to be carried out humanely in a way that would respect the dignity and privacy of the debtor. So these laws address the creditor and call for certain restraints and limits to be observed in the financial transaction, and its social implications. "The bottom line" is not the only thing that counts in God's sight.

Other laws relate to spiritual and attitudinal dimensions of wealth.

Deuteronomy 8 is a chapter that puts all personal wealth in the context of the "prevenient" grace of God's gift of the land. Israel must remember how they were led out of need and poverty into the abundance of the land. The emphasis up to verse 10 is that sufficiency of material goods should generate praise to God. The emphasis shifts somewhat from verses 11–14, with the warning that surplus of goods can quickly generate pride in oneself. That pride is expressed with sharp perception in the boasting of verse 17: "You may say to yourself, 'My power and the strength of my hands have produced this wealth for me.' " But the bubble of self-congratulation is immediately pricked in verse 18, "But remember the LORD your God, for it is he who gives you the ability to produce wealth." The righteous rich remember where their wealth has come from. To forget that is the first step to pride, and all the greed and injustice that flow from it.

Deuteronomy 15 is the warm heartbeat of the whole book, in my view. It expands some basic laws of Exodus concerning sabbatical fallow on the land and the release of Hebrew slaves, but does so in a way that exudes a spirit of generosity and compassion.

> If there is a poor man among your brothers in any of the towns of the land that the LORD your God is giving you, do not be hard-hearted or tight-fisted toward your poor brother. Rather be open-handed and freely lend him whatever he needs.... Give generously to him and so without a grudging eye...there will always be poor people in the land [or in the earth]. Therefore I command you to be open-handed towards your brothers and towards your poor and your needy in your land. (Deut. 15:7–11, my translation).

This text combines a strong use of "body language" (heart, hand/fist, eye), with a strongly relational dimension ("your" is repeated emphatically in a way that some English translations obscure). The righteous rich recognize that the poor are brothers whose need is not only to be helped, but to belong; not to be marginalized into a social category (*the* poor), but to be held within the bonds of community participation (*your* poor). Righteousness is relational, not abstract, impersonal, or arm's-length.

Releasing a Hebrew slave after six years is to be "celebrated" (not begrudged), with a parting gift that will not only sustain him through the transition, but even honors and blesses him in a way that reflects God's blessing on the owner.

When you release him, do not send him away empty-handed. "Garland him" (lit.) from your flock, your threshing-floor, and your winepress. Give to him as the LORD your God has blessed you. (Deut. 15:15, my translation)

That final sentence could have fallen from the lips of Jesus. The righteous rich are consciously motivated by constant recall of how much they themselves owe to God.[4]

Psalms

We have already noticed that lending without interest is one mark of that righteousness that can stand in the presence of God (Ps. 15:5), and Ezekiel confirms this and condemns the opposite as wickedness (Ezek. 18:8, 13, 17).

Psalm 37 is a lengthy reflection, in Wisdom mode, on the contrasting behavior, attitudes, and destiny of the righteous and the wicked. Among other things, it warns the righteous not to envy the prosperity of the unrighteous rich, with the proverbial comparison,

> Better the little that the righteous have
> than the wealth of many wicked. (v. 16)

Like other parts of the Wisdom literature, the psalm deals more with general principles than with all the nasty details of life (v. 25 might lead us to reckon that the author needed to get out more). But it certainly has a view of how the righteous should behave in relation to whatever riches they might have.

> The wicked borrow and do not repay,
> but the righteous give generously. (v. 21)

> [The righteous] are always generous and lend freely;
> their children will be blessed. (v. 26)

Psalm 112 strikes an identical chord, but with the extra harmonics that the generosity of the righteous is a mirroring of the generosity of the LORD himself. Note how Psalm 112:3–5 (and 9), about the righteous wealth, compassion, justice, and generosity of "the person who fears the LORD," echoes quite deliberately the same qualities of the LORD, in the matching acrostic Psalm 111:3–5.

> Wealth and riches are in his house,
> and his righteousness endures for ever.
> Even in darkness light dawns for the upright,
> for the gracious and compassionate and righteous man.
> Good will come to him who is generous and lends freely,
> who conducts his affairs with justice....

> He has scattered abroad his gifts to the poor,
> his righteousness endures for ever.

---

4. For a fuller discussion of the profound social implications of this chapter, see Christopher J. H. Wright, *Deuteronomy,* New International Biblical Commentary on the Old Testament (Peabody and Carlisle: Hendrikson and Paternoster, 1996), 187–97.

Wisdom

Proverbs

The book of Proverbs is a goldmine for the theme of the righteous rich, since so many of its sayings relate in one way or another to the use (or abuse) of material goods.

An early note, consistent with the running thread through the whole book, is that the only acceptable wealth is that which accompanies trust in God, commitment to him, and acknowledgment of him (Prov. 3:5–10). The fear of the LORD is the beginning (or first principle) of wisdom, and also the first requirement for righteous riches. In fact, however, though wealth is a positive good in Proverbs, it is not the only or the greatest good by any means. Far more important is wisdom — the wisdom that comes from God.

> Choose my instruction instead of silver,
>   knowledge rather than choice gold,
> for wisdom is more precious than rubies,
>   and nothing you desire can compare with her.
>   (Prov. 8:10–11, cf. 16:16)

As we saw, Solomon knew this in his humbler youth (1 Kings 3), but sadly forgot it rather quickly.

The upright also recognize that wealth is in any case no protection against death (Prov. 11:4) — a relativizing perception that is amplified in even more melancholy tones in Ecclesiastes 5:13–6:6.

The dominant note in relation to righteous riches in Proverbs, however, is one that is completely consistent with the law and the prophets, namely the requirement to treat the poor with kindness, and without contempt, mockery, or callousness. Interestingly, however, whereas the law and prophets ground such teaching in the history of Israel's redemption (specifically God's saving generosity in the exodus), the Wisdom tradition tends to appeal to the broader foundation of creation. Disparities of human wealth are ultimately irrelevant to our standing before God. Rich and poor have a created equality as human beings before God. Consequently, whatever attitude or action the rich adopt toward the poor, they actually adopt toward God (with all that entails). The righteous rich is therefore one who sees his God when he looks at the poor man made in God's image.

> He who oppresses the poor shows contempt for their Maker,
>   but whoever is kind to the needy honors God. (Prov. 14:31)

This is a note that can be heard echoing through the following texts: Proverbs 17:5; 19:17; 22:2, 22; 29:7, 13.

As we saw in Psalm 37, the Wisdom writers cared more about justice than about prosperity, a perspective that they summarized in the opinion that it was far preferable to be poor but righteous, than to have ill-gotten wealth through injustice and oppression (Prov. 16:8; 28:6).

One final perspective worth mentioning is the value of contentment with sufficiency. Neither excessive poverty nor excessive wealth are desirable, for both are a temptation to behave in ways that disown or dishonor God. The implication seems to be that the righteous rich know when to say, "Enough is enough."

> Give me neither poverty nor riches,
>> but give me only my daily bread.
> Otherwise, I may have too much and disown you
>> and say, 'Who is the LORD?'
> Or I may become poor and steal,
>> and so dishonor the name of my God.
>> > > (Prov. 30:8–9)

Job

For any lingering doubts that righteousness and riches could ever inhabit the same universe, Job is the classic proof. The three opening verses of the book affirm both truths about him: Job was a model of righteousness ("blameless and upright; he feared God and shunned evil"), and he was simultaneously very wealthy — a legend in his own time. The former is the verdict endorsed even by God himself (1:8, 2:3). The latter is cynically offered by the satan as an alleged mercenary motive. Job would not be so righteous, he sneers, if he were not being so richly blessed by God. So the test to which Job is unwittingly exposed is to see if his righteousness (which he more often describes as his integrity) will survive the loss of all his substance, even his health. And it does.

But in the course of his self-defense Job describes the kind of life he had led before the calamity that befell him, and in doing so he sheds considerable ethical light on how those who are blessed by God with wealth beyond what is common can at the same time behave in ways that God himself will own as righteous beyond comparison. Chapters 29 and 31 are particularly rich in righteousness.

Job 29 describes his life "when God's intimate friendship blessed my house," that is, in the days of his wealth and social standing. As one of those who exercised justice in the local courts, Job claims that he had rescued the poor and defended the orphan and widow, that he had been eyes to the blind, feet to the lame, father to the needy, champion of the stranger, and scourge of the wicked (29:12–17). The mark of righteous riches is when those who possess them use the social power they confer for the benefit of the powerless and to confound those who victimize them.

Job 31, Job's final and prolonged moral *apologia,* contains several specific references to his use of, or attitude to, his wealth. In summary: he had used it generously (31:16–20); he had not placed ultimate security in it (31:24–25); he had put it hospitably at the service of others (31:31–32); and he not gained it through merciless exploitation of his own workers (31:38–40). There is much here for ethical reflection, and certainly for those who are blessed with riches and are seeking to act righteously in handling them.

The Prophets

Condemnation by the prophets of those who had gained their wealth by injustice and used their wealth to perpetuate further injustice is pervasive. Only rarely do we get glimpses of prophetic approval of those who are righteous in their attitude and actions in relation to wealth.

There was no love lost between Jeremiah and King Jehoiakim. In condemning his unscrupulous self-enrichment at the expense of unpaid workers, his competitive greed and conspicuous opulence, Jeremiah contrasts the unworthy new king with his godly father, King Josiah. As king, Josiah doubtless also enjoyed his share of royal wealth, but Jeremiah seems to refer to a more modest lifestyle, when he says

> Did not your father have food and drink?
> > He did what was right and just,
> > so all went well with him.
> He defended the cause of the poor and needy,
> > and so all went well.
> Is that not what it means to know me? declares the LORD.
> > (Jer. 2:15–16)

Again, we note that the central key to righteousness in the handling of riches is the doing of justice for the poor. That alone is the path to well-being. These verses also give a sharp insight into what Jeremiah meant by "knowing God" — all the more important since he will later include the knowledge of God as one of the major blessings of the new covenant (Jer. 31:34). Knowing God is not just a matter of personal piety, but the exercise of practical justice.

The link with knowing God is further developed by Jeremiah in a beautifully crafted small poem in which he sets three of God's best gifts on one side of the scales (wisdom, strength, and riches), and declares that none of them (God-given though they may be) are to be boasted of. For they pale in comparison with the privilege of knowing Yahweh as God — and knowing that his primary delight lies in the three things that Jeremiah puts in the other side of the scales, the doing of kindness, justice, and righteousness on earth (Jer. 9:23–24). So the righteous rich do not boast of their riches, rather they relativize them in comparison with knowing God and loving what he loves.

Finally, Ezekiel echoes Psalm 15 when he includes among the characteristics of the model righteous person that all his economic dealings are generous, rather than oppressive, caring rather than self-interested (Ezek. 18:7–8).

A Thematic Summary

As we saw at the very beginning, God may choose (but is not obliged) to make a righteous person rich. But what, in the light of our survey, makes a rich person righteous? At least the following summary points would seem to emerge from the Old Testament's reflections on this matter, with all its different moods and voices. The righteous rich are those who:

- Remember the source of their riches — namely the grace and gift of God himself, and are therefore not boastingly inclined to take the credit for achieving them through their own skill, strength, or effort (even if these things have been legitimately deployed) (Deut. 8:17–18; 1 Chron. 29:11–12; Jer. 9:23–24).

- Do not idolize their wealth by putting inordinate trust in it, nor get anxious about losing it. For ultimately it is one's relationship with God that matters more and can survive (and even be deepened by) the absence or loss of wealth (Job 31:24–25).

- Recognize that wealth is thus secondary to many things, including wisdom, but especially personal integrity, humility, and righteousness (1 Chron. 29:17; Prov. 8:10–11; 1 Kings 3; Prov. 16:8, 28:6).

- Set their wealth in the context of God's blessing, recognizing that being blessed is not a privilege but a responsibility — the Abrahamic responsibility of being a blessing to others (Gen. 12:1–3). Wealth in righteous hands is thus a servant of that mission that flows from God's commitment to bless the nations through the seed of Abraham.

- Use their wealth with justice; this includes refusing to extract personal benefit by using wealth for corrupt ends (e.g., through bribery), and ensuring that all one's financial dealings are nonexploitative of the needs of others (e.g., through interest) (Ps. 15:5; Ezek. 18:7–8).

- Make their wealth available to the wider community through responsible lending that is both practical (Lev. 25) and respectful of the dignity of the debtor (Deut. 24:6, 10–13).

- See wealth as an opportunity for generosity — even when it is risky, and even when it hurts, thereby both blessing the poor and needy, and at the same time reflecting the character of God (Deut. 15; Ps. 112:3; Prov. 14:31; 19:17; Ruth).

- Use wealth in the service of God, whether by contributing to the practical needs that are involved in corporate worship of God (1 Chron. 28–29), or by providing for God's servants who particularly need material support (2 Chron. 31; Ruth).

- Set an example by limiting personal consumption and declining to maximize private gain from public office that affords access to wealth and resources (Neh. 5:14–19).

The person who is characterized in these ways can indeed qualify for the otherwise oxymoronic epithet, "righteous rich." Above all, it is because such a person is marked by the very first principle of wisdom, namely the fear of the LORD, that the blessings he enjoys are not tainted with wickedness and the whiff of oppression. "Blessed is the man who fears the LORD," for if riches also come his way by God's grace, then the double truth can be affirmed of him, without contradiction:

> Wealth and riches are in his house,
> and his righteousness endures for ever.
> (Ps. 112:3)

9

New Testament *Koinonía* and Wealth

Justo L. González

Not until the second half of the first century, some twenty years after its inception, did Christianity emerge from the shadows of literary silence, first in the letters of Paul, then in the synoptic Gospels and Acts, and finally in the rest of the writings of the New Testament. Thus, any attempt to reconstruct the economic life of the early community must rely on these sources and depend on the degree to which they are considered historically accurate. While the synoptic Gospels — Mark, Matthew, and Luke — are the source in which we find most references to the earliest Christian community, even they were written years after the events they portray. Paul's first epistles, on the other hand, are slightly earlier than Mark — probably the oldest of the three synoptic Gospels. But the epistles reflect a different setting and provide little or no information about the earliest Christian community. For these reasons scholars find it difficult or even impossible to agree on which of the sayings or doings attributed to Jesus are historically true and which are not.

No matter what position one takes on those debated questions, one thing is certain: in general, the earliest portions of the synoptic Gospels, especially the materials that scholars call the "Q" source, present us with a social setting and living conditions that are very different from the urban Hellenistic situation that would soon become the setting for Christianity. With the exception of the material that can be attributed to a Hellenistic Christian origin,[1] the synoptics reflect either the very words and actions of Jesus or the words and actions that his earliest followers attributed to him. If our goal is to uncover, not necessarily the very words of Jesus, but the earliest Christian views on wealth and related matters, the

Justo L. González is the editor of *Apuntes,* a journal of Hispanic theology, and of *Comentario Bíblico Hispanoamericano.* He directs the Hispanic Summer Seminary Program of the Fund for Theological Education, Decatur, Georgia, and has published numerous books related to the history of Christianity and Christian thought. This chapter is taken from Justo L. González, *Faith and Wealth: A History of Early Christian Ideas on the Origin, Significance, and Use of Money* (San Francisco: Harper & Row, Publishers, 1990), 71–91. Used with the author's permission.

1. Much of this material consists not of long passages, but rather of changed settings or slight variations which betray a later interpretation.

synoptic Gospels, quite apart from all scholarly debates about Jesus' *ipsissima verba,* provide us with abundant material.[2]

On the other hand, a number of other sources provide information, not directly about the earliest Jesus movement, but about conditions in Palestine, and specifically in Galilee. The works of Josephus, the Dead Sea Scrolls, and numerous bits and pieces that can be gathered from other Jewish and Roman writers comprise such sources. From these and from the Q material in the synoptic Gospels, we draw a picture of an almost exclusively rural society, with significant urban pockets whose leadership had little contact with the peasantry, a society with practically no middle class.

The Setting

As throughout the Roman Empire, the backbone of the economy in first-century A.D. Palestine was agriculture. Here too, latifundia had increased both in size and in number, although the traditional small landholder still survived.[3] Peasants who did not own their plots lived under one of three arrangements: a fixed rent, payment of a predetermined portion of their produce to the owner, or the status of a *colonus.*[4]

The period of the Herodians (37 B.C.–A.D. 70) saw significant change in land tenure, accelerating the dispossession of the local peasantry as well as of many of the former Hasmonean nobility. Many of the latter Herod executed and then either appropriated their lands or redistributed them among his supporters. When Samaria was rebuilt and given the name of Sebaste, six thousand Roman veterans were settled in the area and given land to till.[5] In Galilee itself, most of the better land belonged to large landholders, while the small properties seem to have concentrated on the less fertile hill country. It is also likely that some of the Hasmonean nobles executed by Herod owned land in Galilee and that therefore such land was held either by the royal house itself or by its supporters.[6]

The burden of taxation was heavy, especially for the Jewish population. Foreign conquest had brought no relief from the traditional tithes and other such

---

2. Gerd Theissen, *Sociology of Early Palestinian Judaism,* trans. John Bowden (Philadelphia: Fortress, 1978), 3–4, has expressed this point quite well: "Thus we may leave open the question whether the traditions about Jesus are true or false. If we presuppose that a tradition is genuine, we may assume that those who handed it down shaped their lives in accordance with the tradition. If we assume that it originated within the Jesus movement in the period after Easter, we can presuppose that those who handed it down shaped the tradition in accordance with their lives. In either case the result is the same: there is a correspondence between the social groups which handed down the tradition and the tradition itself. Thus a sociology of the Jesus movement transcends the dispute of both 'conservative' and 'critical' exegetes over the authenticity and historicity of the tradition. It is unaffected by the dilemmas of the quest for the historical Jesus."

3. See M. Gil, "Land Ownership in Palestine under Roman Rule," *Revue Internationale des Droits de l'Antiquité* 17 (1970): 11–53. See also Robert Karl Gnuse, *You Shall Not Steal: Community and Property in the Biblical Tradition* (Maryknoll, NY: Orbis Books, 1985), 87–88.

4. Sean Freyne, *Galilee from Alexander the Great to Hadrian, 323 B.C.E. to 135 C.E.* (Wilmington, DE: Michael Glazier, 1980), 202 n. 16.

5. Josephus, *Ant.* 15.296; *De bel. Jud.* 1.403. All references to Josephus are from *LCL.*

6. Freyne, *Galilee from Alexander the Great to Hadrian,* 164.

obligations and had added the further burden of secular taxation.[7] As elsewhere in the empire, the burden of secular taxation fell on the lower classes, and those under the protection of the authorities paid much less than their just share. Herod himself was one of Rome's richest vassals, if not the richest, and this he owed to the taxes he collected from the local inhabitants.[8] Herod's annual income, which was only a part of the royal revenue, has been estimated at one thousand talents.[9] Eventually his exactions grew to such an extent that a delegation was sent from Palestine to Augustus.[10] The delegation complained about Herod's expropriations, implying that Herod executed people, including members of his own family, in order to disposses them. The delegation also protested against Herod's ruthless and corrupt methods of collecting taxes. Since this was a delegation of Jewish notables, and they felt so oppressed, one can only imagine how the peasantry felt. One indication may be that given the opportunity in the midst of a revolt, the Galileans killed a number of Herod's supporters by drowning them in the Sea of Gennesareth.[11] At any rate, the delegation was generally believed in Rome, where it was said that Augustus had declared that he would rather be Herod's pig than his son, presumably because Herod, being a Jew, would not kill a pig. Still, nothing was done, and Herod continued his extortions.

After the death of Herod the Great in 4 B.C., Judea was formally incorporated into the empire, but the situation did not improve. The procurators and other provincial administrators, expecting that their term of office would be short, sought to enrich themselves as quickly as possible. They found new and more ingenious ways to collect ever more revenue. To this was added the corruption of the tax collectors themselves, whose main source of profit lay precisely in gathering more taxes than they actually paid to the treasury. By the second century, a Roman official is said to have responded to a delegation of Palestinians complaining about increasing taxation: "Verily, if I had my way, I would tax your air."[12] The people made repeated appeals for tax relief, sometimes arguing that such heavy taxation simply forced inhabitants to abandon the land and resort to brigandage.[13]

The peasantry also suffered from the difficulties of competing with larger landowners. In the long run, market fluctuations favored the rich who could afford a smaller margin of profit or even some losses.[14] The peasants, on the other hand, often found that a drop in the price of their produce forced them to

7. A point stressed by F. C. Grant, *The Economic Background of the Gospels* (Oxford: Clarendon, 1923), 89.

8. Josephus, *Ant.* 17.4–5; Horace, *Epod.* 2.2.184; Strabo, *Geog.* 16.2.46.

9. Salo Wittmayer Baron, *A Social and Religious History of the Jews* (Philadelphia: The Jewish Publication Society of America, 1958), 1:262.

10. Josephus, *Ant.* 17.4.204; 11.2.306–7.

11. Ibid., 14.450.

12. Quoted in Baron, *A Social and Religious History of the Jews,* 1:263.

13. Josephus, *Ant.*, 18.274. Cf. Tacitus, *Ann.* ii.42, *LCL.*

14. The question of whether or not markets were actually controlled and manipulated by the wealthy is open to debate. Cf. Heinz Kreissig, *Die Sozialen Zusammenhänge des jüdaischen Krieges* (Berlin: Akademie-Verlag, 1970), 36–51; and Shimon Applebaum, "Economic Life in Palestine," in *Compendia Rerum Judaicarum ad Novum Testamentum,* ed. M. Stern and S. Safrai (Assen: Van Gorcum & Co., 1974), 2:662–66.

sell their land in order to meet expenses and especially to pay taxes. In such cases, the land would be sold to a larger landholder, and the peasant would continue to till it, although now under new conditions. To make matters worse, the three main products of the area — wheat, wine, and oil — were strictly controlled by the government, which made it even more difficult for peasants to find good prices.

War, social unrest, and natural disaster also took their toll. Josephus repeatedly speaks of famine caused by drought, earthquake, or disease. As we shall see later, one of these famines occurred shortly after Pentecost, and may be related to Paul's collection for the poor in Jerusalem. Thus when Mark 13:8 says that "there will be earthquakes in various places, there will be famines," it is not speaking of unknown phenomena.[15]

Around the lake, a goodly number of Galileans made a living by fishing. Connected to fishing was a small industry of salting and preserving fish for market. Again, this appears to have been controlled by wealthy merchants, and the fisherfolk apparently had a minimum margin of profit.[16]

These conditions resulted in a social stratification in which the two extremes of wealth and poverty prevailed. It has been pointed out that the parables of Jesus speak of basically two classes, the rich landholder and the poor peasant or laborer.[17] Indeed, the relationship between creditor and debtor or between employer and day laborer or between rich master and humble servant is the subject of many parables.

The subjects of the parables must have been an important factor in people's reactions to early Christian preaching. It is not difficult to imagine how the peasantry of Galilee would respond to a parable so closely describing their situation and their feelings toward the ruling authorities in Jerusalem and in Rome as the one in Matthew 18, where the rich deal in fabulous sums such as ten thousand talents, while the poor go to jail for a mere hundred denarii:

> Therefore the kingdom of heaven may be compared to a king who wished to settle accounts with his servants. When he began the reckoning, one was brought to him who owed him ten thousand talents; and as he could not pay, his lord ordered him to be sold, with his wife and children and all that he had, and payment to be made. So the servant fell on his knees, imploring him, "Lord, have patience with me, and I will pay you everything." And out of pity for him the lord of that servant released him and forgave him the debt. But that same servant, as he went out, came upon one of his fellow servants who owed him a hundred denarii; and seizing him by the throat he said, "Pay what you owe." So his fellow servant fell down and besought him, "Have patience with me, and I will pay you." He refused and went

---

15. Theissen, *Sociology of Early Palestinian Judaism,* 40. Cf. Josephus, *Ant.* 14.28; 15.299–300, 365; 16.64; 18.8; 20.101.

16. Freyne, *Galilee from Alexander the Great to Hadrian,* 173–74. One should remember, however, that Zebedee, the father of James and John, was sufficiently wealthy to have "hired servants" working in his boat (Mark 1:20).

17. Adrian Nicholas Sherwin-White, *Roman Society and Roman Law in the New Testament* (Oxford: Oxford University Press, 1963), 134–36.

and put him in prison till he should pay the debt. When his fellow servants saw what had taken place, they were greatly distressed, and they went and reported to their lord all that had taken place. Then his lord summoned him and said to him, "You wicked servant! I forgave you all that debt because you besought me; and should you not have had mercy on your fellow servant, as I had mercy on you?" And in anger his lord delivered him to the jailers, till he should repay all his debt. (Matt. 18:23–34)

Such preaching, however, was not the only response to the social tensions of the time. Revolt and rebellion waited always just below the surface, ready to explode at any time. The Zealots kept the flame of nationalism alive, feeding on the people's desire for social redress. Some sources indicate that under Roman rule Galilee fared better than Judea proper,[18] especially during and after the great rebellion against Rome. But even there the spirit of discontent and revolt seethed. Throughout Jewish territory, the memory of the Maccabees still lingered, and much opposition to the Herodians clustered around that memory. Indeed, it is possible to draw a line connecting such Maccabean memories, the many lesser revolts under early Roman rule, and the great war that ended with the fall of Masada in A.D. 72.[19] The first century A.D. clearly saw instability in Palestine, connected both with existing social conditions and with the messianic nationalism that would lead to the great war and its sequels (A.D. 66–135).

In Galilee itself, Herod had executed a certain Hezekiah whom he accused of being a brigand. In all probability Hezekiah was a Hasmonean supporter who resorted to guerrilla tactics.[20] In 4 B.C. Hezekiah's son Judas led a revolt that centered in Sepphoris and spread throughout the land.[21] Ten years later, Judas "the Galilean" led a similar revolt, and his sons and followers kept the flame of resistance alive at least until the fall of Masada.[22] If Judas the Galilean is the same as the son of Hezekiah, this would mean that there was a direct line of Galilean resistance leaders linking the Hasmoneans or Maccabees with the great revolt of A.D. 66.

From the Jesus Movement to the First Urban Churches

In this unsettled atmosphere, full of fear and resentment, of crushing poverty and messianic expectations, the Jesus movement began. It is not surprising, therefore, that Jewish leaders such as the famed rabbi Gamaliel connected it in their minds with the long tradition of revolt (Acts 5:35–38). Nor is it surprising that the Gospels depict the early disciples as expecting the impending restoration of

---

18. Freyne, *Galilee from Alexander the Great to Hadrian,* 57–91.

19. William Reuben Farmer, *Maccabees, Zealots and Josephus: An Enquiry into Jewish Nationalism in the Greco-Roman Period* (New York: Columbia University Press, 1970), argues for such a connection. Freyne, *Galilee from Alexander the Great to Hadrian,* 208–47, tends to downplay it.

20. Josephus, *Ant.* 14.159; *De bell. Jud.* 1.204. Cf. Freyne, *Galilee from Alexander the Great to Hadrian,* 63, 67.

21. Josephus, *Ant.* 17; *De bell. Jud.* 2.43.

22. Josephus, *Ant.* 20.102; *De bell. Jud.* 2.433, 447; 7.253. Cf. J. Kennard, "Judas of Galilee and His Clan," *Jewish Quarterly Review* 36 (1945–46): 281–86.

Israel. While such political matters and expectations are not our central concern here, it is important to keep them in mind, for they are the context of the Jesus movement's treatment of wealth.

All our sources indicate that the core of the preaching both of Jesus and of his early followers was the Kingdom of God. Such preaching bore political and economic implications. On the political side, it is clear that anyone proclaiming the coming of the Kingdom of God is at least by implication criticizing the present kingdom. In conditions such as those prevailing in Palestine at the time, it is not surprising that many, both among the disciples and among the authorities, interpreted the preaching of the Kingdom in the light of the long line of apocalyptic revolts and announcements of the restoration of Israel. Nor is it surprising that eventually Jesus was crucified — as many had been before him — as a pretended restorer of the throne of David.

It is the economic side of the preaching of the Kingdom that interests us here. In the Gospel narratives, the preaching of the Kingdom does indeed have a strong economic or socioeconomic component. It relates to both the justice that the Kingdom requires and the need for drastic action in view of its impending reality. Both themes appear in the preaching of John the Baptist, at least as Luke later reported it:

> "Even now the axe is laid to the root of the trees; . . . He who has two coats, let him share with him who has none; and he who has food, let him do likewise." Tax collectors also came to be baptized, and said to him, "Teacher, what shall we do?" And he said to them, "Collect no more than is appointed you." Soldiers also asked him, "And we, what shall we do?" And he said to them, "Rob no one by violence or by false accusation, and be content with your wages." (Luke 3:9–14)[23]

Themes of economic justice appear repeatedly in the preaching of Jesus and of the early movement. They show up often in the background, as in the many parables that deal with economic matters (the laborers in the vineyard, the unjust steward, the talents, and so forth). And they appear in the foreground, often in starker terms and with more radical demands than those attributed to the Baptist.

First appears the theme of the "great reversal," best summarized in the saying "the last will be first, and the first last" (Matt. 20:16). This saying, which appears in several different contexts in the Gospels (Matt. 19:30; Mark 10:31; Luke 13:30) is generally considered by scholars to have been part of the earliest Christian proclamation and to have existed quite apart from the different contexts in which it now appears. In some of these contexts, it apparently indicates that those who precede others in holiness and religiosity will not necessarily be first in the Kingdom. But in other contexts, and quite probably in its original setting, it means simply that those who are now underprivileged and oppressed will be

---

23. Possibly this passage in Luke reflects a slightly later time than the earliest Jesus movement, a time when there were tax collectors and soldiers in the church. Even if that is the case, the theme of the connection between justice and the Kingdom is clearly part of the earliest proclamation.

first in the Kingdom.[24] Such is also the meaning of the parable of the rich man
and Lazarus, which at least in its core is generally considered to be older than the
Gospel of Luke.[25] But probably the clearest affirmation of such reversal is found
in the Lukan version of the beatitudes, which is probably closer to the original
proclamation of the Jesus movement than the more commonly known version in
Matthew:

> Blessed are you poor, for yours is the kingdom of God.
> Blessed are you that hunger now, for you shall be satisfied.
> Blessed are you that weep now, for you shall laugh.
> But woe to you that are rich, for you have received your consolation.
> Woe to you that are full now, for you shall hunger.
>
> (Luke 6:20b–21, 24–25)[26]

In this connection another of the "harsh sayings" of Jesus must be considered:
his response to the "rich young ruler," and the commentary that follows regarding
the camel and the eye of a needle. The story that appears in all three synoptic
Gospels (Matt. 19:16–29; Mark 10:17–30; Luke 18:18–30) may be seen both as
another example of the great reversal and as a call to renunciation. The reversal
clearly takes place in that, barring a miracle, the rich will be excluded from the
Kingdom. The call to renunciation appears both in Jesus' instructions to the rich
man: "Sell what you have, and give to the poor" (which in Luke's later version
becomes "sell *all* you have and distribute to the poor") and in his response to the
disciples' inquiry about their own rewards: "Truly I say to you, there is no one
who has left house or brothers or sisters or mother or father or children or lands,
for my sake and for the gospel, who will not receive a hundred-fold now in this
time, houses and brothers and sisters and mothers and children and lands, with
persecutions, and in the age to come eternal life" (Mark 10:29–30).

Clearly, by the time these sayings were incorporated into the Gospel of Mark
(and through it into the other Gospels) they were already presenting some difficulties for the Gospel writer. This is probably why we are told that the disciples
were astonished and asked who could then be saved (Mark 10:26).[27] In any case,
it is significant that the other two synoptic writers did not leave it out.

---

24. Luise Schottroff and Wolfgang Stegemann, *Jesus and the Hope of the Poor* (Maryknoll, NY:
Orbis Books, 1986), 24–25.

25. Ibid., 25–28.

26. The blessing and the woe regarding persecution have been omitted, for they are probably
an addition to the earliest proclamation. Cf. Schottroff and Stegemann, *Jesus and the Hope of the
Poor,* 19. It is also possible that the entire "negative" side of woe to the rich and prosperous reflects
Luke's particular interest in calling such people to repentance. In that case, this text would show that
the theme of the great reversal was still central to the understanding of Christianity in Luke's urban
churches.

27. Schottroff and Stegemann, *Jesus and the Hope of the Poor,* 22–23: "We must give Mark
credit for transmitting this saying even though he himself and his community could not identify with
it and must have found it alarming. This is clear in particular from Mark 10:26 where the shock of
the disciples is expressly mentioned. The Markan community lived in a social situation completely
different from that reflected in the earliest Jesus tradition. Rich Christians too now belonged to the
community."

In the story of the rich ruler, a further theme has been added to that of the great reversal: the need for radical renunciation. The passage implies that, if indeed the great reversal can be expected, then what those who are first, the powerful and rich, must do is somehow to join the ranks of the last, the weak and the poor. In twenty-first-century vocabulary, we would speak of "solidarity with the oppressed," but with the caveat that in these stories the solidarity that is envisioned is much more than sympathy or support, for it involves actually becoming poor.

In what context were these words actually taught? In his *Sociology of Early Palestinian Christianity,* Gerd Theissen paints a credible picture of an early Jesus movement composed both of wandering preachers and of a relatively more stable community of "sympathizers."[28] As he sees matters, the bulk of the teachings that have come down to us in the earliest material in the synoptics reflects the kind of preaching that was possible under conditions of wandering rootlessness. Jesus was not the only one who had "nowhere to lay his head" (Matt. 8:20). Those among his disciples who followed him in his wanderings and who, as Peter declared, had left everything in order to follow him continued wandering after the events of Easter. Having given up home, family, and possessions, they were able to speak and repeat the harsh sayings we find in the synoptics, and it was thanks to them that such sayings were preserved.

According to Theissen, the wandering preachers could not have survived without the active support of relatively more established communities and of individuals who had not given up all their riches. In Luke 8:1–3 we are told of a number of women who did follow Jesus, at least in part of his wanderings, but who apparently retained enough wealth to be able to support Jesus and those who followed him. Many others simply remained in their villages, at first hardly distinguishing themselves from the rest of their communities, but providing Jesus and his wandering preachers with shelter, food, and alms. As time passed and the breach between Christians and orthodox Jews became greater, these communities gained a greater sense of identity. The distinction between such communities and the preachers was not rigid. Indeed, one of the themes of the preachers was precisely calling members of the community to take up their style of life. Some did, and thus were the ranks of the wandering preachers replenished. Others did not, and the preachers did not fault them for that, for the simple reason that without the support of those who remained in their villages the preachers themselves would not have been able to continue their ministry. Thus arose ambivalent preaching on possessions as well as on other topics about which the two groups differed. While the wandering preachers and teachers recommended total renunciation, they also made room for those who were not ready to take such a step.

At this point one must take exception with Theissen's reconstruction, for he may be overstating the contrast between the "social rootlessness" of the wandering preachers and the settled life of those who remained in their villages. From

---

28. Theissen, *Sociology of Early Palestinian Judaism*, 9–23. He calls the preachers "wandering charismatics." Since the term "charismatic" today has connotations that Theissen apparently did not intend, I have avoided the confusion that using that term could create.

what we have already seen about conditions in Galilee, it would seem that regarding material wealth and security little difference existed between the preachers and the communities of sympathizers. The poverty of the preachers, perhaps with rare exceptions, was not voluntary. It simply showed their acceptance of a condition that was quite general in their society and their rejection of the anxiety and fear that went along with such a condition. Their appeal to well-to-do sympathizers did not rest on the authority of poverty freely chosen, like Franciscans appealing to members of a tertiary order. The preachers had been born poor; they lived and wandered among others born in equal poverty, proclaiming the message that there is hope for the poor but that this hope must begin by trusting in God and giving up the anxieties that normally accompany poverty.[29] Their supposed "ambivalence" or "lack of principle," allowing for those who were not ready to adopt their way of life, was not a matter of knowing on which side their bread was buttered but simply a matter of understanding the anxieties of the desperately and hopelessly poor and knowing that such anxieties must be met, not with some dogmatic program of renunciation, but rather with a message of hope.

Returning to the passage about the rich young ruler, it should be obvious that in a way this passage is an anomaly. Most of the sayings in the Markan and Q materials are primarily addressed to poor people. What they call for is not a renunciation of goods that such people do not have but a renunciation of fear and anxiety, an affirmation of hope and solidarity. Significantly, even a passage addressed to the well-to-do, such as the story of the "rich young ruler," immediately turns the hearer's attention away from the rich and toward the anxieties of the followers of Jesus. The theme is clear: in most of the Markan and Q materials the context is a situation in which people are truly anxious and have reason to be anxious about what they will eat or wear.

The Growth of the Urban Communities

The situation is different in the material understood as Luke's. Although Luke has often been considered the "Gospel of the poor," because much is said in it about the poor, it could in fact be called the "Gospel of the prosperous," for its purpose is precisely to call to repentance an audience that was almost totally absent from the earliest preaching of the Jesus movement.[30] What we have here is an interpretation of the Gospel in a setting that is mostly urban.[31] In this Christian community the "poor" are spoken of, not as present, but rather as those for whom believers ought to be concerned. In this context poverty as a voluntary choice and renunciation as a virtue become important. The disciples are depicted as

---

29. See the critique of Theissen's depiction in Schottroff and Stegemann, *Jesus and the Hope of the Poor,* 48–51.

30. Such is the thesis of Schottroff and Stegemann, *Jesus and the Hope for the Poor,* 67–120. While I have found their study helpful, and here use it extensively, I disagree with them on a number of points. The most significant is their interpretation of the "commonality of goods" as described in the early chapters of Acts.

31. For a description of such a social setting, although on the basis of the Pauline epistles rather than the Lukan material, see Wayne A. Meeks, *The First Urban Christians: The Social World of the Apostle Paul* (New Haven, CT: Yale University Press, 1983).

leaving *everything* (Luke 5:11, 28); the rich man — now become a "ruler" — is told to "sell *all* you have" (Luke 18:22). Perfect discipleship entails renunciation of goods one could otherwise possess. For others who are not ready to go that far, Luke offers a number of examples of prosperous people whose encounter with Jesus led them to repentance and to sharing their possessions: the wealthy women who supported Jesus and his followers (Luke 8:2–3) and the chief tax collector, who upon meeting Jesus decided to give half of his wealth to the poor and to return to any whom he had defrauded four times as much as he took from them (Luke 19:8). Regarding the preaching of John the Baptist, it is Luke who gives detailed instructions as to what people making their living as tax collectors and soldiers ought to do. If, as is quite possible, the woes on the rich in Luke 6 and the last verses of the parable of the rich man and Lazarus are Lukan additions to earlier materials, they would reinforce the thesis that Luke is addressing a community that includes people for whom possessions are indeed a problem and for whom renunciation and almsgiving have therefore become a necessary sign of repentance. In short, Luke is dealing with the question that will later become a burning issue for Clement of Alexandria: how can the rich be saved?

Luke is not the only place in the New Testament addressing the question of how to deal with a church that includes both rich and poor. Apparently, the church of the epistle of James faces a similar problem, for the text acknowledges the possibility of someone coming to the assembly with gold rings and in fine clothing and the temptation of giving that person special consideration (James 2:1–7).[32] Here one finds once again the theme of the great reversal, with an emphasis on the need to respond in the light of that coming reversal: "Let the lowly brother boast in his exaltation, and the rich in his humiliation" (James 1:9); "Come now, you rich, weep and howl for the miseries that are coming upon you...." (James 5:1). Here again, although indirectly, the question of the salvation of the rich is posed, and the answer appears to be a call (although not only to the rich) to works of mercy:

> What does it profit, my brethren, if a man says he has faith but has no works? Can his faith save him? If a brother or a sister is ill-clad and in lack of daily food, and one of you says to them, "Go in peace, be warmed and filled," without giving them the things needed for the body, does it profit? So faith by itself, if it has no works, is dead. (James 2:14–17)

The Meaning of *Koinonía*

Returning to Luke/Acts, within the context of this economically mixed community we must interpret two of the most debated passages in Acts:

---

32. On the social background and the economic teachings of James, see Pedrito U. Maynard-Reid, *Poverty and Wealth in James* (Maryknoll, NY: Orbis Books, 1987). Although Maynard-Reid places the epistle at an earlier date and more primitive setting than I would, his work does show significant insight into the meaning of its social and economic texts.

And all who believed were together and had all things in common; and they sold their possessions and goods and distributed them to all, as any had need. (Acts 2:44–45)

Now the company of those who believed were of one heart and soul, and no one said that any of the things which he possessed was his own, but they had everything in common.... There was not a needy person among them, for as many as were possessors of lands or houses sold them, and brought the proceeds of what was sold and laid it at the apostles' feet; and distribution was made to each as any had need. (Acts 4:32–35)

As we look at these passages, the first obvious question is, did this actually happen? Did the early Christians practice the sort of commonality described here, or is it a fictional reconstruction of the life of the early church on the part of the author? Some scholars have held the latter, arguing that what is described here is too close to the ideal community of certain Hellenistic traditions — the Pythagorean in particular — and that it is therefore no more than an attempt to depict the early Christian church as an ideal community. Typical of this line of interpretation is Luke T. Johnson, who speaks of the passage in Acts 2 as "idyllic," and of the one in Acts 4 as a literary device to symbolize the authority of the apostles.[33] In another work Johnson points to a series of possible Hellenistic sources that have become standard in supporting this line of interpretation: Plato; a proverb quoted by Aristotle; and the lives of Pythagoras by Diogenes Laertius, Porphyry, and Iamblicus.[34] Briefly, the argument is that the author of Luke/Acts, seeking to describe the earliest Christian community, draws on Hellenistic materials extolling the value of unity and friendship, particularly as expressed in the common possession of goods.

The first difficulty with such an interpretation is that it ignores the obvious contrasts between the Pythagorean ideal and what is described here. One is an elitist association of philosophers who share things because this allows them to devote themselves to the "philosophical life"; the other is an open community that rejoices in adding thousands to its numbers and whose ability to share is the consequence of the outpouring of the Spirit and the resulting vivid eschatological expectation.

A second difficulty is the need to explain why or how the author was able to project into a fairly recent past a practice that did not exist at the time Acts was written. Indeed, one of the basic principles in the interpretation of historical texts is that writers tend to project into the past the practices and conditions of their own time. If at the time Acts was written — say in or around A.D. 80 — commonality of goods was not the practice of the church, why would the author say that it had been before? Perhaps in order to present the early Christian community in ideal terms? That would be possible if Luke could be accused of presenting an ideal picture of the early church. But that is certainly not the case. Indeed, immediately

---

33. Luke T. Johnson, *The Literary Function of Possessions in Luke-Acts* (Missoula, MT: Scholars Press, 1977), 189, 198

34. Luke T. Johnson, *Sharing Possessions: Mandate and Symbol of Faith* (Philadelphia: Fortress, 1981), 119.

after the second of the passages quoted above comes the episode of Ananias and Sapphira, a husband and wife who try to deceive the community precisely on the matter of the use of property. And soon thereafter we are told that "the Hellenists murmured against the Hebrews because their widows were neglected in the early distribution" (Acts 6:1).

A third objection to interpreting these passages as Luke's attempt to idealize the life of the early church is the high probability that these passages themselves — often called the "summaries" in Acts — are pre-Lukan material that the author of Acts incorporated at what seemed to be appropriate places in the narrative.[35] Still, one could argue that, just as Luke introduced or at least reinterpreted the theme of renunciation in the teachings of Jesus in order to shame the rich, so could the second volume of the series, Acts, introduce the theme of common property for the same purpose.

Ultimately, however, the matter of the historicity of the two accounts under discussion can be laid to rest if it can be shown that at the time Acts was written — and indeed for some time after that — what Luke has here described was still practiced. That is indeed the case, as we will show.

Before we turn to that discussion, however, another common interpretation of these passages in Acts must be mentioned. According to this interpretation, the early church did indeed have all things in common at the beginning, but this practice was soon abandoned. Usually, this interpretation includes the notion — with no basis in the texts themselves — that at least one of the reasons the Christian community in Jerusalem was poor and Paul spent so much effort on its relief was precisely the improvidence implied in this failed communistic experiment. This view is succinctly expressed in one of the biblical commentaries most commonly used today by preachers in the United States: "Whatever may have been the extent of this 'communistic' experiment at Jerusalem, it appears very soon to have broken down, first, perhaps on account of the dissension between 'Hellenists' and 'Hebrews' (6:1), and second, because the administrators who had been appointed as a result of the dispute had been driven from the city by the Jews. Probably also the eager expectation of the Parousia led to improvidence for the future, so that the Jerusalem community was always poor."[36]

The notion that the poverty of Christians in Jerusalem resulted from their improvidence in sharing all their goods and using up their capital is fairly common. Yet there is no basis for such an interpretation, either in Acts or in other contemporary records. On the contrary, Acts speaks of a great famine as the reason

---

35. See, for instance, Étienne Trocmé, *Le "Livre des Actes" et l'histoire* (Paris: Presses Universitaires de France, 1957), 195–96. On the other hand, cf. P. Benoit, "Remarques sur les 'Sommaires' de Actes 2/42 à 5," in *Aux sources de la tradition chrétienne, Mélanges offerts à M. Goguel* (Paris: Delachaux & Niestlé, 1950), 1–10. A good discussion of the historical reliability of Acts, although not dealing with the issues we are investigating, is M. Hengel, *Acts and the History of Earliest Christianity* (Philadelphia: Fortress, 1980).

36. G. H. C. Macgregor, in *The Interpreters Bible,* 9:73. Ronald J. Sider, *Rich Christians in an Age of Hunger* (Downers Grove, IL: InterVarsity Press, 1977), 101, quotes a similar view from another contemporary author, J. A. Ziesler, *Christian Asceticism* (Grand Rapids: Eerdmans, 1973), 110: "The trouble in Jerusalem was that they turned their capital into income, and had no cushion for hard times, and the Gentile Christians had to come to their rescue."

relief was needed (Acts 11:27–30). Josephus speaks of a famine in Judea that reached its apex around A.D. 46.[37] And Roman historians Tacitus and Suetonius mention several famines during the reign of Claudius, which is also the time at which Acts dates the famine that produced the need for a collection.[38]

In order to respond both to the "idyllic fiction" view and to the "economic disaster" interpretation, we have to begin by clarifying the commonality of goods to which Acts refers. First of all, the notion that people simply went out and sold all they had in order to share it with the rest is built on an incorrect interpretation of the Greek grammar.[39] The Greek language has two forms of the past tense. One, the imperfect, indicates a continuing past action. The other, the aorist, refers to an action completed once and for all. In the texts under discussion, all verbs appear in the imperfect. Therefore, what the text says is not exactly that "they sold their possessions and goods and distributed them to all, as any had need" (Acts 2:45), but rather that they continued doing this or, as the New American Standard Bible says, "They began selling their property and possessions, and were sharing them with all, as any might have need."

The use of the imperfect tense also points to a major difference between the community described in these texts and the Hellenistic and other communes, including that of Qumran, with which it has been compared. Here the community of goods is not the guiding principle. No matter how much Luke's Gospel has made of renunciation, what is described in Acts is a community where people relinquish their possessions, not for the sake of renunciation, but for the sake of those in need. In both passages under discussion the need of the recipients plays an important role. The goal is not an abstract or dogmatic notion of unity or a principle of purity and renunciation but meeting the needs of others.

It is inevitable in such a community that those who are most generous, such as Barnabas, will arouse the jealousy of others such as Ananias and Sapphira. Yet the very fact that the book of Acts tells the story of both Barnabas's generosity and the deception of Ananias and Sapphira immediately after describing the community of goods indicates that this is neither an attempt to paint the early community in idyllic tones, nor to describe a dogmatically communistic commune. Peter clearly tells Ananias (Acts 5:4) that he was under no obligation to sell his property, and that having sold it he did not have to bring the proceeds to the community. Thus Acts describes an imperfect community with its share of liars and jealousy. In chapter 6 the conflict between the Hellenists and the Aramaic speakers over the distribution of relief to the widows of each group will be further proof of the imperfect nature of this community. The self-understanding of this group, however, is such that "no one said that the things which he possessed was his own." Yet, the actual working out of the sharing that this implied depended both

---

37. *Ant.* 20.5.

38. Tacitus, *Ann.* 12.43, *LCL;* Suetonius, *Claud.* 18, *LCL.*

39. Even though one finds it in the otherwise very careful book by Schottroff and Stegemann, *Jesus and the Hope for the Poor,* 119: "The selling and distribution of proceeds are described as actions done once and for all. Thus there is no reason for assuming that they were done in case after case, whenever someone was in need."

on the needs of those who had no possessions and on the free will to share on the part of the more fortunate.

As we look further at the description of this community in Acts we must pay close attention to the word *koinonía*, by which this community is described in Acts 2:42. The Revised Standard Version and the New American Standard Bible translate it as "fellowship," and the Jerusalem Bible as "brotherhood." This is the common understanding of this word, which is usually taken to refer to the inner disposition of goodwill — "fellowship" — toward other members of the group. Thus taken, what Acts 2:42 says is simply that there were good relationships within the community.

Yet *koinonía* means much more than that. It also means partnership, as in a common business venture. In this way Luke uses the related term *koinonós*, member of a *koinonía*, for in Luke 5:10 we are told that the sons of Zebedee were *koinonoí* with Peter, meaning that they were business partners. The same usage appears outside the New Testament, sometimes in very similar contexts.[40] *Koinonía* means first of all, not fellowship in the sense of good feelings toward each other, but sharing. It is used in that sense throughout the New Testament, both in connection with material goods and in other contexts. In Philippians 3:10, what the Revised Standard Version translates as "share his sufferings" actually says "know the *koinonía* of his sufferings." In 1 Corinthians 10:16, Paul says, "The cup of blessing which we bless, is it not a participation in the blood of Christ? The bread which we break, is it not a participation in the body of Christ?" The term that the Revised Standard Version translates here as "participation," with a footnote explaining that it could also be translated as "communion," is *koinonía*. Paul's letter to the Philippians, which acknowledges receipt of a gift, begins with words in which Paul is thanking the Philippians for their partnership and sharing with him. In 1:5, he says that he is thankful for the Philippians' *koinonía*, and two verses later he declares that they are "joint *koinonoí*" of grace with him, that is, common owners or sharers. At the end of the epistle, he says that they have shared in his trouble (4:14), and the term he uses could be translated as "cokoinonized." All of this leads to the unique partnership "in giving and receiving" that he has enjoyed with the church of the Philippians (4:15), and once again the word he uses literally means "koinonized." In short, *koinonía* is much more than a feeling of fellowship; it involves sharing goods as well as feelings.

Returning to Acts 2:42, it is clear that *koinonía* there is much more than fellowship: "They devoted themselves to the apostles' teaching and *koinonía*, to the breaking of bread and prayers." The four things listed here, the apostles' teaching, *koinonía*, the breaking of bread, and prayers, are taken up in almost the same order in verses 43 to 47, where we are told (1) that fear came upon every soul, and wonders and signs were done through the apostles; (2) that all who believed had all things in common; (3) that they attended the temple and praised God; and (4) that they broke bread in their homes and partook of food with glad

---

40. In *The Amherst Papyri*, ed. Bernard P. Grenfell and Arthur S. Hunt (London: Frowde, 1900), 1:100, no. 4, there is the case where the fisherman Hermes takes another fisherman as his *koinonós* or partner.

and generous hearts. The *koinonía* is not simply a spiritual sharing.[41] It is a total sharing that includes the material as well as the spiritual.

Having clarified the connection of the commonality of goods in Acts 2 and 4 with the idea of *koinonía*, we can now return to the question posed earlier: are there indications that such sharing of goods continued — if it ever existed — after the time that those early chapters of Acts claim to describe? Again, the question is not whether all Christians went out and sold everything at once and put it into a common treasury. As we have seen, that is not the situation that Acts describes. The question is whether we can find indications that, at other times and places in the life of the church described in the New Testament, the Christian community was a partnership that included material as well as spiritual sharing, that this sharing was to be governed by the need of the less fortunate, and that, though voluntary, this sharing and the vision behind it challenged the traditional — particularly the Roman — understanding of private property.

When posed in these terms, the obvious answer is found in the collection for the poor in Jerusalem that plays such an important role in the epistles of Paul. This collection is not a responsibility added to Paul's apostleship; rather it is part and parcel of it. Indeed, as Paul himself describes his authentication by the leaders in Jerusalem, the collection for the poor was an important part of his commission (Gal. 2:10).[42] As we look at that collection and the manner in which Paul describes it in his letters, it is clear that it continues the practice of *koinonía* described in Acts 2 and 4.

Of all the churches among which Paul worked in collecting the offering for Jerusalem, the best known is that in Corinth. Paul's Corinthian correspondence provides much information both about the economic life of Christians in that city and about how Paul understood and interpreted the collection in which he was engaged. The social structure of the Corinthian church has been amply studied.[43] Probably the best conclusion is that of biblical scholar Wayne Meeks, that the prominent members of the Pauline churches, including Corinth, were people of "high status inconsistency."[44] While not all the members of a church such as

---

41. Johnson, *Literary Function of Possessions in Luke-Acts*, 185.

42. It is interesting to speculate on the relationship between Paul's "apostleship" and his commission to collect funds for Jerusalem. "Apostle" is the title given in a number of texts referring to people whom the Jewish patriarchs and other leaders sent to collect funds from Jews in the Diaspora. Eusebius, *In Isa.* 18.1; Epiphanius, *Pan.* 11, 30, PG; *Cod. Theod.* 16.8.14. in *Theodosiani Libri* 16, ed. Th. Mommsen (Berlin: Weidmann, 1962). These descriptions of Jewish "apostles" seem very similar to what Paul was commissioned to do when he went to Damascus before his conversion. Unfortunately, all of these texts, as well as others that speak of Jewish "apostles," come from a later date. In this context, one should note that Paul speaks of his work as "my service for Jerusalem" (Rom. 15:31). Still, one wonders if this is not part of the background of Paul's insistence on his apostolate. Is he only claiming that he has been sent by the Lord, or is he also arguing for his right to collect money for Jerusalem?

43. See especially Gerd Theissen, *The Social Setting of Pauline Christianity: Essays on Corinth* (Philadelphia: Fortress, 1982). Particularly interesting in this study is Theissen's attempt to relate the conflicts within the Corinthian church to the contrast between rich and poor in the community: 99–110, 145–74. Cf. Meeks, *First Urban Christians*, 51–73.

44. Meeks, *First Urban Christians*, 73.

that in Corinth were poor, those who had greater financial resources were people whose status was limited by other factors. In any case, it is clear that marked economic differences existed among members of the Corinthian church and that these differences created difficulties, for Paul says that when they gather for the common meal some are hungry while others are drunk (1 Cor. 11:21).

Paul is clear about the deep contradiction between such behavior, which humiliates the poor, and the very nature of the church. Those who have much to eat while others do not have enough are not only humiliating the poor but also despising the church (1 Cor. 11:22). And a case could be made that Paul is referring to them when he declares that "anyone who eats and drinks without discerning the body, that is, without realizing that this community is the body of Christ, eats and drinks judgment upon himself" (1 Cor. 11:29).

In any case, as Paul speaks of the collection in Corinth, he instructs his readers to set aside a certain amount on the first day every week, so that special contributions will not have to be made upon his arrival (1 Cor. 16:1–4). The phrase that the Revised Standard Version translates "as he may prosper" is difficult to translate. It certainly does not mean that they should contribute only if they prospered. More likely it means that they should set aside as much as they could. These instructions, which Paul says that he has given also to the churches of Galatia, seem to apply to a community most of whose members are neither destitute nor rich.[45] At the same time, Paul expects the total amount he is raising to be liberal, abundant, or even lavish (2 Cor. 8:20).

Paul's theological understanding of the offering for Jerusalem is best seen in 2 Corinthians, chapters 8 and 9. Paul begins by giving the Corinthians news of the collection in Macedonia, where the response was such that "their abundance of joy and their extreme poverty have overflowed in a wealth of liberality on their part."[46] Paul makes clear throughout his argument that the gifts he is requesting should be made voluntarily. The Macedonians have given "of their own free will" (8:3). Paul stresses that his asking the Corinthians for an offering is not a command (8:8). Their offering should be "ready not as an exaction but as a willing gift" (9:5). And "each one must do as he has made up his mind, not reluctantly or under compulsion, for God loves a cheerful giver" (9:7). Thus, just as in Acts the giving was voluntary, and Peter told Ananias that he had been under no obligation to give, so here Paul makes it clear that giving must be from the heart and not out of an exterior compulsion or a dogmatic understanding of the community of goods.

The voluntary nature of the gift does not mean, however, that no goals or guidelines apply. In this text, the goal is equality: "I do not mean that others should be eased and you burdened, but that as a matter of equality your abundance at the present time should supply their want, so that their abundance may supply your want, that there may be equality. As it is written, 'He who gathered much had nothing over, and he who gathered little had no lack'" (2 Cor. 8:13–15).

---

45. Ibid., 65.
46. Meeks suggests the literal translation, "abysmal poverty," but then (ibid., 66) suggests also that this may be hyperbole.

The text is unclear as to how the abundance of the recipients will supply the want of the givers. Possibly it means that the Christians in Jerusalem, though materially poor, are spiritually rich, and that from this abundance the Corinthians will profit. The idea is fairly common in later patristic thought, that the prayers of the poor have greater efficacy, and that when the rich give to the poor the latter repay their benefactors by praying for them. This may be what Paul means here. Another option, however, would be to take a clue from the phrase "at the present time" and to interpret the text as meaning that when, at some future date, the Corinthians are in need, those in Jerusalem will come to their aid.

Whatever the case may be, Paul clearly says that the purpose of the offering is to promote equality. At present, the Corinthians enjoy relative abundance, at least of material wealth. It is clear from 1 Corinthians 1:26 that the church in Corinth did not include the aristocracy of that city. Still, in comparison with those in Jerusalem they lived in abundance. It is the contrast between the need in Jerusalem and the abundance in Corinth that must be overcome by the offering. The Corinthians are to give because those in Jerusalem are in need. Thus, as in the case of the original commonality of goods in Acts 2 and 4, what controls the giving is the need of the poor.

In this context, and to strengthen his argument, Paul cites the miracle of the redistribution of manna. In Exodus 16:16–18, when God provided manna, the Israelites were ordered to go and collect a certain measure of it (an omer) for each member of the household. As so often happens in human societies, "some gathered much and some little." Yet, when they measured what they had gathered, they found that it had been redistributed, so that each household had the amount that God had ordered. This is the miracle of equality, which shows the will of God and which Paul is exhorting the Corinthian Christians to imitate.

The Corinthian discussion displays a remarkable similarity to what the book of Acts describes as having taken place in the early church. True, the text does not say, "They had all things in common." But the spirit and practice are certainly similar to that found in Acts, especially if we read, not only the brief account of the commonality of goods, but also the examples of how this actually worked — or did not work — in the cases of Barnabas and of Ananias and Sapphira.

Luke/Acts was written after the epistles of Paul, in a circle with strong Pauline influence. Actually, the vast majority of the book of Acts is devoted to Paul's ministry. Therefore, rather than suggesting that the description of the commonality of goods in Acts is due to Hellenistic influences and to the idealizing of the early community, it seems possible to take the opposite view: even though some of the phrases used in Acts 2 and 4 may have parallels in earlier Greek literature, what Luke was describing here was the understanding of the Christian *koinonía* that had been at the very heart of Paul's ministry. If so, Acts is not speaking about a brief idyllic moment in the early life of the church or of something limited to the Jerusalem community but of something that, fully practiced or not, was still part of the self-understanding of the church — at least of the Pauline churches — everywhere. This continued to be the case for several generations.

The Later Books of the New Testament

In the later books of the New Testament we find both the continuation of themes already present in the early Christian movement and the first adumbrations of themes and situations that would become clearer in later times.

The theme of *koinonía* continues in the Johannine Epistles. Indeed, 1 John begins by declaring that the epistle itself is written "so that you may have fellowship *koinonía* with us; and our fellowship *koinonía* is with the Father and with his Son Jesus Christ" (1 John 1:3). The writer then goes on to say that it is impossible to have *koinonía* with God unless we have it among ourselves (1:6–7). The entire epistle leads to the conclusion that "if anyone has the world's goods and sees his brother in need, yet closes his heart against him, how does God's love abide in him? Little children, let us not love in word or speech but in deed and in truth" (3:17–18).[47]

The existence of wandering preachers and the need to support them are reflected in 1 John 5–8. In the Deutero-Pauline literature (Titus 1:7–11) a problem appears that we shall find again in our next chapter, namely, preachers who are upsetting and exploiting the community "by teaching for base gain" (cf. Phil. 1:15–18).

Also in the Deutero-Pauline epistles appear a number of references to the temptation involved in riches. The evil of the "last days" includes people who will be "lovers of self, lovers of money, proud, arrogant, abusive..." (2 Tim. 3:1–2). And the following passage clearly reflects a church in which some have, or at least are seeking, more than they need:

> There is great gain in godliness with contentment; for we brought nothing into the world, and we cannot take anything out of the world; but if we have food and clothing, with these we shall be content. But those who desire to be rich fall into temptation, into a snare, into many senseless and hurtful desires that plunge men into ruin and destruction. For the love of money is the root of all evils; it is through this craving that some have wandered away from the faith and pierced their hearts with many pangs. (1 Tim. 6:6–10)

Along the same lines, Hebrews 10:34 praises believers who "joyfully accepted the plundering of your property, since you knew that you yourselves had a better

---

47. A text often quoted in modern times but much less in the patristic period, is John 12:8: "The poor you always have with you." This text must not be interpreted, as is often the case, in the sense that Christian should be reconciled to the existence of poverty and should not seek to alleviate it. In its proper context, this text means exactly the opposite. First of all, it is a quotation from Deuteronomy 15:11. The entire passage in Deuteronomy affirms that, were the people of God to obey God's law, there would be no poor among them; but that, since perfect obedience will never take place, "the poor will never cease out of the land; therefore I command you, You shall open your hand to your brother, to the needy and to the poor, in the land." Second, in the passage in John, Jesus is responding to Judas, who has commented that Mary's extravagance in anointing the feet of Jesus with costly ointment would have been better spent on the poor. In that context, Jesus' response means that, now that he is with his disciples and is preparing for death, it is proper for Mary to be extravagant in her gift to him. After he is gone, there will be ample opportunity to practice equal liberality toward the poor.

possession and an abiding one." They are also told that Moses "considered abuse suffered for the Christ greater wealth than the treasure of Egypt, for he looked to the reward" (Heb. 11:26). And they are exhorted: "Keep your life free from love of money, and be content with what you have" (Heb. 13:5).

The theme of a reward for those who do not cling to their wealth but employ it for good deeds sounds most clearly in 1 Timothy 6:17–19: "As for the rich in this world, charge them not to be haughty, nor to set their hopes on uncertain riches but on God who richly furnishes us with everything to enjoy. They are to do good, to be rich in good deeds, liberal and generous, thus laying up for themselves a good foundation for the future, so that they may take hold of the life which is life indeed."

Here we find not only the notion that by making good use of treasures on earth one can acquire treasures in heaven, but also the contrast between two kinds of riches. Some are "rich in this world"; others are "rich in good deeds." While the two are not mutually exclusive, they are quite distinct. A fairly common theme in early Christian literature is that those who apparently are rich are in truth poor and vice versa. This theme appears already in the book of Revelation, where the words to the church in Smyrna, "I know your tribulation and your poverty (but you are rich)" (Rev. 2:9), contrast with the message to the church in Laodicea: "For you say, I am rich, I have prospered, and I need nothing; not knowing that you are wretched, pitiable, poor, blind, and naked. Therefore I counsel you to buy from me gold refined by fire, that you may be rich" (Rev. 3:17–18).

These are only a few of the many passages that should be explored in a fuller investigation of issues of faith and wealth in the New Testament. They are offered here not in an attempt at exhaustiveness, but they should suffice to show that the matter of the relationship between faith and wealth is not foreign to the New Testament.

10

Wealth in the Subapostolic Church

Justo L. González

By the second century, the writing of the books that now form the New Testament was coming to a close. Christian literary activity, however, did not abate. On the contrary, Christians wrote letters, and sermons, manuals of discipline, and, by the middle of the second century, they were also writing learned defenses of their faith. It is to these writings that we now turn.

The *Didache*

One of the most tantalizing historical discoveries of the nineteenth century took place in a library in Istanbul in 1875, where an ancient manuscript was found containing a document that had long been considered irretrievably lost. The *Doctrine of the Twelve Apostles,* usually known as the *Didache,* is repeatedly quoted by Christian writers from the second to the fifth centuries. After that time, most quotes seem to be secondhand, and therefore one can presume that the document was lost at some point in the early Middle Ages. It finally resurfaced in 1875 in the library of the Knights Hospitaller of the Holy Sepulchre in Istanbul. It was then added to the list of writings that are presumed to date from the subapostolic period and are usually called the "Apostolic Fathers."

Scholars disagree on the date of composition of the *Didache.*[1] Although its author had apparently read the synoptics, the setting of the *Didache* is still very similar to the early days of the Jesus movement. By this time, however, wandering "apostles" or preachers have begun to present a problem of accreditation. The same is true of "prophets," although the relationship between these two titles is not clear. How is one to know that they are legitimate? The *Didache*'s answer reveals a fear that some people might seek to profit from the preaching of the

From Justo L. González, *Faith and Wealth: A History of Early Christian Ideas on the Origin, Significance, and Use of Money* (San Francisco: Harper & Row, Publishers, 1990), 92–105. Used with the author's permission.

1. Jean-Paul Audet, *La Didachè: Instructions des Apôtres* (Paris: J. Gabalda, 1958), argues that it is earlier than the fall of Jerusalem in A.D. 70, while Jean Colson, *L'évêque dans les communautés primitives* (Paris: Editions du Cerf, 1951), argues for the third century and claims that the archaicism of the *Didache* is forged. It is also possible that the document actually includes layers from different periods, as suggested by Stanislas Giet, *L'énigme de la Didachè* (Paris: Ophrys, 1970).

Gospel. An apostle or prophet who asks for more than bread for the road —
especially one who asks for money — or one who asks to be put up for more
than two days is false.[2] The content of the text points to a fairly early time in the
development of church structure. On the other hand, some of the members of the
communities to which the *Didache* is addressed owned slaves, pointing to a time
when the church is making inroads into the middle economic strata.

Since some clues in the text point toward semidesert or arid conditions,[3] it
seems safe to assume that the *Didache* reflects life in a non-Pauline church,
perhaps in the semidesert zones of Syria or Palestine, at a time that is impossible
to determine precisely, perhaps between A.D. 70 and 140.[4] The communities to
which it is addressed are not rich; yet in addition to slaves, some members own
flocks, and others have grapes to press and wheat to thresh.[5]

The *Didache* includes the earliest reference outside the New Testament to the
commonality of goods of which Acts speaks:

> Be not a stretcher forth of the hands to receive and a drawer of them back
> to give. If thou hast aught, through thy hands thou shalt give ransom for
> thy sins. Thou shalt not hesitate to give, nor murmur when thou givest;
> for thou shalt know who is the good repayer of the hire. Thou shalt not
> turn away from him that is in want, but thou shalt share all things with thy
> brother, and shalt not say that they are thine own; for if ye are partakers in
> that which is immortal, how much more in things which are mortal?[6]

The last few lines of this quote closely parallel Acts 4:42, where we are also
told that the first Christians had all things in common and that they did not claim
what they had as their own. Here again, readers are commanded not to say that
things their own. They are to share (*synkoinonein*, "cokoinonize") all things
with those in need. In order to support this, the writer introduces a new argument:
Christians who share — literally, who are common owners, partners, *koinonoí* —
in immortal things should be ready to share likewise in the less important things
that are mortal.[7]

The *Didache* also agrees with Acts in that the basis for this sharing is the
other's need: "Thou shalt not turn away from him who is in want." In another
passage, it lists among those who follow the "way of death," besides murderers,
adulterers, and thieves, those who do not respond to the needy, "not pitying a
poor man, not labouring for the afflicted, not knowing Him that made them [the

---

2. *Did.* 11.4–6, 9, 12. All references to the Apostolic Fathers and the Apologists are to *ANF.*
The Greek text employed is from *BAC.*

3. Especially the instructions regarding baptism in cases where water is scarce. *Did.* 6.2.

4. By the mid-second century, Hermas, in Rome, quotes the *Didache.* Shepherd of Hermas,
Mandate 2.4; *Did.* 1.5.

5. *Did.* 13.3.

6. *Did.* 4.5–8. The phrase that is here translated "If thou hast aught, through thy hands thou
shalt give ransom for thy sins" is probably better translated: "If thou has aught through the work of
thy hands, thou shalt give of it as ransom for thy sins." In other words, that what one makes through
labor is to be shared.

7. A passage that is reminiscent of Luke 16:11–12: "If then you have not been faithful in the
unrighteous mammon, who will entrust to you the true riches? And if you have not been faithful in
that which is another's, who will give you that which is your own?"

afflicted], murderers of children, destroyers of the handywork of God, turning away from him that is in want, afflicting him that is distressed, advocates of the rich, lawless judges of the poor, utter sinners."[8]

Apart from the passing reference to material goods as "mortal," there is in the *Didache* no indication that one should dispossess oneself of such goods for the sake of renunciation, nor that one should give them to the community for the sake of a principle of shared property. The reason that one should not claim the rights of private property is the need of the other. The governing principle in giving is neither a communistic ideal nor an ascetic renunciation, but the need of the other. Apparently this is the meaning of the saying which the *Didache* quotes: "Let thine alms sweat in thy hands, until thou know to whom thou shouldst give."[9] This again is very similar to what we found in the two passages in Acts referring to the commonality of goods.

As in Acts, what is envisioned here is not the abolition of property, but its subordination to the claims of those in need. The *Didache* gives instructions for the offering of first-fruits for the support of the local prophets — or, if there are no prophets, for the support of the poor.[10] Obviously, such instructions imply that those who own fields or flocks will not necessarily rid themselves of such property, but put it at the disposal of the needy.

Finally, also like Acts, the *Didache* is not speaking of an ideal community, in which love and sharing are such that all difficulties are overcome. Just as Acts knew of Ananias and Sapphira, and of the murmurings regarding the distribution of support for the widows, the *Didache* knows of those who will try to take advantage of the community and its *koinonía*. After quoting the words of Jesus to the effect that one should give to any who ask, the *Didache* continues:

> Happy is he that giveth according to the commandment; for he is guiltless. Woe to him that receiveth; for if one having need receiveth, he is guiltless; but he that receiveth not having need, shall pay the penalty, why he received and for what, and coming into straits [confinement], he shall be examined concerning the things which he has done, and he shall not escape thence until he pay back the last farthing.[11]

Those who seek to take advantage of the community are warned by the text quoted above (4.5): "Be not a stretcher forth of the hands to receive and a drawer of them back to give." Likewise, the *Didache* warns against newcomers who abuse the community's hospitality, and it gives instructions for dealing with wayfarers who desire to settle in the community.

---

8. *Did.* 5.2.

9. *Did.* 1.6.

10. *Did.* 13.1–4. "But every true prophet that willeth to abide among you is worthy of his support [meaning his food]. So also a true teacher is himself worthy, as the workman, of his support. Every first fruit, therefore, of the products of the wine press and threshing floor, of oven and of sheep, thou shalt take and give to the prophets, for they are your high priests. But if you have not a prophet, give it to the poor."

11. *Did.* 1.5.

If he who cometh is a wayfarer, assist him as far as ye are able; but he shall not remain with you, except for two or three days, if need be. But if he willeth to abide with you, being an artisan, let him work and eat; but if he hath no trade, according to your understanding see to it that, as a Christian, he shall not live with you idle. But if he willeth not so to do, he is a Christ-monger.[12]

In conclusion, regardless of the date of the *Didache,* the self-understanding of the Christian *koinonía* that appears in it is similar to that found in Acts 2 and 4. The one element added — foreshadowed already in the New Testament — is that what is given serves also as a ransom for the giver's sins.[13] As we shall see, using a promise of reward as a motivation for aiding the needy will become increasingly common throughout the patristic period.

Pseudo-Barnabas

The manuscript discovered in Istanbul in 1875 contained also another document that had been lost until the nineteenth century, the so-called *Epistle of Barnabas.* Scholars already knew this text, for in 1859 in the library of the monastery of St. Catherine on Mount Sinai, Konstantin von Tischendorf had discovered another manuscript, now known as the *Codex Sinaiticus,* which also included — besides the Old and New Testaments and part of the *Shepherd of Hermas* — this so-called *Epistle of Barnabas.* Like the *Didache,* the *Epistle of Barnabas,* probably written in or near Alexandria around the year 135,[14] was frequently quoted in antiquity but was apparently lost in the Middle Ages, in this case, probably in the ninth century.

The *Epistle* interests us here because it shows the wide dissemination of the understanding of the *koinonía* of goods found in the *Didache.* The last chapters of the *Epistle* so closely parallel the early chapters of the *Didache* that a connection between the two is beyond doubt. The common material is what scholars have dubbed the "Document of the Two Ways." Whether such a document actually existed independent of the *Didache* or whether the author of the *Epistle of Barnabas* took this material from the *Didache* does not concern us. The important point is that, either quoting from a common source or repeating the words of the *Didache,* the *Epistle of Barnabas* includes the crucial text of the *Didache* on the commonality of property:

Thou shalt communicate [practice *koinonía*] in all things with thy neighbour; thou shalt not call things thine own; for if ye are partakers in common

---

12. *Did.* 12.2–5.

13. *Did.* 4.6–7, quoted above: "Give ransom for thy sins" and "thou shalt know who is the good repayer of the hire."

14. This is a matter of conjecture. There is much uncertainty about the date of composition of the *Epistle.* The date 135 is based on a passage in chapter 16 that seems to refer to Hadrian's project of building a temple to Jove on the site where the Jewish temple had stood. So Adolf von Harnack, *Die Chronologie der altchristlicher Literatur bis Eusebius* (Leipzig: J. C. Hinrichs, 1897), 423–27. Others, on the basis of cryptic references in chap. 4, date the *Epistle* during the time of Nerva, in A.D. 98.

[*koinonoí*] of things which are incorruptible, how much more [should you be] of those things which are corruptible![15]

Although this text and many others in which the *Epistle of Barnabas* parallels the *Didache* add little as far as content is concerned, they prove that the view of *koinonía* — the sharing of possessions — that appears in Acts and in the *Didache* was shared by other Christians, perhaps as far away as Alexandria and as late as A.D. 135.

Epistle to Diognetus

The final text dealing with common property in the Apostolic Fathers is the *Epistle to Diognetus*. This document, which should be classified with the apologists of the second century rather than with the Apostolic Fathers, probably dates from the time of Emperor Hadrian (A.D. 117–38).[16] Describing the life of Christians to an outsider, the *Epistle to Diognetus* declares that they "share a common table, but not a bed."[17] This is probably a brief way of contrasting the common life of the Christians with what had been advocated by Plato and others. Outsiders, acquainted as they were with the communistic utopias of antiquity, and having heard rumors of immorality among Christians, might confuse their commonality of goods with promiscuous sexual behavior. Later, and for the same reasons, Tertullian makes a similar statement. In any case, here we find once again the practice of *koinonía*, although not as explicitly as in the other texts we have studied.

A significant detail is that the author of this treatise bases this *koinonía* on the imitation of God's goodness, a theme that will appear repeatedly in later Christian writings. According to this treatise, God's majesty does not consist so much in power and riches as in love and giving, and these qualities Christians are called to imitate:

Do not wonder that a man can become an imitator of God. He can, if he is willing. For it is not by ruling over his neighbor, or by seeking to hold the supremacy over those that are weaker, or by being rich, and showing violence towards those that are inferior, that happiness is found; nor can anyone by these things become an imitator of God. But these things do not at all constitute His majesty. On the contrary he who takes upon himself the burden of his neighbor; he who, in whatsoever respect he may be superior, is ready to benefit another who is deficient; he who, whatsoever things he

---

15. *Barn.* 19.8. Other sections of the *Didache* we have quoted appear also, with slight variations, in the *Epistle:* "Do not be ready to stretch forth thy hands to take, whilst thou contractest them to give.... Thou shalt not hesitate to give, nor murmur when thou givest. 'Give to everyone that asketh thee,' and thou shalt know who is the good Recompenser of the reward.... There are those who attend not with just judgment the widow and the orphan, ... pity not the needy, labour not in aid of him who is overcome with toil; ... who turn away him that is in want, who oppress the afflicted, who are advocates of the rich, who are unjust judges of the poor" (19.9, 11; 20.2).

16. Its date, however, is much controverted. See Justo L. González, *A History of Christian Thought,* 2nd ed. (Nashville: Abingdon, 1989), 1:116 n. 83.

17. *Diog.* 5.7.

has received from God, by distributing these to the needy, becomes a god to those who receive [his benefits]: he is an imitator of God.[18]

Hermas

With the *Shepherd of Hermas,* we approach the middle of the second century. Hermas was a brother of Pius, bishop of Rome from 141 to 155, and it was probably during this time that the *Shepherd* was written.[19] Thus, just as Aelius Aristides was delivering his famous *Oration to the Romans* (in A.D. 143 or 144) Hermas may have been writing his *Shepherd.* Yet the world of Hermas is very different from that of Aelius Aristides. While Aristides speaks of a prosperous world, to which Rome had brought peace and prosperity, Hermas sees a world divided between rich and poor:

> For some through the abundance of their food produce weakness in their flesh, and thus corrupt their flesh; while the flesh of others who have no food is corrupted, because they have not sufficient nourishment. And on their account their bodies waste away. This intemperance in eating is thus injurious to you who have abundance and do not distribute among those who are needy.[20]

None of the Apostolic Fathers devotes as much attention to this problem as does Hermas. Indeed, while his central theme is the possibility of a second repentance after baptism, the question of riches and their use is constantly interwoven with this topic. The texts that we shall study in the following pages are just a few of many that could be cited to show this interest and how Hermas deals with it. At the same time, however, the *Shepherd*'s main concern is not the well-being of the poor but the salvation of the rich. The primary question is not, How can the poor be helped? It is rather, How can the rich be saved? Naturally, this requires helping the poor, and the rich are given some guidelines for doing it. But in general the book addresses the rich. The poor are spoken *about,* usually in the third person.[21] The writer's concern for a second repentance, inasmuch as it relates to riches and their entanglement, is a pastoral concern for the salvation of the rich or of those who desire to be rich.[22] The social milieu in which Hermas is writing

---

18. *Diog.* 10.4–6.

19. The unity of the *Shepherd* has been much debated, with a number of ingenious theories proposed as to the number of possible authors and their dates. I am inclined to think that the book contains a number of visions and other elements from various times, and perhaps even from different sources, all put together into approximately its present form in the dates given. As to the role of Hermas in this process, there is no reason to doubt that when the book was published it was considered his, and that therefore he is probably the author of most of it and the compiler and editor of the rest.

20. *Shepherd of Hermas, Vision* 3.9.3–4.

21. Carolyn Osiek, *Rich and Poor in the Shepherd of Hermas: An Exegetical-Social Investigation* (Washington, DC: Catholic Biblical Association of America, 1983), 47: "The poor and the needy are spoken of only as foils for elaborating on the responsibilities of the rich." While this is true, it is probably overstated on 133: "Economic poverty and the plight of the poor were not major concerns of Hermas."

22. It may be illuminating to compare Hermas with Heb. 10:26–36, where sins committed after repentance, possessions, and the willingness to part with them are also at issue.

is very different from that of the early Jesus movement or even of the *Didache* or the *Epistle of Barnabas.*[23]

Hermas's pastoral concern for the rich does not mean that he simply seeks to comfort them in their riches. On the contrary, he feels strongly that riches are an impediment to salvation. In one of the visions he records, the church shows him a great tower that is being built — the church itself. As a multitude of angels brings stones to the building site, the six angels in charge of construction place some stones directly on the wall, and cast aside others. Some of the cast-off stones are hopelessly shattered, while others await another opportunity to be brought to the tower. Among the latter are some white and round stones that do not fit the construction precisely because they are round. Hermas asks his guide,

> "But who are these, Lady, that are white and round, and yet do not fit into the building of the tower?" She answered and said, "How long will you be foolish and stupid, and continue to put every kind of question and understand nothing? These are those who have faith indeed, but they also have the riches of the world. When, therefore, tribulation comes, on account of their riches and business they deny the Lord." I answered and said to her, "When, then, will they be useful to the building, Lady?" "When the riches that now seduce them have been circumscribed, then they will be of use to God. For as a round stone cannot become square unless portions be cut off and cast away, so also those who are rich cannot be useful to the Lord unless their riches be cut down."[24]

For several reasons Hermas views riches and especially the quest after riches as impediments to salvation. First of all, concern over business keeps attention away from the faith, making it difficult for those who are so obfuscated to understand the teachings of the church. Some have believed and then "devote themselves to and become mixed up with business, and wealth, and heathen friends, and many other actions of this world." Such people do not understand the teachings of the church, "for their minds are corrupted and become dried up," and they "go astray in their minds, and lose all understanding in regard to righteousness."[25]

A second reason riches are dangerous has to do with the company kept by those who seek them. The reference to "heathen friends" in the previous paragraph points in this direction. In another passage, Hermas seems to distinguish between the rich and those "who are immersed in much business." Apparently the distinction is between those who are comfortably rich and the social climbers who are trying to get ahead through business ventures. In any case, the problem with both groups is that they keep the wrong sort of company. Those who are entangled in business do not "cleave to the servants of God, but wander away,

---

23. There is no doubt that Hermas knew either the *Didache* or the "Document of the Two Ways" (if such a document ever existed), for Herm. *Mand.* 2.4–5 is a collection of phrases from *Did.* 1.5 and 2.6–7. Significantly, Hermas does not go on to quote *Did.* 4.8, which is a sharp statement in favor of radical *koinonía.*

24. Herm. *Vis.* 3.6.5–6.

25. Herm. *Mand.* 10.1.4.

being choked by their business transactions." The others, the comfortably rich, "cleave with difficulty to the servants of God, fearing lest these should ask something of them."[26] The tendency of those who are in business to avoid offending others may be what Hermas has in mind when he says "on account of their desire of possessions they became hypocritical, and each one taught according to the desires of men who were sinners."[27]

Yet the most important reason that riches are an obstacle to faith is that they involve a commitment to the present order, and in a time of persecution such commitment makes it very difficult to stand firm.

> He says to me, "You know that you who are the servants of God dwell in a strange land; for your city is far away from this one. If then," he continues, "you know your city in which you are to dwell, why do you here provide lands, and make expensive preparations, and accumulate dwellings and expensive buildings? He who makes such preparations for this city cannot return again to his own.... Dost thou not understand that all these things belong to another, and are under the power of another? For the lord of this city will say, 'I do not wish thee to dwell in my city; but depart from this city, because thou obeyest not my laws.' Thou therefore, although having fields and houses, and many other things, when cast out by him, what wilt thou do with thy land, and house, and other possessions which thou hast gathered to thyself? For the lord of this country justly says to thee, 'Either obey my laws or depart from my dominion.' ... Thou shalt altogether deny thy law, and walk according to the law of this city. See lest it be to thy hurt to deny thy law; for if thou shalt desire to return to thy city, thou wilt not be received, because thou hast denied the law of thy city.... Have a care, therefore: as one living in a foreign land, make no further preparations for thyself than such merely as may be sufficient; and be ready, when the master of this city shall come to cast thee out for disobeying his law, to leave his city, and to depart to thine own, and to obey thine own law without being exposed to annoyance, but to great joy."[28]

Clearly, what most concerns Hermas is the price Christians pay for social climbing. Hermas himself was a freedman. At some point he had been rich, but apparently at the time the book was written he was not wealthy. In the vision of the tower, after telling him that the wealth of the rich has to be cut away before they can be useful to God, the church reminds Hermas, "Learn this first from your own case. When you were rich, you were useless; but now you are useful and fit for life."[29] How this change in station came about is not known. Naturally, it is possible that Hermas lost his wealth through an unfortunate turn of events. But it is also possible that he gave up much of it for the sake of the Gospel, as he called others to do. We know that many among the freedmen and women in the

---

26. Herm. *Sim.* 9.20.1–2, Also Herm. *Sim.* 8.8.1: "Those who are immersed in business, and do not cleave to the saints." This and all future references to the *Shepherd* are from *ANF.*

27. Herm. *Sim.* 9.19.3.

28. Herm. *Sim.* 1.1–6.

29. Herm. *Vis.* 3.6.7.

Roman Empire became wealthy. Trimalchio, the freedman in the *Satyricon,* is the successful social climber par excellence. It is quite possible that many among Hermas's audience are freedmen and women like himself, and that these are the people he considers unduly entangled in their business affairs and whom he calls to repentance. One can hear a note of pain as he speaks of

> those that were faithful indeed; but after acquiring wealth, and becoming distinguished amongst the heathen, they clothed themselves with great pride, and became lofty-minded, and deserted the truth, and did not cleave to the righteous, but lived with the heathen, and this way of life became more agreeable to them. They did not, however, depart from God, but remained in the faith, although not working the works of faith.[30]

Hermas advises such people to share with the needy: "Do not partake of God's creatures alone, but give abundantly of them to the needy. . . . Ye, therefore, who are high in position, seek out the hungry as long as the tower is not finished."[31] The passage quoted above, which compares the Christian life with living in a foreign city, leads to the following exhortation: "Instead of lands, buy afflicted souls, according as each one is able, and visit widows and orphans, and do not overlook them; and spend your wealth and all your preparations, which ye received from the Lord, upon such lands and houses. For to this end did the Master make you rich."[32]

A specific suggestion for sharing with the needy — and one that has become quite popular among antihunger activists in modern times — is that when fasting one should set aside the amount that would otherwise have been spent on food and give it to someone in need.[33] In so doing, Hermas asserts, the givers will also receive a benefit, for the poor will pray for them.

This symbiosis between the rich and the poor, so that one contributes material goods and the other contributes special prayers and piety, will become a fairly common theme in later Christian literature on almsgiving. Hermas expresses it by using the image of vines growing amid elm trees — what the Romans called the *arbustrum* method of growing vines. He says that he was once walking in the countryside and thinking about how the elms and the vines helped each other, when the "Shepherd" — his guide in the later part of the book — appeared to him and told him that there was a lesson in the vines and the elms. The vine cannot yield much fruit when it trails on the ground without the support of the elm, and whatever fruit it produces rots. The elm, on the other hand, is by nature a fruitless tree, but by supporting the vine it is as if it too produced fruit. Likewise, the rich have much material wealth but are poor in matters relating to God, precisely because their wealth impedes them.

> But when the rich man refreshes the poor, and assists him in his necessities, believing that what he does to the poor man will be able to find its reward

---

30. Herm. *Sim.* 8.9.1.
31. Herm. *Vis.* 3.9.2, 5.
32. Herm. *Sim.* 1.8–9.
33. Herm. *Sim.* 5.3.7.

with God — because the poor man is rich in intercession and confession, and his intercession has great power with God — then the rich man helps the poor in all things without hesitation; and the poor man, being helped by the rich, intercedes for him, giving thanks to God for him who bestows gifts upon him.... Both, accordingly, accomplish their work. The poor man makes intercession; a work in which he is rich, which he received from the Lord.... And the rich man, in like manner, unhesitantly bestows upon the poor man the riches which he received from the Lord.[34]

Here we find two themes interwoven. The ancient theme that the poor are somehow closer to God or that God listens to their prayers as if a preferential manner joins the notion that the existence of some who are poor and some who are rich produces an ideal balance. In this context Hermas uses the ancient notion of *koinonía,* for he declares that, just as the elm and the vine are partners in producing grapes, so are the rich and the poor partners — *koinonoí* — in the work of justice. Needless to say, this is a step removed from the *koinonía* of Acts, which resulted — at least as Luke describes it — in "not a needy person among them," or from the *koinonía* that Paul advocates in 2 Corinthians 8, whose result is equality.

Yet, once again, this does not mean that the rich are free to continue enjoying their riches in the midst of want, simply on the basis that the poor are a necessary part of the landscape. On the contrary, the image of the elms and the vines is addressed precisely to *those* among the rich who believe they can ignore the need of the poor. It may leave something to be desired as a manifesto of social justice, and it certainly implies that poverty exists because God wills it. Yet those are not the points that Hermas is trying to make. He is not addressing the poor and telling them that their poverty is willed by God. He is addressing the rich and telling them that their wealth is fruitless unless it is shared with the needy. Indeed, as he concludes his book he declares that everyone must be spared want. To be in need is a torture, and therefore to rescue another from such conditions is to earn great joy. Not to do so, on the other hand, is a great crime, for the pain of poverty sometimes leads the poor to seek their own deaths. In such cases, those who could have helped and did not are guilty of the blood of the poor.[35]

Other Apostolic Fathers

Among the Apostolic Fathers, Hermas deals most extensively with the responsibilities of the rich. However, the other Apostolic Fathers do touch on them in passing and do not contradict what has been drawn from the more explicit texts. Late in the first century Clement of Rome, writing in support of order and authority, counsels, "Let the rich man provide for the wants of the poor; and let the poor man bless God, because He hath given one by whom his need

---

34. Herm. *Sim.* 2.5–7.
35. Herm. *Sim.* 10.4.2–3.

may be supplied."[36] Early in the second century, Ignatius of Antioch character-izes heretics as those who "have no regard for love; no care for the widow, or the orphan, or the oppressed; of the bond of the free; of the hungry, or of the thirsty."[37] He also exhorts slaves not to try to buy their freedom "at the expense of the common," lest they become slaves of greed.[38] Apparently, this is another reference to the *koinonía,* which will suffer if one slave's desire for freedom is put ahead of all the needs of the poor. Yet, the very fact that Ignatius mentions this seems to indicate that, at least in some cases, the *koinonía* was understood in terms of helping some of its members who were slaves buy their freedom. Polycarp, writing shortly after Ignatius, in passing equates greed with idolatry.[39] Finally, the so-called *Second Epistle of Clement* calls for mutual compassion[40] and declares that "almsgiving . . . is a good thing, as repentance from sin; fasting is better than prayer, but almsgiving than both."[41]

This may be the place to say a word about the doctrine of the *Pseudoclementine Homilies.* This document, although from a later date,[42] probably reflects ideas circulating in Jewish Christian gnostic circles by the beginning of the second century. Here we find a negative view of property based not on questions of the just distribution of wealth or the needs of the poor but on a radical dualism that sees the present world as belonging to evil powers. The true believers are in an alien world. Therefore what they have is not properly theirs, and those who take it away from them are not acting unjustly. "And Peter said: 'Are not those, then, who you said received injustice, themselves transgressors, inasmuch as they are in the kingdom of the other, and is it not by overreaching that they have obtained all they possess? While those who are thought to act unjustly are conferring a favour on each subject of the hostile kingdom, so far as they permit him to have property.' "[43]

The conflict between these two kingdoms is so great that one has to choose between having things of the present order and having a share in the future kingdom. Therefore, having — or desiring — anything beyond the bare minimum is sin.

> Those men who choose the present have the power to be rich, to revel in luxury, to indulge in pleasures, and to do whatever they can. For they will possess none of the future goods. But those who have decided to accept the blessings of the future reign have no right to regard as their own the things that are here, since they belong to a foreign king, with the exception only of water and bread, and those things procured with sweat to maintain life

---

36. *Clem. ad Cor.* 37.2.
37. *Ad Smyr.* 6.2.
38. *Ad Pol.* 4.3.
39. *Pol. ad Philip.* 11.2.
40. *2 Clem.* 4.3.
41. Ibid., 16.4.
42. See González, *A History of Christian Thought,* 1:62 n. 5.
43. *Clem. Hom.* 15.7.

(for it is not lawful for them to commit suicide), and also one garment, for they are not permitted to go naked on account of the all-seeing heaven.[44]

To all of us possessions are sins. The deprivation of these, in whatever way it may take place, is the removal of sins.[45]

Against such views, basing poverty and renunciation on a dualism that tends to deny the doctrine of creation, later Christian writers, such as Clement of Alexandria, will argue that the things that constitute wealth are not in themselves evil. They do not belong to another god or principle, these writers will say, but to the same God who has been revealed in Jesus Christ. If evil is connected with them, it resides not in the things themselves but in the greed that leads some to seek after them with an inordinate desire.

The Apologists

The only two writings of the early Apologists that deal significantly with the subject of wealth and its use are the *Apology* of Aristides and the *First Apology* of Justin.[46] Aristides, writing at approximately the same time as Hermas,[47] affirms that among Christians "the one who has gives liberally to the one who has not."[48] Also, it is interesting to note that what Hermas orders regarding the use of the proceeds of fasting, Aristides describes as the practice in his own community (although in this case those who fast are too poor to feed both themselves and the needy): "If one of them is poor or in need and they have no abundance of resources, they fast two or three days in order to supply the food that the poor need."[49]

Finally, three passages in Justin's *First Apology* deserve our attention. The briefest one is an introduction to a summary of some of the teachings of the Sermon on the Mount. Justin's words are: "We should communicate [*koinoneîn*] to the needy."[50] The second passage expresses the same idea more explicitly: "We who valued above all things the acquisition of wealth and possessions, now bring what we have into a common stock, and communicate to [i.e., 'share with'] everyone in need."[51] Thus in Justin we find once again the theme of *koinonía* as sharing that we have found repeatedly in early Christian tradition. The third passage confirms that this *koinonía* is voluntary and is carried out in a similar

---

44. Ibid.

45. Ibid., 15.9.

46. However, on the general social background and significance of the Apologists, see Robert Louis Wilken, "Toward a Social Interpretation of Early Christian Apologetics," *Church History* 39, no. 1 (1970): 1–22.

47. Eusebius of Caesarea (*H. E.* 4.3.3; *Chron.*, 01.226, Chr. 125, Adr. 8). *PG* affirms that the *Apology* of Aristides was addressed to Hadrian, who reigned from 117 to 138. Johannes Geffcken, however, argued that it was actually addressed to Antoninus, who reigned from 138 to 161: *Zwei griechische Apologeten* (Leipzig: Teubner, 1907), 28–31. Most modern critics agree with Geffcken.

48. Arist., *Apol.* 15.7. The Syriac version speaks not of the liberality of the gift, but of its willingness.

49. Arist., *Apol.* (Syr.) 15.7.

50. *1 Apol.* 15.10. Clearly, better translations would be "share with the needy," "be partners with the needy," or even "have things in common with the needy."

51. Ibid., 14.2. The same corrections apply to this translation as to the previous one.

fashion to that of Acts. In Acts, voluntary contributions were laid at the feet of the apostles and distributed according to need:

> Those of us who have assist those who are in need, and we help one another.... Those who can and will, according to their own decision, give what they consider fitting, and what is collected is given to the president who succors orphans and widows, those who are in need for reason of illness or any other cause, those who are in prison, and sojourners. In a word, it is he who provides for those who are in need.[52]

In summary, as we look at the subapostolic church through the writings of the Apostolic Fathers and the Greek Apologists, we find numerous indications that the *koinonía,* or partnership in goods, was still practiced, at least to a degree. As from the beginning, it did not require selling all and putting it into a common treasury. It did, however, require considering all members of the church as partners not only in spiritual things but in the totality of life. For this reason, while wealth as such was not condemned, wealth that was unavailable for the succor of the needy was considered a hindrance to the salvation of its owner. Among all the writings studied, the *Shepherd of Hermas* stands out as the one that, while dealing most extensively with matters of wealth and its use, says least about *koinonía* or partnership in earthly goods.

---

52. Ibid., 67.1, 6. In this case, the translation is mine, for the *ANF* changes the meaning by translating "those who have" as the "well to do," which gives the impression that only the wealthy are expected to contribute.

Select Bibliography

General Reference

Aikman, J. Logan. *Cyclopaedia of Christian Missions: Their Rise, Progress, and Present Position.* London: Richard Griffin and Co., 1860.

Barrett, David B., and Todd M. Johnson, with Christopher R. Guidry and Peter F. Crossing (Associate Editors). "Part 22. Evangelism: Numerical Analysis of Ongoing Evangelism Worldwide." In *World Christian Trends AD 30–AD 2200: Interpreting the Annual Christian Megacensus.* Pasadena, CA: William Carey Library, 2001.

Barrett, David B., George T. Kurian, and Todd M. Johnson. *World Christian Encyclopedia: A Comparative Survey of Churches and Religions in the Modern World.* 2nd ed. 2 vols. New York: Oxford University Press, 2001.

Beach, Harlan P., and Charles H. Fahs, eds. *World Missionary Atlas; Containing a Directory of Missionary Societies, Classified Summaries of Statistics, Maps Showing the Location of Mission Stations Throughout the World, a Descriptive Account of the Principal Mission Lands, and Comprehensive Indices.* New York: Institute of Social and Religious Research, 1925.

Bread for the World Institute. *A Program to End Hunger. Hunger 2000. Tenth Annual Report on the State of World Hunger.* Silver Spring, MD: Bread for the World Institute, 2000.

Buttrick, George Arthur. *The Interpreters Bible.* Nashville: Abingdon Press, 1952.

Cornelius, Peter K., ed. *The Global Competitiveness Report 2002–2003.* New York and Oxford: Oxford University Press, 2003.

International Schools Services. *The ISS Directory of Overseas Schools.* 1987/88 Edition. Princeton, NJ: International Schools Services, 1987.

Jacquet, Constant H., Jr., ed. *Yearbook of American and Canadian Churches, 1987.* Annual. Fifty-fifth Issue. Nashville: Abingdon Press, 1987.

Kravis, Irving B., Alan Heston, Robert Summers. *World Product and Income: International Comparisons of Real Gross Product.* Produced by the Statistical Office of the United Nations and the World Bank. Baltimore: Published for the World Bank by the Johns Hopkins University Press, 1992.

Kravis, Irving B., Zoltan Kenessey, Alan Heston, Robert Summers. *Phase IV: World Comparisons of Purchasing Power and Real Product for 1980.* New York: United Nations, 1986.

Lindner, Eileen W., ed. *Yearbook of American & Canadian Churches, 2006.* Annual. Seventy-fourth Issue. Nashville: Abingdon Press, 2006.

McEvedy, Colin, and Richard Jones. *Atlas of World Population History.* Harmondsworth, UK: Penguin Books, 1978.

The New Dictionary of New Testament Theology. Ed. Colin Brown. Grand Rapids: Zondervan, 1975–78.

Ronsvalle, John L., and Sylvia Ronsvalle. *The State of Church Giving through 2002.* 14th ed. Champaign, IL: Empty Tomb, Inc., 2004.

Smith, Dan. *The State of the World Atlas: New Edition for the 21st Century.* 6th ed. London: Penguin Books, 1999.

United Nations. *Report on the World Social Situation 2005: The Inequality Predicament.* New York: United Nations, Department of Economic and Social Affairs (DESA), 2005.

United Nations Department of International Economic Affairs. Various Years. *Statistical Yearbook.*

U.S. Bureau of Economic Analysis, Survey of Current Business, April 2005. *www.census .gov/compendia/statab/tables/06s0663.xls.*

U.S. Census Bureau. *Statistical Abstract of the United States, 1981.* Washington, DC: U.S. Census Bureau, Government Printing Office, 1981.

U.S. Department of State. *Compensation of American Government Employees in Foreign Countries.www.state.gov/m/a/als/qtrpt/2005/42204.htm.*

———. *Indexes of Living Costs Abroad and Quarters Allowances: A Technical Description.* Washington, DC: U.S. Department of Labor, Bureau of Labor Statistics, April 1980. Report 568.

———. *Indexes of Living Costs Abroad, Quarters Allowances, and Hardship Differentials. www.state.gov/m/a/als/qtrpt/2005/.*

Welliver, Dotsey, and Minnette Northcutt, eds. *Mission Handbook 2004–2006: U.S. and Canadian Protestant Ministries Overseas.* 19th ed. Wheaton, IL: Evangelism and Missions Information Service (EMIS), 2004.

World Bank. *Poverty and Hunger: Issues and Options for Food Security in Developing Countries.* Washington, DC, 1986.

———. *World Bank Atlas, 2000.* Washington, DC: The World Bank, 2000.

———. *World Bank Development Report: Attacking Poverty.* World Development Report 2000/2001. New York: Oxford University Press, 2000.

———. *World Development Indicators, 2000.* Washington, DC: The World Bank, 2000.

———. *World Development Report 1987.* "Barriers to Adjustment and Growth in the World Economy; Industrialization and Foreign Trade; World Development Indicators." Published for the World Bank [by] Oxford University Press, 1987.

———. *World Development Report 2006: Equity and Development.* Washington, DC and New York: World Bank and Oxford University Press, 2006.

World Commission on Environment and Development. *Our Common Future.* New York: Oxford University Press, 1987.

World Resources 1987. A Report by the International Institute for Environment and Development and the World Resources Institute. New York: Basic Books, 1987.

Books

Ahlstrom, Sydney E. *A Religious History of the American People.* New Haven, CT: Yale University Press, 1972.

Allen, Roland. *The Ministry of the Spirit: Selected Writings of Roland Allen.* London: World Dominion Press, 1960.

———. *Missionary Methods: St. Paul's or Ours?* London: World Dominion Press, 1912.

———. *The Spontaneous Expansion of the Church and the Causes Which Hinder It.* London: World Dominion Press, 1927.

Almquist, Arden. *Missionary Come Back!* New York: World Publishing Co., 1970.

Applebaum, Shimon. "Economic Life in Palestine." In *Compendia Rerum Judaicarum ad Novum Testamentum,* ed. M. Stern and S. Safrai, vol. 2:662–66. Assen: Van Gorcum & Co., 1974.

Arnott, Neil. *A Survey of Human Progress, from the Savage State to the Highest Civilization yet Attained: A Progress as Little Perceived by the Multitude in any Age, as Is the Slow Growing of a Tree by the Children who Play under Its Shade — but which Is Leading to a New Condition of Mankind on Earth.* London: Longman, Green, Longman, and Roberts, 1861.

Audet, Jean-Paul. *La Didachè: Instructions des Apôtres.* Paris: J. Gabalda, 1958.

Axling, William. *Kagawa.* New York: Harper & Bros., 1932.

Bales, Kevin. *Disposable People: New Slavery in the Global Economy.* Berkeley: University of California Press, 1999.

Barnett, Mrs. H. O. (R.) *Canon Barnett: His Life, Work, and Friends,* by his wife. London: John Murray, 1918.

Baron, Salo Wittmayer. *A Social and Religious History of the Jews.* Philadelphia: The Jewish Publication Society of America, 1958.

Barton, James L. *Human Progress through Missions.* New York: Fleming H. Revell Co., 1912.

———. *The Missionary and His Critics.* New York: Fleming H. Revell Co., 1906.

Bassler, Jouette M. *God & Mammon: Asking for Money in the New Testament.* Nashville: Abingdon Press, 1991.

Beaver, R. Pierce. *The Missionary between the Times.* Garden City, NY: Doubleday, 1968.

———, ed. *The Gospel and Frontier Peoples.* South Pasadena, CA: William Carey Library, 1973.

Bellah, Robert N. *The Broken Covenant: American Civil Religion in Time of Trial.* New York: Seabury Press, 1975.

Bellah, Robert N., Richard Madsen, William N. Sullivan, Ann Swidler, and Steven M. Tipton. *Habits of the Heart: Individualism and Commitment in American Life.* Berkeley: University of California Press, 1985.

Bendix, Reinhard, and Seymour Martin Lipset, eds. *Class, Status, and Power: Social Stratification in Comparative Perspective.* 2nd ed. New York: Free Press, 1966.

Bernikow, Louise. *Alone in America: The Search for Companionship.* New York: Harper & Row, 1986.

Black, Jan Knippers. *Inequity in the Global Village: Recycled Rhetoric and Disposable People.* West Hartford, CT: Kumarian Press, 1999.

Blomberg, Craig L. *Neither Poverty nor Riches: A Biblical Theology of Possessions.* Downers Grove, IL: InterVarsity Press, 1999.

Boerma, Conrad. *Rich Man, Poor Man — and the Bible.* London: SCM, 1979.

Bonk, Jonathan J. *Missions and Money: The Role of Affluence in the Christian Missionary Enterprise from the West.* Maryknoll, NY: Orbis Books, 1991.

————. *"Not the Bloom, but the Fruit..." Conversion and Its Consequences in Nineteenth-Century Missionary Discourse.* Yale Divinity School Library, Occasional Publication no. 17. New Haven, CT: Yale Divinity School Library, 2003.

————. *The Theory and Practice of Missionary Identification, 1860–1920.* Vol. 2 in the History of Missions series. Lewiston, NY: Edwin Mellen Press, 1989.

————, ed. *Between Past and Future: Evangelical Mission Entering the Twenty-First Century.* Evangelical Missiological Society Series, Number 10. Pasadena, CA: William Carey Library, 2003.

Brattgård, Helge. *God's Stewards.* Trans. G. J. Lund. Minneapolis: Augsburg Press, 1963.

Brewster, E. Thomas, and Elizabeth S. Brewster. *Bonding and the Missionary Task: Establishing a Sense of Belonging.* Pasadena, CA: Lingua House, 1982.

Brookes, Martin. *Extreme Measures: The Dark Visions and Bright Ideas of Francis Galton.* London: Bloomsbury Publishing, 2004.

Brown, Robert McAfee. *Unexpected News: Reading the Bible with Third-World Eyes.* Philadelphia: Westminster Press, 1984.

Brown, Roger William. *Words and Things.* Glencoe, IL: Free Press, 1958.

Buchan, James. *The Expendable Mary Slessor.* Edinburgh: Saint Andrew Press, 1980.

Burke, Kenneth. *A Grammar of Motives and a Rhetoric of Motives.* New York: World Publishing Co., 1962.

Burkett, Larry. *What the Bible Says about Money.* Brentwood, TN: Wolgemuth & Hyatt, Publishers, 1989.

Calder, Lendol G. *Financing the American Dream.* Princeton, NJ: Princeton University Press, 2001.

Campolo, Anthony. *The Success Fantasy.* Wheaton, IL: Victor Books, 1980.

Carey, William. *An Enquiry into the Obligations of Christians to Use Means for the Conversion of the Heathen.* London: Hodder & Stoughton, 1891 [reprint of the 1792 edition].

Centenary Missionary Hymnal. Compiled and ed. Stanley Rogers. London: London Missionary Society, 1895.

Chirgwin, A. M. *Arthington's Million: The Romance of the Arthington Trust.* London: Livingstone Press, 1935.

Chrysostom, Saint John. *On Wealth and Poverty.* Translated and intro. Catharine P. Roth. Crestwood, NY: St. Vladmir's Seminary Press, 1984.

Clough, Shepard B. *Basic Values of Western Civilization.* New York: Columbia University Press, 1960.

Coles, Robert. *Privileged Ones: The Well-Off and the Rich in America.* Vol. 5 of *Children in Crisis.* An Atlantic Monthly Press Book. Boston: Little, Brown and Company, 1977.

Collins, Marjorie A. *Manual for Today's Missionary: From Recruitment to Retirement.* Pasadena, CA: William Carey Library, 1986.

Colson, Jean. *L'évêque dans les communautés primitives: tradition paulinienne et tradition johannique de l'épiscopat des origines a saint Irénée.* Paris: Editions du Cerf, 1951.

Cone, Orello. *Rich and Poor in the New Testament.* New York: The Macmillan Co., 1902.

Conference on Missions Held in 1860 in Liverpool: The Papers Read, the Conclusions Reached, and a Comprehensive Index, Showing the Various Matters Brought under Review. London: James Nisbet & Co., 1860.

Conn, Harvie. *Bible Studies on World Evangelization and the Simple Lifestyle.* Phillipsburg, NJ: Presbyterian and Reformed Publishing Company, 1981.

Considine, John J., ed. *The Missionary's Role in Socio-Economic Betterment.* Published under the sponsorship of the Fordham University Institute of Mission Studies and the International Rural Life Movement with the aid of the Bruno Benziger Fund of Maryknoll. New York: Newman Press, 1960.

Countryman, L. William. *The Rich Christian in the Church of the Early Empire: Contradictions and Accommodations.* Lewiston, NY: Edwin Mellen Press, 1980.

Cowen, Benjamin R. *The Miracle of the Nineteenth Century. Do Missions Pay?* Cincinnati: Cranston and Sons, 1891.

Cross, Gary S. *An All-Consuming Century: Why Commercialism Won in America.* New York: Columbia University Press, 2000.

Cullmann, Oscar. *Message to Catholics and Protestants.* Trans. Joseph A. Burgess. Grand Rapids: William B. Eerdmans, 1959.

Cumming, John. "God in History." *Lectures Delivered Before the Young Men's Christian Association 1848–1849.* Vol. 4. London: James Nisbet and Co., 1876.

Cust, Robert Needham. *Essay on the Prevailing Methods of the Evangelization of the Non-Christian World.* London: Luzac & Co., 1894.

———. *Notes on Missionary Subjects.* London: Elliot Stock, 1889.

Danker, Frederick W. *Benefactor.* St. Louis: Clayton Publishing House, 1982.

Davey, Cyril J. *Kagawa of Japan.* Nashville: Abingdon, 1960.

David, Paul A., and Melvin Reder, eds. *Nations and Households in Economic Growth.* New York: Academic Press, 1974.

Davis, J. Merle, ed. *The Economic Basis of the Church. Preparatory Studies and Findings, Meeting of the International Missionary Council, at Tambaram, Madras, India, December 12th to 29th, 1938.* "The Madras Series," Volume 5. New York: International Missionary Council, 1939.

———. *The Economic and Social Environment of the Younger Churches. The Report of the Department of Social and Economic Research of the International Missionary Council to the Tambaram Meeting — December 1938.* London: Published for the International Council by the Edinburgh House Press, 1939.

De Graaf, John, et al. *Affluenza: The All-Consuming Epidemic.* San Francisco: Berrett-Koehler, 2001.

Dennis, James S. *Christian Missions and Social Progress: A Sociological Study of Foreign Missions.* 3 vols. Edinburgh: Oliphant, Anderson and Ferrier, 1898.

Dickinson, Richard D. N. *Poor, Yet Making Many Rich: The Poor as Agents of Creative Justice.* Commission on the Churches' Participation in Development. Geneva: World Council of Churches, 1983.

Dostoyevsky, Fyodor. *The Brothers Karamazov.* Trans. Constance Garnett. New York: Random House, 1950.

Drohan, Madelaine. *Making a Killing: How and Why Corporations Use Armed Force to Do Business*. Toronto: Vintage Canada, 2004.

Drummond, Henry. *Tropical Africa*. 3rd ed. London: Hodder & Stoughton, 1889.

East, David Jonathan. *Western Africa: Its Condition, and Christianity the Means of Its Recovery*. London: Houlston & Stoneman, 1844.

Edmond, Mrs. A. M. *Memoir of Mrs. Sarah D. Comstock, Missionary to Arracan*. Philadelphia: American Baptist Publication Society, [1854].

Ehrenreich, Barbara. *Nickel and Dimed: On (not) Getting By in America*. New York: Metropolitan Books, Henry Holt and Company, 2001.

Ela, Jean-Marc. *African Cry*. Trans. Robert R. Barr. Maryknoll, NY: Orbis Books, 1980.

Ellul, Jacques. *The Technological Society*. Trans. John Wilkinson. New York: Knopf, 1964.

Fabian, Johannes. *Out of Our Minds: Reason and Madness in the Exploration of Central Africa*. Berkeley and London: University of California Press, 2000.

Fargher, Brian. *Philip: An Ethiopian Evangelist*. Ethiopia: Addis Ababa, 1985.

Farmer, William Reuben. *Maccabees, Zealots and Josephus: An Enquiry into Jewish Nationalism in the Greco-Roman Period*. New York: Columbia University Press, 1970.

Ferkiss, Victor C. *Technological Man: The Myth and the Reality*. New York: George Braziller, 1969.

Finley, Allen, and Lorry Lutz. *The Family Tie*. Nashville: Thomas Nelson Publishers, 1983.

Flannery, Tim. *The Eternal Frontier: An Ecological History of North America and Its Peoples*. Melbourne, Australia: Text Publishing, 2001.

———. *The Weather Makers: How Man Is Changing the Climate and What It Means for Life on Earth*. New York: Grove/Atlantic, 2006.

Fleming, Daniel Johnson. *Ethical Issues Confronting World Christians*. Published for the International Missionary Council, New York, by the Rumford Press, Concord, NH, 1935.

———. *Living as Comrades: A Study of Factors Making for "Community."* Published for the Foreign Missions Conference of North America by Agricultural Missions, Inc., New York, 1950.

———. *Ventures in Simpler Living*. Printed for the International Missionary Council, by the Polygraphic Company of America, New York, 1933.

Foster, George M. *Traditional Societies and Technological Change*. 2nd ed. New York: Harper & Row, Publishers, 1973.

Frank, Thomas. *The Conquest of Cool*. Chicago: University of Chicago Press, 1998.

———. *One Market under God: Extreme Capitalism, Market Populism, and the End of Economic Democracy*. New York: Anchor Books, 2001.

———, and Matt Weiland, eds. *Commodify Your Dissent: Salvos from the Baffler*. New York: W. W. Norton & Company, 1997.

Freyne, Sean. *Galilee from Alexander the Great to Hadrian, 323 B.C.E. to 135 C.E.: A Study of Second Temple Judaism*. Wilmington, DE: Michael Glazier, 1980.

Galbraith, John Kenneth. *The Affluent Society*. 3rd ed., rev. New York: New American Library, 1976.

———. *The Culture of Contentment*. Boston: Houghton Mifflin Company, 1992.

———. *The Nature of Mass Poverty*. Cambridge, MA: Harvard University Press, 1979.

Galton, Francis. *The Art of Travel; or, Shifts and Contrivances Available in Wild Countries.* London: John Murray, 1855.

Gandhi, Mohandas K. *The Mahatma and the Missionary: Selected Writings of Mohandas K. Gandhi.* Ed. Clifford Manshardt. Chicago: Henry Regnery Company, 1949.

Gateley, Edwina. *I Hear a Seed Growing: God of the Forest, God of the Streets.* Trabuco Canyon, CA: Source Books, 1990.

Geffcken, Johannes. *Zwei griechische Apologeten.* Leipzig: B. G. Teubner, 1907.

Gerber, Vergil, ed. *Missions in Creative Tension.* South Pasadena, CA: William Carey Library, 1971.

Gesch, Patrick F. *Initiative and Initiation: A Cargo Cult-Type Movement in the Sepik Against Its Background in Traditional Village Religion.* St. Augustin, West Germany: Anthropos Institut, 1985.

Giet, Stanislas. *L'énigme de la Didachè.* Paris: Ophrys, 1970.

Glickman, Lawrence B. *Consumer Society in American History: A Reader.* Ithaca, NY: Cornell University Press, 1999.

Glyn-Jones, Anne. *Holding Up a Mirror: How Civilizations Decline.* London: Century Books, 1996.

Gnuse, Robert Karl. *You Shall Not Steal: Community and Property in the Biblical Tradition.* Maryknoll, NY: Orbis Books, 1985.

González, Justo L. *Faith and Wealth: A History of Early Christian Ideas on the Origin, Significance, and Use of Money.* San Francisco: Harper & Row, Publishers, 1990.

———. *A History of Christian Thought.* 2nd ed. Nashville: Abingdon Press, 1989.

Gore, Al. *An Inconvenient Truth.* New York: Rodale, 2006.

Goudzwaard, Bob. *Aid for the Overdeveloped West.* Toronto: Wedge Publishing Foundation, 1975.

Grant, Frederick Clifton. *The Economic Background of the Gospels.* Oxford: Clarendon Press, 1923.

Grenfell, Bernard P., and Arthur S. Hunt. *The Amherst Papyri: Being an Account of the Greek Papyri in the Collection of the Right Hon. Lord Amherst of Hackney, F. S. A. at Didlington Hall, Norfolk.* London: H. Frowde, 1900.

Grigg, Viv. *Companion to the Poor.* Sutherland, NSW, Australia: Albatross Books, 1984.

———. *Cry of the Urban Poor.* Monrovia, CA: MARC, 1992.

Guinness, Mrs. Gratan. *The New World of Central Africa, With a History of the First Christian Mission on the Congo.* London: Hodder & Stoughton, 1890.

Hancock, Graham. *Lords of Poverty: The Power, Prestige, and Corruption of the International Aid Business.* New York: Atlantic Monthly Press, 1989.

Hands, A. R. *Charities and Social Aid in Greece and Rome.* Ithaca, NY: Cornell University Press, 1968.

Harnack, Adolf von. *Die Chronologie der altchristlicher Literatur bis Eusebius.* Leipzig: J. C. Hinrichs, 1897.

Hastings, Adrian. *A History of African Christianity 1950–1975.* London: Cambridge University Press, 1979.

Heider, Fritz. *The Psychology of Interpersonal Relations.* New York: John Wiley & Sons, 1958.

Heilbroner, Robert L. *The Quest for Wealth: A Study of Acquisitive Man.* New York: Simon and Schuster, 1956.

Hengel, Martin. *Acts and the History of Earliest Christianity.* Philadelphia: Fortress Press, 1980.

———. *Property and Riches in the Early Church: Aspects of a Social History of Early Christianity.* Philadelphia: Fortress Press, 1974.

Henry, Jules. *Culture Against Man.* New York: Random House, 1963.

Heslam, Peter, ed. *Globalization and the Good.* London: SPCK, 2004.

Hesselgrave, David J. *Communicating Christ Cross-Culturally: An Introduction to Missionary Communication.* Grand Rapids: Zondervan Publishing House, 1978.

———. *Paradigms in Conflict: 10 Key Questions in Christian Missions Today.* Grand Rapids: Kregel Publications, 2005.

Heuver, Gerald Dirk. *The Teachings of Jesus Concerning Wealth.* New York: Fleming H. Revell, 1903.

Hoagland, Edward. *African Calliope: A Journey to the Sudan.* Harmondsworth, UK: Penguin Books, 1978.

Hobsbawm, E. J. *The Age of Empire, 1875–1914.* New York: Pantheon Books, 1987.

Hocking, William Ernest. *Re-thinking Missions: A Laymen's Inquiry after One Hundred Years.* New York and London: Harper & Brothers, Publishers, 1932.

Hoppe, Leslie J., O.F.M. *There Shall Be No Poor among You: Poverty in the Bible.* Nashville: Abingdon Press, 2004.

Horney, Karen. *The Neurotic Personality of Our Time.* New York: W. W. Norton & Company, 1937.

Huffington, Arianna. *Pigs at the Trough: How Corporate Greed and Political Corruption Are Undermining America.* New York: Crown Publishers, 2003.

Hughes, Dewi, with Matthew Bennett. *God of the Poor: A Biblical Vision of God's Present Rule.* Carlisle, UK: OM Publishing, 1998.

Hunter, James Davison. *American Evangelicalism.* New Brunswick, NJ: Rutgers University Press, 1983.

Hvalkof, Soren, and Peter Aaby, eds. *Is God an American? An Anthropological Perspective on the Missionary Work of the Summer Institute of Linguistics.* Copenhagen: International Work Group for Indigenous Affairs, and London: Survival International, 1981.

Illich, Ivan D. *Celebration of Awareness: A Call for Institutional Revolution.* Garden City, NY: Doubleday, 1970.

———. *The Church, Change and Development.* Chicago: Urban Training Center Press, 1970.

Jaher, Frederic Cople, ed. *The Rich, the Well Born, and the Powerful: Elites and Upper Classes in History.* Urbana: University of Illinois Press, 1973.

Jencks, Christopher. *Inequality.* New York: Basic Books, 1972.

Jewett, Robert. *The Captain America Complex: The Dilemma of Zealous Nationalism.* Philadelphia: Westminster Press, 1973.

John, Griffith. *A Voice from China.* London: Religious Tract Society, 1907.

Johnson, Luke T. *The Literary Function of Possessions in Luke-Acts.* Missoula, MT: Scholars Press, 1977.

———. *Sharing Possessions: Mandate and Symbol of Faith.* Overtures to Biblical Theology. Philadelphia: Fortress Press, 1981.

Johnston, Harry H. *A History of the Colonization of Africa by Alien Races.* Cambridge: Cambridge University Press, 1899.

Johnston, James. *A Century of Christian Progress and Its Lessons.* London: James Nisbet & Co., 1888.

Johnstone, Patrick, and Jason Mandryk, with Robyn Johnstone. *Operation World: 21st-Century Edition.* Carlisle: Paternoster Lifestyle, 2001.

Jones, David Picton. *After Livingstone: The Work of a Pioneer Missionary in Central Africa.* London: Privately Published by Dorothy Picton Jones, 1968.

Jones, Landon Y. *Great Expectations: America and the Baby Boom Generation.* New York: Coward, McCann & Geoghegan, 1980.

Kagawa, Toyohiko. *Brotherhood Economics.* New York: Harper & Bros., 1936.

———. *Meditations on the Cross.* Trans. Helen F. Topping and Marion R. Draper. Chicago: Willett, Clark & Co. 1935.

———. *The Religion of Jesus.* London: SCM Press, 1931.

———. *Songs from the Slums.* Nashville: Cokesbury, 1935.

Kennedy, Gail. *Democracy and the Gospel of Wealth: Problems in American Civilization.* Readings Selected by the Department of American Studies, Amherst College. Boston: D. C. Heath and Company, 1949.

Kennedy, Paul. *The Rise and Fall of the Great Powers: Economic Change and Military Conflict from 1500 to 2000.* New York: Random House, 1987.

Kenney, Betty Jo. *The Missionary Family.* Pasadena, CA: W. Carey Library, 1983.

Kinsler, Ross, and Gloria Kinsler, eds. *God's Economy: Biblical Studies from Latin America.* Maryknoll, NY: Orbis Books, 2005.

Kinzer, Stephen. *Overthrow: America's Century of Regime Change from Hawaii to Iraq.* New York: Times Books, 2006.

Klassen, A. J., ed. *The Church in Mission: A Sixtieth Anniversary Tribute to J. B. Toews.* Fresno, CA: Board of Christian Literature, Mennonite Brethren Church, 1967.

Knitter, Paul F., and Chandra Muzaffar, eds. *Subverting Greed: Religious Perspectives on the Global Economy.* Maryknoll, NY: Orbis Books, 2002.

Knollys, Henry. *English Life in China.* London: Smith, Elder & Company, 1885.

Koyama, Kosuke. *Fifty Meditations.* Maryknoll, NY: Orbis Books, 1979.

———. *Mount Fuji and Mount Sinai: A Critique of Idols.* Maryknoll, NY: Orbis Books, 1985.

———. *No Handle on the Cross: An Asian Meditation on the Crucified Mind.* London: SCM Press, 1976.

———. *Theology in Contact.* Madras: Christian Literature Society, 1975.

———. *Three Mile an Hour God: Biblical Reflections.* Maryknoll, NY: Orbis Books, 1980.

———. *Waterbuffalo Theology.* Maryknoll, NY: Orbis Books, 1974.

Kreissig, Heinz. *Die Sozialen Zusammenhänge des jüdaischen Krieges.* Berlin: Akademie-Verlag, 1970.

Landes, David S. *The Wealth and Poverty of Nations: Why Some Are So Rich and Some Are So Poor.* New York and London: W. W. Norton & Company, 1998.

Lane, Stewart. *Weep You Rich!* Limbe, Malawi: The Cornelius Fellowship, n.d.

Lapierre, Dominique. *The City of Joy.* Trans. from the French by Kathryn Spink. Garden City, NY: Doubleday & Company, 1985.

Latourette, Kenneth Scott. *History of the Expansion of Christianity.* Vol. 4. *The Great Century, A.D. 1800–1914: Europe and the United States of America.* London: Eyre and Spottiswoode, 1941.

———. *The Unquenchable Light.* London: Eyre and Spottiswoode, 1940.

Laurie, Thomas. *The Ely Volume; or, The Contributions of our Foreign Missions to Science and Human Well Being.* Boston: ABCFM, 1881.

Lausanne Committee for World Evangelization. Occasional Paper no. 2, *The Willowbank Report. Report of a Consultation on Gospel and Culture* held at Willowbank, Somerset Bridge, Bermuda, from January 6–13th, 1978. Sponsored by the Lausanne Theology and Education Group. Wheaton, IL: Lausanne Committee for World Evangelization, 1978.

———. Occasional Paper no. 22, *The Thailand Report on the Urban Poor. Report of the Consultation of World Evangelization Mini-Consultation on Reaching the Urban Poor* held in Pattaya, Thailand, June 16–27, 1980. Sponsored by the Lausanne Committee for World Evangelization. Wheaton, IL: Lausanne Committee for World Evangelization, 1980.

Lennox, William G. *A Comparative Study of the Health of Missionary Families in Japan and China and a Selected Group in America.* Denver: University of Denver Department of Economics, 1922.

———. *The Health of Missionary Families in China: A Statistical Study.* Denver: University of Denver Department of Economics, 1921.

———. *The Health and Turnover of Missionaries.* Published by the Advisory Committee (J. G. Vaughan, M.D., Chairman; E. M. Dodd, M.D.; P. H. J. Lerrigo, M.D.; M. H. Ward, M.D.), the Foreign Missions Conference, New York, 1933.

Liggins, John. *The Great Value and Success of Foreign Missions. Proved by Distinguished Witnesses: Being the Testimony of Diplomatic Ministers, Consuls, Naval Officers, and Scientific and other Travellers in Heathen and Mohammedan Countries; Together With that of English Viceroys, Governors, and Military Officers in India and in the British Colonies; also Leading Facts and Late Statistics of the Missions.* London: James Nisbet & Co., 1889.

Lilly, William Samuel. *Christianity and Modern Civilization: Being Some Chapters in European History with an Introductory Dialogue on the Philosophy of History.* London: Chapman & Hill, 1903.

Limburg, James. *The Prophets and the Powerless.* Atlanta: John Knox Press, 1977.

Lissner, Jorgen. *The Politics of Altruism: A Study of the Political Behaviour of Voluntary Development Agencies.* Geneva: Lutheran World Federation, Department of Studies, 1977.

Livingstone, David. *Missionary Travels and Researches in South Africa; Including a Sketch of Sixteen Years Residence in the Interior of Africa and a Journey from the Cape of Good Hope to Lands on the West Coast; thence across the Continent, down the River Zambesi, to the Eastern Ocean.* London: J. Murray, 1857.

Loewen, Jacob A. *Culture and Human Values: Christian Intervention in Anthropological Perspective. Selections from the Writings of Jacob A. Loewen.* South Pasadena, CA: William Carey Library, 1975.

Lovett, Richard. *James Gilmour of Mongolia: His Diaries, Letters and Reports.* London: Religious Tract Society, 1893.

Lutz, Jessie G. *Christian Missions in China: Evangelists of What?* Boston: D. C. Heath and Company, 1965.

Macdonald, Allan J. M. *Trade Politics and Christianity in Africa and the East.* London: Longmans, Green and Co., 1916.

Mackenzie, W. Douglas. *Christianity and the Progress of Man as Illustrated by Modern Missions.* Edinburgh: Oliphant, Anderson and Ferrier, 1898.

Mander, Jerry, and Edward Goldsmith, eds. *The Case against the Global Economy and for a Turn toward the Local.* San Francisco: Sierra Club Books, 1996.

Maranz, David. *African Friends and Money Matters: Observations from Africa.* Dallas: SIL International, 2001.

Maung She Wa, G. Edwards, and E. Edwards. *Burma Baptist Chronicle.* Rangoon, 1963.

May, Elizabeth. *Central Africa.* Handbooks to Our Mission Fields Series. London: LMS, 1908.

Maynard-Reid, Pedrito U. *Poverty and Wealth in James.* Maryknoll, NY: Orbis Books, 1987.

McGilvary, Daniel, et al. *Counsel to New Missionaries from Older Missionaries of the Presbyterian Church.* New York: Board of Foreign Missions of the Presbyterian Church in the U.S.A., 1905.

Meeks, Wayne A. *The First Urban Christians: The Social World of the Apostle Paul.* New Haven, CT: Yale University Press, 1983.

Melville, Herman. *Moby Dick or The White Whale.* New York: Dodd, Mead and Company, 1922.

Michie, Alexander. *Missionaries in China.* London: Edward Stanford, 1891.

Miller, Vincent J. *Consuming Religion: Christian Faith and Practice in a Consumer Culture.* New York: Continuum, 2005.

Milner, Don, and John Wesson. *God or Mammon? A Christian Ethic for the Market-Place.* Grove Booklet on Ethics no. 10. Bramcote Notts, UK: Grove Books, 1976.

Missionary Service in Asia Today. A Report on a Consultation Held by the Asia Methodist Advisory Committee, February 18–23, 1971, in cooperation with the Life, Message, Unity Committee of the East Asian Christian Conference. Kuala Lumpur: University of Malaysia, 1971.

Mitchell, Lawrence E. *Corporate Irresponsibility: America's Newest Export.* New Haven, CT: Yale University Press, 2002.

———. *Stacked Deck: A Story of Selfishness in America.* Philadelphia: Temple University Press, 1998.

Mittelman, James M. *The Globalization Syndrome.* Princeton, NJ: Princeton University Press, 2000.

Moffat, Robert. *A Missionary Prize Essay on the Duty, the Privilege, and Encouragement of Christians to Send the Gospel to the Unenlightened Nations of the Earth.* Newcastle: Pattison and Ross, 1842.

Mommsen, Th., ed. *Theodosiani Libri* 16. Berlin: Weidmann, 1962.

Mooneyham, Stanley. *What Do You Say to a Hungry World?* Waco, TX: Word Books, 1975.

Muggeridge, Malcolm. *Chronicles of Wasted Time. Part I. The Green Stick.* London: Collins, 1972.

Mullin, Redmond. *Present Alms: On the Corruption of Philanthropy.* Birmingham, UK: Phlogiston Publishing, 1980.

———. *The Wealth of Christians.* Maryknoll, NY: Orbis Books, 1983.

Mumford, Lewis. *The Transformations of Man.* Vol. 7 of World Perspectives Series. Planned and ed. Ruth Nanda Anshen. New York: Harper & Brothers, 1956.

Myers, Bryant L. *Walking with the Poor: Principles and Practices of Transformational Development.* Maryknoll, NY: Orbis Books, 1999.

Nee, Watchman. *Concerning Our Missions.* Shanghai: Gospel Book Room, 1939.

Nelson, Marlin. *The How and Why of Third World Missions.* South Pasadena, CA: William Carey Library, 1976.

New Directions in Missions: Implications for MKs. Ed. Beth A. Tetzel and Patricia Mortenson. West Battleboro, VT: International Conference on Missionary Kids (ICMK), 1986.

Nicgorski, Walter, and Ronald Weber, eds. *An Almost Chosen People: The Moral Aspirations of Americans.* Notre Dame, IN: University of Notre Dame Press, 1976.

Nicholls, Bruce J., and Beulah R. Wood. *Sharing the Good News with the Poor: A Reader for Concerned Christians.* London and Grand Rapids: Published on behalf of the World Evangelical Fellowship by Paternoster Press and Baker Book House, 1996.

Nickle, Keith F. *The Collection: A Study in Paul's Strategy.* Studies in Biblical Theology 48. Naperville: Alec R. Allenson, 1966.

Nida, Eugene. *Message and Mission: The Communication of the Christian Faith.* New York: Harper & Row, 1960.

Niles, D. T. *Upon the Earth: The Mission of God and the Missionary Enterprise of the Churches.* New York: McGraw-Hill, 1962.

Nisbet, Robert A. *History of the Idea of Progress.* New York: Basic Books, 1979.

Nissen, Johannes. *Poverty and Mission: New Testament Perspectives on a Contemporary Theme.* IIMO Research Pamphlet no. 10. Leiden: Interuniversity Institute for Missiological and Ecumenical Research, Department of Missiology, 1984.

Noll, Mark A. *God and Mammon: Protestants, Money, and the Market, 1790–1860.* New York: Oxford University Press, 2001.

Nurnberger, K., ed. *Affluence, Poverty and the Word of God: An Interdisciplinary Study-Program of the Missiological Institute, Mapumolo.* Durban, South Africa: Lutheran Publishing House, for the Missiological Institute at Lutheran Theological College, Mapumolo, Natal, 1978.

O'Brien, Niall. *Revolution from the Heart.* New York: Oxford University Press, 1987.

Orwell, George. *England Your England and Other Essays.* London: Secker & Warburg, 1953.

Osiek, Carolyn. *Rich and Poor in the Shepherd of Hermas: An Exegetical-Social Investigation.* Washington, DC: Catholic Biblical Association of America, 1983.

Palmer, Ray. *The Highest Civilization a Result of Christianity and Christian Learning,* a Discourse Delivered at Norwich, CT, November 14, 1865, on behalf of the Society for Promoting Collegiate and Theological Education at the West, in Connection with the Annual Meeting of the Board of Directors. Albany: J. Munsell, 1866.

Peabody, Francis Greenwood. *Jesus Christ and the Social Question.* New York: Macmillan, 1900.

Pfaff, William. *The Wrath of Nations: Civilization and the Furies of Nationalism.* New York: Simon & Schuster, 1993.

Phillips, Keith W. *They Dare to Love the Ghetto.* Los Angeles: World Impact, 1975.

Piggin, Stuart. *Making Evangelical Missionaries 1798–1858: The Social Background, Motives and Training of British Protestant Missionaries to India.* With texts of David Bogue's *Missionary Appeal,* 1794; Charles Buck on *Philanthropic Movements,* 1800; Sydney Smith on *Evangelical Missionaries,* 1808. Number 2 in the *Evangelicals and Society from 1750* series. Ed. G. E. Duffield. London: Sutton Courtenay Press, 1984.

Pilgrim, Walter E. *Good News to the Poor: Wealth and Poverty in Luke and Acts.* Minneapolis: Augsburg, 1981.

Pollock, David C., and Ruth E. Van Reken. *The Third Culture Kid Experience: Growing Up among Worlds.* Yarmouth, ME: Intercultural Press, 1999.

Potter, David M. *People of Plenty: Economic Abundance and the American Character.* Chicago: University of Chicago Press, 1954.

Putnam, Robert D. *Bowling Alone: The Collapse and Revival of American Community.* New York: Simon & Schuster, 2000.

Ranulf, Svend. *Moral Indignation and Middle Class Psychology: A Sociological Study.* Copenhagen: Levin & Munksgaard, 1938.

Ratneshwar, S., ed. *Why of Consumption: Contemporary Perspectives on Consumer Motives, Goals and Desires.* Routledge Interpretive Market Research Series. New York: Routledge, 2000.

Reade, W. Winwood. *The Martyrdom of Man.* London: Kegan Paul, Trench, 1909 [1872].

Rempel, Henry. *A High Price for Abundant Living: The Story of Capitalism.* Waterloo, Ontario: Herald Press, 2003.

Report of the Rev. R. Price of His Visit to Zanzibar and the Coast of Eastern Africa. London: LMS, 1876.

Reynolds, Lloyd G. *Economic Growth in the Third World: An Introduction.* New Haven, CT: Yale University Press, 1986.

Riesman, David. *Abundance for What? And Other Essays.* New York: Doubleday & Company, 1964.

Robb, Alexander. *The Heathen World and the Duty of the Church.* Edinburgh: Andrew Elliott, 1863.

Roberts, Paul. *The End of Oil: On the Edge of a Perilous New World.* Boston and New York: Houghton Mifflin Company, 2004.

Ronsvalle, John, and Sylvia Ronsvalle. *The Hidden Billions: The Potential of the Church in the U.S.A.* Champaign, IL: C-4 Resources, Inc., 1984.

Russell, W. E. *Sydney Smith.* London: Macmillan & Co., 1905.

Ryan, William. *Blaming the Victim.* New York: Pantheon Books, 1971.

Samuel, Vinay, and Chris Sugden. *Evangelism and the Poor: A Third World Study Guide.* Rev. ed. Bangalore: Partnership in Mission-Asia, 1983.

Sanneh, Lamin. *Whose Religion Is Christianity? The Gospel beyond the West.* Grand Rapids: Wm. B. Eerdmans, 2003.

Sayers, Dorothy. *Letters to a Post-Christian World: A Selection of Essays.* Selected and introduced by Roderick Jellema. Grand Rapids: Wm. B. Eerdmans Publishing Co., 1969.

Schlabach, Gerald W. *And Who Is My Neighbor? Poverty, Privilege, and the Gospel of Christ.* Scottdale, PA: Herald Press, 1990.

Schneider, John R. *The Good of Affluence: Seeking God in a Culture of Wealth.* Grand Rapids: Wm. B. Eerdmans, 2002.

Schoeck, Helmut. *Envy: A Theory of Social Behaviour.* London: Secker & Warburg, 1969.

Schottroff, Luise, and Wolfgang Stegemann. *Jesus and the Hope of the Poor.* Trans. Matthew J. O'Connell. Maryknoll, NY: Orbis Books, 1986.

Schweiker, William, and Charles Mathewes. *Having: Property and Possession in Religious and Social Life.* Grand Rapids: William B. Eerdmans Publishing Company, 2004.

Shames, Laurence. *The Hunger for More: Searching for Values in an Age of Greed.* New York: Times Books, 1989.

Sheils, W. J., and Diana Wood, eds. *The Church and Wealth. Papers Read at the 1986 Summer Meeting and the 1987 Winter Meeting of the Ecclesiastical History Society.* Studies in Church History, Vol. 24. Oxford: Published for the Ecclesiastical History Society by Basil Blackwell, 1987.

Sherwin-White, Adrian Nicholas. *Roman Society and Roman Law in the New Testament.* Oxford: Oxford University Press, 1963.

Shi, David. *The Simple Life: Plain Living and High Thinking in American Culture.* New York: Oxford University Press, 1985.

Sider, Ronald J. *Cup of Water, Bread of Life: Inspiring Stories about Overcoming Lopsided Christianity.* Grand Rapids: Zondervan Publishing House, 1994.

———. *Rich Christians in an Age of Hunger.* Downers Grove, IL: InterVarsity Press, 1977.

Sider, Ronald J., ed. *Cry Justice! The Bible Speaks on Hunger and Poverty.* Downers Grove: InterVarsity Press, 1980.

———. *Living More Simply: Biblical Principles and Practical Models.* Downers Grove, IL: InterVarsity Press, 1980.

Simon, Arthur. *How Much Is Enough? Hungering for God in an Affluent Culture.* Grand Rapids: Baker Books, 2003.

Simon, Charlie May. *A Seed Shall Serve: The Story of Toyohiko Kagawa, Spiritual Leader of Modern Japan.* London: Hodder & Stoughton, 1959.

Slater, Philip E. *The Pursuit of Loneliness: American Culture at the Breaking Point.* Boston: Beacon Press, 1970.

———. *Wealth Addiction.* New York: E. P. Dutton, 1980.

Smalley, William A., ed. *Readings in Missionary Anthropology II.* Enlarged 1978 ed. South Pasadena, CA: William Carey Library, 1978.

Smith, George Adam. *The Life of Henry Drummond.* New York: Doubleday & McClure, 1898.

Smith, Stephen C. *Ending Global Poverty: A Guide to What Works.* New York: Palgrave Macmillan, 2005.

Stavrianos, L. S. *Global Rift: The Third World Comes of Age.* New York: William Morrow and Company, 1981.

Stearns, Peter N. *Consumerism in World History: The Global Transformation of Desire.* Themes in World History. New York: Routledge, 2002.

Stiglitz, Joseph E. *Globalization and Its Discontents.* New York and London: W. W. Norton & Company, 2002.

———. *Making Globalization Work.* New York: Norton, 2006.

Stoll, David. *Fishers of Men or Founders of Empire? The Wycliffe Bible Translators in Latin America.* London: Zed Press, 1982.

Strong, Josiah. *The New Era; or, The Coming Kingdom.* New York: Baker & Taylor Co., 1893.

Tawney, R. H. *The Acquisitive Society.* New York: Harcourt, Brace & World, 1920/1948.

Taylor, Michael. *Christianity, Poverty and Wealth: The Findings of "Project 21."* Geneva, Switzerland: World Council of Churches, 2003.

Tetzel, Beth A., and Patricia Mortenson, eds. *New Directions in Missions — Implication for MKs.* Compendium of International Conference on Missionary Kids, Manila, Philippines, November 1984. Farmington: Missionary Internship, 1984.

Theissen, Gerd. *The Social Setting of Pauline Christianity: Essays on Corinth.* Philadelphia: Fortress, 1982.

———. *Sociology of Early Palestinian Judaism.* Trans. John Bowden. Philadelphia: Fortress Press, 1978.

Thomas, Jacob. *From Lausanne to Manila: Evangelical Social Thought. Models of Mission and the Social Relevance of the Gospel.* Delhi: Indian Society for Promoting Christian Knowledge, 2003.

Thompson, J. Milburn. *Justice and Peace: A Christian Primer.* 2nd ed., rev. and expanded. Maryknoll, NY: Orbis Books, 2003.

Thompson, R. Wardlaw. *Griffith John: The Story of Fifty Years in China.* London: Religious Tract Society, 1906.

———. "Self Support and Self Government in the Native Church as Affected by Considerations of Race, Previous Religion, and Present Social Conditions." In *Centenary of the London Missionary Society. Proceedings of the Founders' Week Convention, at the City Temple, Holborn Viaduct, London, E.C., September 21st to 27th, 1895. Papers and Speeches in Full.* London: LMS, 1895.

Thornton, A. P. *Doctrines of Imperialism.* New York: John Wiley & Sons, 1965.

Tiberondwa, Ado K. *Missionary Teachers as Agents of Colonialism: A Study of Their Activities in Uganda.* Lusaka: National Educational Company of Zambia, 1978.

Tocqueville, Alexis de. *Democracy in America.* The Henry Reeve text as revised by Francis Bowen now further corrected and edited with introduction, editorial notes, and bibliographies by Phillips Bradley. 2 vols. New York: Alfred A. Knopf, 1956 [1835].

Trocmé, Étienne. *Le "Livre des Actes" et l'histoire.* Paris: Presses Universitaires de France, 1957.

Trollope, Frances. *Domestic Manners of the Americans.* Ed., with a history of Mrs. Trollope's adventures in America, by Donald Smalley. New York: Alfred A. Knopf, 1949 [1832].

Trout, Jessie M., ed. *Kagawa, Japanese Prophet: His Witness in Life and Word.* World Christian Books, no. 30. London: Lutterworth, 1959.

Turow, Joseph. *Breaking Up America: Advertisers and the New Media World.* Chicago: University of Chicago Press, 1998.

Vallely, Paul. *Bad Samaritans: First World Ethics and Third World Debt.* Maryknoll, NY: Orbis Books, 1990.

van den Berg, Johannes. *Constrained by Jesus' Love: An Inquiry into the Motives of the Missionary Awakening in Great Britain in the Period between 1698 and 1815.* Kampen: J. H. Kok N.V., 1956.

VandenBroeck, Goldian, ed. *Less Is More: An Anthology of Ancient and Modern Voices Raised in Praise of Simplicity.* Rochester, VT: Inner Traditions, 1996.

Wallis, Jim. *Agenda for Biblical People: A New Focus for Developing a Life-Style of Discipleship.* New York: Harper and Row, 1976.

————. *The Call to Conversion: Why Faith Is Always Personal but Never Private.* Rev. ed. New York: Harper Collins, 2005.

————. *Faith Works: How to Live Your Beliefs and Ignite Positive Social Change.* New York: Random House, 2000.

Walsh, Michael, and Brian Davies, eds. *Proclaiming Justice & Peace: Documents from John XXIII-John Paul II.* Mystic, CT: Twenty-Third Publications, 1984.

Walsh, William Pakenham. *Christian Missions: Six Discourses Delivered before the University of Dublin; Being the Donnellan Lectures for 1861.* Dublin: George Herbert, 1862.

Warneck, Johannes. *The Living Forces of the Gospel: Experiences of a Missionary in Animistic Heathendom.* Authorized translation from the 3rd German edition by Neil Buchanan. London: Oliphant, Anderson & Ferrier, 1909.

Warren, William. *These for Those: Our Indebtedness to Foreign Missions; or, What We Get for What We Give.* Portland, ME: Hoyt, Fogg and Breed, 1870.

Webster, Donovan. *Aftermath: The Remnants of War.* New York: Random House, 1996.

Wheeler, Sondra Ely. *Wealth as Peril and Obligation: The New Testament on Possessions.* Grand Rapids: William B. Eerdmans Publishing Company, 1995.

White, John. *The Golden Cow: Materialism in the Twentieth-Century Church.* Downers Grove, IL: InterVarsity Press, 1979.

Whybrow, Peter C. *American Mania: When More Is Not Enough.* New York & London: W. W. Norton and Company, 2005.

Wolff, Edward N. *Top Heavy: The Increasing Inequality of Wealth in America and What Can Be Done about It.* New York: New Press, 2002.

Wong, James, ed., with Peter Larson, Edward Pentecost. *Mission from the Third World.* Singapore: Church Growth Study Center, 1972.

Woolman, John. *The Journal and Major Essays of John Woolman.* Ed. Phillips P. Moulton. New York: Oxford University Press, 1971.

World Missionary Conference, 1910. To Consider Missionary Problems in Relation to the Non-Christian World. Edinburgh: Oliphant, Anderson & Ferrier, 1910.

World Wide Fund for Nature (WWF, formerly World Wildlife Fund). *Living Planet Report 2004.* Gland, Switzerland: WWF, 2004. *www.assets.panda.org/downloads/lpr2004.pdf.*

Worsley, Peter. *The Trumpet Shall Sound: A Study of "Cargo" Cults in Melanesia.* 2nd augmented ed. New York: Schocken Books, 1968.

Wright, Christopher J. H. *God's People in God's Land.* Carlisle: Paternoster, 1990.

————. *Old Testament Ethics for the People of God.* Leicester and Downers Grove: IVP and InterVarsity, 2004.

Wuthnow, Robert. *God and Mammon in America*. New York: Free Press, 1994.

Yohannan, K. P. *The Coming Revolution in World Missions*. Altamonte Springs, FL: Creation House, 1986.

Young, Robert. *The Success of Christian Missions: Testimonies to Their Beneficent Results*. London: Hodder & Stoughton, 1890.

Ziesler, J. A. *Christian Asceticism*. Grand Rapids: William B. Eerdmans Publishing Company, 1973.

Zinbarg, Edward D. *Faith, Morals, and Money: What the World's Religions Tell Us about Ethics in the Marketplace*. New York: Continuum International, 2005.

Articles and Book Chapters

Addleton, Jonathan S. "Missionary Kid Memoirs: A Review Essay." *International Bulletin of Missionary Research* 24, no. 1 (January 2000): 30–34.

Ahlstrom, Sydney E. "*Annuit Coeptis:* America as the Elect Nation. The Rise and Decline of a Patriotic Tradition." In *Continuity and Discontinuity in Church History: Essays Presented to George Huntston Williams on the Occasion of his 65th Birthday,* ed. F. Forrester Church and Timothy George. Vol. 19 of *Studies in the History of Christian Thought,* ed. Heiko A. Oberman, et al., 315–37. Leiden: E. J. Brill, 1979.

ARICCIA 2006. SEDOS Residential Seminar. "Mission and Money: Perspectives from Religious Life." *SEDOS* 38, nos. 5/6 (May/June 2006): entire issue.

Barrett, David B., Todd M. Johnson, and Peter F. Crossing "Missiometrics 2006: Goals, Resources, Doctrines of the 350 Christian World Communions." *International Bulletin of Missionary Research* 30, no. 1 (January 2006): 27–30.

Beidelman, Thomas O. "Contradictions between the Sacred and the Secular Life: The Church Missionary Society in Ukaguru, Tanzania, East Africa, 1876–1914" *Comparative Studies in History: An International Quarterly* 23, no. 1 (January 1981): 73–95.

Benoit, Pierre. "Remarques sur les 'Sommaires' de Actes 2/42 à 5." *Aux sources de la tradition chrétienne: mélanges offerts à M. Maurice Goguel à l'occasion de son soixante-dixième anniversaire.* Paris: Delachaux & Niestlé, 1950.

Blasi, Joseph, and Diana L. Murrell. "Adolescence and Community Structure: Research on the Kibbutz of Israel." *Adolescence* 12, no. 46 (Summer 1977): 165–73.

Bleek, Wolf. "Envy and Inequality in Fieldwork: An Example of Ghana." *Human Organization* 38, no. 2 (Summer 1979): 200–205.

Bloom, Leonard. "Psychological Aspects of Wealth in Poorer Societies." *Journal of Psychoanalytic Anthropology* 7, no. 2 (Spring 1984): 189–208.

Bonk, Jonathan J. [with responses by Stan Nussbaum and James E. Pluddemann]. "Affluence: The Achilles' Heel of Missions." *Evangelical Missions Quarterly* (October 1985): 382–90.

———. "'All Things to All Persons?' — The Missionary as a Racist-Imperialist, 1860–1910." *Missiology: An International Review* 8, no. 3 (July 1980): 285–306.

———. "'And They Marveled...': Mammon as Miracle in Western Missionary Encounter." In *Evangelical, Ecumenical, and Anabaptist Missiologies in Conversation: Essays in Honor of Wilbert R. Shenk,* ed. James R. Krabill, Walter Sawatsky, and Charles E. Van Engen, 78–87. Maryknoll, NY: Orbis Books, 2006.

————. "Between Past and Future: Non-Western Theological Education Entering the Twenty-first Century." In *Between Past and Future: Evangelical Mission Entering the Twenty-first Century*. Evangelical Missiological Society Series, no. 10, 121–46. Pasadena, CA: William Carey Library, 2003.

————. "Contextualizing Theological Education and Mission outside the United States." In *Be My Witnesses: Essays in Honour of Dr. Sebastian Karotemprel, SDB,* ed. Dr. Jose Varickasseril, SDB, and Dr. Mathew Karaipuram, SDB, 79–87. Shillong: Vendrame Institute Publications and Don Bosco Centre for Indigenous Cultures, Sacred Heart Theological College, 2001.

————. "Doing Mission out of Affluence: Reflections on Recruiting *'End of the Procession'* Missionaries from *'Front of the Procession'* Churches. (1 Corinthians 4:1–13)." *Missiology: An International Review* 17, no. 4 (October 1989): 427–52.

————. "Mission and the Problem of Affluence." In *Toward Century 21 in Christian Mission*. Essays in Honor of Gerald H. Anderson, Director, Overseas Ministries Study Center, New Haven, Connecticut, Editor, *International Bulletin of Missionary Research*. Ed. James M. Phillips and Robert T. Coote, 295–309. Grand Rapids: Wm. B. Eerdmans, March 1993.

————. "Missions and Mammon: Six Theses." *International Bulletin of Missionary Research* 13, no. 3 (July 1989): 174–81.

————. "Missions and Money: Affluence and the Communication of the Gospel." Part 2 of a Two-Part Series, *World Christian* 8, no. 10 (December 1989): 22–28.

————. "Missions and Money: Relational Costs of Missionary Affluence." Part One of a Two-Part Series, *World Christian* 8, no. 9 (November 1989): 30–33.

————. "Reflections on Recruiting Missionaries Today." *SEDOS Bulletin* 22 (February 15, 1990): 42–47.

————. "The Role of Affluence in the Christian Missionary Enterprise from the West." *Missiology: An International Review* 14, no. 4 (October 1986): 437–61.

————. "Singing the Spirit's Song: Finding Freedom from Affluence." *Health and Development* 1 (1997): 3–10.

————. "Small Is [Still] Beautiful in Missions." *Transformation: An International Dialogue on Evangelical Social Ethics* 8, no. 1 (January/March 1991): 26–31.

————. "Thinking Small: Global Missions and American Churches." *Didaskalia: The Journal of Providence Theological Seminary* 9, no. 1 (Fall 1997): 1–25.

————. "Wanted: 'End of the Procession' Apostles." *His Dominion: Journal of the Faculty of Canadian Theological Seminary* 15, no. 1 (1989): 2–16.

————. "We Can't Afford Affluence: We Must Not Confuse the Good News of the Gospel with the Good News of Plenty." *Advance* (Spring 1989): 5–7.

Bosch, David J. "The Missionary: Exemplar or Victim?" *Theologia Evangelica* 17, no. 1 (March 1984): 9–16.

————. "Vision for Mission." *International Review of Mission* 76, no. 301 (January 1987): 8–15.

Brown, Arthur Judson. "A Serious Problem in Missions: Salaries and the Increased Cost of Living in Asia." *The Missionary Review of the World* 27 (June 1904): 408–13.

Bruner, Frederick Dale. "The American Missionary Problem: An Essay in Conscience." *Christian Century* 85, no. 23 (June 5, 1968): 751–53.

Callahan, Daniel. "Doing Well by Doing Good: Garrett Hardin's 'Lifeboat Ethic.' " *The Hastings Center Report* 4, no. 6 (December 1974): 1–4.

Cohen, Lizabeth. "The Politics of Mass Consumption in America." *The Chronicle of Higher Education* (January 3, 2003): B7–B9.

Cole, Arthur H. "The Relations of Missionary Activity to Economic Development." *Economic Development and Cultural Change* 9, no. 2 (January 1961): 120–27.

Conn, Harvie M. "The Money Barrier between Sending and Receiving Churches." *Evangelical Missions Quarterly* 14, no. 4 (October 1978): 231–39.

Coote Robert T. "Taking Aim on 2000 AD," 35–80. In *Mission Handbook: North American Protestant Ministries Overseas,* 13th ed., 57, 79–80. Monrovia: Missions Advanced Research and Communication Center, 1986.

Dahl, Nils Alstrup. "Paul and Possessions." In *Studies in Paul: Theology for the Early Christian Mission,* 22–39. Minneapolis: Augsburg Publishing House, 1977.

Dennis, James S. "The Social Influence of Christianity as Illustrated by Foreign Missions." In *Christ and Civilization: A Survey of the Influence of the Christian Religion upon the Course of Civilization,* ed. John Brown Paton, Percy William Bunting, and Alfred Ernest Garvie. London: National Council of Evangelical Free Churches, 1910.

DeVoss, David. "The New Breed of Missionary." *Los Angeles Times Magazine* (January 25, 1987), 14–23, 34–35.

Domingues, Fernando, MCCJ. "Poverty and Mission." *SEDOS* 38, nos. 5/6 (May/June 2006): 129–36.

Dow, James. "The Image of Limited Production: Envy and the Domestic Mode of Production in a Peasant Society." *Human Organization* 40, no. 4 (Winter 1981): 360–63.

Doxiadis, C. A. "Three Letters to an American." *Daedalus: Journal of the American Academy of Arts and Sciences* 101, no. 4 (Fall 1972): 163–83.

Drewnowski, Jan. "The Affluence Line." *Social Indicators Research* 5, no. 3 (July 1978): 263–78.

Ellinwood, F. F. "Asceticism in Missions." *The Chinese Recorder and Missionary Journal* 22, no. 1 (January 1891): 1.

Feagin, J. R. "We Still Believe That God Helps Those Who Help Themselves." *Psychology Today* 6 (November 1972): 101–29.

Feather, N. T. "Explanations of Poverty in Australian and American Samples: The Person, Society, or Fate?" *Australian Journal of Psychology* 24, no. 3 (December 1974): 199–216.

Flannery, Tim. "Endgame." *The New York Review of Books* 52, no. 13 (August 11, 2005): 26–29.

Foyle, Marjorie. "Missionary Relationships: Powderkeg or Powerhouse?" *Evangelical Missions Quarterly* 21, no. 4 (October 1985).

Frazier, William B. "Where Mission Begins: A Foundational Probe." *International Bulletin of Missionary Research* 11, no. 4 (October 1987): 146–56.

Fuellenbach, John, SVD. " 'You Cannot Serve God and Money' (cf. Mt. 6:24): Some Biblical and Theological Considerations Concerning Mission and Money." *SEDOS* 38, nos. 5/6 (May/June 2006): 101–10.

Fukada, Robert M. "The Legacy of Toyohiko Kagawa." *International Bulletin of Missionary Research* 12, no. 1 (January 1988): 18–22.

Furnham, Adrian. "Why Are the Poor Always with Us? Explanations for Poverty in Britain." *British Journal of Social Psychology* 21, no. 4 (November 1982): 311–22.

Galbraith, John Kenneth. "The 1929 Parallel." *The Atlantic Monthly* 259, no. 1 (January 1987): 62.

Gil, M. "Land Ownership in Palestine under Roman Rule." *Revue Internationale des Droits de l'Antiquité* 17 (1970): 11–53.

Grigg, Viv. "The Urban Poor: Prime Missionary Target." *Evangelical Review of Theology* 11, no. 3 (July 1987): 261–72. Reprinted from *Urban Mission,* March 1987.

Guarda, Alessandro, MCCJ. "Economy for Mission: Religious Life's Prospects." *SEDOS* 38, nos. 5/6 (May/June 2006): 138–47.

Haley, Doris. "Ralph and Roberta Winter: A Wartime Lifestyle." *Family Life Today* (March 1983): 29–33.

Hallowes, J. F. T. "The Expansion of England in Relation to the Propagation of the Gospel." *Chronicle of the London Missionary Society* 51 (May 1886): 197–200.

———. "Our World-Wide Empire." *Chronicle of the London Missionary Society* 59 (October 1894): 225–26.

Heaps, Richard A., and Stanley G. Morrill. "Comparing the Self-Concepts of Navajo and White High School Students." *Journal of American Indian Education* 18, no. 3 (May 1979): 12–14.

Honeycutt, James M. "Altruism and Social Exchange Theory: The Vicarious Rewards of the Altruist." *Mid-American Review of Sociology* 6, no. 1 (Spring 1981): 93–99.

Horder, W. Garett. "Prophecy of a Positivist." *Chronicle of the London Missionary Society* 59 (November 1886): 455–59.

"An Indictment of the Way in Which Science and Technology Have Become Instruments of a Global Structure of Inequity, Exploitation and Oppression..." *International Development Review* 21, no. 2 (1979): 13–15.

Jethani, Skye. "All We Like Sheep." *Leadership* (Summer 2006).

Joes, Anthony James. "Fascism: The Past and the Future." *Comparative Political Studies* 7, no. 1 (April 1974): 107–33.

John, Griffith. "North China-Hankow." *The Chronicle of the London Missionary Society* (July 1891): 166.

Kane, J. Herbert. "My Pilgrimage in Mission." *International Bulletin of Missionary Research* 11, no. 3 (July 1987).

Kelly, Erin. "Mac in the USSR." *The New Journal* 20, no. 2 (October 16, 1987): 6–7.

Kennard, J. Spencer. "Judas of Galilee and His Clan." *Jewish Quarterly Review* 36 (1945–46): 281–86.

Keys, Lawrence E. "Third World Missionaries: More and Better" *Evangelical Missions Quarterly* 18, no. 4 (October 1982): 216–24.

Krugman, Paul. "For Richer: How the Permissive Capitalism of the Boom Destroyed American Equality." *New York Times Magazine* (October 20, 2002), 62–67, 76–77, 141–42.

Lasch, Christopher. "The Narcissistic Personality of Our Time." *Partisan Review* 44, no. 1 (1977): 9–19.

Latourette, Kenneth Scott. "Christian Missions as Mediators of Western Civilization." In *Christian Missions in China: Evangelists of What?* ed. Jessie G. Lutz, 83–95. Boston: D. C. Heath and Company, 1965.

Latshaw, Greg. "Missionaries Make Short Trips to Teach Gospel." *Pittsburgh Tribune-Review,* June 25, 2006.

Loewen, Jacob A. "Missionaries: Drivers or Spare Tires?" *International Review of Mission* 75, no. 299 (July 1986): 253–60.

Lundberg, Isabel Carey. "World Revolution, American Plan." *Harper's Magazine* 197 (December 1948): 38–46.

MacDonald, G. Jeffrey. "Rise of Sunshine Samaritans: On a Mission or Holiday?" *The Christian Science Monitor* (May 25, 2006). *www.csmonitor.com/2006/0525/p01s01-ussc.html.*

McCracken, John. "Underdevelopment in Malawi: The Missionary Contribution." *African Affairs* 76, no. 303 (April 1977): 195–209.

Miller, Elmer S. "The Christian Missionary: Agent of Secularization." *Missiology: An International Review* 1, no. 1 (January 1973): 99–107.

The Missionary Visitor: Presenting Church of the Brethren Mission Fields 32, no. 6 (June 1930).

Monroy, Juan Antonio. "Why Do Protestant Missionaries Fail in Spain?" *Milligan Missiogram* 6, no. 3 (Spring 1979): 1–9.

Mullen, Redmond. "The Roles of Private Funding in the Context of International Voluntary Activity." *International Transnational Associations,* no. 4 (April 1980): 176–79.

Mutch, W. J. "Adaptation in Missionary Method." *Review of Reviews* 6 (June 1897): 324–32.

Neimark, Jill. "The Power of Positive Thinkers: How One Company Created a Work Force Full of Optimists." *Success* (September 1987).

Packer, George. "When Here Sees There." *New York Times Magazine* (April 21, 2002).

Parshall, Phil. "How Spiritual Are Missionaries?" *Evangelical Missions Quarterly* 23, no. 1 (January 1987): 10–16.

Pate, Larry D., with Lawrence E. Keyes. "Emerging Missions in a Global Church." *International Bulletin of Missionary Research* 10, no. 4 (October 1986): 156–65.

Pearce, T. W. "Western Civilisation in Relation to Protestant Mission Work." *Chronicle of the London Missionary Society* 55 (August 1890): 239.

Pierson, A. T. "The Needless Sacrifice of Human Life in Mission Work." *The Missionary Review of the World* 27, no. 2 (Old Series) (February 1904): 81.

Porter, Andrew. "Cambridge, Keswick, and Late-Nineteenth-Century Attitudes to Africa." *The Journal of Imperial and Commonwealth History* 5, no. 1 (October 1976): 5–34.

———. "Evangelical Enthusiasm, Missionary Motivation and West Africa in the Late Nineteenth Century: The Career of G. W. Brooke." *The Journal of Imperial and Commonwealth History* 6, no. 1 (October 1977): 23–46.

Pritchett, Lant. "Divergence: Big Time." *Journal of Economic Perspectives* 11, no. 3 (Summer 1997): 3–17.

"A Prophecy According to Roland Allen." *Laity* no. 12 (October 1961): 38–43.

Rakowski, Helmut, OFM Cap. " 'A Mission for Money': An Interpretation of the Prohibition of Money by Francis of Assisi Seen Against the Economic-Social Background of His Time." *SEDOS* 38, nos. 5/6 (May/June 2006): 112–22.

"Rianto and Ratna" (pseudonyms). "Millionaire Missionaries' Principles for Giving." *Evangelical Missions Quarterly* 41, no. 4 (October 2005): 466–71.

Robert, Dana L. "Shifting Southward: Global Christianity since 1945." *International Bulletin of Missionary Research* 24, no. 2 (April 2000): 50–58.

Rydell, Lars H., and Charlene B. Rydell. "Poverty: Waning or Waxing?" *Social Praxis* 1, no. 4 (1973): 389–97.

Silver, Maury, and John P. Sabini. "From Christ's Church to iChurch: How Consumerism Undermines Our Faith and Community." Posted on *Christianity Today*'s summer 2006 LeadershipJournal.net Web site: *www.christianitytoday.com/leaders/newsletter/2006/cln60710.html.*

———. "The Perception of Envy." *Social Psychology* 41, no. 2 (June 1978): 105–17.

———. "The Social Construction of Envy." *Journal for the Theory of Social Behaviour* 8, no. 3 (October 1978): 313–32.

Smith, Edwin W. "The Earliest Ox-wagons in Tanganyika: An Experiment Which Failed." *Tanganyika Notes and Records* no. 40, 1–14, and no. 41, 1–15 (1955).

Smith, Kevin B. "I Made It Because of Me: Beliefs about the Causes of Wealth and Poverty." *Sociopolitical Spectrum* 5, no. 3 (1985): 255–67.

Smith, Sydney."Critique." *Edinburgh Review* (April 1809): 40, 42.

Strachan, Hew. *The First World War.* Vol. 1, *To Arms.* London: Oxford University Press, 2002; reviewed by Niall Ferguson in the February 13, 2003, issue of the *New York Review of Books,* 21–23.

Sweeney, Vernon E. "A Note on Classical Economics." *Social Science* 52, no. 2 (Spring 1977): 90–93.

Taylor, Isaac. "The Great Missionary Failure," and "Missionary Finance." *The Fortnightly Review* 44 (July–December 1888): 488–500, 581–92.

Thayer, C. C. "Missionary Economics: Personal Efficiency." *Missionary Review of the World* 26 (July 1903): 516–20.

———. 'Missionary Health Economics." *Missionary Review of the World* 26 (February 1903): 128.

Thompson, Joseph P. "Christian Missions Necessary to a True Civilization." *Bibliotheca Sacra* 14, no. 56 (October 1857): 818–54.

Townsend, Meredith. "Cheap Missionaries." *The Contemporary Review* 56 (July 1889): 1–9.

Vanier, Jean, interview by the editors. "Expert Witness." *U.S. Catholic* 71, no. 8 (August 2006): 18–22.

Verryn, Trevor D. "What Is Communication? Searching for a Missiological Model." *Missionalia* 11, no. 1 (April 1983): 17–25.

von Keuhnelt Leddihn, Erik. "La Morale du Travail: Un Probleme Mondial." *Cahiers de Sociologie Economique* 2, no. 2 (December 1971): 215–27.

Wallis, Jim. "A Bible Full of Holes." *The Mennonite* (November 21, 2000): 6–7.

Walls, A. F. "Black Europeans, White Africans: Some Missionary Motives in West Africa." In *Religious Motivation: Biographical and Sociological Problems of the Church Historian,* ed. D. Baker, 339–48. Cambridge: Cambridge University Press, 1978.

———. "The Legacy of David Livingstone." *International Bulletin of Missionary Research* 11, no. 3 (July 1987): 125–29.

————. "Missionary Vocation and the Ministry: The First Generation." In *New Testament Christianity for Africa and the World: Essays in Honor of Harry Sawyerr,* ed. M. E. Glasswell and E. W. Fasholé-Luke, 141–56. London: SPCK, 1974.

Warneck, Johannes. "Are African Native Races Profited by Foreign Rule?" *The Illustrated Missionary News* 22 (July 1888): 111.

Wilken, Robert Louis. "Toward a Social Interpretation of Early Christian Apologetics." *Church History* 39, no. 1 (1970): 1–22.

Williamson, H. G. M. "The Old Testament and the Material World." *The Evangelical Quarterly,* 57, no. 1 (January 1985): 5–22.

Wuthnow, Robert. *Global Issues Survey.* Princeton, NJ: Princeton University Center for the Study of Religion, 2005.

Pamphlets

American Board. "Preparations and Outfit. A Letter to New Members Joining the North China Mission of the American Board." Shanghai: American Presbyterian Mission Press, 1886.

American Board of Commissioners for Foreign Missions. "Manual for Missionary Candidates, and for Appointed Missionaries before Entering their Fields." Revised Edition. Boston: Printed for the Board, Beacon Press, 1877.

Kagawa, Toyohiko. "A Significant Word from Asia." Published by Bishop Brenton Thoburn Badley, Episcopal Residence, Byculla, Bombay, India, n.d.

Makanzu, Mavumilusa. "The Twentieth-Century Missionaries and the Murmurs of the Africans." *Apophoreta of African Church History* 3. Aberdeen: Department of Religious Studies, University of Aberdeen, in association with the Scottish Institute of Missionary Studies, 1974.

"Remarks on the Provision that Should be Made for the Children of Missionaries." New York: Anson D. F. Randolph, 1855.

Shenk, Wilbert R. "God's New Economy: Interdependence and Mission." Elkhart, IN: Mission Focus, 1988.

Southon, E. J. "Hints for Missionaries Proceeding to Central Africa." London: Printed for the Directors of the London Missionary Society by Yates & Alexander, 1880.

Whately, Richard, "On the Origin of Civilization. A Lecture by His Grace the Archbishop of Dublin. To the Young Men's Christian Association." London, December 1854.

Unpublished Sources

Manuscripts

Moore, Tom. "The Support Role to the Bible Translation Task." A workpaper prepared for the November 1985 S.I.L. branch conference, Pucallpa, Peru.

Quick, Bernard E. "He Who Pays the Piper...: A Study of Economic Power and Mission in a Revolutionary World." With a foreword by Dr. M. Richard Shaull. Princeton Theological Seminary, n.d.

Song, Choan-seng. "The System, Missionaries and the Future of the Christian Mission." n.d. [ca. 1971] Yale Divinity School Pamphlet Collection, Box 359, Folder 2465.

Walls, Andrew F. "The Voice of One Crying in the Supermarket: The West as the Prime Field for Christian Mission." University of Aberdeen, n.d.

Williams, Cecil Peter. "The Recruitment and Training of Overseas Missionaries in England between 1850 and 1900, with special reference to the records of the Church Missionary Society, the Wesleyan Methodist Missionary Society, the London Missionary Society and the China Inland Mission." M.Litt. Dissertation, University of Bristol, 1976.

Letters

August 10, 1881, Letter from David Williams to Ralph Wardlaw Thompson.

September 21, 1881, Letter from Walter Hutley to home secretary.

February 26, 1985. Johnstone to Bonk.

February 26, 1985. Fort Wayne. Nussbaum to Bonk.

July 26, 1985. Youngman to Bonk.

December 11, 1985. Moore to Bonk.

December 23, 1985. Ward to Bonk.

February 28, 1986. Fargher to Bonk.

September 12, 1986. Culver to Bonk.

November 7, 1986. Waddell to Bonk.

December 17, 1986. Strickland to Bonk.

January 14, 1987. Wheaton. Hill to Bonk.

Fall 1987. Letter of Hardy to Bonk, Mozambique.

January 29, 1987. Geysbeek to Bonk.

April 16, 1987. Irian Jaya. McAllister to Loge.

August 28, 1987. Japan. Hederstedt to Bonk.

October 1987. Nairobi. Cassette tape letter. Nelson and Peters to Bonk.

November 17, 1987. Singapore. Harrison to Bonk.

December 1987. Roy Larson, Kinshasa, Zaire, to Trinity Evangelical Free Church, Woodbridge, Connecticut.

January 26, 1988. Pasadena. McGavran to Bonk.

World Council of Churches, Commission on World Mission and Evangelism. "A Monthly Letter on Evangelism," no. 8, August 1985.

Consultations

Missionary Service in Asia Today. A Report on a Consultation Held by the Asia Methodist Advisory Committee February 18–23, 1971, in cooperation with the Life, Message, Unity Committee of the East Asian Christian Conference. Kuala Lumpur: University of Malaysia, 1971.

WCC World Consultation on Resource Sharing. El Escorial, Spain, October 24–31, 1987.

Index

Numbers in *italics* indicate tables.

money. *See also* missionary affluence
 ambiguous relationship of, with spiritual
  ideals, xi
 changes in approach to, by missionaries,
  xiii
 having too much and not enough, 13
 North-to-South flow of, xiii–xiv
 raising, for missionary ventures, xiii
Monroy, Juan Antonio, 54
Moravians, 176
mortality and morbidity, among
 missionaries, 39–42
Mother Teresa, 178
Muggeridge, Malcolm, 59–60

national evangelists, 15, 80
nationalism, 26
needs, defined by local conditions, 173
Nehemiah, righteousness in use of wealth,
 194
New Testament teachings, reassuring for
 the wealthy, 105–7
 Jesus, parables of, featuring astute
  businessmen, 106–7
 private property, 105
 wealth, among Jesus' followers, 106
New Testament teachings, on the righteous
 rich, 170
New Testament teachings, troubling for the
 wealthy, 127–56
 Christ identified with poor, 139–47
 Christ pronouncing woes on the wealthy,
  130–31
 Christ's followers called to self-denial,
  148–50
 Christ's followers identified with the
  poor, 141–44
 Christ's followers in the world, not of it,
  133
 demands of the Kingdom of God, wealth
  interfering with, 137–38
 generosity of Christ's followers to
  be uncalculating, and to extend to
  enemies, 150
 genuine repentance, features of, 147–48,
  151–52

New Testament teachings, troubling for the
 wealthy (*continued*)
 God working through the poor and the
  weak, 144–46
 holding out hope that disciples will be
  resistant to wealth's effects, 138
 identification with the involving relations
  with specific people, 146–47
 love of money by religious leaders and
  missionaries, 152–53
 love of property leading to temptation to
  betray Jesus, 139
 obedience distinguishing true follower
  of Jesus, 153–56
 one's treasures reflecting heart's
  position, 133
 personal possessions of Christ's
  followers regarded as a trust, 128
 poverty and hardship as consequence of
  obedience, 128–30
 prayer, made difficult by wealth, 136–37
 preoccupation with self, money, and
  pleasure, 133
 pride and self-deluding sense of security,
  134
 prosperity and wealth as signs of greed,
  128–30
 relationship with the needy as indicator
  of one's standing with God, 146
 sins of the rich associated with idolatry,
  impurity, and immorality, 131–33
 spiritual dangers of wealth and
  prosperity, 133–39
 spiritual sterility, resulting from wealth,
  138
 wealth and possessions as subordinate
  goods, 127–28
 wealth distorting perspective on life,
  134–35
 wealth fostering alienation from God,
  135–36
Nida, Eugene, 46, 72
Nisbet, Robert, 23
nonconformity, 179, 180
non-Westerners, missionaries' solutions
 for troubles of, 29–30

Previously published in
the American Society of Missiology Series